IDENTITY
THROUGH
PROSE

RICHARD PAUL JANARO

Miami-Dade Junior College

IDENTITY THROUGH PROSE

HOLT, RINEHART AND WINSTON, INC.

New York   Chicago   San Francisco
Atlanta   Dallas   Montreal   Toronto

The photographs are by Philip Obrecht.

Copyright © 1971 by Holt, Rinehart and Winston, Inc.
All rights reserved
Library of Congress Catalog Card Number: 79–138443
SBN: 03–083628–X
Printed in the United States of America
1234   090   9 8 7 6 5 4 3 2 1

To Darwin, Gwynne, and Estelle,
who kept the faith going

The next thing most like living one's life over again seems to be a recollection of that life, and to make that recollection as durable as possible by putting it down in writing.

BENJAMIN FRANKLIN

FOREWORD
TO THE
STUDENTS

(But Teachers May Read It Too)

This is a composition book, not because I think writing compositions is important in and for itself, but because I believe writing is one of the best ways of coming to grips with who you are, where you are, and what all of us are up to at the present time. I also think it's exciting to discover things about yourself. And since it so happens I teach writing, prose seems to me the logical medium through which self-analysis should be carried on.

In a way, it figures. I mean, it's one thing to experience sudden and occasional insights into yourself. It's quite another to get these down in some definite place—like on a piece of paper—where you can find them and refer to them again and where you can show them to others so that they'll come to know you better too.

Have you shied away from prose? Was part of the reason that too much stress was placed on the *mechanics* of writing? diction? spelling? grammatical structure? vulgarisms? groundrules of style? "Don't ever end a sentence with a preposition or begin one with a conjunction." Was it topic sentence after topic sentence? outline after outline?

Well, what about it?

I have nothing much to say about spelling in this book. As far as I'm concerned, it's one of the social graces—like waiting for everyone to be seated before you eat. It's as important as you and the circles in which you travel care to make it. Since it *is* a convention, a social contract most people agree to abide by, it can be learned. Like the rules of a card game, it can be looked up so you needn't even carry it around with you if it proves too much of a burden. Whether you lose credit for unfashionable spelling is a matter that had best be left up to you and your teacher for negotiation.

Just what grammar is, I'm not really certain. I have no intention of defining it anywhere in this book. I have a suspicion it has something to do with the way each of us tends to put his words and thoughts together. Maybe it isn't possible to be truly *un*-grammatical. Maybe it's just a matter of communicating or not communicating. Maybe it's more important to make sense than it is to follow some rules to the letter, if, when you do follow the rules, you're only writing a lot of nice-sounding but essentially unfelt and dishonest sentiments. If I had to take a stand, I'd say bad grammar was communication that didn't make the grade, either because of unclear thinking or a failure to care very much about what you were writing.

Which brings us back to the real purpose of this book: *getting you to care*. I have a theory—and considerable evidence—that the more you write, the better you tend to do it. So this book puts the emphasis on writing and I'm trying to coax you to write more than you'll think you want to. How? By suggesting writing assignments built around the subject most likely to be of concern: YOURSELF. And by YOURSELF I don't mean casual topics like "What I Did Last Summer" or "My Favorite Sport." I'm talking about really getting in there and trying to find some words with which to express hard-to-express feelings about love or your relationship with your parents or what it means to be in the minority in your part of town.

Don't be alarmed by the number of suggested assignments. There are hundreds of them. But they're there because I wanted to make a wide range of options available so that, somewhere in this book, you might find the issues that are of genuine interest to *you*.

Some of the exercises are accompanied by specific guidelines and examples of how different writers—sometimes professionals, sometimes students—have done certain things in prose. With others, you will be much more on your own, often because the idea for a particular exercise occurred to me in the context of recalling an experience I had and there just weren't any examples readily available. Some exercises I'm not even sure will work very well. But it may be fun for you and your class to try.

I think this "experimental" aspect of writing is most important of all. The surest sign you're on the track of something pretty good is that you're enjoying yourself. If your search for identity in prose gets to seem a chore, it may be an indication you're getting off the track— exploring somebody else's identity, kidding yourself, pretending to be involved with something that you don't care about. What you're looking for is a feeling of ease, a sense that what is happening in your writing is as much you as your characteristic way of dressing or wearing your hair. Your writing needs to feel good to you, and, when it does, you should be feeling the joy of knowing you're *together*. It comes down to the fact that no book or teacher can be your best guide or critic. Only you can know when you feel this joy.

So, I hope you'll take my examples and guides in the proper spirit. They are *only* suggestions. Ignore them if they do nothing for you. Make up other exercises. Perhaps you, the class, and the teacher can collaborate, negotiate, compromise—until you've found a series of writing assignments that feel right to you and seem to point toward self-awareness. After all, the specimens of prose that I include all came from those who were making the search for identity in ways that seemed important to them, and in many cases the exercises use those specimens as models. Perhaps you can create new models.

This book doesn't claim to have authority. A book can be an authority on grammar or vocabulary building. But if prose is employed as the means of understanding and expressing oneself, then each of us becomes an authority on writing just as soon as he starts communicating himself to others. How this happens, as often as not, is a mystery. The best this writing book can do is hope that it touches upon some aspects of the search for identity that will prove valuable to you.

To help you on the way, I have gathered up some of my own experiences, some of my students' experiences, and some vivid reflections of the thought and feelings of a number of famous writers. I think you'll find that they, you, and I all share some common hopes, fears, anxieties, and joys. I hope you'll find yourself mirrored here, and, if you do, you'll realize the true message of this book.

Everyone is important. Everyone has much to offer. You should get down to writing, not because you're forced to do it, but because this is a solid way to measure your importance and to make your offering.

R.P.J.
December 1970.

ACKNOWLEDGMENTS

During the last couple of years I have been accumulating more than the material for this book. I have been incurring debts of gratitude to many friends and colleagues who have encouraged, aided, and inspired me in too many ways that I could ever fully acknowledge. I would like, however, to give special thanks to Professors Darwin E. Gearhart and McGregor Smith, Jr. of Miami-Dade Junior College for the hours they have selflessly given to the care and feeding of an often unruly manuscript; to Sally Arbuthnot of Holt, Rinehart and Winston for sharing the minute concerns that I had thought only authors care about; and to my editor Jane Ross for her wisdom and patience, without which my own identity in prose might still be questionable.

PRELIMINARY
EXERCISE

WHO ARE YOU?

Before you read one word of the text, before you get into the numerous writing exercises that will be placed before you, write a brief paper on the subject WHO AM I? You should have no discussion about it in class nor receive any guidance whatever from the teacher. Don't ask how long or how many paragraphs.

Just imagine that there's a group of people standing inside your mind, crying out WHO ARE YOU? They keep saying this over and over no matter how frequently you answer. They appear never to be satisfied, though they hear each reply you give. Your paper should be made up of all the answers to this question that you can think of.

For example, to the question WHO AM I? a rather obvious answer might be your name. But then the group cries "Yes, but who are you?" Then you say: A STUDENT. Again: "Yes, but who are you?" Answer: A TEENAGER. Same question. Answer: AN AMERICAN. Same question. A CHEMISTRY MAJOR. Same question. AN EX-METHODIST. Same question. AN INTRAMURAL BASKETBALL PLAYER. Same question. Over and over.

If there *were* such an insistent group and you were being given such a going-over, could you become increasingly detailed in your explanations? Could you come ever closer to the true answer? Or is there one?

CONTENTS

PART ONE

THE SELF

"It should have a poetic mist about it; you should have poetic feelings toward it that you can't quite describe."

1

WRITING AS

SELF-INDULGENCE

OR

YOU TOO CAN

BE BRILLIG

Writing begins with the simple decision that you are going to do it. It is not necessary to start your writing career with definite ideas. You don't have to spend years in meditation figuring out the world in advance before bursting into prose with profound opinions that will immediately change everything. Whether your writing will ever matter very much to anyone but yourself is totally irrelevant at the outset.

Pleasing yourself, however, *is* important, and it is the first step toward that eventual thing we call communication. Others will be interested in what you write only when you have a unique and exciting identity to translate into prose. In order to reach others through the written word it is first essential that you use it to reach yourself.

The exercises in this first chapter are not designed to "make you think"—at least not in the traditional sense. You will be invited to indulge shamelessly in memories of your past, whether they make sense or not. You will have a chance to make up your own language, give yourself and your friends new names, invent fantasy countries and even new species of life, and, in fact, weave a little mythology all around yourself.

3

How will such self-indulgent writing help you to discover your identity? The first exercises mainly require you to trust your instincts, to do the verbal thing that comes into your head without going through the process of constructing an outline, developing a topic sentence, and so on. In other words, you will be sneaking in on yourself through a side door, sometimes catching yourself in the act of dreaming away the hours and trying to put the dream into words; sometimes making a conscious effort to find new ways of saying something, even if it means making up language nobody has ever used before.

The more outrageously wild and untraditional your first papers are, the more will you appreciate the difference between the you and the not-you. It's a sure bet your verbal fantasies can't sound like anybody else's, and that's the whole point. Self-indulgent writing is like the infant's wiggling his toes, stretching, yawning, and rolling luxuriously around in his crib. It's the dawning awareness of an existence, a being that is simply *there*, and if anybody doesn't like it, that's too damned bad.

A PLACE TO WANDER IN

The big difference between dreaming on paper and dreaming in your armchair is that, as soon as you commit your wildest fancies into prose, you are conscious of the urgent need for some means of containing them. You can't just tell your imagination, "All right, start working!" Your mind will jump around so uncontrollably that you can scarcely remember from one minute to the next what you've been fantasying about. Idle reverie does no harm and can even be a pleasant form of semiconscious relaxation, but when you attempt to translate yourself into words on paper, you must think of the reader. Even if you are your own "ideal" reader, you incur no less an obligation to provide a rudimentary shape or form to your shadowy imaginings.

Indeed it is this very realization of the need for a form that marks the beginning of the writer's outlook. It can be your outlook as easily as anybody else's. All you have to do is want to hold onto your fancies, and in order to do that, you need to put them in a container of some kind where you can readily get your hands on them.

The container I heartily recommend is *a place you remember*. Close your eyes. Think of some place that has a special significance in your past—preferably a place to which you return in spirit from time to time: a park, a lonely lighthouse on a windswept coast, the old barn at the southeast corner of grandfather's farm, a country store. It should NOT be a place you visit every day in real life. It should have a poetic mist about it; you should have poetic feelings toward it that you can't quite describe. It has to be a secret refuge where, in imagination, you can feel safe and secure. Ideally it is a place you can find *only* in your innermost dreams. Perhaps they've torn it down. Or you've moved far away and may never see it again. It all begins here. . . .

The Phantom Park

Perhaps it's a peculiarity of mine, but I have the distinct feeling that parks offer the writer a great opportunity to put his fancies together into a basic structure. Parks seem to have special significance for almost everyone. All of us played games in a favorite park, and many of us had our first amorous experiences in the same place.

Contemporary writers are very fond of parks as the setting for stories or plays. Samuel Beckett's *Waiting for Godot* uses a park to symbolize the whole human condition: two tramps hang around there, waiting for a mysterious person named Godot who may or may not exist and who may or may not be about to arrive. Edward Albee's *The Zoo Story* brings two strangers together in a park and ends on a tragic note as we learn how impossible it is for people really to reach and communicate with each other. In both plays the park becomes a concrete means whereby the author is able to think about and describe the eternal loneliness of people. Maybe the author in each instance recalls having wandered in parks, seeing so many people, but finding none who cared deeply about him.

But don't worry about what the park might secretly mean to you. If you have one in your past and you find yourself returning to it in spirit, just concentrate on it and try writing whatever occurs to you. Chances are the memory of the park will bring back with it certain associations and meanings that will drift to the surface quite effortlessly.

I asked an advanced writing class to begin the semester by finding the Phantom Park in their buried past and using it as their first subject. One student remembered Tompkins Park in New York, a place that has recently been the scene of quite a few confrontations between cops and hippies. Though the author is writing about two little girls, it seems obvious that she is one of them and that this is something she remembers from her past. The point is that the concentration on the park helped her to remember. It gave her memories a form.

The Haunted Park

Two Related Vignettes about Tompkins Park [1]

Compared to Prospect Park, Tompkins Park was small and scraggly. Its yellowed grass was contained behind rusted green rails. Its trees were stunted and mean. But sometimes, in the late Spring, at twilight, after the grass had been cut and fresh rain had washed the air, a fragrance would rise from the steaming earth and sweeten the tired streets.

To the two figures shuffling along a cement walk, the Park was not there. The shabby bushes and sprouting trees were only shadows across a golden path. Their goal lay at the end of the path: a self-contained, compact Castle—a dream world where illusion dispelled reality and fulfillment awaited every wish.

As the two figures approached, their steps quickened and they shifted the burdens in their arms. The tall, skinny one smiled and looked down at her short, chubby companion. "I can hardly wait," she said. "I'm dying to see if they've got anything new."

"Yeah," the little one replied, "I'm sick of the same old stuff."

And sliding her glasses up on her slippery, freckled nose, she skipped to catch up with her friend, and together they mounted grey stone steps to the entrance of the Tompkins Park Branch of the Brooklyn Public Library.

After dark, Tompkins Park became a jungle. On hot summer nights children climbed its rails and raced over its grass. Young couples strolled through its outer paths. Some sat on benches and held hands, talked, kissed, took their first steps toward love. Some sat in shadows.

There were rumors that in the heart of the Park were rape and rumbles. On some nights Tompkins Park was ringed with police cars and patrolmen. No one could say for sure why they were there, but conjecture usually was that they had come to prevent or to break up a fight—the blacks against the whites—again.

One night the two girls stood in front of the entrance to Tompkins Park. Their arms were laden with books. A policeman blocked their way. They asked why, but he only shook his head and pointed with his nightstick toward the street. The girls turned and started to walk away. They circled the Park,

[1] Printed by permission of the author, Alice Lee.

weaving their way through inquisitive children and dispossessed lovers. Some leaned over the rails and peered curiously into the Park; others stood indifferently against parked cars, or shrank into the shadows of a tree.

The girls looked at them enviously, pretending not to see, discussing their disappointment, the closing of the Park, the presence of the police, and their plans for the evening. They would go home and trade. Each would read the other's books.

They reached the corner. They turned and took one last look at the Park. They heard the shouting children and caught glimpses of cool-seeking couples and shadowy lovers. They crossed the street.

ALICE LEE

The author probably didn't know what she was going to say about her youth when she started writing this short piece. She never *does* say anything directly, but Tompkins Park serves her as a focal point for what might otherwise have been some disconnected memories: her childhood love of reading, the kind of sheltered background she came from, the fact that she saw little of the exciting sort of life that went on in the park, her book-reading friend, and so on.

EXERCISES

1. Locate your Phantom Park in your memory. Take an imaginary walk through it, starting at one point and ending at another, or else circle the entire park, returning to your place of origin. This will give you an initial sense of form. It will prevent your jumping from one memory to another. Perhaps you will want to imitate Alice Lee and objectify yourself at a younger age, seeing yourself as if you were another person and using the pronoun "he" or "she." This is a marvelous way to develop a "structure": to actually *see* a character, who is you, walking through the scenes of memory from place to place.

   Or perhaps you will want to keep humanity out of the scene altogether. Your mind's eye simply travels about the park, recalling things—an old drinking fountain—or animals or the weather —the skating pond, for example.

2. Play the Park Game. Close your eyes. Find the park. Then give your imagination free play and start listing the crazy images that

come to mind—as long as they are seen in the setting of the park. They don't have to be things you actually experienced in that very place. What do you see?

a nun bouncing a basketball
a Salvation Army band
a clown on a unicycle

Or perhaps your images will take on significance, and the park will provide you with a stable means of thinking about things that might otherwise be too scattered in your mind to put together on paper. Without consciously striving for meaning, you might become aware of a certain focus to your park imaginings, such as

a straight-laced high school teacher taking a drink
a policeman disturbing the peace by driving his motorcycle about on public walks
a group of nonviolent protestors fighting furiously among themselves
three nonconformists dressed exactly alike
a philosopher mounted on a soap box speaking in a very obscure language about the difficulty of communicating

All of these images, which are off the top of my head, relate to the general idea of *inconsistency*—the fact that people so often proclaim a belief in one thing and practice another. Let's say you were upset because of a bad deal at the hands of such a person. You might discover that your "idle fancies" weren't so idle after all but were really communicating something you deeply felt.

At any rate, the Phantom Park supplies you with the "glue" for your imagination.

Early Geography

One of the primary purposes served by self-indulgent writing is to encourage a sense of your existence as opposed to anyone else's. When you stop to think about it, you could as easily have been someone else but you weren't. You might now be somewhere else but you're not. In fact, you could as easily not have been at all anywhere or anytime. But you managed to overcome all those obstacles and turn into the present phenomenon that is sitting there reading this book (which could as easily never have been printed!).

Place strikes me as being so much more logical as a starting point for self-awareness than abstract ideas. Whatever accidental chain of circumstances has led to your present existence, it is absolutely impossible to divorce this from a sense of place. It is always *where* we have been that strikes the vivid note in the memory—not *what* we have been. The "what" is so complicated we come to it, if at all, much, much later. But each of us is filled with concrete images of the places of our past. In other words, what I definitely know of myself is that I am a something born into a certain year (not saying which one) in a very specific building (Prospect Heights Hospital) on a specific street (Washington Avenue) in Brooklyn, New York. If I let my mind relax and luxuriate in the memories of youth, it is PLACE that I find most definite and easiest to recall. (Faces are far more difficult *and vague.*)

Not to be associated with particular places, not to have this "early geography," is to be missing the very foundations of your identity. Not surprisingly, the autobiographies of many famous personalities usually start off with this early geography, and how eagerly do we soak it up! How exciting does it seem when it serves to locate an important identity! But, of course, yours can be, *should* be just as important.

Here's how the singer Lena Horne locates herself with respect to her neighborhood and her house.

> The house I lived in until I was six or seven, and to which I returned time and again as I grew up, belonged to my paternal grandparents. It was the first in a row of four brownstones on Chauncey Street. Two doors down was a "Boy's Welcome Hall," a youth center to which I can remember my Uncle Burke going to practice basketball. Next to it was a frame house occupied by an Irish family whom I didn't know very well, though I remember liking their front yard, which was much deeper than ours and had flowers. Then came our house, then the other three in our brownstone row and then a garage owned by a Scandinavian family. Their children were real towheads and seemed nice, although I was not allowed to play with them because the car grease could get you so dirty. Nevertheless, I was always instructed to be very polite to them. Across the street were three-story frame houses, mostly occupied by poor Irish people who were supposed to be the less privileged people of the neighborhood.
>
> Our house was four stories and narrow, as most brownstones are. The thing I always remember first about it was the iron fence that separated our yard from the sidewalk and from the houses on either side. What the white picket fence was to some parts of America, the iron fence was to Brooklyn in those days. Painted shiny black, each spike topped by a neat, arrow-shaped point, I suppose those fences were supposed to tell the world, This is Ours; we must have arrived at the point where there is property that must, at least symbolically, be marked off and protected. Anyway, you opened the gate in the fence, crossed a little patch of paved yard and then fol-

lowed a walk around the left side of the house, went down a couple of steps and arrived at another bit of fancy iron work, the grille door to the basement. The front sitting room lay just beyond that door. I would come home from school (during the few times during my school years that I lived in this house) and take the key off the chain on which I always wore it around my neck and let myself in this door. Waiting for me on the kitchen table would be an apple and a Hershey bar. If the weather was good I would go out into the back yard and play under the cherry tree, by myself, until someone came home. I had a little table and chair out there and I would sit there quietly and read or just think. Sometimes I would take some clothes of my mother's or my grandmother's and play dress up. Every now and then I'd run to peer through the iron grille door to see if my Uncle Burke (the youngest of my grandmother's boys and a teen-ager then) had come home from school and had time to talk to me before he ran out again to play basketball or whatever.[2]

What is striking about this excerpt is that the author makes her early geography seem interesting and relevant even though, in actuality, the specific details would not be important to anyone except Lena Horne. The secret lies in those very details. They keep the reverie from getting out of hand and losing itself in abstractions. They teach us a very fundamental principle of all good writing: SEE IT ALL CLEARLY AND SAY IT AS YOU SEE IT. You can interest almost any reader in almost anything so long as you give his imagination something concrete to work with. And the same clarity of image—as you visit the innermost places of your mind—will begin to strengthen your sense of identity.

EXERCISE

Write a short paper describing some special place or connected series of places. Don't give a lot of explanation, and don't flood the scene with remembered people. For now just concentrate on the less complicated business of transferring memory to paper as simply and as directly as possible. It is helpful to find some principle to follow in order to keep this visit to the past from getting out of focus. For example, Lena Horne first imagines her street, going from house to house in order, finally locating her own, and then allowing her mind's eye to close in on its object. Then she revisits the remembered details as you might find them in reality: the fence, opening the gate, going into the front sitting room, then the kitchen, and so on.

[2] From *Lena* by Lena Horne & Richard Schickel. Copyright © 1965 by Lena Horne & Richard Schickel. Reprinted by permission of Doubleday & Company, Inc.

DELIBERATE MADNESS AND NONSENSE

Fantasy isn't always this controlled, because you're not always making an effort to give it a stable background like a park or the house
of your childhood. Sometimes fantasy is literally that, and you can't
nail it down to concrete images borrowed directly from reality. When
you find yourself getting far out, it isn't always necessary to call a
screeching halt to the reverie. There are other ways of exploring your
fancies than the memory of place.

The Enjoyment of Oddity

One particularly pleasant form of self-indulgence, which transfers
rather readily into prose, is to dwell on one's peculiarities. If you
recall, the preliminary exercise suggested that you try at the very
outset to think of all the answers you could to the question, WHO ARE
YOU? To prepare for the next exercise, sort of lie back, relax, and make
a mental list of the answers you might give to the question, WHAT
IS THERE ABOUT ME THAT IS ODD? Do you

wear your hair, as a boy, in a pony-tail?

wear, as a girl, leather jackets and hip boots?

wear around your neck beads or medallions which possess mystic
significance?

belong to an out-of-the-ordinary religious or nature cult?

dress and behave in a way that is so square you're considered "out"
and are therefore proud of the peculiarity?

Whatever the form of oddness, you won't be dwelling upon it unless
you wear it like a badge. To be conscious, then, of being odd is to
take another definite step on the road to identity.

Read the following newspaper account of a meeting of the American Psychiatric Association and its discussion of the relationship between creativity and peculiarity.[3]

MANIC-DEPRESSION 'HEALTHY' FOR ARTISTS

Plato Called It 'Divine Madness'
PEGGY BLANCHARD
Herald Staff Writer

The artist's fits of melancholy, the writer's periods of inspiration and the musician's bursts of creativity all could be symptoms of mental illness.

[3] From *The Miami Herald*, May 8, 1969. Reprinted by permission of *The Miami
Herald*.

The American Psychiatric Association's annual meeting at the Americana Hotel Wednesday was told that such creative fits and starts are often indications of a manic-depressive personality.

The subject under discussion was "Are There Benefits of Mental Illness?" The connection between mental illness (particularly the manic-depressive state) and creativity was apparent from the start.

"The association of creativity and psychiatric illness has been discussed for many years," said Dr. Myron H. Marshall of New Canaan, Conn., and Buffalo, N.Y. He added that this combination has been associated with artists' "varying periods of increased productivity and creativity associated with mood swings."

The connection has been studied in more than psychiatric terms over the years. Dr. Eugene T. Hupalowsky of New Canaan quoted Plato's belief in a "divine madness," "for a poet is indeed a thing ethereally light, winged and sacred, nor can he compose anything worth calling poetry until he becomes inspired, and as it were, mad," said Plato. "The God seems purposely to have deprived all poets, prophets and soothsayers of every particle of reason and understanding."

Oddness Society?

It's not just poets that are afflicted with this "divine madness," the doctors stressed. Through studies at the Silver Hill Foundation, where all the panelists have some connection, these traits were noticed in successful writers, theatrical producers, inventors, musicians, and others.

"Those who are creative," said Dr. Marshall, "are expected to be a little odd. Consequently their actions are labeled as characteristics of a creative person. Even industry has recognized this creativity and gives these people more leeway. But these traits could frequently be called mental illness in other people."

Their patients recognize these traits and they know they do their best work, creatively, when they are on the high swing of a manic-depressive. They also know they could become so depressed as to contemplate suicide. These are the risks some patients are willing to make to keep that creative spark alive.

"Drug treatment is successful in keeping these people on an even keel," said Dr. Marshall. But some patients—and in particular a best-selling writer—prefer the up and down route because they feel the problems are worth it in terms of creativity achieved during the up-swing.

Robbing Expected

"There's something about psychic suffering and artistic talent," said Dr. Marshall. "Art flourishes among the least happy people. If we work on a neurotic creativity, will we be robbing society of this artist's ability?"

"Creative individuals speak of producing by intuition and impulse," said Dr. Hupalowsky. "The period of creativity is preceded by withdrawal, apathy, and irritability. During this time he may complain of finding himself unable to concentrate and work, become obsessed with grave doubts about his ability and fearful that he has lost his creative power."

In discussing case histories of manic depressivism Dr. Charles P. Neumann of New Canaan commented, "It should be noted that the great creativity of these persons was always associated with a manic or high phase—in sharp contrast to the lack of productivity associated with their depressed or low periods."

EXERCISES

1. To what extent do you find that manic-depression or other forms of oddness in your own behavior have a direct bearing on your creative side? Have you, for example, developed acting talent as a consequence of maladjustments in your family or social life? Have you turned to music as a consolation for something that is missing in your life? What is it? Has your creative oddness caused you any anguish because of opposition from your family, school, or circle of friends? Do you have an inner driving force that has directed you into creative activities but that at the same time has become a source of despair? Try to explain the conflict.

2. Perhaps you are not especially creative nor even especially odd and rather enjoy your normality (assuming for the moment that both "odd" and "normal" are perfectly clear and useful terms). Let your mind have some fun with the subject of the creative oddballs and how you feel about them. Do you, for example, believe their creativity is enough to warrant their antisocial behavior? Or are you normal because you want to be and not because you are strongly opposed to what the others do? If this is so, make a case for the normal person. Can you be happy without being odd or even trying to be? Maybe you think the creative-but-odd person has to sacrifice too much to maintain his oddness and can't truly be happy.

3. If you have peculiarities and are proud of it, write a paper in defense of oddness and its consequence: the risk of becoming alien-

ated from the groups in which one lives. Suggested aspects of the problem:

a) Does alienation depend upon the kind and degree of the peculiarity?

b) Is a peculiarity defensible regardless of its consequences so long as the peculiar person is content? Or are there larger considerations?

c) How important is it to have the esteem of one's peers? To what extent is compromise necessary or desirable?

d) Describe one of your peculiarities and amuse the reader with a few dramatic examples of confrontations between you and society to which it has led.

e) Describe a peculiarity you once nurtured but were forced to abandon because of external influences. Are you glad or sorry you did?

f) Describe a peculiarity you once nurtured but were forced to abandon when you discovered that it had itself become a norm.

4. We're just relaxing and having fun with notions that come and go in the mind. That is, we're not at the moment terribly concerned about expository form or putting down ideas in a logical order. But it would be a shame to leave the subject of oddness without trying to pin down some significant or widespread oddity that has reached the status of a fad or style or even a whole subculture. Take something like the hippie movement. Break it down into two or three of its most obvious components and then try to trace them to their source. Did a good deal of the movement originate with the Beatles? Or was the war in Vietnam responsible, and, if so, in what way? If an entire movement proves too complex, take some aspects of it. For example, body painting; Indian dress; psychedelic posters, lettering, or color schemes; psychedelic influence on dress styles in general or automobile design or architecture, and so on.

Being Verbally Different

When I was growing up during and just after World War II, the older generation was doing its best to train us kids to be as "corny as Kansas in August" and "normal as blueberry pie." If the generation with which I entered college deserves any label at all, I suppose it must be something like the Howard Johnson Generation; certainly we did very little except sip coffee in one of those thousand orange-roofed establishments with their clean tables, nicely starched waitresses, and unimaginative menus, and talk about remote and abstract things like dialectical materialism. More boys had crew cuts than didn't, and the college girls we dated came in two varieties only: snooty WASPs from proper families, who dressed with overdone and expensive simplicity (collars raised at the neck and two deep, plunging pockets on either side of the skirt); or pallid intellectuals with figures like ironing boards, who dressed like cross-country coaches in British girls' schools.

Our professors were well known throughout the length and breadth of the academic world, which means that their books had average sales of ten copies. Their lectures were letter perfect, like crisp lettuce, and if you blundered into the wrong room by accident, you might never be aware you were listening to someone else. (In the early 1950s a three-volume study of American writers was published—the work of over thirty contributors; but the reviewer remarked that each of them sounded exactly like the other!)

As every Howard Johnson is constructed from the same blueprint, as every one of my professors sounded like every other professor, so too did every coffee-drinking undergraduate in those days look and sound very much alike. And that is what our parents wanted. Each of us was to bring home exactly the same sheepskin and enter at once the permanent Establishment, where a little niche had been waiting all along, much as they used to keep some snug nook vacant in Westminster Abbey for the remains of a nobleman, who probably never enjoyed life just thinking about it.

But now you can dress and sound like nobody but yourself if that is your wish and if you can arrange to escape the influences of whatever groups you may travel with. This freedom includes the right to express yourself on paper in your own inimitable way, and I would think you need to take being a verbal weirdo very seriously. If your speech is filled with "hey man" and "groovy" and "oh wow"; if you find yourself picking up the same verbal patterns as everyone else around you, then you are in dire peril of founding a neo-Howard Johnson cult!

One thing I *will* say for the Howard Johnson set, however, is that we all loved Gertrude Stein, probably America's first official hippie back in the 1920s. With Ernest Hemingway, F. Scott Fitzgerald, Sherwood Anderson, and a number of others, including the secretary with the unusual name of Alice B. Toklas, Gertrude led her literary guerillas in attacks against the permanent Establishment—and is about ready for a large-scale revival. Certainly nobody today expresses himself with more originality.

If we don't want to (or can't) exactly imitate her, we can draw a measure of inspiration from her example. Remember the passage I quoted a few moments ago from Lena Horne's recollections of her childhood house? Though it *was* an illustration of somebody indulging in reverie on paper, the language and the grammar were both pretty straightforward, orthodox, *square*. Here's how Gertrude Stein recalls her past. Note that she refers to herself in the third person.

> She was born in Allegheny, Pennsylvania, of a very respectable middle class family. She always says that she is very grateful not to have been born of an intellectual family, she has a horror of what she calls intellectual people. It has always been rather ridiculous that she who is good friends with all the world and can know them and they can know her, has always been the admired of the precious. But she always says some day they, anybody, will find out that she is of interest to them, she and her writing. And she always consoles herself that the newspapers are always interested. They always say, she says, that my writing is appalling but they always quote it and what is more, they quote it correctly, and those they say they admire they do not quote. This at some of her most bitter moments has been a consolation. My sentences do get under their skin, only they do not know what they do, she has often said.[4]

Nonsense Rather than the Cliché

> "It seems very pretty," she said when she had finished it, "but it's *rather* hard to understand!" (You see she didn't like to confess, even to herself, that she couldn't make it out at all.) "Somehow it seems to fill my head with ideas—only I don't exactly know what they are!"
>
> ALICE IN WONDERLAND

One way to avoid the constant danger of sounding like everyone else both in speaking and writing is to make a conscientious list of the stereotyped words and phrases, the clichés, you find yourself using all the time. In addition to "hey man," "groovy," and "out of sight," do you speak about the "straight truth"? Do you ask people to "tell it like it is"? Do you keep saying "my own thing" so often that you haven't any idea what it is anymore? In short, do you and your friends sound too much alike?

Everyone today speaks of the Communication Gap. "Getting through" to others is said to be of utmost importance. Hearing people "coming through loud and clear" is enough to "turn you on." But

[4] Gertrude Stein, *The Autobiography of Alice B. Toklas* (New York: Vintage Books, 1960), p. 70.

you can "tune them out" when they turn into "drags." It's supposedly better to "drop out" altogether than to try to get on "the same wave length" as a "sick society."

Because linguistic clichés are like contagious diseases—airborne and almost impossible to resist—it is talk itself that creates the Communication Gap. It isn't a lack of opportunity to reach people. We reach people entirely too much. We never shut up. Why is it nobody—at least to my knowledge—has pointed out the glaring fact that the less we read and the more we tend to mingle and converse with people instead, the greater has been our failure to reach them?

I think children seem to have less trouble communicating to themselves or with each other than adults do. Children frequently understand complicated adult writers better than their elders. I recall once having to babysit with a four-year-old girl and entertaining her thoroughly with readings from Gertrude Stein. "A rose is a rose is a rose" made perfect sense to her. Like Hercules having to return to the earth in order to regain his strength, perhaps each of us has to cultivate "nonsense" deliberately and for the pure joy of becoming friends once more with language *as* language. Before we can learn to use words effectively, we have to imagine ourselves as Adam and Eve on the world's first day, gathering the first words that ever dropped from the sky. Maybe we have to regress even more than that; maybe we need to revert to our own childhoods and learn once again to babble and gurgle from the pure delight of making sounds no matter what they signify. Is that what Lewis Carroll was doing when he inserted this poem in *Alice in Wonderland?*

> 'Twas brillig, and the slithy toves
>   Did gyre and gimble in the wabe:
> All mimsy were the borogoves,
>   And the mome raths outgrabe.
>
> "Beware the Jabberwock, my son!
>   The jaws that bite, the claws that catch!
> Beware the Jubjub bird, and shun
>   The frumious Bandersnatch!"
>
> He took his vorpal sword in hand:
>   Long time the manxome foe he sought—
> So rested he by the Tumtum tree,
>   And stood awhile in thought.
>
> And, as in uffish thought he stood,
>   The Jabberwock, with eyes of flame,
> Came whiffling through the tulgey wood.
>   And burbled as it came!
>
> One, two! One, two! And through and through
>   The vorpal blade went snicker-snack!

He left it dead, and with its head
  He went galumphing back.
"And hast thou slain the Jabberwock?
  Come to my arms, my beamish boy!
O frabjous day! Callooh! Callay!"
  He chortled in his joy.
'Twas brillig, and the slithy toves
  Did gyre and gimble in the wabe:
All mimsy were the borogoves,
  And the mome raths outgrabe.

Here's a little piece of verse written by one of my students whose close friend was a writer of technical material. I think she was less interested in the content of her friend's articles than in the punctuation marks. At any rate, she wrote me this delightful bit of nonsense:

PRINTS CHARMING [5]

I love each glowing asterisk
Made by your gentle touch,
And each sweet little semi-colon
Warms my heart so much.
Your ampersands are dear hello's,
Each tilde leaves me numb.
Your circumflex is simply great,
And, oh, what a vinculum!

CEIL KATCHEN

EXERCISES

1. Let your mind wander back into your past, as you did for a previous exercise. Only, this time, have a little fun with the language. One way to do this is to take each sentence that you write and repeat it aloud over and over again until the words seem to lose their meaning for you. Then see whether you can find different words without changing the rhythm pattern.
Suppose, for example, my paper began with this statement:

  "The street where I spent my childhood
  was lined with elms and maples."

Repeating it over and over, I become numb to the words as words, but the rhythm and the sounds remain as a fixed pattern. Soon I find myself saying,

  "The deet fair indent why mile cobras
  bind mig als in grappled."

[5] Printed by permission of the author, Ceil Katchen.

You do it. No doubt you'll come up with different words. That scarcely matters. Fun, isn't it? But what does it mean?

All right. Now we've got at least something to work with, something new and fresh, nonsensical but out of the ordinary, to say the least. If you go back and read Carroll's *Jabberwocky* carefully, you will note that a semblance of meaning begins to emerge, even though the specific terms are mainly very strange indeed. One of the wildest sentences, "And the mome raths outgrabe," tells us more than we might at first think. We know that "mome" is an adjective and describes some things called "raths." We also know that they have a habit of "outgrobing," which explains why, in the past, they "outgrabe."

Back to our sentence: How about "fair" as a subject? Okay? And a "deet" fair, at that. But since fair is singular, the verb has to be "indents." The "why" makes no sense at all, but how about combining "why" and "mile" into "while?" "Cobras" can stay, but suppose we make them "wind," as is proper for snakes? If we change "mig" to "big" all we need is something to be an object for wind. How about "alsin grapples?" Somehow I seem to think a cobra could have a grapple, and the mysterious "alsin" makes it doubly scary. Our sentence now reads:

"The deet fair indents while cobras wind big alsin grapples." If I let my mind play around foolishly with this sentence, I begin to supply further meanings, don't you?

For your exercise, write a series of such sentences, translating them into a nonsense language. Then see whether you can link them all up in a short paper that "almost" tells a story, as *Jabberwocky* does. Instead of pointedly trying for nonsense language through sound and rhythm, try doing a nonsense fantasy—such as Carroll's account of the killing of the Jabberwock. That is, work from a general idea, except that you will employ only unfamiliar terms in all the key places. (Don't forget "And the mome raths outgrabe.") Perhaps you can persuade the teacher to read a number of the papers to the class, and then you can all have fun trying to guess what the writer is really talking about.

2. It should be clear by now that the cultivation of nonsense in language is one sure way of cultivating a more immediate awareness of self, for you'll soon find out how different you're sounding from anybody else. This can open up entirely new worlds. You can, for example, rip open the channels of communication between people by inventing new terms for the purpose. Go up to someone right this instant and say "Perdlunck!" or any other word that you feel like saying.

If you're in love, are you deep in the rut of traditional sweet nothings? How about doing a paper designed to be spoken by a lover to his beloved, filled with inventive and original cooings and carryings-on? Or, if you're not so disposed, you might still attempt a new way to express feelings of affection, such as by cataloging your loved one's worst faults as a way of showing how totally you are accepting this person without blinding yourself to the realities.

3. Your name is probably the first identity in prose of which you become conscious. Yet, when you stop to think about it, what control did you exercise over your name? Are you John or Pete or Sandra or Joan? Are you one of those old standbys, a Linda or a Gary? With the unimaginative names most of us carry around, it's impossible to say that our labels are symbols of our uniqueness. Wouldn't you rather be called Goriathlazur or Eldrinbog?

Write a paper about your family life, removing all the names the various people now have and substituting names for which you think they are better suited. Name yourself, your mother, your father, and any other kin you wish to include. Indicate what sort of dwelling you inhabit ("house" is too common). What do you drive around in? (A zoomershtoond?) Do you own any pets? (A Klopperhound? A purreyshticktail?) Where do you get your education? What is it called? Who is your favorite teacher? Your unfavorite teacher?

In short, pretend you are Adam or Eve, having all the fun of renaming everything.

VOYAGES INTO NEW WORLDS

Once you start fantasying in prose, it's hard to stop. It's fun to visit all the strange and secret places that exist inside you. For this reason many of the world's most famous writers have gone all the way and remained deep in their innermost selves long enough to bring to the surface entire countries and even new species of human and animal life that inhabit them.

Such "escapism" often turns out to be not a true rejection of reality, but rather a way of *rediscovering* it. Fantasy landscapes often bear a disguised resemblance to one's familiar surroundings. But one alters them for various reasons to emphasize certain characteristics—perhaps like creating a mythical country that gets buried in smog and other forms of air pollution and then inventing all sorts of wonderful devices to purify the atmosphere. This is *wish-fulfillment*, but sometimes fairy tales bring to light useful ideas.

They can also make it possible for us to express secret fears or hopes. Sometimes reality becomes so depressing it's a pleasure to turn away from it for a time and idly daydream, spinning fables of unknown terrains and peoples. But, if the things that bother us are strong enough, they'll invade our subconscious selves and make their way into our Never-Never Lands.

Without working very hard at it, you'll find it quite easy to turn the fantasy exercises in this section into meaningful commentaries on current issues. At the same time, you'll be continuing to indulge yourself in the luxury of imagination, continuing to develop a sense of identity through exploiting rather than denying your peculiarities. If nothing else, fantasying carries you away from the direct confrontation of reality long enough to get you rested, ready, in short, to plunge back into battle refreshed and invigorated.

The Secret Country

We began this chapter by remembering actual places from our past, such as parks and old houses. But the imagination is also capable of putting together a brand new countryside out of bits and pieces from actuality: a tree from a farm in Georgia, a flower-covered hillside from Wisconsin, a quaint fishing dock from Oregon. Nearly everyone has awakened from a profound sleep and seen traces of that private land.

It may be that the secret landscape beckons to us because it is not where we really are, and everyone must dream of some alternative to his existence. The dweller in the urban ghetto dreams of a spring countryside with clean air and lots of room to wander in, but just as assuredly does the Madison Avenue executive gaze down at the tangle of New York from his high-rise apartment and wonder how he can escape from his complex problems, some unpleasant associates, and the same buildings, cabs, restaurants, and lounges to which his profession takes him day after day. No doubt he too has a private little paradise (perhaps a Tahitian lagoon?) where he sometimes hides.

One of the most obvious uses of the secret country is compensation. If you live in a cold climate and finally become exasperated with the snow, ice, and sleet, you may shut your eyes and feel yourself floating ever so gently in a pool of the clearest blue tucked away in the heart of some forgotten island. If you live in a hot climate and become fed up with the humidity and the mosquitoes, you may shut your eyes and suddenly find yourself the master of a quaint chalet looking down upon a Swiss valley.

If it were not for the phenomenon of the secret land, the cumulative body of human folk lore, mythology, and religious fable would be almost bankrupt. The visitation has its practical side. What did the ancient Hebrews do while they were in exile and leading such miserable existences in the arid desert? Throw up their hands and resign themselves to their thirsty fate? Not at all. They told each other and their children wondrous stories of a land of milk and honey, a land that was green and wet from the waters that rolled down from the mountains. One of the earliest visions of heaven is that of the famous secret country described in the Twenty-third Psalm, the land of green pastures and still waters and a cup that runs over.

In 1933 James Hilton wrote a famous novel called *Lost Horizon*, which told of a far country hidden deep in the Himalayas, a place to which he gave the immortal name Shangri-La. You don't even need to be told of its beauty. The very sound of the word falls softly and exquisitely upon the ears. Shangri-La is a land of unending spring, spared by the high mountains from the wintry blasts and blinding snowstorms of the outer world. It is a land of mystical climate, where people live to incredible ages so long as they never set foot again in the world beyond. Shangri-La became the official refuge for America's reading public from the grim Depression years, but, more than that, it became a lasting symbol of every man's private dream. Ever since Plato told mankind that there are two planes of reality—one, the actual world of birth, growth, and death; the other, an eternal world beyond the senses where change is unknown—men have longed for the something over the rainbow.

You may argue that it is foolish to close your eyes and visit such a land, that it is better to face reality no matter how harsh it may be. Many have contended that imagination solves no problems and only makes everything worse. But others have insisted that whatever is experienced is a reality, whether it is "out there" or not.

EXERCISE

Let your imagination take a trip into its own far country. Don't think about utopias for the moment: that is, mythical lands where people lead an ideal existence. Just enjoy the scenery. Provide yourself with a sensuously beautiful background for your dreams. Strive in particular for exotic sound effects, such as the poet Keats achieved in his poem *Ode to a Nightingale*, when he describes the marvelous landscape he visits while in the throes of poetic inspiration:

I cannot see what flowers are at my feet
  Nor what soft incense hangs upon the bough,
But, in embalmed darkness, guess each sweet
  Wherewith the seasonable month endows
The grass, the thicket, and the fruit-tree wild,
  White hawthorn, and the pastoral eglantine;
    Fast fading violets cover'd up in leaves;
    And mid-May's eldest child,
  The coming musk-rose, full of dewy wine,
    The murmurous haunt of flies on summer eves.

Don't be afraid of anything you may see, regardless of how wild it may seem. Put it down as faithfully as possible. It is often during those times when we think we have totally lost contact with sense that we are being most creative and perceptive.

The Far Country as Utopia

Sometimes, however, there seems to be no point in idly dreaming of a secret land unless you make the dream really worth your while by giving this country all of the qualities you most desire. This Never-Never Land, this perfect place over the rainbow, was called Utopia by Sir Thomas More in his book of that title written in 1516. Long before that, poets and philosophers had conjured up visions of ideal societies where people achieved limitless happiness and governments existed solely to that end. Plato's Republic, a community presided over by the wisest man alive, the Philosopher-King, was an early milestone in the literature of utopias.

Hilton's Shangri-La is a perfect society in addition to being a paradise of exotic beauty. Its mild climate allows for year-round cultivation of the land. No struggle for food exists, and all that is grown is distributed equally among the inhabitants. Nobody needs (and therefore wants) to possess material goods merely for their own sake. The people turn to loftier pursuits, such as seeking each other's intellectual companionship.

In 1921 there appeared a beautiful book by the poet Walter de la Mare. Called *Memoirs of a Midget*, this fragile novel has for its protagonist a freak named Miss M., who stands just three feet high and has no visible beauty about her person. Forced by circumstances to earn her living in a carnival sideshow, Miss M. in her agony symbolizes everyone who must endure adversity, even the jeers and taunts of the insensitive, and hide from the harsh world in a dream of the secret land.

Miss M.'s dream becomes personified when a stranger named Mr.

Anon appears one night out of nowhere to befriend her and console her with wonderful stories of his far country:

> This was a land, he said, walled in by enormous, ice-capped mountains couching the furnace of the rising sun, and yet set at the ocean's edge. Its sand-dunes ring like dulcimers in the heat. Its valleys of swift rivers were of a green so pale and vivid and so flower-encrusted that an English—even a Kentish—spring is but a coarse and rustic prettiness by comparison. Vine and orange and trees of outlandish names gave their fruits there; yet there also willows swept the winds, and palms spiked the blue with their fans, and the cactus flourished with the tamarisk. Geese, of dark green and snow, were on its inland waters, and a bird clocked the hours of the night, and the conformation of its stars would be strange to my eyes. And, such was the lowliness and simplicity of this people's habitations that the most powerful sea-glass, turned upon and searching their secret haunts from a ship becalmed on the ocean, would spy out nothing—nothing there, only world wilderness of snow-dazzling mountain-top and green valley, ravine, and condor, and what might just be Nature's small ingenuities—mounds and traceries. Yet within all was quiet loveliness, feet light as goldfinches', silks fine as gossamer, voices as of a watery beading of silence. And their life being all happiness they have no name for their god.[6]

Much more recently the film *Easy Rider* (1969), written by Peter Fonda and Dennis Hopper, contained a utopia of contemporary character: a commune hidden away on a mountain plateau in a western state. As in Shangri-La, the youthful inhabitants grow their own food, producing only what will satisfy their needs. Since those who live here have come of their own free will, they enter voluntarily into communal fellowship, having already renounced the pursuit of wealth as a goal of life and success and failure as the only standards by which to judge life.

In addition to food, the residents grow pot and smoke it together in fraternal ritual. If it appears that they live only for pleasure, they would be the first to admit it and argue that the only sensible motto for living is, "Do your thing."

The utopia created by some writers is thought of as a place that no longer exists, that has vanished from the earth because something went wrong. In suggesting reasons for its failure the writer is thus able to make a powerful statement about the weaknesses in human beings, either singly or collectively. Also, the idea of a past utopia offers a chance for showing up by contrast what one thinks is all wrong about the present.

[6] (New York: Alfred A. Knopf, 1921), pp. 221–222.

Sometimes known as the "Golden Age" fable, this particular kind of utopian myth is found in the folklore and literature of most religions. There is, for example, the Greek story of Pandora, the girl whose fatal curiosity drove her to open the forbidden chest containing the evils, like war and famine, which have continued to plague human existence ever since. The story of Adam and Eve, their eventual fall from innocence, and the loss of Eden and its joys is probably the most famous single way of accounting for the sorrow and imperfection of human life.

A great many people continue to think of the past as having been a whole lot better than the present. The utopian yesterday is one more fantasy escape route from the stark reality of today. Everyone has heard his parents sigh, "In our day, we knew how to live; you kids don't." Besides, the past that never was can be a kind of poetic consolation prize for the present that never is, and both could have an effect on a future that yet might be.

Here's an example of what I mean. Toward the end of the eighteenth century the French philosopher Rousseau wrote many books that, in a manner that sounds amazingly contemporary, decry the decadence and corruption of his age. By way of strengthening his case against the present, he wove for his readers a Golden Age myth tracing the evolution of robbery, murder, and the police state from a utopian past in which men lived close to nature in peace and harmony. In the beginning, says Rousseau, man was involved solely in those activities that insured his survival: that is, gathering food from the earth's plenty, and procreating the species. Equality and mutual trust and respect were instinctive to this primitive being. The trouble all started on the day when somebody invented the notion of private ownership:

> The first man, who, after enclosing a piece of ground, took it into his head to say, "This is mine," and found people simple enough to believe him, was the true founder of civil society. How many crimes, how many wars, how many murders, how many misfortunes and horrors, would that man have saved the human species, who pulling up the stakes or filling up the ditches should have cried to his fellows: Be sure not to listen to this imposter; you are lost, if you forget that the fruits of the earth belong equally to us all, and the earth itself to nobody!

> From DISCOURSE ON THE ORIGIN OF INEQUALITY

Rousseau's Golden Age fable was one of the strong influences on a "back to nature" movement that saw its followers forsaking the crime and pollution of the cities and setting up, in some cases, rural communes that resembled those of the present day.

EXERCISES

1. Create a far country of your own imagining, using vivid images and sensuous sounds, but make it a utopia. Describe the inhabitants, their way of life, their customs, their forms of pleasure, and their political structure or any of these things in detail. Everything you describe should be consciously a foil for the current state of society. Your utopia, in other words, should represent an effort to correct what you consider to be the glaring mistakes of the real society in which you live.
Here are some questions to consider:

   a) Are there families, or do the people constitute one super-community?

   b) If there are families, do the men take only one wife as in our system? Do the women take only one husband?

   c) Are there laws, or are these unnecessary? How are things run otherwise?

   d) What is the educational system like?

   e) Describe a typical ruler or leader.

   f) What do the people do for amusement?

   g) Has life any purpose here? If so, what is it? If not, how do the people keep from getting bored?

2. Showing the evolution from a utopian yesterday to a corrupt today is an effective means of making significant commentary on the state of the world or at least the society in which you live. Rousseau attributes the reason for crime and other human ills to the law that was created to protect private property after the first free citizen grabbed a stick and outlined the boundaries of his land.

   Think about the idea for a while. Try to imagine your own Rousseauistic primitive society in which people are living and working side by side in peace and harmony. Create your own version of the "man with a stick." As Rousseau does not, explain what makes him set off his own estate.

   Your paper should embody your deepest convictions about the main causes of the corruption in society. Of course, the man with the stick is just one possibility. You may, for example, not believe with Rousseau that *he* is the culprit who started it all. Maybe your version will have a "man with a nightstick"—the world's first cop —a tribesman who gets the notion that a police force is necessary. Your myth may show crime as a response to the law. But, again, you have to explain what made the first person deviate from the others.

You may also find, upon reflection, that the things that corrupt, such as the desire for money or power, are positively basic to all men and that it was only a matter of time before the "nasty" side of man would assert itself. In this case, your paper should give one or two examples of how it began to emerge. What did somebody do or say that brought forth the earliest indications of what society was eventually going to be like? Did a fight break out over whose piece of ground would have the better view? The richer soil? Did somebody up and crack somebody else over the head just for the fun of it? Did somebody have to miss a harvest because of illness and then realize it was just as easy to steal somebody else's?

3. Imagine a commune such as the one shown in the film *Easy Rider*. Your ideas can come from your reading or possibly your actual experience. More than likely, however, you will be imagining the ideal commune you would want to inhabit if you had your choice. In your description of this commune, correct all the major flaws you find in the communal system as you know it to be in reality.

INVENTING PEOPLE AND OTHER BEINGS

The Mysterious Stranger

Sometimes our fantasies create, in addition to the secret land itself, the vision of a mysterious figure who hails from there and comes into the midst of our world. Almost from the beginning of man's literary record of himself, there have been myths and legends, stories, poems, plays, novels, and operas on the subject of the visitation of the Stranger and the effect he has on a certain person or group of persons.

The Mysterious Stranger is the symbol of the qualities we would like others to possess or to find in ourselves. He is usually super-cool, marvelously capable of doing just the right thing in any crisis. Often he is made to save an entire community from some disaster—like St. George slaying the dragon, for a medieval example, or the cowboy Shane, created in modern times by Max Brand, riding his snow-white horse out of the faraway hills and disposing of the bad guys who have been plaguing a settlement of basically decent and gentle folk. In his haunting autobiographical play *The Glass Menagerie*, Tennessee Williams describes the Gentleman Caller, who comes to dinner and provides the crippled Laura with the only tenderness she has ever known,

in this manner: ". . . since I have a poet's weakness for symbols, I
am using this character also as a symbol; he is the long delayed but
always expected something that we live for."

Whether we embody them in a person or not, our fancies are filled
with such phantoms; they sometimes provide us with the strength to
carry on. They offer glimpses of things that might be: solutions to
problems that appear hopeless; or a totally new pattern of life just
when we feel we are mired in a deep, muddy rut. We slip into dreams
as the Mysterious Stranger's shadow is turning the corner.

To call him forth from the dim regions of our minds is to take a
long stride toward self-discovery. Whatever Mysterious Stranger will
come to visit us will represent many of our most intense hopes, and
we can tell a good deal about how we really feel about our lives by
the way this figure is handled. There are just so many possibilities:

1) The Stranger is long awaited and talked about, but he never actually shows up.

2) The Stranger, representing exactly those qualities we feel are
necessary to solve all our problems, shows up, sets everything
right, but then disappears as mysteriously as he came. (This ending helps to remind us that the Stranger is a poetic figment of
our imagination.)

3) The Stranger has a hard time adjusting to our way of life and at
length either gives up or is somehow defeated by it. (This is perhaps a more realistic use of this figure.)

4) The Stranger arrives, pure and innocent, from his far country but
becomes corrupted, or at all events radically altered, by his experiences in "our world." (You could have some fun with science
fiction if you select this possibility.)

5) The Stranger is unseen by and therefore unknown to anyone
except you, and this creates a conflict with an unsympathetic
environment.

This last possibility has provided the theme for a number of both
amusing and touching stories and plays. One in particular was *Harvey*, which won for its author Mary Chase the Pulitzer Prize for
drama in the mid-1940s. The title character is an invisible six-foot
rabbit, who enjoys his nips and is a constant companion to a good-
natured drunk named Elwood P. Dowd. That Harvey doesn't actually
exist seems immaterial, as the audience observes the beneficial effect
that believing in him seems to have on Elwood. But an inevitable
conflict arises between the demands of reality and the sweet pleasures
of illusion. While believing implicitly in Harvey, Elwood is kind,
thoughtful, and gallant. Near the end of the play his sister has him
committed to a sanitarium for "the cure" but is stopped at the eleventh
hour from making this dreadful mistake by the cab driver, who de-

scribes how the people who take this cure arrive as happy saints and leave as miserable "bastards."

The value of not only illusion but of idealism in general is questioned and examined when you indulge yourself in the myth of the Stranger, for he is everything you feel is required to make this a better world. The often heartbreaking need for such phantom hopes provides the theme for this tender little story by one of my students:

Randy Bulmer and Frankie did everything together. From the first thing in the morning until the last thing at night Randy and Frankie were side-by-side. To Frankie, there was no one in the whole world who was as "big and strong" and could do everything as well as Randy.

Randy's world, Frankie's world, was the big house on Skippack Pike. It was an old farm house with peeling paint and pale green shutters. On the front porch were two rocking chairs. Aunty Helen's cat, Cinnamon, slept in one, and Uncle Lou rocked in the other.

Behind the house, the yard stretched all the way back to the creek. When the creek had water in it, Randy and Frankie would take off their shoes and socks and spend the morning jumping from one slippery gray stone to another. Sometimes Frankie would slip and the bottom of his pants would get wet, but Randy never missed. At lunch time Randy tried to sneak Frankie into the house without Aunty Helen seeing his wet pants, but he usually got caught. Randy tried not to listen when Frankie got yelled at. He would stand next to him so that he wouldn't be afraid and cry, but he wished Frankie was as good as he was.

After lunch Randy and Frankie had to take naps. Randy liked it when it rained. Before he got into bed, he and Frankie would sit on the window seat wrapped up in a quilt and watch the rain. It made Randy feel very warm and safe to know he was inside and the cold windy rain was outside.

When he got tired of looking outside and seeing nothing but rain, he would climb into the big double bed and pull the quilt up around him. The sound of the rain on the roof made him think of soldiers marching and reminded him of the picture of his Daddy in his uniform on the table downstairs. One day he would be a soldier too, and Randy would fall asleep dreaming of soldiers, and his Daddy going off to war.

Randy and Frankie spent the early afternoon swinging. The swing was a wooden seat with a rope on each end, and was tied to a branch in the oak tree. It swung out over the rose garden which was down the hill. When Randy swung on it he could just imagine how a bird must feel when it flies. He didn't like to look down, though, because he was afraid that he would fall into the rose bushes. Frankie couldn't swing very high by himself, in fact, he could barely move the swing at all. So Randy had to push him. They took turns on the swing, first swinging sitting down and then lying flat on their stomachs on the seat and flying out over the garden like birds.

When Randy got tired of swinging he and Frankie would pick some daisies from the lower field for Aunty Helen. They would take them up to the house when they went in for a snack. Aunty Helen fixed the flowers for the dinner table while Randy had his milk and cookies. She always forgot about Frankie so Randy would share his snack with him.

Then with a straw picnic basket, Randy and Frankie made the inspection of the fruit vines. The grapes on the arbor in the back were still green so after eating a few hard, sour grapes they gave up and tried the mulberry bush by the drive.

Randy liked to go inside the bush and stand and look out. It was almost like having an umbrella and all the rain falling all over. One day when he was big he would let his hair grow long and it would hang all around like a mulberry bush, and he would be able to look out at people, but they wouldn't be able to see him.

It was cool sitting under the bush with the breeze blowing and the vines scraping the ground sounded like a broom sweeping a rug. He always ate more mulberries than he put in the basket and they made him thirsty. So when no one was looking, he and Frankie would get a drink of water from the hose.

Randy and Frankie took their baths early and came down to dinner in their pajamas. After eating they would help Aunty Helen clear off the table. Sometimes Frankie would drop a plate and it would break, but he tried to be very careful. After they dried the dishes, Randy and Frankie went in and watched television with Uncle Lou. Randy's favorite program was cartoons but they never came on at night, only on Saturday morning.

At eight o'clock Randy and Frankie would hop one step at a time up the stairs to bed. After Randy said his prayers Aunty Helen would tuck him in and kiss him goodnight. Lying in his bed in the dark, for the first time all day Randy felt alone. He turned over and put his arm around the other pillow lying empty next to him and said, "Goodnight Frankie."

EXERCISES

1. Like Randy in the above story, did you ever create an imaginary friend? If you don't remember, ask your parents. Write a paper describing him. Indicate the reasons you brought him into being. Describe some of your activities together. Did any conflicts ever arise between your friend and the "real" world? How were they resolved? Finally, under what circumstances were you and your friend forced to part?

   This writer's story is somewhat effective in its simplicity, but I'm sure the assignment can be done more skillfully. For example, the reader isn't really moved by Frankie's need for Randy because not enough details are given. If you select this assignment, make certain that you emphasize the conditions of the "real" world that drive you to fantasy, though the student no doubt intended to show only that making up such companions is a normal part of growing up. Still, I think the vacuum they fill has to be indicated, and why not take advantage of a good chance to move your reader by describing the day you finally "grew up" and never saw your friend anymore?

2. Make up a fable about today. Describe a person or group of persons with a problem that really exists. For example:

   a) They live in a polluted environment, and their days are numbered.

   b) They have been arrested for setting up a commune on the outskirts of an unfriendly town that denies squatters' rights to vagrants.

   c) They are blacks seeking homes in an all-white neighborhood.

   d) They are American diplomats who must decide whether to commit American troops to support the non-Communist side in a civil war in a remote country no one has ever heard of.

   They are trapped in their problem until the Mysterious Stranger arrives. You can take it from there. He will, of course, represent some course of reason that is really *yours*. Through such a paper you can project yourself into the world of actual and excruciating dilemmas and see how you would solve them. By what happens to your Stranger, the reader should be able to tell exactly how you feel about the chances for the problem's ever being solved. Even if he is successful, it may be that the means used are obviously not available in the "real" world or else depend upon some aspects of human nature you feel can never exist. If pollution, for example, is finally stopped when the

Stranger persuades everyone to stop driving cars, the reader will *know* you're deep in fantasy. In other words, you can have a "happy ending" without suggesting you naïvely believe it can happen. Or, you can make the Stranger fail in order to bring your message home to the reader.

New Species

One of the delights of fantasying either in your armchair or on paper (where it counts) is the inalienable right to bring new orders of beings into existence whenever you choose. Even the Mysterious Stranger has to abide by the restrictions of humanity. That is, he is imagined as walking upright, conversing in our tongue, and so on. (This goes for Harvey, the six-foot rabbit, who otherwise has all human characteristics.) The laws of human experience therefore place limits around what you can do with your fancies—*unless* you go outside these laws. And why not?

Jonathan Swift is the name that perhaps comes most readily to mind in this regard. Maybe *Gulliver's Travels* was written to give mankind a good scolding and make it conscious of its outrageous follies, but the author had himself a fine time in the process of writing his book.

As everyone recalls, Gulliver travels first to the country of the Lilliputians, six-inch men who measure the universe in their own terms and, like humankind itself, are swollen with unjustifiable pride in their achievements. The whole point of creating such a tiny species was to show how foolish it is for man to boast and swagger over his prowess and his supposed importance in the universe, when, for all we know, we are infinitesimal beings ourselves. It takes the arrival of Gulliver on their shores to bring the Lilliputians face to face with a new possibility for human size and power.

Don't get the impression, however, that, if you indulge yourself with such creations, you have to be primarily concerned with making a point. The whole premise of the assignments in this chapter is that you are to have fun with them. Sacrifice meaning for charm, if necessary.

Swift's Lilliputians are memorable as achievements of the imagination, quite apart from what they have to say to us as symbols. Literature contains few moments as vivid and delightful as this famous account of Gulliver's awakening on the Lilliput coast after his shipwreck:

> I heard a confused noise about me, but in the posture I lay, could see nothing except the sky. In a little time I felt something alive moving on my left leg, which advancing gently forward over my

breast, came almost up to my chin; when bending mine eyes downwards as much as I could, I perceived it to be a human creature not six
inches high, with a bow and arrow in his hand, and a quiver at his
back. In the mean time, I felt at least forty more of the same kind (as
I conjectured) following the first. I was in the utmost astonishment,
and roared so loud, that they all ran back in a fright; and some of
them, as I was afterwards told, were hurt with the falls they got by
leaping from my sides upon the ground. However, they soon returned; and one of them, who ventured so far as to get a full sight
of my face, lifting up his hands and eyes by way of admiration,
cryed out in a shrill, but distinct voice, 'Hekina degul': the others
repeated the same words several times, but I then knew not what
they meant.

Swift has a passion for giving his readers not only the physical description of his new beings, but their language as well.

All is not charm in *Gulliver's Travels*, however. In the final book,
Swift creates the Yahoos, a race of apelike creatures with filthy and
loathsome habits. Vaguely resembling mankind in their general con-
tours, the Yahoos are mentally so retarded and morally so degenerate
that they exist as the slaves of a different race—beautiful horses,
called the Houhynmhnms and possessed of an exquisite refinement of
reason that Gulliver realizes puts man to shame. In fact, Gulliver decides he wants nothing more than to disappear from human society
altogether and spend the rest of his life among these marvelous and
rational horses. The most tragic moment of the whole story occurs
when Gulliver makes the appalling discovery that he is really a Yahoo,
for all his pretense at being civilized. Here is the description of how
that discovery is made:

> Being one day abroad with my protector the sorrel nag, and the
> weather exceeding hot, I entreated him to let me bathe in a river that
> was near. He consented, and I immediately stripped myself stark
> naked, and went down softly into the stream. It happened that a
> young female Yahoo standing behind a bank, saw the whole proceed-
> ing; and inflamed by desire, as the nag and I conjectured, came running
> with all speed, and leaped into the water within five yards of the place
> where I bathed. I was never in my life so terribly frighted; the nag
> was grazing at some distance, not suspecting any harm; she embraced
> me after a most fulsome manner; I roared as loud as I could, and the
> nag came galloping towards me, whereupon she quitted her grasp,
> with the utmost reluctancy, and leaped upon the opposite bank,
> where she stood gazing and howling all the time I was putting on
> my cloaths.
> This was matter of diversion to my master and his family, as well
> as of mortification to my self. For now I could no longer deny, that I
> was a real Yahoo, in every limb and feature, since the females had a
> natural propensity to me as one of their own species: neither was the
> hair of this brute of a red colour (which might have been some excuse
> for an appetite a little irregular) but black as sloe, and her countenance

did not make an appearance altogether so hideous as the rest of the kind; for, I think she could not be above eleven years old.

Since he doesn't make the grade, Gulliver is forced to pay the consequences of his humanness. He must depart forever from the utopia of the white horses and return to human "civilization," which fills him with the same horror and disgust as had the first sight of the dreaded Yahoos.

The Swift of the twentieth century is undoubtedly J. R. R. Tolkien, author of the great epic of Middle-earth and all its marvelous inhabitants, the trilogy *The Lord of the Rings* and *The Hobbit*, which serves as its prelude. Written in the 1930s, the Middle-earth novels have recently enjoyed a considerable vogue and continue to be among the most widely read books on college campuses.

The dominating species of Tolkien's tales are the hobbits, who grow to about three feet in height and resemble neither humans nor animals. Indeed controversy has raged over just what a hobbit might look like. If *The Lord of the Rings* were ever turned into a movie, for example, what sort of makeup and costumes would the director use to create an accurate visual counterpart of these delightful creatures, who continually tease the imagination?

> I suppose hobbits need some description nowadays, since they have become rare and shy of the Big People, as they call us. They are (or were) a little people, about half our height, and smaller than the bearded Dwarves. Hobbits have no beards. There is little or no magic about them, except the ordinary everyday sort which helps them to disappear quietly and quickly when large stupid folk like you or me come blundering along, making a noise like elephants which they can hear a mile off. They are inclined to be fat in the stomach; they dress in bright colours (chiefly green and yellow); wear no shoes, because their feet grow natural leathery soles and thick warm brown hair like the stuff on their heads (which is curly); have long clever brown fingers, good-natured faces, and laugh deep fruity laughs (especially after dinner, which they have twice a day when they can get it).[7]

The most irresistible thing about the hobbit is that he is by no means one of your Walt Disney creations. He is not nauseatingly sweet and adorable, like the thousands of chipmunks, squirrels, and skunks with cute faces and scented with Chanel No. 5 with which the Disney staff has filled its enchanted forests. (Not that such sweetness and light have no place in the world of everyone's childhood, but hopefully we are all a little past that stage by now.) The Disney animals have the function with respect to utopian fantasies. They are what we, in our less sophisticated moments, would like to think people can always be: loyal, considerate, sacrificing. Hobbits, on the

---

[7] J. R. R. Tolkien, *The Hobbit* (Boston: Houghton Mifflin Co., 1937). Reprinted by permission of Houghton Mifflin Co. and George Allen & Unwin Ltd.

other hand, throw tantrums, nurse secret grudges, get drunk on beer, and can be envious, greedy, jealous, and downright selfish. The fact that they are not saints endears them to us.

Tolkien has repeatedly denied having any other aim in creating all of the species of Middle-earth than that of entertaining his readers and himself. Swift is more obviously moralistic. What makes both *The Hobbit* and *The Lord of the Rings* such absorbing reading is, as I have hinted, the overwhelming feat of the imagination which they represent. The frailties and problems of these fantasy creatures are the very reasons we can identify with them. They are, in a sense, far more real than even Swift's beings because they appear to belong to a world that has the same ups and downs as our own. Maybe that's why we enjoy spending so many hours in Tolkien's company.

The hero of *The Hobbit*, for example, is Bilbo Baggins, a middle-aged bachelor of settled ways and decided preferences, who dislikes having his placid mode of existence intruded upon. He is especially averse to taking on responsibilities (like most of us, of course). Nevertheless he is asked to accompany a band of dwarves and elves on a perilous sort of Mission Impossible to retrieve a lost treasure from a dragon's underground hideout. They need a hobbit because he's wiry and agile enough to get into tiny crevices and quiet enough to elude detection even from the ears of a dragon.

In the course of the harrowing journey, Bilbo finds a magic ring, which makes the wearer invisible and grants him almost limitless powers. The only trouble is that the ring also corrupts whoever owns it, causing the lust for power to eat away any noble tendencies he may ever have had. So Bilbo decides having the ring isn't worth the trouble, even though Gandalf the magician has warned him the ring will bring devastation to all of Middle-earth if it should fall into the wrong hands. In other words, Bilbo is made to feel it is his mission in life, his sacred duty, to save the world by guarding the ring. (You can well imagine how many evil creatures try to steal it in the course of the four novels, and you can understand how unpeaceful will be the life of its guardian.)

What does Bilbo do, the sly old codger? He bequeaths it to his nephew Frodo to dispose of as he can. He passes the buck, as any of *us* might very well do. Frodo, for his part, becomes an unwilling hero, a hobbit who happened to be in the right place at the wrong time and now must face the awful prospect of getting rid of the ring or being responsible for the doom of the whole world. Frodo, in short, has to ask the question familiar to everyone: WHY ME?

To attempt a summary of Frodo's arduous journey to locate the Mountain of Doom and cast the ring back into the fires from which it was originally forged is beyond the scope of this book. If the reader hasn't made friends with the hobbits and their world, he is urged to do so with dispatch. But even without having read Tolkien's masterpiece, one can understand what makes it "go." It throbs with life because its species—not only the hobbits, but elves, dwarves, orcs (a weird type of wolf), talking trees, and countless other things sometimes too odd even to have a name—are created thoroughly and not symbolically. Tolkien has fully indulged himself with his fantasy and, in so doing, has given his readers a huge present.

Still, what he accomplishes beyond entertainment is *insight*. By spinning a myth, the writer can be more objective when the problems are not those of his own family or the people across the street. He isn't going to be able to turn off his integrity at will. Whatever he writes about must embody certain awarenesses that are very close to him. Tolkien, for example, seems to be hung up on the problem of responsibility. Perhaps he has himself been in a position where he was supposed to carry the ball and didn't especially relish having this "privilege" foisted upon him.

Contemporary parallels immediately suggest themselves. One can fancy a modern-day Tolkien spinning a yarn about mythical creatures who have to face the problem of being drafted in order to defend another country, inhabited by other kinds of creatures, with whom they have little in common. One can fancy the question arising "Why must we be the ones to do it? Why don't they help themselves? They can't? They won't? They don't care anyway? If so, why should we?"

It helps to put such problems off at a distance. Not only do we get a better perspective, but we can bear to face them when they seem to belong to unreal beings. Insight, in other words, may come easier when you're not so close to something. Besides, there's always the charm of the creation itself to compensate for whatever depressing conclusions you may reach. You can always console yourself for the hopelessness of some real situation by reminding yourself that you're still in a fantasy world.

EXERCISES

1. The hobbit books tantalize the imagination with more possibilities for writing than anyone could have time for, but here is one obvious response:

    Create a species with the appeal of hobbits. That is, its members should have characteristics and qualities that make them delightful in themselves. *Don't try to mean anything by them.* If possible, read at least *The Hobbit* in preparation for this exercise. (Don't scream.) Ask yourself what it is that makes Bilbo Baggins so irresistible. Perhaps his name (what about it?)

his size (why are small things appealing?)

his age (he is getting on in years, but maybe this is better than if he were young; why?)

his traits (he likes to eat; he is not very altruistic; he is seldom a good sport and doesn't adjust readily to unpleasant circumstances but gripes as much as anyone else).

The main point of this assignment is to avoid Disney like the Black Death. Delight, but don't nauseate, the reader. Give your new beings some nasty habits or a few mean streaks.

2. But if you want to be more serious—that is, use your new species to help you get at some important insights—do so by all means. Here are some guidelines you may want to follow:

   a) Imagine a being, like Frodo.

   b) Describe the species to which he belongs, indicating its habitat, appearance, diet, customs, and general characteristics.

   c) Describe some problem with which this species is faced, but make the problem center around your hero. (Frodo's being the one to have to get rid of the ring, for example.)

   d) Describe some adventures the hero has in the course of trying to solve the problem. (Does he, for example, defect to another country to avoid the draft, and does he run into assorted goblins and witches?)

3. There's nothing to stop you from being even more relevant if you have a mind to. You may, for example, create a species that discriminates against another species, or one whose older members become nuisances and have to be gotten rid of, or one whose younger members rebel against the customs of their ancestors, or one that develops so much clever scientific technology that it puts itself altogether out of existence. You can have fun creating, but be pointed and meaningful at the same time.

4. Invent a species like Swift's Lilliputians. That is, they should be tiny beings who believe they have accomplished a good deal. (If they resemble modern man, who can stop you?) Then have their country invaded by a Gulliver figure or alien group (perhaps a super-race from another planet, though this device has been used a little too often). What do they discover about themselves as a result? What happens to them? Do they change their proud ways after this encounter?

5. If you remember, Gulliver, after discovering he himself was a Yahoo, was forced to leave the Houyhnmhnm utopia, but he was also unable to adjust to his own kind after coming back home.

(He tells us he can't stand the Yahoo stench of his family and takes refuge in the stable with the horses.) Following this model, write a paper about somebody (you—who else?) who takes a journey and finds himself, quite by accident, in a utopia, but can't stay there. Describe carefully the utopia and the person's reasons for preferring it to the world he has just come from. After he is cast out, what does he do? Does he readjust to his former life, or does he become, like Gulliver, a real oddball, sleeping in stables and the like?

6. Another use of the imaginary species is to throw some serious light on humanity by comparison. Many years ago Al Capp, creator of L'il Abner, Daisy Mae, and all the unkempt inhabitants of Dogpatch, invented the Schmoo, a kind of animal with the most beguiling face and beautiful disposition you have ever known. The Schmoo's main characteristic was his utter adoration of man (somewhat unjustified!) and a natural instinct that told him that he and his kind existed solely for man's pleasure. If you looked hungrily in a Schmoo's direction, he would literally die of joy to think you wanted to devour him. (I have no doubt hundreds of people became vegetarians during the height of the Schmoo's popularity.) In creating the Schmoo, Capp was able to imply many things about man. Was he, in fact, a cannibal? Did the Schmoo's almost divine willingness to sacrifice himself put man's egotism to shame? In any event, Capp was able to give us the sheer delight of associating with his beautiful creation and at the same time make us realize he had a more serious purpose. (Many great fantasies have this dual quality.) Create your own Schmoo. He doesn't have to be as wonderful as Capp's little creature: he can be anything you like. Your objective is to shed some light on mankind through his relationship with your new kind of being. If you have artistic talent, you might draw a picture to accompany your paper.

7. Since we've mentioned the Disney world quite a bit, let's have some fun with it. Take a traditional fairy tale of the sort that the Disney establishment usually treats, such as "Cinderella" or "Snow White" or "Sleeping Beauty," and treat both the characters and events as you think they should be treated. If current issues creep into your fables, I suppose that can't be helped.

Hints:

a) Cinderella's foot doesn't fit the slipper.

b) Haven't Cinderella's stepsisters been discriminated against just because they're ugly?

c) Isn't Cinderella's stepmother entitled to some understanding?

She's got two unmarried daughters on her hands. Why has she always been so unflatteringly portrayed?

d) What, in the long run, really recommends Cinderella? What can she do? Why does she deserve success merely because she's pretty?

e) How about the later life of Cinderella and Prince Charming? ("Don't you ever read a book?" "You never asked me if I was smart!")

f) The real story of the witch in "Snow White." (How would *you* like to be told by your mirror that you'd had it and some-one else was taking your place?)

g) The moral problems involved in Snow White's residency in the same house with seven bachelors. What does the community say? What pressures do they apply to rectify this appalling setup?

h) The curse on Sleeping Beauty is invoked by another witch, this one because she hadn't been invited to the christening. Why wasn't she?

i) Why not write a short history of the witch as a misunderstood victim of prejudice?

8. Since it traditionally embodies wish-fulfillment, it is necessary to keep bringing the fairy tale up to date. It's too bad that nobody does this and that we still rely on the brothers Grimm, Andersen, and Mother Goose. So I hereby nominate *you* to contribute a new fairy tale to the world's tired old supply. Here are some things to consider:

a) The hero (or heroine) should embody what you consider ideal physical or moral qualities.

b) There's got to be an antagonistic force that represents all the wrong values.

c) There's got to be suspense. The villain(s) should seem to be winning.

d) There's got to be a happy ending. The forces of right should triumph or else be saved by some "higher" force (like the old fairy godmother).

e) Try to be as up to date as possible. Is the hero an IBM computer? Is the villain an IBM computer? Is the hero the man in the moon who finally outwits the astronauts and regains the peace and solitude he has always enjoyed? Or is he perhaps a student who undoes the educational establishment by some brilliant strategy?

"You have a philosophy and a morality that determine what you say to and how you feel about other people."

2

THE SELF
IN SPACE

Each of us inhabits two worlds. The one we have just been exploring
is the world of the inner self: of dreams, fantasies, and all sorts of
oddball notions. It is as limitless as we care to make it, and though
it is inhabited by a great many phantom creatures, it is as private as
a padded cell. So long as we choose to remain deep within its confines, we are safe from the prying eyes of intruders and the incessant
knockings on the door of our awareness.

But it can't last. Sooner or later it is necessary to awaken from the
dream and come back to the reality of yourself as a being in space,
one who belongs to the world of commerce and human relationships
where there are problems and pain and joy.

In this world of space you operate as a particular individual. You
already have an identity here, whether you fully understand it or not.
You act, react, and interact in characteristic ways. You have a philosophy and morality that determine what you say to other people and
how you feel about them. You fall in and out of love in this world.
You eagerly seek out or else run away from encounters and even
closer relationships. You belong to a society; you are a citizen of a

country. Such membership imposes certain obligations upon you that you may sometimes accept willingly and sometimes reject angrily. You may even be called upon to make sacrifices, rising above narrow self-interest and giving up money, time, perhaps even your life in a cause that is bigger or higher than your own well-being.

Because of your continual entanglements with others, you may sometimes reach a breaking point and rebel, either loudly or silently, either actively or passively. You may find that nonconformity to the demands made upon you by the others is the only answer. Then again, you may come to a realization that identity *means* making some compromises. You may find out that it is all but impossible to isolate yourself in space, and that even if you had a choice, you might not want to do without the society of your fellow men.

The exercises in this chapter are intended to help you explore many facets of the problems created by occupying space in the real world, beginning with the discovery of your characteristic nature and ending with the decision whether you want to play the game along with the others or not.

YOU ARE YOU

> I celebrate myself, and sing myself,
> And what I assume you shall assume,
> For every atom belonging to me as good belongs to you.
> WALT WHITMAN

It is sheer hypocrisy to believe you can begin your search for identity by an awareness of yourself as just another member of society and that you can (or even should) first be interested in "the others." True, they are out there, and they are real. Oh, are they ever! You can't get very far into this book without opening the door to their knocks and coming to terms with their existence. But there's little point in learning how to live more effectively in society if you don't come to it with some idea of your own importance. If you don't enjoy existing at all, why would you want to do it with more awareness?

You Have a Way of Life

You are relatively new to this world, and you have many years ahead of you in which to change, refine, and improve your life style. One day you may look back upon yourself as you are at this moment and wonder how you could ever have been whatever you now are. The fact remains that, as far as anybody is concerned, *now* is the time that counts. It makes no sense at all to live only for what was better yesterday or may be better tomorrow. Hope has its place, but it is no substitute for living.

In other words, what you want to do is pretend for the moment that your life is a movie you are looking at. Never mind the other movie you could have gone to see across the street or the feature attraction that is coming up next. Never mind that it's not a wide-screen, super-color-super-stereophonic spectacular. Whatever it is, that's what you're looking at. And you're the star of it. Never mind that you're not blonde or that you're light black, not dark black, or that your nose is a trifle too long for comfort or that you think your hands are not delicate and aristocratic. There's the star, and it's the star we've all come to see.

Now stop the camera. Right here, this instant. What's up there on the screen? It's you. Take it as you find it. This is how it all begins.

I asked a class to do an assignment in which each person wrote down his way of life exactly as it occurred to him. The only requirement I made was that it be written PROUDLY, as if each member of the class were indeed the star of the only film that for the moment was playing in any theater of the world. Here's what one student wrote: [1]

They look at me with concern in their eyes and say "You know you're not bad looking but why don't you do something with yourself?" The question annoys and bores me. Don't they know that there are a million different things to be concerned about other than makeup and beauty parlors? How can they be concerned with the shade of a lipstick when the Fall has come and the leaves are reaching for the cool firm earth with soft rustling signs and there are dragonflies in the air resting on silent wings and the greens are slipping into gold and maybe even orange?

They sadly touch the grey hairs at my temples and mumble something abut Clairol but there is a wide-eyed bright green lizard on that branch and he has something very important to say and I must go and listen to him and there is not time to be thinking about Clairol.

"You simply must do something about your hair," they say. But the rain is ending and the snails will come out and greet

[1] Printed by permission of the author, Ceil Katchen.

each other and touch and make love and you will be able to hear the deep echoing call of the frogs and the bold crows will argue and the gentle sparrows will be looking for food and I just do not have the time to have my hair done.

"There is a new kind of spray-on rouge," they tell me. But the sun is going down over the bay and the clouds are changing from white to pink to grey and the terns are flying across the sky in a perfect V formation and two wild ducks on a rock are speaking to me and who has the time to waste on rouge?

"What, no stockings?" they say in horror. But if you wear stockings you can't take off your shoes whenever you want to dig your toes into the sweet moist grass and splash through the puddle that the pigeons are drinking from and feel the tall slender grass moving against your legs.

"There is a gorgeous shade of nail polish called Iridescent Passionate Pink," they say. But I have to feel the bark of the trees and the sea grapes need tasting and some driftwood has been washed up on the beach that I have to feel and the hermit crabs want to run across my fingers and nail polish simply will not do.

"You mean you never wear a girdle or high heels?" they say and raise carefully arched eyebrows. But I have to walk for miles along the beach to look for jellyfish and at low tide the shells are best and there are skates egg cases to examine and seaweed that rattles when you shake it and now and then a baby sea cucumber that squirts purple ink and has to be put back into the sea before it dies and there is no need for a girdle or high heels.

How can you screen your vision with mascara and false eyelashes and dull your skin with creams and makeup and encase your body in all sorts of unnecessary things when what we really have to do is see and smell and taste and listen to and touch and feel everything in the whole world with all of ourselves?

CEIL KATCHEN

EXERCISES

1. Borrowing the main idea from the above example, write a paper about your way of life, as if someone had just criticized you and you were proudly defending yourself.

In order to prepare for the assignment, make a list of things you enjoy doing, things you feel are fundamental to your life style. Whether they "add up" is immaterial at the moment. That is, don't worry about having a pattern or a sense of purpose. Don't try to interpret your entire life. Just defend your peculiarities. It is enough that you emphatically believe in what you are doing.

Next to each activity you list jot down one or more objections that others have actually raised or that you think others might raise. Next to the objections jot down your answer or defense. Put the lists together, and you're got your paper written.

For example:

I Like	They Say	But I Say
To skip over puddles after a rain.	I go foolishly out of my way to find them.	If I don't go out of my way, I don't have a way.
To go for long drives with no destination.	I waste time and gas in so doing.	Think of what I would never see if I only went where I had to.
To practice shuffling decks of cards so fast they seem to be made of water.	I'll probably end up being a gambler or n'er-do-well of some kind.	If I could count on becoming an expert gambler, it wouldn't be a gamble, would it?

I'm sure you can think of much cleverer retorts than I have done, but I just wanted to start the ball rolling. The longer your list gets, the more ingenious your defense will undoubtedly be, and then your paper can hardly miss.

2. Another way of finding intense joy in your own existence is to translate the idea of yourself into some other terms: that is to find symbols for yourself. In this way you become, in a sense, a spectator of your own being. Some possibilities are to think of yourself as

a) an animal (cat, basset hound, bear, chipmunk)

b) a bird (falcon, dove, sea gull)

c) a sound (lark song, automobile horn, outboard motor)

d) an object (tree stump, rocky crag, flagpole, windowpane)

e) a season

f) a plant (cactus, Venus flytrap, fern)

g) a fruit (pear, strawberry, tomato)

Your paper takes the form of a catalog of all the things you are. Again, there need be neither rhyme nor reason to any of it. The very fact that certain symbols occur to you is enough to justify putting them down.

Plead with the teacher to read the papers aloud to the class *without indicating who the author is in each case.* As the papers are read, write down who you think wrote them. You'd be surprised how often you'll be right and even more surprised when a majority of your classmates guess *you* from the the symbolic description you give of yourself.

3. Your characteristic way of life determines your preferences in clothes, automobiles, leisure time activities, and so on. Make a list of such preferences and then try to find some appropriate reasons for them. This will provide the basis for another interesting paper about your unique existence.

EXAMPLES:

I Drive: MG's, Mustangs, Porches, Falcons, Impalas

Because: I admire English things

I believe in supporting American industry

I derive a high degree of excitement, even sexual pleasure, from zooming down the freeway

I attach no importance to a car and only require that it go

I am basically conservative and want a car that has prestige and is a solid buy

I Enjoy: flying kites, fishing, playing golf, skindiving, bowling

Because: the kite is a symbol of freedom, which I crave

I love to be challenged by an "uncatchable" fish and to be the winner

I love to be be challenged and to win out: the golf course is like nature herself, throwing in my way obstacles like sandy bunkers and waterholes; whether I play against an opponent or not, I have the excitement of trying to outwit nature

it's a real escape from this sick world to get under the water where it's quiet and (seemingly) unpolluted and almost like the dawn of creation again

in bowling, as in playing pool, you get to assert your will and to check out the results immediately; you know what pins you need to knock out or what ball goes in what pocket and the only thing that makes it happen is you

I Read: detective stories, crime stories, sex stories, seldom any stories, poetry

Because: I have an active mind and love to match wits with criminals

I like to identify with the criminal; it gives me a sense of freedom and not being hemmed in by rules and regulations

I'm so shy I doubt I will ever enjoy real sex with anyone

I'm too busy doing the things other people read about so I have no time to read myself

I love beautiful words and images; poetry is an ultimate trip, a great escape from reality

If you are absolutely honest about your preferences and your analysis of your motives, you are bound to find out a great deal about yourself from this exercise. You are also bound to learn about your classmates. Perhaps the teacher can read some papers, omitting the author's name, to see whether the rest of the class believes each writer is telling the truth about himself.

You Have a Philosophy

Whether you are conscious of it or not, your way of life inevitably becomes a pattern whose nature is determined by a certain philosophy or combination of several philosophies. You may never have given a single direct thought to what that philosophy is, but all the same you have preferences and characteristics that need to have a basis in an outlook, a fundamental set of attitudes that should add up, complement each other, be compatible. Otherwise you could be in for some unresolved tensions. But at the moment we're not really concerned with anything except locating and defining them. That is, you are you, remember? You are your actions and your beliefs. The point of the exercises in this section is to make certain you know what these are—particularly, that you aren't somebody else's beliefs.

My classes and I have worked up something we call the *philo-profile*, which we'd like to share with you now. It's a relatively simple way of determining what kind of person you are, and you can use it as the foundation for the next set of writing assignments.

The labels we developed are not those of *formal* philosophy. It should be made extremely clear that when professional philosophers do their thing, they are a totally different breed from the rest of us. Theirs is an intellectual fraternity that seeks answers to lofty and eternal problems such as "What is the nature of the mind?" or "Is time real or an illusion?" Whatever label they apply to themselves as professional thinkers is determined by their characteristic way of solving intellectual problems, but, over and above that, one or more of our informal labels could apply to their private lives as functioning human beings.

Here are the labels together with the sort of outlook they tend to characterize. No doubt you can find yourself here somewhere, perhaps in more than one place.

Idealist: expects a great deal from people

constantly being disappointed

expects much from himself; drives himself

never satisfied; always trying to improve things

can't take the world as it's found; finds it hard to be happy, but hopes for better things

doesn't always look where he's going; his mind is on other things

Realist: takes the world as he finds it without too much anger or joy either way

knows his own limitations and those of others and doesn't look for much improvement

does what he can when he can; takes advantage of opportunities but doesn't particularly create them

is generally distrustful, or at least cautious, when it comes to believing what politicians and other leaders promise

tends therefore not to be much of a joiner

Stoic: expects and generally finds the worst in people and events

therefore is immune to being hurt by them; has learned to endure pain and anxiety

derives great satisfaction from self-control and not being one to deliberately add to the world's harm—has a high sense of duty even though he expects none from others

tries to keep his emotions under wraps; stays calmer than most; seldom argues or gets violent; seldom allows himself to be deliriously happy for fear of the inevitable crash on the other side

tends to be a loner and individualist

Hedonist: lives mainly for pleasure and the satisfaction of his every need

is not deliberately cruel to others but doesn't tend to put himself out in their interest

outgoing and affectionate, deriving his pleasure from loving and being loved; craves the company of others

doesn't wait to take his pleasures as he finds them (like a realist) but makes his opportunities for pleasure whenever and wherever he can believes that a day without noticeable pleasure will never come again

believes he exists for no other purpose than such pleasure; is not religious or humanitarian in his habits

enjoys competition and winning—believes in getting ahead at all costs

Activist: espouser of causes and joiner of movements

constantly critical of government programs that are not for the people

cannot be happy in his own private daily pleasures when he thinks about hunger, poverty, and other social evils

cannot take his associates as he finds them but is critical of them whenever they show a lack of interest in his causes

finds himself continually angry; unlike the idealist, doesn't waste time hoping but believes in doing

As I indicated before, nobody is necessarily all one thing to the exclusion of the others. An activist can take time out from his crusades to enjoy the pleasures of an evening and for a few hours can even change his whole outlook. He may find his companion so delightful to be with that he may be willing to forget about his causes and movements. Similarly, a Stoic can throw an occasional tantrum, whereas a hedonist may do a big favor for a friend that involves a great personal sacrifice. Still, you can run a philo-profile on yourself to discover what label *in general* seems to fit you best.

THE PHILO-PROFILE OF ————————

This morning I woke up (reluctantly; enthusiastically; indifferently) and lay there in bed (wondering why I should bother getting up; thinking of another exciting day ahead; luxuriating in the sensuous comfort of the bed). At length I rose and dressed (with great care; without noticing what I was putting on; making sure I was reasonably coordinated but not being overly concerned with my appearance). I came down to breakfast (which I ate with great gusto and appreciation; which I barely noticed; which I gulped down while quickly scanning the paper or listening to the news on TV). Toward my parents and brothers or sisters (I was somewhat indifferent; I was deliberately guarded so as not to start a fight with them again; I tried to be pleasant but ended up fighting as usual; I was upset because they just won't ever change and see things my way; I was as usual warm and affectionate).

I got in my car (without noticing it; with great enthusiasm, ready to enjoy the pleasures of the road) and drove to school (oblivious to my surroundings and the other drivers; after a number of infuriating incidents during which I cursed and screamed at other drivers; after an aggressive and highly successful bout with traffic; after an extremely long trip during which I continually let others get ahead of me, backing down from any hint of a struggle).

I went to my classes (fully prepared after having studied diligently; unprepared because I am bored by the whole outmoded educational establishment; unprepared because doing homework does not afford me much pleasure) and found myself (alert and involved in the learning process; angered by my instructors' irrelevance and blindness to social realities; respectful toward my instructors' superior knowledge, vowing to know as much some day; unable to keep my mind on the subject, always thinking of coming pleasures or else the more important activities for the day, such as a meeting of a crusading group).

Throughout the day I (eagerly sought and enjoyed the companionship of my friends; interacted with almost nobody but went my silent way unnoticed—distinctly the way I like it; found myself, once again, the center of attraction, a dominant and dominating figure—distinctly the way I like it; wheeled and dealed and maneuvered, always looking out for my own interests, ready to seize upon every chance to move ahead; spent as much time as I could enjoying each passing moment, staring at the water of the lake, watching a flower open, just looking at and appreciating the spectacle of people passing by).

I have presented here only the barest beginnings of a philo-profile. I took a few basic activities that you probably engage in during the course of a typical school day, but, if you didn't especially find yourself anywhere, run your own profile. Perhaps you live in a domitory and haven't seen your family for months. Perhaps you live entirely alone and aren't able to interact with anyone just after getting up in the morning (too bad, because let me tell you: *that* can be the supreme test of how you relate to others!).

EXERCISES

1. After running your philo-profile, write a paper in which you give yourself an appropriate philosophical label, explain it, defend it,

enjoy it. The important thing is honesty. If you really retrace your actions in any given day, you cannot help seeing a pattern emerging, allowing for a certain number of human inconsistencies. If you drove to school as if you were competing in the Indianapolis 500, it is highly doubtful that you spent the rest of the day gazing poetically at flowers or sat back passively while your friends tried to dominate you and give you orders. If you endured your father's morning lecture without any comeback at all, you probably didn't rush to an activist group meeting and make a stirring speech in defense of tomorrow's protest march. If you couldn't stay awake or keep your mind on somebody's lecture, you probably didn't (or probably shouldn't have) taken part in a sit-in in the Dean's office.

Of course, there's no law that says your life needs to have a pattern to it. If you gave your mother a good verbal lacing, you could have driven murderously to school as a way of relieving your tensions, and you could have been all sweetness and affection for the rest of the day. You might have locked the Dean in his office because you're a born follower of somebody else's movements, not because you have any specific ideas about what your education ought to be like.

If you find glaring inconsistencies in your actions, you have a perfect right to describe them proudly and to enjoy them on *that* basis. The main thing is to be able to put your philosophy down on paper, and the philo-profile is an effective way to discover just what you're all about.

2. It is possible that the philo-profile will cause you to confront some aspects of yourself that are not to your liking. Perhaps you never realized some of your inconsistencies until you tried to retrace an entire day and look at it analytically. Perhaps you *can't* be one hundred percent proud of yourself, even though you realize you're not required to be an idealist or an activist or a Stoic. Therefore, another writing assignment is to describe the faults you have located in yourself and that you think you want to do something about. That is, you find you're tending toward activism, but there are some things you need to come to terms with in your life, such as a frequent sense of indifference to others (it is possible to join causes for theoretical reasons but not to care that much about actual people). Even at that, you must realize some of the greatest progress has come about because of a philosophy held by someone whose actions did not always exemplify it. It all depends on what you want yourself to be. Nobody should require you to do this exercise at all if you don't believe you have any faults or if you don't intend to change your ways.

3. You can't run a philo-profile on yourself without becoming aware of the general outlook of other people who are close to you. A spin-off exercise is thus to do a paper on your mother or father, your sister or brother, or perhaps a teacher. Show that there is a gap between what this person expects *you* to be and what this person seems to be himself. Do you, for example, have a teacher who appears to be a hedonist (dressing with meticulous care, driving a flashy sports car, acting like quite the ladies' man, apparently devoting most of his time to the good things of life) while at the same time he continually lectures to you on the unimportance of material pleasures? Perhaps you can put together a number of "cracked profiles" in one (amusing?) paper.

You Have a Morality

You can't have a philosophy without at the same time having a morality that determines what value you place on actions, events, and people and also what kind of treatment you expect from others. You may think you have freed yourself from allegiance to a specific moral code. You may have rebelled against the moral traditions of your family, church, or ethnic group. You may suppose you belong to the ranks of the "enlightened few," but you just can't get away from the fact that you do what you do because of its value for you and that you adore or despise the actions of others toward you because of the high or low value you attach to them.

Thus, if you have become a free soul in your family—rising when you please, eating when you please, going out when you want to, coming home as late as you desire, associating with people of your choice and no one else's—you are declaring these things "Grade A." At the same time you are labeling your parents' efforts to intervene as "Grade D. Unfit for Use."

As simply as possible: morality involves your distinction between good and bad, or, if you will, right and wrong. No one can live his life by hanging totally loose and never valuing anything. No one can take the world and the people in it precisely as he finds them. Everyone rises every day with certain expectations, and he is going to be pleased or offended, overjoyed or angered many times before he shuts his eyes once more in sleep. You evaluate living *in terms of* something, and that something is your morality.

It is important to understand your characteristic moral values and moral expectations of others. To do so is to take one more step in the direction of identity. Not to confront such issues is to lose ground in the search, so let's have some fun with another kind of profile:

THE MORAL PROFILE OF ———————————

1. I am in school because
   a) learning is good
   b) working is bad
   c) it uses up time, and it's bad to have to decide to *be* something
   d) it will prepare me for a high-paying job, and money is good

2. My favorite subject is ——————— because
   a) I can get "A" without much trouble, and success is good
   b) it challenges me, and the satisfaction of not ducking the challenge is good
   c) with other subjects I run the risk of failing, and failing is bad
   d) I know that it has a direct bearing on the work I shall be doing, and making good money is good

3. My constant companion is ——————— because
   a) sex is good
   b) intellectual rapport is good
   c) (he, she) accepts me, and rejection is bad
   d) (he, she) boosts my ego by allowing all conversations to revolve around me

4. I spent (a lot of time, not much time) reading because
   a) intellectual stimulation is good
   b) I'm not accepted by others anyway
   c) I don't enjoy thinking
   d) I *do* enjoy the active pleasures

5. I (seek, avoid) many outside associations with people because
   a) to be alone is to be bored, and being bored is not good
   b) when I am with other people, I don't have to think or wonder who I am
   c) knowing too many people becomes confusing, and it is bad not to know who I am
   d) I become easily bored in the company of others because nothing is ever accomplished

6. I (intend, don't intend) to get married someday because
   a) the social system that requires people to restrict themselves to one mate for life is silly and outmoded
   b) I want children
   c) at the eleventh hour I know I wouldn't have the nerve to be all *that* antisocial and unwilling to conform to the traditions of my family and society
   d) I believe marriage is a sacrament and intended as a gift for mankind

e) I secretly fear I'm ugly, and I don't want to seek marriage only to be badly hurt

7. If my (male, female) companion throws me over for somebody else without warning, I tell myself that
   a) this is the way of society and think nothing of it
   b) *nobody does this to me!*
   c) I am ecstatic that (she, he) has found someone whose company is more delightful
   d) it is unfair of any person not to give warning

8. If I fail a course I expected to pass without cracking the book, I tell myself that
   a) I thoroughly deserved to do so
   b) the instructor, knowing I seldom attended and never studied, was out to teach me a lesson
   c) grades should be given on the basis of actual merit, not the whim of the instructor
   d) passing a stupid course makes no difference to my life anyway

9. As a matter of fact, I am even thinking of quitting school because
   a) I know I can't do the work and it's good to find this out at this stage
   b) I can succeed without a degree, and success is the ultimate good
   c) I will never be an intellectual, and therefore intellectualism is bad
   d) I am basically lazy and have decided that applying oneself is bad

10. I may even drop out of organized society altogether because
    a) I cannot tolerate anybody else's "thing" that interferes with mine in the slightest
    b) it has too many restrictions, and all restrictions are automatically bad
    c) I like to have sex whenever I choose and get high wherever and with whomever I please, and it is good to fulfill one's every desire

The Moral Profile is something that each person inevitably constructs to his own specifications. It is not intended that the ten value indicators listed above should be applicable to every reader. In fact, no one really needs to know exactly what indicators you finally use. I hope, of course, that you will be as honest as possible. That is, if you *are* liberal in your sexual habits and *do* indulge in certain extracurricular activities that are not quite legal, you will want to analyze your true reasons and determine where the values lie. Are you smoking pot, for example, because the act *in itself* is pleasurable and pleasure is good (regardless of risks and consequences)? Or are you smoking pot because it's your way of giving your family the old what-for? If you're female and are sexually promiscuous, is it that the sex act is good *in itself* (and then good for what reason?) or are you secretly afraid you won't be accepted if you're not permissive in such matters? If you're a male and are sexually promiscuous, again is it the intrinsic value of the sex act you're after, or, because you know many girls who are permissive, are such "conquests" a means of satisfying your ego?

It takes considerable courage to be honest about your value indicators, let alone about the values themselves. Some people would hesitate to use terms like "drop out" or "promiscuous," and it's one of humanity's oldest games to evade a confrontation of one's moral code by refusing to examine issues that might lead to the place where the real money is hidden.

Such things as unrestricted sexual activity, pot-smoking, or dropping out may not apply in your case (cross your heart and all that). I will always remember one line from the musical play *Fanny* a number of years ago. The sixteen-year-old heroine has been a bit too friendly with the lad next door and has suffered the frequent consequence of such friendliness. Unfortunately, however, the young man has been shipped out to sea for three years and is therefore unavailable for the required hasty marriage. All is saved when an elderly merchant of the town offers to marry Fanny and overlook the half-century gap between their ages. Fanny, for her part, is not quite so liberal and objects to the marriage on the grounds that, after all, she might turn out *not* to be pregnant. At that point her mother with magnificent cool declares: "But, Fanny, it is not necessary to be pregnant in order to get married. Many girls aren't."

We are probably well into a period when, in certain circles, it is as embarrassing to discover how traditionally moral one is as it used to be to learn the opposite. Recognizing this fact, you must try to be as honest as you can when you make a list of the value indicators you believe will relate most significantly to your own way of life.

For all that, I don't believe I've ever gone into such matters with my own classes without having some people object. Such discussions appear to them to be an outrageous violation of their privacy. They feel they ought not to be expected to reveal to the world their private moral secrets. The morality of asking for this I cannot, of course, justify if the reader is determined to protest.

Perhaps it is better not to look too closely at one's values. Perhaps it is better to live one's life with a certain amount of illusion, just as there are some who will tell you it's better not to look too closely at the morality of *other* people, especially those with whom one is very close.

Accordingly, you will find a number of alternate exercises in this section, exercises allowing you to examine some general principles regarding morality rather than getting overly personal.

EXERCISES

1. If you are so inclined—that is, if you've got the nerve and truly don't care what others may think—write a paper explaining and illustrating your own morality. Be sure to run a thorough moral profile on yourself before embarking on the project. This way you can scan your moral code carefully beforehand and determine how honest you are being. You ought, especially, to try to balance your value indicators. Don't ignore some aspects of your life that may be quite pertinent. It *is* possible, after all, to decide in advance what "moral image" you wish to have in the eyes of other people. One good way to achieve a high degree of honesty is to use a method similar to the one we employed in the philo-profile. That is, go over the events of a recent day in your life and list the important actions in which you took part, especially those that most clearly involved the application of values.

   Optional: You can make your paper even more interesting by showing you understand how your moral code strikes other, perhaps more "traditional" types. Indicate what aspects of your morality they tend to object to the most; then defend your values against these charges.

2. Take one or two persons whom you have the opportunity to study carefully and regularly: your mother, father, teacher, minister, priest, or rabbi, perhaps. Run a moral profile that represents, to the best of your knowledge, a faithful analysis of the moral code of these people. Your paper will be most fascinating if it could represent a moral portrait of someone who stands for one set of values, only to practice another.

3. The fact that a person is not always consistent in his morality does not necessarily indict him for a crime. You may be aware of such discrepancies in your own life. You may, for example, lie to your parents about some of your behavior because you feel it is kinder to do so in the long run. Your decision in this matter could be considered Judeo-Christian, in that it represents the

desire to love and protect those who are, in a sense, "moral enemies" to your way of life. On the other hand, your own moral code in all remaining respects may be the very opposite of Judeo-Christian in its values. Or you may be aware of the inconsistent values of, say, your parents. They may, for example, object to your drinking around the house but indulge heavily themselves. They may question you closely and appear suspicious of your social behavior, perhaps because they remember quite clearly how they themselves carried on when they were your age. (The premise of the play *Anniversary Waltz* is that parents who are strict moral disciplinarians may have been wildly undisciplined themselves at an earlier stage.) Yet, even though the discrepancy is painfully obvious, you also realize the necessity for parents' having strict views.

Every day of our lives we are faced with such inconsistencies. The policeman, rushing to apprehend a speedster who is endangering life and property, will in all probability have to drive even faster himself. The lazy teacher, who spends little time preparing for his lectures, may demand much work from you—and be justified! Nonviolent protestors have been known to get very violent on the subject of "Peace At All Costs." Remember the irrational bumper sticker—SUPPORT MENTAL HEALTH OR I'LL KILL YOU? Does this argue against the need for mental health? In other words, the end may sometimes cause you to be lenient in evaluating the means. Write a paper discussing such moral inconsistency in yourself or in other people, showing why it may be a necessity after all.

4. Your analysis of your own moral code and that of people close to you may awaken a more intense concern for the moral values of the society in which you find yourself, though the difficulty of running a moral profile on even one person should persuade you that generalizations in this area are quite dangerous. At any rate, if you wish to generalize, you might give it a try. Here's a suggested guideline to follow:

> *The Establishment:* dedicated to affluence and to success as highest good
>
> gives lip service to Judeo-Christian values but practices direct opposite
>
> so intent on preserving itself that it must consider any threat automatically bad
>
> *The Resistance:* dedicated to idealism but inevitably becomes aggressive with respect to Establishment

demands the right to "own thing" and therefore cannot tolerate anyone whose "thing" is opposition to "own thing"

against the doctrine that success and failure are the main criteria and so takes a more charitable view of failure

deplores what it considers the traditional racism of the Establishment

White community: skin color is significant, and white color is automatically good, whereas black is bad

puts affluence and material possessions at top of list of goods

often disguises its racism behind "virtue" words like "freedom of choice" and "individual rights"

Black community: skin color is significant, and black is automatically good

nonviolence is the answer; we don't want to commit the same sins we are charging the white community with

militant activism is the only answer; an eye for an eye is the world's oldest and most logical morality

we are interested in accumulating the very same material possessions we condemn the white community for pursuing

poverty and persecution have made us more tolerant and humanitarian than the whites in our views

Understand: I am not presenting my own moral views in all these matters. I am merely suggesting a broad spectrum of possibilities, should you wish to try a moral analysis of the society in which you live. The different aspects of the problems are stated in order to encourage you to be as honest as you can. Your paper may show that, after all, a moral utopia is hardly likely. If you are black, for example, and decide that militancy is necessary because the whites have been asking for it, you can also decide such a position would not need to exist in your ideal society. If you are white, you may side with black militancy but at the same time recognize the degree to which you yourself have been guilty of discrimination. Your "moral socio-profile" may lead you to the conclusion that moral progress is relatively hopeless. If so, what course would you suggest? Do you believe the government is going to have to make the moral decisions for society? The courts? But to what extent does the human fallibility of people in high places argue against moral progress even on such an impersonal basis?

YOU LOVE AND ARE LOVED

If there's anything that is universal about being a self in space, it's that you're not alone. *You can't be if you try.* The rest of this chapter has to do with the consequences of this important principle.

I don't mean that the world will constantly beat a path to your door. You can build a better mousetrap, and assuredly the very first person you describe it to will ask you "But what's a mousetrap?" You can be desperate for a match and not find one person in a thousand who smokes. Your car can break down, and you can pick up the trusty black book next to the phone and find not a single friend who is able to go three minutes out of his way to drive you where you have to go. Day after day people let you down. Day after day you find more and more evidence of the fact that people hate to get involved, even when they know you. You've probably heard about that girl in New York who got stabbed to death in full view of about eighteen neighbors, not one of whom came to her assistance or even called the police. It is relatively simple to reach a point where you want to chuck it all and have nothing whatever to do with people.

But precisely at that very moment, the pattern of your life will change. Just as you curl up in your favorite armchair to begin enjoying your solitude, the doorbell will ring and nineteen friends will show up for a surprise party, having mistaken the date of your birth. Just as you have reconciled yourself to living without your girlfriend or boyfriend and really don't *mind* that you're never going to see him or her anymore, the phone will ring—guess who? The merry-go-round starts once more.

The Great Love Debate

> There are people who would never be in love if they had never heard of love.
>
> LA ROUCHEFOUCAULD
> *Eighteenth-century French philosopher*

The great question surrounding love is whether indeed such a thing exists—at least as the poets and song writers speak of it. The dictionary won't help to define it, and if you look to the literary greats, you will come up with as broad a spectrum of definitions as any single term could ever yield. One cynical writer, for example, thinks of love as a purely chemical equation, such as $2H_2 + O_2 \rightarrow 2\ H_2O$. A man and a woman pass each other in the street. Some physical phenomenon occurs within them; they are driven toward each other. They stop and chat. He asks her to view his etchings. She accepts, knowing perfectly well his intentions and hoping she isn't wrong. They play a game for a time, and sooner or later they go to bed. They throb with passion. They exchange many kisses. They may even vow undying devotion and talk marriage. But, according to our cynic, they are mechanical victims of chemistry, and what has been poetically termed "romance" has nothing to do with it.

On the other hand, the poet e. e. Cummings, this time using a *mathematical* formula, tells us that love is "1×1." Another, Archibald MacLeish, sees love in this romantic way: "The leaning grasses and two lights above the sea. . . ."[2]

Sex, of course, is part of the whole problem. Although even Christianity poses no objection to sexual relations, these are made inseparable from a social institution, marriage. For centuries our civilization has nurtured a healthy neurosis over the issue. Since marriage is supposed to be more than a sexual union, the idea of "love" as something that transcends sex has been inescapable.

Yet one need have only a meager sense of history to be aware that love, like any other idea, has definite roots in time. It appears to be unknown before the Greeks, who invented the word itself, except that they divided it into two classes: physical love (*eros*) and spiritual love (*agape*). The division has been with Western man ever since, greatly solidified by Christianity throughout the Middle Ages.

The Christian Middle Ages maintained and strengthened the separation. Physical passion and sexual union were acceptable only within the sacred confines of marriage. Otherwise, they were the sinful inspiration of the devil. If you weren't or couldn't be married, you could love, but only in a Platonic sense.

Marriage wasn't entered into lightly, for there were issues at stake, especially for the nobility, that were probably more important than the sacrament itself. Money and property were two such issues. Marriageable young ladies of good background were hardly expected to be "easy to get," and so a whole elaborate tradition, known as *courtly love*, arose. Its rituals—such as the young man's serenading the young lady beneath her balcony—became indispensable preludes to the eventual consummation. The lady was supposed to be lofty, unreachable, even nasty; and her persistent purity was supposed to

[2] From "Ars Poetica," *Collected Poems 1917–1952* by Archibald MacLeish. Reprinted by permission of the publisher, Houghton Mifflin Company.

further ennoble the relationship. Thus was "courtship" or "romance" born—the time of wooing without winning. It was "going together" before marriage, and it didn't include (supposedly) sex.

That physical union and the desires of the flesh were in themselves dirty and deplorable is made abundantly evident in the literature and folklore of the Middle Ages. This was, after all, the era of gallant knighthood, when every knight worth his crest rode into battle and braved danger and death for his lady fair; and, if she tossed him an occasional rose for his pains, he was more than satisfied. Otherwise, we are warned of the grim tragedies wrought by the flesh. A famous medieval tale tells of the unhappy love of Eloisa, a nun, for Abelard, a priest. Forced to separate when each must enter religious life, they are reunited on the occasion of Eloisa's vow-taking ceremony, iron-ically presided over by Abelard. Throughout her short and wretched existence, the unhappy nun tortures herself by trying to rise above her suppressed passion. The moral is clear: without marriage, one must love spiritually, or not at all.

The ideal of the pure and untarnished relationship—of "romance" as opposed to sex—has been around ever since. Keats' famous poem "Ode on a Grecian Urn" contains a passage that suggests a lower and a higher form of love. The lower or physical side is brief and passing; only the higher or spiritual side can endure. The narrator of the poem, looking at the pictures painted on an ancient jug, sees one depicting a young lover and his lass almost, but not quite, in the act of kissing. Since they are not human but figures in a work of art, they'll never get any closer than they are now, which is, he tells them, all to the good.

> Bold Lover, never, never canst thou kiss,
> Though winning near the goal—yet, do not grieve;
> She cannot fade, though thou has not thy bliss,
> For ever wilt thou love, and she be fair!

Of course, the big question is whether the young lovers would experience so uplifting a relationship if they were real, *not* figures on a jug, and free to sport in the hay whenever they wished. In other words, is this whole idea of romance or nonphysical love derived from a longing for the flesh? Not having it, have frustrated couples since time immemorial projected their physical passions into airy myths of poetic, but unrealistic, Platonic affairs?

Novelist and story-teller Somerset Maugham, in a story called "Red," adopts the view that love is nothing *but* the yearning of the flesh, and that once this is satisfied, love flies out the window. In his tale a pair of young lovers who meet on a Pacific Island *do* get together, unlike Eloisa and Abelard; they do consummate their desires, settle down together, and in time grow older, fatter, and altogether indifferent to each other.

Many other writers have been inspired by the same theme: not love's undying beauty, but its quickly burnt out fury and passion. Another popular subject has been the keen disappointment experienced by those who hoped for more from love: the contrast between the romantic expectation and the physical reality.

The problem is complicated by the fact that what is termed "love" sometimes means an ideal believed in and dreamed about *before* the fact, an ideal entertained by an individual that shapes his hopes and causes him to enter into actual relationships with certain prejudgments and emotional needs; and sometimes it can mean the relationships themselves with all of their many-sided, multi-leveled misunderstandings, coming-togethers, drifting-aparts, endless telephone calls, sleepless nights, long soul-searching letters, confused answers, no answers, resolves never to see people again, hours of loneliness, but also hours of quiet companionship when all the world once again seems so right.

Psychology and divorce courts can supply abundant statistics to show what often happens to those who approach an amorous relationship on *their* terms only or who have spun airy dreams about love based on the mythology of romance. Members of older generations, in particular, sometimes became neurotic and unhappy when the reality of marriage clashed with their expectations of it. The popular literature of love that so abounded in novels, movies, and songs in early decades of this century—what one writer has so aptly described as the Moonlight and Poison Ivy tradition—usually described its subject in metaphorical terms not remotely connected with the actual facts later to be encountered in marital privacy. A gentle kiss between lovers standing by the sea while a full moon cast a glimmering light on the water, may have been many a young person's idea of the complete fulfillment of his dreams.

An older, married woman in one of my classes once wrote a paper on the difference between the expectation and the reality of her marriage. Here's how she describes the honeymoon fantasy she wove while eagerly awaiting her wedding day:

> Then I saw myself clad in a gossamer nightgown, white, with hundreds of diamonds sparkling in the seams. I was as graceful as a ballerina. I saw myself dancing in some great courtyard where an orchestra played Strauss' *Rosenkavalier Waltzes*. In and out of the olive groves I danced, while my prince-lover followed at a respectful distance.

Love may well be neither the expectation nor the objective fact of a relationship, but rather a strong force existing in all of us, impelling us toward others in order to satisfy a deep-rooted, intensely personal need. Perhaps this is the need not to be lonely, not to be apart, and it is always there, whether one has found a partner or not. If this is the case, love may not be something that "happens" when two people find each other mutually pleasant to be with. It may be the highly selfish need which requires the presence of another in order to gratify itself. Is love, in other words, an "ego trip"? Is it to be measured in terms of approval and acceptance rather than the joy of giving, of making a sacrifice, as some of the philosophies of love—especially the Christian view—would demand? Or, if we *do* sacrifice and feel a selfless dedication to another, is the reason perhaps that we are paying off a debt of gratitude for ego-services already rendered? Are we showing approval to another because the other has shown approval to *us*? And which comes first?

If one reads Freud and more recent psychologists like Erich Fromm, one finds that what is really happening when we fall in love is something quite different from what we sometimes tell ourselves about it. Freud says no one ever truly recovers from the shock of becoming separated from the mother at birth. Many of our later and supposedly mature activities represent efforts to return to the comfort and security we have lost. Fromm tells us, further, that what is called love is actually a way of overcoming the shame and guilt we experience whenever we feel that we are separate from others; we can't stand to be different. We feel too insecure; hence, the reaching out to another or to others so we can become *unseparate*. But love can, according to this theory, take many forms—from an ancient tribal orgy to the need felt by the modern citizen to conform to the mores of society. Whatever makes us feel less cut off from the others can be "love."

Your generation seems to have mixed feelings on the subject. On the one hand, there is an undeniable trend toward holding frank and realistic views about sex and accepting sex as an integral, natural, and beautiful aspect of the love relationship. There is a rebellion against the classic separation of love and sex. But sometimes there is also the feeling that love is a delusion, that sex is all, and that it is to be accepted and indulged in as casually as possible without emotional entanglement and guilt. Many of today's views add up to the belief that the present marriage system, as it has been known, will inevitably decay. Sometimes there is added, however, the belief in a utopian future in which people will live together in large communes, loving freely and ecstatically, without ever feeling tied down to one mate for life.

Views like these create alarm within the Establishment, which has always relied upon stable moral laws governing sex and upon the health of marriage as an institution in order to preserve itself. Some sociologists point toward a depressing tomorrow when the full impact of today's so-called Sexual Revolution will begin to be felt: illegitimate children adding to the burdens of the welfare rolls; illegal, unsanitary abortion clinics springing up everywhere because legislation will not be able to keep up with the rising birth rate among the unwed; neurosis and guilt increasing because the law and the social mores may be offering even stiffer resistance; and thus, drug addiction and alcoholism increasing at ever more fantastic rates. And perhaps all of the unhappiness, all of the conflict will have grown out of the painful elusiveness of that one word—love.

One of my students brought in a brief list of how a few personalities of past and present have regarded love. The breadth of definition is staggering indeed. *Love is*

1) for Dante: a macrocosmic force that moves the sun and other stars;

2) for Samuel Johnson: of no great influence upon the sum of life;

3) for H. L. Mencken: a state of perpetual anesthesia;

4) for Wilhelm Bolsche: spiritual impetuosity;

5) for Ovid: a delicious game of seduction;

6) for Plato: an appreciation of beauty;

7) for Descartes: an emotion in which the soul is incited to join itself willingly to objects which appeal agreeably to it;

8) for Morton M. Hunt: any and every form of relationship between human beings which makes sense when used in conjunction with the phrases "falling in love" or "being in love";

9) for Freud: aroused from inhibited or delayed sexuality;

10) for Ortega y Gasset: a centrifugal act of the soul in constant flux that goes toward the object and envelops it in warm corroboration, uniting us with it and positively reaffirming its being.

You can tell from the foregoing list of possibilities that men have experienced one whale of a time trying to get together on the subject. No wonder people get confused. No wonder more time is spent walking the floor about this one problem than almost any other known to the human race. Surely no search for identity can ever be complete until one has given serious thought to what love means to *him*.

EXERCISES

1. If you disavow any faith in marriage as an institution, why not do a paper stating the reasons for arriving at so drastic a view? Try to be as broad as possible. That is, consider such issues as the following:

   a) Can society survive without it?

   b) Even assuming you don't want society to survive in its present form, do you have a clear and workable alternative?

   c) Would the care and disciplining of children become the responsibility of the "super-state"?

   d) Would such a state allow the individual the kind of freedom you may want?

   e) Would you, instead, have a collection of large communal families?

   f) Do you think large communal families are eligible to develop the same internal problems as smaller families?

   g) Would your system be to live with the same mate in this marriageless society or to keep moving on when the fancy strikes you?

   h) Would such a "rotation" system make raising children highly inconvenient?

   Perhaps you secretly believe that the majority of those in your generation are or will become conventional by the time they are ready to settle down and will therefore see to it that the institution of marriage survives. In this case, do you see yourself as a conscientious nonconformist? Will you observe the rotation system mentioned above, changing mates as often as you please? Will you bring illegitimate children into the world? Will this be fair to them? Perhaps, on the other hand, you have already had your fill of sexual freedom and find that you are ready to settle down. Have you come to view your contemporaries in a different light? If you have become disillusioned by the Sexual Revolution, speak your mind.

2. One way of clarifying one's own thoughts about love is to submit, instead of a regular paper, a list of twenty-five or thirty sentences, each beginning "Love is . . ." What follows should not be an adjective but a noun or noun clause. The reason is that too many people make the mistake of merely *describing* love, instead of

trying to define it clearly to themselves. Strive, above all, to be as concrete and specific as possible. Avoid vagueness, no matter how poetic you may think you're being. To call love a "many-splendored thing" may have some advantages in a popular song, but it doesn't really help much in solving the problem, does it?

To start you off, here's a random selection of student definitions:

some happy children

Shelley's poems

a corruption of clear thought

a friendly smile of approval

controlling your anger when somebody does something that disturbs you deeply

something the world can't do without

the beauty one sees when he goes to the beach on a clear and sunny day

the pleasant feeling you have when you do something nice for someone

that which is usually absent from a marriage

caring if something is wrong with another person

the synthesis of two people's efforts not to be alone

joining 100% to 100% and coming up with 100%

teasing your younger sister

having someone watch over you so you don't get in trouble with cops

EVOL spelled backwards

choosing the right one in a process of elimination

the need that binds compatible people together

riding to school with Don

buying a pantsuit for $35.00

kissing her when she has a cold

Perhaps your teacher will talk about these definitions with you. In discussing these or the ones your class will eventually write, why not set up a list of categories, such as

Eros: involved with purely physical relationships

Agape: involved with purely spiritual relationships

Tradition-Breaking: mainly concerned with smashing old ideals rather than contributing new thoughts

Psychological: concerned with the effort to be realistic and un-emotional or nonpoetic on the subject; stressing an individual's personal needs

If you want to, use these or similar categories as guidelines when compiling your own sentences and label each one as you write it. Then ask the teacher to read some of the lists or have each student read his own and see whether everyone agrees with the definition or with the proposed category.

It's also fun to have others tell you what general impression they get from your list: that is, how you came across on the subject of love. Perhaps you will discover that it wasn't exactly the way you thought it might be.

3. a) You must have seen scores of old "late" movies on television— those tired products of the thirties and forties, in which a married man meets another woman and falls "madly" in love with her, though there isn't even the remotest suggestion that anything physical transpires between them. You know the rest. He's got an invalid wife or a money-grubbing wife who knows he's got a girlfriend but won't give him a divorce. The plot was always guaranteed to extract the last possible tear from the ladies in the audience. (The critics used to call this a four hankie movie.) The two "lovers" end up in a hopeless stalemate. They can never marry, but there is the poetic suggestion that their "love" will go on forever. There is even the suggestion that this "love" is endorsed by heaven, whereas the legal marriage to the hateful wife is not. Do you think the old movie makers were pulling everyone's leg? Can such a thing as a purely nonphysical relationship exist, and can it be called "love"?

   b) Everyone is familiar with the world's most famous love story, that of Romeo and Juliet. The poetry of love in this play and the sentiments it expresses are so pure that not even a newborn baby is too innocent to listen. But consider: Romeo and Juliet meet at a party and are instantly "attracted" to each other in this most celebrated of all examples of so-called love at first sight. What do you think this means? Was it a purely physical attraction masquerading as poetry? Or has Shakespeare captured the very essence of a relationship that contains equal parts of physical and spiritual love and deserves to be labeled "romance"? Have *you* experienced emotions such as those felt by Romeo and Juliet? Describe them as precisely as you can. If you have not but consider yourself pretty worldly-wise, give your impressions of what the "romance" of Romeo and Juliet was really all about.

4. Perhaps you are already married and therefore feel more qualified than some of your classmates to write on the subject. Do a paper

setting forth your own premarital expectations contrasted with the reality. If you are aware of no difference in expectations between the "before" and "after," indicate clearly how you managed to bring such harmony about. If there *is* a difference, indicate the source of your premarital expectations. That is, was it literature? your own fantasies? your parents' lectures on the subject?

5. Do you consider your present knowledge of sex adequate? Do you have any difficulties adjusting to the society of your peers because of inadequate sex education? If so, where do you place the blame for this? On the schools, or on your parents? Write a paper outlining a workable plan for improving the chances of young people for a healthy and normal adjustment to the many problems sex presents.

6. Perhaps you are a product of an academic experiment in sex education, and perhaps you have definite feelings about the advantages or disadvantages of early and systematic training in sex. Do any amusing incidents come to mind concerning either the classes themselves or some later consequences of them?

7. A female student happened, in the course of a discussion, to mention that she intended never to have any babies. Her reason was the Population Explosion. She insisted it was the responsibility of enlightened youth to do what it could to stem the tide, even if it meant checking her own maternal instincts. She considered such instincts to be purely animal in nature and therefore to be entirely under the control of the will, if one chose to place them there. Several other members of the class objected on the grounds that it was healthy and normal for a woman to desire children and very dangerous to try to subvert the maternal instinct. The "enlightened" young lady replied that such thinking was old-fashioned and dangerous to the future of the world. She even went on to say that the desire for children had nothing to do with the need to procreate the race but was only another form of ego-fulfillment. "If you really cared for the human race," she argued, "you'd get married and adopt orphans from all the wars in Asia." Do you find any merit in such arguments? Do you think we may reach a critical point at which the "normal and healthy" instincts, which used to take care of the need to procreate the race, *have* to be curtailed in a cold-blooded and deliberate effort to save it from reproducing itself out of existence? What about the student's suggestion that women should adopt war orphans instead of adding to humanity's burdens? How do you feel about

your own plans for parenthood? Do you want children? Why? Do you believe this is just "ego-fulfillment?" Is there anything wrong with that? Do you believe some limits should be placed upon the number of children a person has? If so, who would decide? Has anybody any *right* to decide?

8. The subject is a pretty trite one by now, but it is almost impossible to leave the area we're in without considering the classic problem of the Pope vs. the Pill. If you are Catholic, you may surely want the chance to add your sentiments on this highly inflammatory topic. Today, when some of the highest-ranking clergymen have openly disagreed with the papal decision on birth control, it is no longer assumed that a devout churchgoer is necessarily against the Pill. Compelling statistics show how many married Catholics do practice nonapproved birth control methods. As a Catholic, will you have the Pill in your home when you are married? If the answer is yes, how can you reconcile your decision with other Catholic beliefs? If you are not a Catholic, what is your feeling about the Pope's stand? Do you believe he had any other choice?

9. Even as we go to press, the Pill is under close scientific—and even Congressional—investigation. No guarantee exists that it won't someday be found to yield harmful consequences, possibly leading to birth defects in the children that are finally allowed to be born. Conceivably the Pill could be outlawed. If this happens, there is bound to be renewed pressure on Congressmen everywhere to push for a liberalization of abortion laws.

   Write a paper arguing for or against legalized abortion, using religious, scientific, humanitarian, or other arguments.

10. It was inevitable that the Sexual Revolution and the demand for greater permissiveness in all sexual matters should give rise to a push for the relaxation of the restraints traditionally placed on homosexuality and other so-called "unnatural" expressions of sexual desire. For example, homosexual societies are already in existence, openly campaigning for the legalization (as in Great Britain) of sexual activity between members of the same sex. Demonstrations, protest marches, and manifestations of so-called Gay Power have brought dramatic attention to the cause of the sexual deviant as a minority group member whose civil rights are supposedly being denied when he is forced to live an underground existence.

   Do you think our society has been just in its treatment of the homosexual? What do you think accounts for the traditional abhorrence of sexual deviations? Do you believe legalization would make a difference in the number of people that practiced homosexuality? (One argument against legalization has always been that boys and girls can easily be led into homosexuality through early encounters with older members of their own sex and that the removal of restrictions would encourage homosexuals to keep making converts.)

Love for Humanity

As we have seen, the issue is still very much in doubt whether the total separation of the physical from the spiritual in love is anything but a poetic dream. But men have had even more profound dreams. They have sung songs and made inspiring speeches about a love that transcends the desire, either physical or spiritual, for just one person: a love that reaches out for and embraces all mankind. Thus we are told that Jesus loved man so much he offered his own death on the cross as a sacrifice. If this is too supernatural for you, what of the countless tales of battlefield heroics, in which one person gives up his life to save a battalion?

It's easy enough to be cynical and deny that "love" can also mean caring enough about others to renounce pure self-interest. Many contend that man is basically selfish and that any reason given for actions that deny the selfish motive are fraudulent. The German philosopher Nietzsche saw Jesus as a superman, a powerful leader whose method was love, someone who preached a gospel of humility and self-effacement but who nonetheless attracted more devoted followers than any other leader. To Nietzsche it was the power that Jesus wanted—and got. But to the religious, the power of love is truly different from the power of self-interest.

However we wish to explain the phenomenon, it is difficult to dismiss the overwhelming evidence of man's capacity for showing concern for others. If it *is* self-interest, it must exist on a higher plane than the one most of us know. It is a burning compulsion to be needed, perhaps, and a feeling of emptiness, of worthlessness unless one is richly and completely fulfilled. For the lover of humanity, perhaps, such fulfillment comes only when he has performed some great service for society.

The ultimate power figures may well be lonelier than you or I will ever be. It's one thing to say that everyone is motivated by the desire to better himself, but surely, wouldn't most of us stop far short of aspiring to be generals, college presidents, or corporation heads, not to mention world leaders? My point is that the pursuit of *that much power* may need to be explained in terms of motives that go a bit deeper than self-love. After the assassination of John F. Kennedy in 1963, one heard comments like, "I wouldn't be President for the world." Yet *somebody* had to be. Nobody panicked. You knew that there would always be someone willing to take on the job.

The personality of the compulsive *sacrificer*—the man or woman who is unfulfilled in taking care of only his private needs—has fascinated me for many years. If you read carefully this moving selection by Martin Luther King, you may find a clue to such behavior. King's struggle against fear is almost the legendary struggle of the born leader, striving to rise above self-interest, for what is fear *but* self-interest, and what is courage but a genius for forgetting about oneself?

DARK YESTERDAYS, BRIGHT TOMORROWS: [3]

After a particularly strenuous day, my wife had already fallen asleep at a late hour and I was about to doze off when the telephone rang. An angry voice said, "Listen, nigger, we've taken all we want from you. Before next week you'll be sorry you ever came to Montgomery." I hung up, but I could not sleep. It seemed that all of my fears had come down on me at once.

I began to walk the floor. Finally, I heated a pot of coffee. I was ready to give up. I tried to think of a way to move out of the picture without appearing to be a coward. In this state of exhaustion, I determined to take my problem to God. My head in my hands, I bowed over the kitchen table and prayed aloud. The words I spoke to God that·midnight are still vivid in my memory:

"I am here for what I believe is right. But now I am afraid. The people are looking to me for leadership, and if I stand before them without strength and courage, they too will falter. I am at the end of my powers. I have nothing left. I've come to the point where I can't face it alone."

At that moment I experienced the presence of the Divine as I had never before experienced Him. I seemed to hear the quiet assurance of an inner voice, saying, "Stand up for righteousness, stand up for truth. God will be at your side forever." Almost at once my fears began to pass from me. My uncertainty disappeared. I was ready to face anything. The outer situation remained the same, but God had given me inner calm.

Three nights later, our home was bombed. Strangely enough, I accepted the word of the bombing calmly. I knew now that God is able to give us the interior resources to face the storms and problems of life.

Let this affirmation be our ringing cry. When our days become dreary with low-hovering clouds and our nights become darker than a thousand midnights, let us remember that there is a great benign Power in the universe who is able to make a way out of no way, and transform dark yesterdays into bright tomorrows.

Realizing that fear drains a man's energy and depletes his resources, Emerson wrote, "He has not learned the lesson of life who does not every day surmount a fear."

But I do not mean to suggest that we should seek to eliminate fear altogether from human life. Were this humanly possible, it would be practically undesirable. Normal fear protects; abnormal fear paralyzes. Normal fear motivates us to improve our individual and collective welfare; abnormal fear constantly poisons and distorts our inner lives. Our problem is not to be rid of fear but rather to harness and master it. How may it be mastered?

First, by looking squarely and honestly at our fears, we learn that many of them are residues of some childhood need and apprehension. A person haunted by a fear of death or the thought of punishment in the afterlife discovers that he has unconsciously projected into the whole of reality the childhood experience of being punished by parents, locked in a room, and seemingly deserted. Or a man plagued by the fear of inferiority and social rejection discovers that rejection in childhood by a self-centered mother and a preoccupied father left him with a self-defeating sense of inadequacy and a repressed bitterness toward life. By bringing our fears to the forefront of consciousness, we may find them to be more imaginary than real.

Second, we can master fear through one of the supreme virtues known to man: courage. The determination not to be overwhelmed by any object, however frightful, enables us to stand up to any fear. Courage faces fear and thereby masters it; cowardice represses fear and is thereby mastered by it. Courageous men never lose the zest for living even though their life situation is zestless; cowardly men, overwhelmed by the uncertainties of life, lose the will to live. We must constantly build dikes of courage to hold back the flood of fear.

Third, fear is mastered through love. The New Testament affirms, "There is no fear in love; but perfect love casteth out fear." Racial segregation is buttressed by such irrational fears as loss of preferred economic privilege, altered social status, intermarriage, and adjustment to new situations. White people attempt to combat these corroding fears by diverse methods. Some seek to ignore the question of race relations. Others counsel massive resistance. Still others hope to drown their fear by engaging in acts of violence and meanness toward their Negro brethren. But instead of eliminating fear, these remedies instill deeper and more pathological fears. Neither repression, massive resistance, nor aggressive violence will cast out the fear of integration; only love and goodwill can do that.

Only through Negro adherence to love and non-violence will the fear in the white community be mitigated. A guilt-ridden white minority fears that if the Negro attains power he will without restraint or pity act to revenge the accumulated injustices and brutality of the years.

The Negro must show white men that they have nothing to fear, for the Negro forgives and is willing to forget the past. *The Negro must convince the white man that he seeks justice for both himself and the white man.* A mass movement exercising love and non-violence and demonstrating power under discipline should convince the white community that were such a movement to attain strength its power would be used creatively and not vengefully.

Fourth, fear is mastered through faith. All too many people attempt to face the tensions of life with inadequate spiritual resources. When vacationing in Mexico, Mrs. King and I wished to go deep-sea fishing. For reasons of economy, we rented an old and poorly equipped boat. We gave this little thought until, ten miles from shore, the clouds lowered and howling winds blew. Then we became paralyzed with fear, for we knew our boat was deficient. Multitudes of people are in a similar situation. Heavy winds and weak boats explain their fear.

One of the most dedicated participants in the Montgomery bus protest was an elderly Negro whom we affectionately called Mother Pollard. Although poverty-stricken and uneducated, she possessed a deep understanding of the meaning of the movement. After having walked for several weeks, she was asked if she were tired. With ungrammatical profundity, she answered,

"My feets is tired, but my soul is rested."

On one particular evening, following a tension-packed week, I spoke at a mass meeting. I attempted to convey an overt impression of strength and courage, although I was inwardly depressed and fear-stricken. Mother Pollard came to the front of the church afterward and said . . . "You didn't talk strong tonight. I know something is wrong. Is it that we ain't doing things to please you? Or is it that the white folks is bothering you?"

Before I could respond, she looked directly into my eyes and said, "I done told you we is with you all the way." Then her face became radiant, and she said in words of quiet certainty, "But even if we ain't with you, God's gonna take care of you." As she spoke these consoling words, everything in me quivered and quickened with the pulsing tremor of raw energy.

Since that dreary night in 1956, Mother Pollard has passed on to glory, and I have known very few quiet days. But as the years have unfolded, the eloquently simple words of Mother Pollard have come back again and again to give light and peace and guidance to my troubled soul. "God's gonna take care of you."

This faith transforms the whirlwind of despair into a warm and reviving breeze of hope. The words of a motto which a generation ago were commonly found on the wall in the homes of devout persons need to be etched on our hearts:

Fear knocked at the door.

Faith answered.

There was no one there.

EXERCISES

1. Throughout the centuries men have spun legends around the special leaders. Call them saints or martyrs or whatever term suits you. Besides extraordinary leadership ability, these figures are supposed to have possessed the rare and uncanny capacity for rising above self-interest and devoting their lives to the good of their people. Thus is Moses alleged to have led the children of Israel to the banks of the Jordan but not to have been able to cross himself. We have already cited the example of Jesus. We have thought about Martin Luther King as a modern legend. There are others. Both John and Robert Kennedy have been accorded places in this sparse but noble company; they have been described as men flirting with doom yet driven on by a sense of obligation to serve their country. But some people remain skeptical about such

men. Unable to see beyond their own narrow sphere of self-interest, they cannot imagine how anybody else could.

Here's a chance for you to add your valuable opinion to an area of considerable controversy. Write a paper giving your own views about the saint or martyr (it is evident that I am not using "saint" in any official, sectarian sense). What do you think moves such a person? Is it a fanatic desire for self-fulfillment, so that even self-destruction does not seem to be too high a price to pay? Or is it some deep-rooted psychological compulsion that forces some people to do the job if nobody else will? Or is it, indeed, love of humanity? Can you imagine such a love? Is it too abstract and remote to conceive of? If so, can you account for the martyr's martyrdom in any way that hasn't been mentioned?

2. If real sacrifice is undeniably rare, fake sacrifices are fairly common. What I'm talking about here is, for example, the mother who makes her children's life a living hell by constantly reminding them of the sacrifices she has made for them—so often that they cannot help wondering whether it is not *they* who are making the sacrifice, giving up their right to complain in order to allow her to pat herself on the back. There are people who go out of their way to make "sacrifices" just so they can tell everyone and receive their applause. You must have known such a person. Why not do a verbal sketch of one?

3. What about compulsive buying at Christmastime? showering everyone you can think of with gifts you can't really afford? that they can't return? It is said, " 'Tis more blessed to give than to receive." Perhaps this really means, " 'Tis more *enjoyable*." Wouldn't it be more like a sacrifice to make a Hate List and buy presents only for your worst enemies? If you want to have a little fun while we're on the subject of sacrifices, how about a paper on what the Christmas spirit is actually about?

4. One of the most famous quotations in modern American politics is from President Kennedy: "Ask not what your country can do for you. Ask rather what you can do for your country." This might have been put down as nothing but waxy rhetoric had it not been for the fact that Kennedy did indeed give up his life for his country.

In addition, thousands of young men have died on foreign battlefields, and their families for the most part take some consolation from knowing that they have sacrificed "for their country." But even when they enter the armed forces, many young men say, and probably believe, that they are more than willing to give up two or four years "for their country."

Write a paper setting forth your ideas about "country" and the responsibility one should or should not feel toward it. Consider, especially, the all-important issue of patriotism in times of national emergency and what might happen if everyone decided at the same time to protest a certain administration's policy and refuse to fight or in any other way "inconvenience" himself for the benefit of "country."

Remember: this is not to be a paper about protest, the right of dissent, or your attitude toward the current administration. This exercise asks you to face the question of *loyalty when the chips are down.*

YOU VS. SOCIETY

So far in this chapter we have considered the self in the pure act of *being* itself—that is, becoming aware of its way of life and its basic attitudes. We have considered the problems created when that self gets entwined, entangled, and otherwise involved with others in those complex relationships that are often called "love." We have delved into the possibility of that self's having some feelings of obligation toward society or humanity or country. All of these issues inevitably arise when one considers the self as a thing existing in space, for it is not possible to occupy space without being *near* other beings.

But it should be obvious that there has to be a conflict between the self in the act of trying to be itself and the self that loves or in some way feels obligated to some other person or persons. You can't, in short, be in space without at the same time feeling the friction of contact with all the others. Sometimes this friction is warm and pleasant; sometimes it is even glorious; and then again, sometimes it is downright painful. It is then that the self may long for and even practice nonconformity.

Writing the Angry Outburst

Nonconformity or individualism or "doing one's own thing" doesn't always need motivation. Sometimes we need to indulge in it simply because the tensions of living have mounted inside us, and we get "ornery" for the sake of orneriness. At such times nothing appeals to us. We watch television and downgrade everything we see. We can't find a book or magazine that seems worth reading. We become hypersensitive to the faults of family and friends. We like to be alone, and nothing anyone can say or do can bring us around until we are quite ready.

If such a mood ever hits you, you can derive a large measure of satisfaction from taking out a piece of paper and letting out your aggressions in words. It can be soul-satisfying therapy, if nothing else; but it can also bring to light some deep-rooted and reasonable gripes. You never can tell when you might have a real chance to *do* something about them. At any rate, it's better to put them all in one place than to waste a lot of time and energy fuming and fretting and snarling. Perhaps we can call this *creative nonconformity*.

The Angry Outburst is the basic kind. I remember a vivid example of its effectiveness. In one of my classes there once sat a student of the kind who always sit in the back row, slumped in their seats, occasionally dozing, and never, never taking a single note. Sometimes they are called "unmotivated" students. Still, if a teacher is a dedicated professional he will try to "communicate."

One day I happened to catch my dozer doodling. He was apparently refreshed after a brief nap during a discussion of underground movies. Looking directly at him, I suddenly said, "By the way, there are a number of you who haven't yet turned in a single film report. Are you seeing any movies?"

"Yeh, yeh, all the time," the doodler muttered.

I felt like crying out "Lo, he speaketh!" but thought better of it and merely asked, "Well?"

"Well, what?"

"Where's my paper?"

He caught my eye, for the first time. I swear real contact was made, and it jolted me. I have never seen such an expression; if my life depended on it, I could not describe it accurately. His look told me exactly what he thought of my dumb course, my dumb assignments, and, in fact, the whole dumb world.

"You want a paper? You'll get it."

At the very next class session he shuffled in, stopped by the desk, opened a spiral notebook, which a furtive glance told me was filled with very avant-garde doodlings, ripped out about four sheets, and handed them to me. Then he smiled. A sign of triumph over my disbelief? An attempt at establishing a friendly truce at long last? At any rate, I had gotten the longest paper he had ever penned.

Of course it was a poison-pen letter to me, but that scarcely mattered. His paper told me the real reason for his academic delinquency. The kind of movie I had been sending him to see was, in his opinion, boring, stupid, and a thorough waste of his valuable time. And now he had had enough.

The movie on which he was reporting was Luis Buñuel's *The Exterminating Angel*, certainly not the most comprehensible of foreign films for beginning viewers. Among other minus factors it has the quality that students find particularly irksome—length, combined with slow-moving, symbolic action. But it proved to be beautiful in arousing the wrath of a student who had probably never felt impelled to write anything before.

Since I know very little, in fact nothing about directing a film, I couldn't tell you what I thought of the directing so I won't. As far as the acting goes, I believed it not to be acting in the sense of acting, but real life acting.

I would most assuredly recommend this film to someone who has nothing else better to do, which they usually don't. At this point I would like to ask a question. How is a person like me going to be able to tell someone else what the director of this film was trying to say or to put forth when the director more than likely didn't or doesn't know what the person who wrote the play was trying to say? Each person no matter who or what he is, is going to get something entirely different from the film, from what I got from it. This and all means of entertainment is no more than a way for people to pass time or make a living. If someone has something to say or wants to express himself in some way, let him come out and say it and not beat around the bush, by a film that is going to mean something entirely different to anyone who sees it. Everybody in this world is different from the next guy, and each person has his own wants, beliefs, fears, and thoughts, and you're not going to be able to tell someone to see the same thing that you see in something, he might say he does, but he doesn't. He's just trying to be his surface personality. Sometimes you'll find a person who has only one personality, his real one. This kind of person you usually have a hatred for, but deep down you admire him for being able to say what he really thinks and not what society would require him to say.

I have nothing against anyone who wants to express himself, because everybody does, by the way you drive a car or mostly in your own way of making a living. For example, take two carpenters, one carpenter is going to do his work differently from the next, the same goes for teachers, office workers, etc. In conclusion everybody has his own wants, beliefs, fears and thoughts, and you're not going to be able to change all of them, or force something you believe in on him when it doesn't agree with his beliefs.

In its own way this paper is probably as profound as the film which inspired it. My doodler couldn't be bothered with grammatical structure. That would have meant conformity, and so it was inevitable that he should have created his own grammar and manner of putting a paper together. It's difficult to analyze his method, but at the same time, it's impossible to avoid getting the boy's point. It surely sobered *me* considerably. Since the day I received the paper, I have revised the film report assignments considerably and greatly liberalized them.

I had a colleague who bought a Ford station wagon new and complained to me that within two months, it sounded as if it were getting ready to fall apart. I told him to complain instead to his salesman, but somehow he never could reach the man on the telephone. "Okay," I suggested half in jest, "write to Mr. Ford."

A few weeks later we saw in the paper that the Ford Foundation had granted the college where we both worked a million dollars for increasing faculty salaries. My friend had an idea. He wrote a letter to the president of the Ford company, thanking him for the generous grant but pointing out that it would take his entire raise to keep up with the repairs on his station wagon. Guess what happened? Right! The president wrote back personally and authorized a couple of hundred dollars' worth of free service. It's silly to mope around in your anger when you *can* convert it into profit.

EXERCISES

1. Perhaps you too, like my doodling student, have a teacher whose methods of teaching or assignments anger you. Why hold it in? Use this exercise as an opportunity to let your feelings out. Of all papers, the Angry Outburst requires the least amount of structuring. Anger, almost by definition, knows no bounds. The important thing is to get it all said.

   How will you get a grade? How will you succeed or fail in such an assignment? You guessed it. You've got to come up with a blast. It can't be polite, and there should be no doubt left in the reader's mind how you feel toward this teacher and why he has inspired such strong emotions in you.

2. If your anger is aimed at a state of affairs in society or in the government, why not write a protest or poison-pen letter instead of the conventional theme? Why not write directly to the President of the United States or a Congressman or the local mayor or the governor of your state? Why not write a letter to the editor of your local paper? *Time* magazine? *The New York Times*? And if you

actually do this assignment, why not really mail the letter and see what happens? (You may get free auto repair service.)

Try the one-sentence outburst. See how much you can pack into a sentence without putting a period on it. You might use an opening like, "If there's anything I can't stand, it's . . ." or "Oh, there's nothing very much wrong with the Establishment, except . . ." Take a gander at the following sentence written in response to this assignment by one of my students:

When anthropologists talk of men as being animals, they should apologize to the beasts who have not had the advantage of the education and cultural evolution which man enjoys; they are not ignorant, superstitious, self-deceptive, supercilious, vain-glorious, sanctimonious, conniving, vindictive, brain-washed, prejudiced, vengeful, wrathful, bigoted, as man is; they do not blindly accept mythological, superstitious, dark-age theology as being heavenly inspired by a god or collection of gods nor damn those who don't to eternal hell, purgatory and worse or, to quote Dante's Inferno, to "hang by their heels eternally with their heads dipped in hot pitch"; they don't have a false sense of flag, boundary, amulet, ecclesiastic fairy-tale worship; they don't spend a good portion of their lives promoting, revering, believing and practicing a caste system of race, color, ethnic, religious and nationalistic hatred and annihilism; they don't expend the great-est portion of their educational, scientific, financial and man-power resources to the cause of mutual, wholesale extermination of their own species; they don't murder, torture, starve, burn, disintegrate, hang, electrocute, gas, cripple, blind, mutilate, dis-embowel endless numbers of men, women and children in the holy name of god, country and politics, all blessed by tax-paid chaplains representing tax-free churches; they don't claim to be made in god's image or to be god's chosen people or as being in the highest echelon of civilization and culture while practicing cannibalistic rituals among themselves; they don't believe that their particular miracle-endowed, ghost-worshipping fetishism is a tribal carry-over or that their particular one and only true god has endowed only them with his exclusive brand of holiness and righteousness; they don't attach an all-believing sanctity to the printed word that would have them accept and have faith in ghosts, hobgoblins, seraphim, immaculate conceptions, mes-siahs, peaceful or warlike gods, heavenly hereafters for the gullible and hell-fire and brimstone for the questioners; the dead brought to life, parting of the waters, burning stones, faith-healing and other tricks commonly practiced by stage magicians and indian fakirs; they don't offer animal and people blood-sacrifices to their omnipotent, omnipresent, omniscient holy ghosts; they don't consider it their holy duty to brain-wash their progeny with their vestigial, retrogressive beliefs.

You and the Law

Chicago police beat protesters back with nightsticks. . . . Cambridge police called in to disperse rioters in front of MIT laboratory. . . . Berkeley police use water hoses and tear gas to force angry students into submission. So flash the news reports week after week, day after day. The American cop has suddenly found himself the center of attention, controversy, praise, and scorn. The protesters often call him "pig" and delight in stirring him into a frenzy by shouting "oink!" at him. Television commentators often show him in closeup, wielding his stick, his jaws grimly set, his eyes cold and determined. But school principals sometimes call him in to speak before assemblies, where he can be soft-spoken and kind-looking. You can see him on street corners, helping small children and old ladies to cross. You can see him at the side of the road, lecturing a traffic violator solemnly and firmly, much like a father who must regretfully administer discipline. And you can see him coming on strong to break up a riot, his hand all too ready to seize the club, and sometimes he seems (or is made to seem) to be enjoying himself.

Bumper stickers urge you, SUPPORT YOUR LOCAL POLICE. Recruiting campaigns are being stepped up considerably, and in some areas— notably the big northern industrial centers—the shortage is fast reaching the critical stage. The law has come under fire so often in recent years that one wonders how anybody at all can be attracted to the job, with its rigorous training, long hours, short pay, and constant hazards. (Insurance companies tend to regard cops as something less than excellent risks.)

Protesters, many of whom say they have been victims of "police brutality," warn of a coming police state. They speak of the possibility of concentration camps to be erected for militant blacks, potsmoking hippies, and even innocent flower children who desire only to do their thing in peace.

However, the current concern over and distrust for the law, which are very intense in some quarters, are nothing very new on the

American scene. In fact, if you wanted to make a verbal portrait of the "traditional American" from the beginning to the present, you'd probably end up with a schizophrenic who was half solid middle-class citizen, wanting nothing more than to earn a peaceful living and willing to pay his taxes and do what the police tell him, and half rugged "hands-off-me" individualist. In other words, there seem to be two kinds of Americans. One sees freedom as a matter of getting ahead and living in the suburbs and doesn't mind at all conforming: in fact, he is often motivated by the desire to be just like the rest. The other interprets freedom literally and cannot tolerate any restrictions, including those that come from the cops.

A dramatic example of our national conflict is provided by the contrast between two famous residents of Concord, Massachusetts: one, Ralph Waldo Emerson, a philosopher who preached nonconformity in his writings but who otherwise led a pretty respectable life; the other, Henry David Thoreau, a philosopher who preached civil disobedience in his writings and then went out and practiced it. On one occasion Thoreau stood boldly up to the Massachusetts government by refusing to pay a six-year accumulation of poll taxes and got himself thrown in jail for it. When a friend (who happened to be Emerson) bailed him out, he disappeared into the woods to pick berries, totally unchanged by his brush with the law—totally unrepentant and totally committed to remaining outside the fold. Here's how Thoreau describes his experience and also his scorn for the goody-goody middle-class citizen who won't follow his example:

> . . . as I stood considering the walls of solid stone, two or three feet thick, the door of wood and iron, a foot thick, and the iron grating which strained the light, I could not help being struck with the foolishness of that institution which treated me as if I were mere flesh and blood and bones, to be locked up. I wondered that it should have concluded at length that this was the best use it could put me to, and had never thought to avail itself of my services in some way. I saw that, if there was a wall of stone between me and my townsmen, there was a still more difficult one to climb or break through before they could get to be as free as I was. I did not for a moment feel confined, and the walls seemed a great waste of stone and mortar. I felt as if I alone of all my townsmen had paid my tax . . .
>
> The night in prison was novel and interesting enough. The prisoners in their shirtsleeves were enjoying a chat and the evening air in the doorway, when I entered. But the jailer said, "Come, boys, it is time to lock up", and so they dispersed, and I heard the sound of their steps returning into the hollow apartments. My room-mate was introduced to me by the jailer as "a first-rate fellow and a clever man." When the door was locked, he showed me where to hang my hat, and how he managed matters there. The rooms were whitewashed

once a month; and this one, at least, was the whitest, most simply furnished, and probably the neatest apartment in the town. . . .

When I came out of prison,—for some one interfered, and paid that tax,—I did not perceive that great changes had taken place on the common, such as he observed who went in a youth and emerged a tottering and gray-headed man; and yet a change had to my eyes come over the scene,—the town, and State, and country,—greater than any that mere time could effect. I saw yet more distinctly the State in which I lived. I saw to what extent the people among whom I lived could be trusted as good neighbors and friends; that their friendship was for summer weather only; that they did not greatly propose to do right; that they were a distinct race from me by their prejudices and superstitions, as the Chinamen and Malays are; that in their sacrifices to humanity they ran no risks, not even to their property; that after all they were not so noble but they treated the thief as he had treated them, and hoped, by a certain outward observance and a few prayers, and by walking in a particular straight though useless path from time to time, to save their souls.[4]

The pattern of American life is basically the same as it was in Concord a century and a quarter ago—only more intensely so. One can still be a solid citizen, perhaps even believing in the Emersonian theory of nonconformity but not straying very far from the herd; or a Thoreau, making the commitment all the way even if it means jail. The continuing conflict between the two attitudes keeps making the law flex its muscles: on the one hand, to show the solid citizen he's being protected; on the other, to show the resister he dare not go too far. The flexing of the muscle continues to inflame the dissenters and add to their unrest. The unrest inevitably leads to confrontations. And then there's bound to be violence on both sides. Sometimes the law gets nervous and overreacts or reacts before there's any violent expression of dissent at all. Sometimes the Thoreau figure—who nowadays may like to freak out with long hair, beards, beads, Afros, and bizarre clothing—can get rough treatment just because of how he looks.

Here's how one student describes his encounter with the law.

"Get yo' head back in the car, Boy," the officer bellowed. Perhaps he didn't realize the type of day I'd been through; certainly he didn't care. In fact, the sickened look on my face and my feeble attempt at getting a little fresh air seemed to give the men great pleasure. Dulcet tones of laughter resounded through my already splitting head.

[4] From "Civil Disobedience" by Henry David Thoreau.

And what a day it had been. Ten minutes late to Traffic Court and you got long hair, too, eh? The judge wouldn't hear the case. Fifty dollars cash bond and re-schedule the hearing. Well, this just wasn't one of the days I happened to have fifty dollars in my pocket. So, go directly to jail; do not pass go. Before Officer DiCaccio escorted me to jail, I requested to see the judge in his chambers to explain my situation. DiCaccio assured me the judge wasn't interested in my problems, and off we went.

So this is what a hold cell looks like. Rather small. Nice of them to include a toilet, in case you felt like vomiting, or something. The jingle of keys made me look up in time to see Shapiro enter the cell.

Shapiro was from Israel. To no one in particular he said, "The Judge should only drop dead before I vould give him ten cents. If mine son was here, he vould have the judge sveeping floors, the son of a gun!" Shapiro adjusted the "yarmolke" on the crown of his head and sat down. From within his wrinkled, oversized suit jacket he produced a copy of the *Israeli News* and a small magnifying glass.

"This is justice in America. For a lousy ten dollars they put me in here. They should come and take a picture of Shapiro in jail."

A face in the desert is a true oasis. Thus it was that Shapiro and I spent the next couple of hours in idle conversation touching on topics from the democratic convention to those dogs in Egypt. Then the jingler returned and DiCaccio was ready to march us to the regular jail.

A few dimly lit winding corridors and three jail doors later, we were ready to be frisked.

"All right you two, empty out your pockets, put your hands up on the table and spread your legs apart."

I followed instructions and glanced over at Shapiro. He had an ungodly collection of things in his pockets, from four handkerchiefs, to a "ram's horn" like the type used on high Jewish Holy Days.

"Hey, Joe, look at Schwartz, here. He plays the flute and everything."

"That's not a flute, that's what he uses to call his gefilte fish with. When they come to the surface, he catches them with the beany on his head."

So that's where the cops are at. Figures. I made my one phone call and my friend said he would try to raise the fifty dollars to bring to me as soon as possible. A few fingerprints and mug shots later (smile pretty), I was hustled off to another hold cell with five other men, separated for good from Shapiro.

Lunch time at last. Through it all, I was pretty hungry. The mud sandwiches, passed off as peanut butter and jelly, were handed through the bars. I waited patiently in line to flush this delicacy down the toilet. Shortly, we were escorted in single file to a little room where we all stripped down and had our clothes searched for L.S.D. After a few probes into rather personal areas, our clothes were returned minus belts, combs, and other dangerous weapons. Now the big moment drew near; the moment we had all been waiting for; the assignment of cell blocks.

"Jones, McCullough and Washburn, Cell A-1. Rivers and Levy, B-1. And you, Hippie, you take C-1. They have a nice psychedelic light show in there for you."

Well, for sure one needn't lack for company in the county jail, what with about forty inmates per cell. Eighteen bunks for forty men showed a definite oversight on the part of our city planners, but a cement floor isn't really that bad for sleeping on. After all, the place was steam heated (rather strange for the month of August), and one could watch Hubert Humphrey's smiling face talk about the American way (though once in awhile a brave cameraman would scan the much more interesting events outside the convention hall). A drunk vomited in a corner as I set about making new friends.

At first it didn't seem as if there was anyone I had too much in common with. Then I noticed Dan; thirtyish, bearded, and fairly intelligent looking. If taken at his word, Dan was a rather comfortable local business man who held the unfortunate desire to legalize marijuana in this country. Finding nothing better, they had picked him up on a deportation charge and forced him to close his place of business (a local psychedelic shop; they even passed a law outlawing such shops of ill-repute).

So the afternoon passed with Dan and I trying to work out some of the world's problems. I began to doubt that my rescue would be effected before having to spend a night in my new-found haven. Alas, though, I heard my name echo down the corridor and hollered, "Here!"

The jailer opened the cell and suggested I follow him. I waved good-bye to Dan and tossed my half pack of cigarettes to eager hands. Picking up my personal belongings on the way, I was led to a room with a long desk where my friend stood grinning at me.

Freedom at last. Ah, the sweet smell of Mother Earth; the tingling crispness of green grass on my barefeet. There was even still time to drive my cab for a few hours before calling it a day.

I guess maybe because I was tired and anxious to get home and it was after midnight that I didn't notice I was going sixty in a fifty-five zone. And I guess that's why that nice officer pulled me over; or maybe it had something to do with the banner blatantly displayed on the trunk of my car "Your local police are armed and dangerous."

The officer apparently wasn't too adept at making conversation as he wrote the ticket. My driver's license informed him that I was a student.

"A student, eh? What school do you go to?"

"City Junior College, Sir."

"Yeah, well then let's see your student I.D. card."

"For what purpose, Sir?"

"Oh, a wise guy, huh? Get in the backseat of the car. You're under arrest."

The smoke from his cigar didn't seem quite as pleasant as the sweet smell of Mother Earth; the carpet in the patrol car didn't feel quite as tingly as fresh grass; and my head throbbed violently. Perhaps the nice officers wouldn't mind if I just opened this back window and stuck my head out for a little fresh air.

I believe the most solid of citizens would agree that the writer, *as he describes his experiences,* was pushed around unnecessarily by the law. But I also have a suspicion the citizen, in all conscience, would argue that such stories represent the unfortunate consequences of the "present state of things" and that police overreaction doesn't justify the dissenters' disrespect for the law.

Perhaps the tragedy in this whole cycle (nonconformity → law enforcement → resistance → reaction and overreaction → increased resistance, and so on) is that neither the protestor nor the solid citizen is in a position to appreciate the other's viewpoint. The citizen says, "I've worked hard to get what I have, and I need the law to help me protect my interest." The protestor says, "The law is preventing me from fulfilling myself and isn't helping my interests at all. Isn't this unfair?"

It is hard for either one to see that both of them are vital to the preservation of America: the one, because this country was founded for the individualist and everything he stands for; the other, because some degree of conformity is apparently needed to make society work, to make it jell, to give it organization and order. No doubt Emerson thought to himself, "What if everyone were a Thoreau and practiced nonconformity? Would this not end up jeopardizing the rights of all of us?" No doubt Thoreau thought to himself, "What if everyone were an Emerson and were afraid to take that first drastic step against the Establishment? What would happen to American freedom?" It may be that the two questions, both so reasonable when placed side by side, create a stalemate, and the law is caught somewhere in the middle, unable to serve both masters adequately.

EXERCISES

1. When Thoreau made his famous decision to abandon organized society and go live all alone in a hut by Walden Pond, I wonder whether he asked himself the obvious question, "What if everybody did just what I'm doing?" That is, nonconformity must depend upon the conformists in order to be what it is. Protest loses meaning when there is no Establishment.

   It is sobering to imagine what life would be like if all of a sudden everyone became a nonconformist. Write a paper describing a day in a town in which all the people stop doing their jobs and in which the moral and legal stronghold of the Establishment is completely abandoned. Everything goes. Nothing is prohibited. At the same time, not even the most practical and necessary functions—like the collection of garbage and the operation of phones and electric plants—are performed. If you regard yourself as a dedicated nonconformist and have no use for the Establishment, indicate how such a town would strike you. Would this be truly a liberation? How would you and the others survive? Perhaps you would return to nature and adapt to the circumstances in a way that even Thoreau would heartily applaud. But if you are not a dedicated nonconformist, this topic could provide you with a way of pointing out how dependent we all are on the fact that others will conform to their functions and stay pretty squarely within the confines of social expectation.

2. Describe an encounter you may recently have had with the police for some petty or major violation of the law. Describe in detail the manner in which you were treated. Try to be perfectly honest. If you are vehemently anti-cop, you should have good

reasons. Were you unjustly charged? Were you behaving in a blameless manner? If so, why were you treated unjustly?

But if you secretly believe the policeman was just doing his duty, be honest about that too. Perhaps you recognize the need for police but feel that they are sometimes arbitrary in their enforcement of the law. (Who has not been stopped for excessive speed only to see other cars whizzing by unmolested?)

3. Rather than rely on hearsay or your own instincts, why not go directly to the source of the police controversy? Find a policeman who is willing to be interviewed. Use his answers as the basis for a serious paper about the role (or plight) of the cop in American society today. Here are some suggested questions:

a) Why did you join the force?

b) How do you feel about violence, especially the possibility of your having to use it in order to apprehend someone?

c) Do you have a sense of serving society, or is this just a job?

d) Do you consider yours a thankless role?

e) In order to apprehend lawbreakers, is it necessary to detach yourself from any tendency to "understand" them or see them as victims of, say, poverty or other conditions?

f) Do you ever help to recruit new members for the force? What incentive do you offer them?

g) Do you approve of the stop-and-frisk law? Or do you agree with those who say it is a violation of civil rights?

4. Thoreau had no use for the self-righteous citizens of his town. Such persons, who comprise the middle-class bulwark of any community, tend to be law-abiding and exemplary in their actions. Often they pride themselves on their perfect driving records and their general Johnny-on-the-spot handling of all legal obligations, such as debts incurred.

In your opinion, are such citizens truly commendable? Are they law-abiding because they are too "chicken" ever to be nonconformists? Are they exemplary in their conduct because it is in their best interests to be so? Who gets elected president of the Rotary Club? The man who is known to be in and out of court? In other words, do you see the self-righteous person as one who deeply believes in law, or one who conforms to the letter of the law because it will advance his own cause?

Do you know any such "perfect" citizen? Paint a verbal picture of him.

5. Of course, it's easy to protest and to criticize the entire Establishment when it isn't up to you to run the store. If you are against
   the principle of "law and order," as this is generally understood in
   society today, write a paper stating your alternatives. Can you
   conceive of a society without *any* such principle? Would you want
   to live in it?

   Assuming that most people agree that some law and order must
   be maintained, how would you propose to modify the present system? In your ideal society, who would be the police? How would
   they be selected? trained? What would be their proper function?
   What would be considered illegal, and what would typical punishments be like?

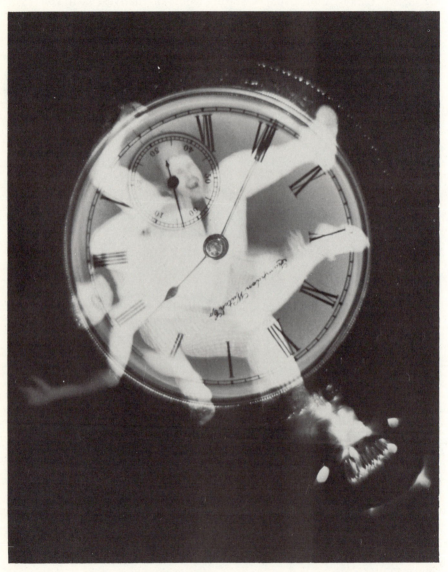

"If time exists, Yesterday was real also and has left its calling card with us somewhere."

3

THE SELF
IN TIME

In the last chapter we looked at the problems created by the existence of the self in space. You had a chance to analyze your fundamental attitudes toward life and society, including your moral values; and you found out whether you are now, or have ever been, in love and perhaps whether you intend to marry. In order to confront such problems, it was necessary to treat the self in space as if it were at any given moment something static, somebody *here* with somebody else *there*. You saw yourself taking a certain stand, and that was that. In this chapter we must now look more closely at the self as a fluid, continually changing entity.

You exist in time as well as space. Sometimes it's easy to lose consciousness of the fact, it's true. When, for example, you associate with the same people day after day, year after year, you seldom notice how you and they are changing. But if you suddenly run into someone you haven't seen for a year or so, you are usually shocked by how *much* he seems to have altered or else how *little*. Either way, you notice it. You become directly aware of the physical nature of time.

This very moment is affecting you, changing you in some way, and its influence may be felt tomorrow. Day by day your identity alters, grows, develops. Your identity in time is a living record of the events through which you have lived and are living. It is like a tape recorder that can never be turned off. All your experiences are on the reel, whether you admit it or not.

How important is time to you personally? I would gladly agree with students who argue that one needn't ever play the tape if it were not for the fact that what's already on the tape helps determine everything that is about to be recorded. In other words, it is necessary from time to time to rewind it and play it back, to see where one has been and what forces have contributed to one's being.

You may even discover that you are the accumulation of many things you can justly be proud of. Your ethnic heritage, for example: your family tradition or the regional customs of the part of the country (or the world) from which you hail.

In this chapter let's consider two basic things about you in time: your feelings about how one should live with respect to time and the knowledge of what time does; and your feelings about tradition, including the importance or unimportance of history and the observances and rituals people take part in that are rooted in history. You can then decide whether it is at all possible to live with no regard for time.

NOW OR TOMORROW?

Two men—call them Mr. Boggs and Mr. Twill—live next door to each other on Day-by-Day Avenue. Each has a project house that costs approximately the same amount of money. But that was ten years ago. If you looked only at the house of Mr. Boggs now, you'd think the neighborhood must be an expensive Los Angeles suburb. Its glistening new coat of paint, its neat white shutters, its evenly mowed, green lawn, its sparkling window panes—all testify to the homeowner "who cares." Whenever a civic issue arises, the men of the neighborhood call upon Mr. Boggs for help, and invariably he becomes their leader. Thanks to his efforts in collecting 4,000 signatures on a petition, a cement batching plant was not allowed to be built six blocks from his street, and a much-needed children's playground became a reality.

Next door, Mr. Twill and his wife live in comparative squalor. Their house still bears the original, faded, and peeling coat of paint. The windows are thick with grime. The uncared-for lawn has long since given up and died, and in its place are tall weeds, crabgrass, and sandspurs. If it had been up to Mr. Twill, the cement plant would have become a reality, and the playground would never have materialized.

Mr. and Mrs. Boggs have tried, unsuccessfully, to get the Twills evicted from the neighborhood. They have tried, unsuccessfully, to get the Twills to upgrade their property. Mr. and Mrs. Boggs stare through their clean windows in dismay and curse the day they acquired such neighbors. But Mr. and Mrs. Twill, inside their seldom-cleaned house, play their stereo, smoke their pot, paint pictures, entertain continually, and lead what they consider an ideal existence.

The Twills aren't just lazy people. They do nothing about their property except live inside their house because they don't believe in working today for a future they may not be here to enjoy. They don't care that their property may depreciate in value. They don't care about cement plants or children's playgrounds. They don't even *have* any children because the care and feeding of offspring represent to them time- and money-consuming investments that, again, depend too heavily on future rewards. They don't want to waste time going to civic functions and listening to a lot of talk about neighborhood problems. They don't want to attend PTA meetings and go to banks and insurance companies and worry about trust funds and annuities. They want to catch a big piece of the action—NOW!

The Boggs believe people get caught short when they live only for the NOW. Their motto is, "Tomorrow will come, in all probability, and if you have wasted today, you'll be sorry when you see the dawn after all." The Boggs never seem to stop working. Mr. Boggs, for example, holds down three jobs so he can save money to educate four children. The family seldom takes a vacation, and the Twills have never known them to give a party.

The Boggs are confident the Twills will gnash their teeth in sorrow and repentance when they find themselves old and gray—without children to care for them, money in the bank, or equity in valuable property. The Twills are confident the Boggs will die, like everyone else, when the atmosphere gets a bit more polluted, unless all-out or civil war happens first. The Boggs pity the Twills, and the Twills are sorry for the Boggs.

Between the two couples and their way of life there exist a thousand variations. Somewhere you may find your parents, and somewhere you may find yourself. The older one becomes and the more responsibilities he has, the more he may inch toward the Boggs position. The younger one is and the fewer responsibilities he needs to shoulder, the more his sympathies are likely to lean toward the Twill position. Neither in its purest form may appeal to you entirely, but, for the sake of determining just how you *do* feel about time—about the relationship between Now and Tomorrow—let's look at each extreme.

"Carpe Diem," or the Creed of Pleasure

There is a philosophy that teaches that only the present moment is real, that there is only Now, that, if tomorrow comes at all, it becomes Now. This philosophy goes on to say that the reality of Now can only be experienced directly and through the five senses. It does not exist in the memory of yesterday or the anticipation of tomorrow. If this is so, the philosophy adds, it means there is little point to living if one isn't using the senses to absorb the moment. Living in terms of yesterday's debts and tomorrow's promises is to lose contact with the senses and therefore with reality itself.

But what is gained by getting absorbed in the moment? By looking, listening, tasting, smelling and touching the people and the things surrounding us? Nothing but the joy that these offer in themselves. They exist as objects of pleasure, and we fulfill ourselves in the moment only insofar as we are able to find this pleasure. So if somebody depresses you or you can't bear his company for any reason, you find somebody else. If your surroundings don't please you, you go somewhere else, and if you can't do that, you stop looking at them and try to gratify another sense. The main thing is to find pleasure. A moment of emptiness and boredom, a moment without a piece of the action, is lost forever, and that much of your life has been a waste.

This philosophy goes by the name of *carpe diem*, which is Latin for "seize the day," or hedonism, which comes from a Greek word meaning "delight." Both the Greeks and the Romans were specialists in the creed of pleasure, and both had their Now Generations. The first major hedonist was Aristippus, a young man who followed Socrates around Athens and apparently enjoyed eating, drinking, and having long and profound discussions with Socrates and others on deep and weighty matters. Aristippus really dug this drop-out existence, and after the death of his idol, he went back to his home in North Africa to open a wildly progressive school where he created more Now Generations.

Aristippus taught, among other things, these three doctrines:

1) There is no point to life except to enjoy it.
2) Pleasure, to be real, has to be physical (that is, sensory).
3) Pleasure has to be constant (that is, once you commit yourself to the enjoyment of Now, it is meaningless to stop).

Aristippus couldn't see any point in saying that one should have a few pleasures and also spend much time in working diligently for the future. Either you went all the way or you might as well be dead. To emphasize the necessity of pleasure's being physical and nothing else, he even defined it as a "tingling of the spine."

But a total commitment to the *carpe diem* ideal does have its problems, and even Aristippus didn't quite know how to resolve them. He knew, for example, there had to be intervals between pleasures. You couldn't go around tingling all the time. You have to sleep, and that's eight hours shot right there. Also, there's nothing about discipline in his philosophy. Where do you draw the line? How many pleasures are ever "enough"? Obviously no number can be given. A perfect life would require the perfect number of pleasures —an impossibility. So you keep pushing yourself, keep seeking more and more. Then what happens? As Epicurus, a critic of Aristippus, pointed out, you become depressed by worrying about the pleasures you're *not* having or the short time you have to live.

Throughout history the writers and philosophers who have been most committed to hedonism have shown an unusual preoccupation with the themes of aging and dying: mournful subjects for pleasure-oriented people! One of the world's most celebrated poems expressing the philosophy of *carpe diem*, Andrew Marvell's "To His Coy Mistress," deals in equal measure with the joys of sexual union and the inevitability of death. In the first part, the poet is discreetly asking his lady friend the big question, but she apparently is standoffish, requiring the romantic preliminaries that refined young ladies of the seventeenth century had come to expect: namely, sonnets, songs, and endless words of love. The poet tells her to forget this nonsense:

> Had we but world enough, and time,
> This coyness, lady, were no crime.
> We would sit down, and think which way
> To walk, and pass our long love's day.
> Thou by the Indian Ganges' side
> Should'st rubies find: I by the tide
> Of Humber would complain. I would
> Love you ten years before the Flood:
> And you should if you please refuse
> Till the conversion of the Jews.

The poet's reason for desperate haste is this frightening specter of time:

> But at my back I always hear
> Time's winged chariot hurrying near:

> And yonder all before us lie
> Deserts of vast eternity.
> Thy beauty shall no more be found;
> Nor, in thy marble vault, shall sound
> My echoing song: then worms shall try
> That long preserved virginity:
> And your quaint honor turn to dust;
> And into ashes all my lust.

One wonders whether Mr. and Mrs. Twill are fully enjoying the swinging parties inside their devalued house. In the middle of the music and the dancing, do they sometimes think of the cold and empty morning after? Do they sometimes catch glimpses of their faces in the mirror and realize they're not young any more? One of the requirements of *carpe diem* has always been the wave of the hand, the broad smile, and the cry, "Heigh-ho! There's no tomorrow." Does this suggest underlying *fear* of tomorrow? If so, is the unending pursuit of pleasure the only answer, the only way to control the fear?

EXERCISES

1. Do you know anyone who appears to be devoted to nothing except the unending pursuit of pleasure? Describe him (or her). Give some examples of how (s)he lives and what (s)he lives for. Do you consider this person happy or unhappy? What are your reasons? Do you intend to live your own life this way? Why? Or do you reject this in favor of a different creed? If so, which one? Why is it preferable?

2. There is said to be a very high suicide rate among members of your generation. Two possible explanations occur to me:
   a) Life has no purpose, not even pleasure; all is futile.
   b) Certain pleasures—notably the use of drugs—come on too strong and create a terrific depression from which the only escape is self-destruction.

   How do you, personally, react to the suicide statistics? Are they a sign, to you, that your generation is totally disillusioned and no longer can locate the source of pleasure? Are they a sign, instead, that your generation has discovered the ultimate truth that there is only pleasure and it's better to take one's own life at the height of one's pleasure than to wait around, growing older and facing the decay and pain of age? Or is suicide a sign of cowardice? the ultimate cop-out? Or does the suicide rate have to do with urban as opposed to rural areas? middle-class status? below-middle-class status? racial factors? It might be interesting to do a little research and try to discover whether suicide statistics reveal any sort of pattern, especially one that relates to the subject of pleasure.

I once had a student who believed the high suicide rate was a sign that his generation had made the most intelligent commitment in the history of mankind: namely, to play the game for the highest stakes and pull out before one could become a loser. I thought his attitude frightening, but there were others in the class who said the idea of suicide was definitely not frightening to them. I decided to include an exercise such as this in order to bring the issue to the surface.

If you choose this subject, take any viewpoint you honestly hold. You can, of course, take this as an opportunity to express your disapproval of those persons of your generation who seem not to place a high value on living a long life. Or else defend those who, like Andrew Marvell, continually hear "time's winged chariot" and prefer not to wait to be a victim of time.

3. Apart from those few who contemplate the idea of suicide without flinching, there are an enormous number of persons who tend to follow the *carpe diem* philosophy because they are still young, and whose creed is: UNLIMITED PLEASURE UP TO AGE THIRTY, AND THEN WHO KNOWS? They admit they don't expect to end their own lives, but at the same time they find it difficult to talk about what the future may hold for them. One substitute for thinking about the years beyond thirty is the familiar one: namely, that all civilization probably has less than ten years to go, and so what does it matter anyway?

Write a paper projecting yourself ahead to your thirtieth birthday. Try as honestly as you can to believe you are in this situation. Try to look at the people with whom you associate, many of whom will be younger than thirty, as you would then, not as you do now. Here are some questions to ask:

a) Do you find that you're prepared for this milestone in your life? Why or why not?

b) Do you find it makes no difference and that you will continue to pursue the immediate pleasures of the moment?

c) Do you find that you have less and less in common with the pleasure-seekers?

d) Do you find yourself changing the definition of pleasure? That is, are there "higher" pleasures, such as art, music, or religion?

e) On the other hand, are you alienated both from your contemporaries and from those who are under thirty? Do you find there's no place for you at all?

f) Will you use your more venerable age to work toward specific goals—things you always believed in, such as changing the system and ending war? How will you do this?

4. People committed to nothing but the *carpe diem* approach to life can seldom endure the long stretches of time between pleasures: the morning after the party, time spent in school or in performing the endless but necessary little tasks of daily living (household chores, washing the car, going shopping, and so on). The more pleasure-oriented you are, the more boring these stretches seem. On the other hand, people whose life isn't geared to many pleasures appear to be able to take boredom more in stride.

Almost anyone is capable of having a good time at a party. It takes a "discipline fanatic" to deny himself pleasure when the opportunity arises. But not everyone requires that his life be one long party. You can find out a great deal about your own commitment to pleasure—the extent to which you need pleasure and the intensity of pleasure it takes to satisfy you—by finding out how you stand on the subject of boredom.

Answer the following questions, and then write a paper analyzing your capacity for "holding up" during the stretches between pleasures:

a) At such times, do you find yourself planning what your next source of pleasure might be?

b) Do you have a tendency to instantly convert a boring moment into a pleasurable one? How do you do this? By joking with others? By smoking a cigarette? Taking a drink? Watching television? Reading?

c) Do you derive pleasure from performing the tasks that have to be done? Why? Because it is enjoyable in itself to perform certain duties? Because performing them will lead to future benefits? If you don't, is it because you're basically lazy? because only "actual" pleasures turn you on?

d) Do you find these moments unbearable? Why? Because you then come face to face with your lack of purpose in life? Because you realize pleasure is your only purpose? Does it make you unhappy to face this last possibility, or are you unhappy only because there's no pleasure around at the moment?

e) Are you seldom conscious of being bored because you are continually working toward specific objectives, such as planning a protest demonstration or doing schoolwork diligently because you know exactly what you want from life after graduation? If this is the case, are you actively finding pleasure in such work, or do you feel you are sacrificing immediate for long-range pleasures?

f) If you're committed to long-range pleasures, what happens when they don't materialize? Do you suffer from acute depression? Or are you capable of bearing up under extreme disappointment and immediately working toward other goals? If these questions don't seem to get the job of analysis done for you, by all means find some that will lead you to a better grasp of how you feel about operating within time and without those stimuli that are normally considered pleasures.

5. In your opinion, does the average American citizen have many or few pleasures in his life? To prepare for this assignment, observe someone you consider typical, perhaps a member of your own family or a neighbor or a roommate. The closeness will give you a chance to spend a couple of days watching his daily activities and jotting down some notes.

Here are some sample questions to ask yourself; choose those that are relevant:

a) How does he begin the day? (Describe what he is like in the morning; how he greets other members of his family, or his roommates; how he notices or fails to notice the immediate prospects for pleasure.)

b) Does he seem always to be living ahead of himself? Gloomily complaining about the agonizing day's work ahead; excitedly planning a big business deal or a fraternity election or a campus beauty queen pageant; worrying about unpaid bills or yet unflunked exams, and so on?

c) How does he come home from his day at work or school? Is he now living behind himself, or can he shed the accumulated tensions and relax into the present moment?

d) How does he spend the evening; half asleep in a chair before the television set, having had little or no contact with his family or roommates? Worrying about tomorrow? Out on dates? (If this last is the case, you are not, presumably, along, but nonetheless you can speculate on the kind of date he has.)

Put your notes together and write a sketch of a day in the life of an American businessman or businesswoman, white-collar or blue-collar worker, or student.

Expanding the Moment

The pleasure-oriented people of the past found themselves, like those of the present, investigating ways of getting the most out of each moment, including "freezing the action," so to speak; of making it seem as though a moment really lasts a lot longer than that. Time, it has been argued, is a state of mind. If you can lose track of it, will you not be unaware of its passing? And if you can forget about "time's winged chariot," won't you also be less concerned about getting old and dying? Or certainly about the empty stretches between pleasures? Pleasure people have long been experimenting with ways of expanding their moments.

Sexual union, as intense and as often as possible, has, of course, been a popular way. So has the use of drugs and alcohol. During the nineteenth century, for example, opium and laudanum were widely indulged in among poets and writers—and, presumably, by others who didn't leave behind a record of their "trips." Records we do have, such as Thomas De Quincey's *Confessions of an English Opium Eater* and most of the poetry and prose of Samuel Taylor Coleridge. The popular "Ancient Mariner" could easily pass for something written during a trip, and the sensuous "Kubla Khan" is thought by some to have been an experiment in writing a poem while under the influence of a drug. Coleridge denied having any conscious meaning to communicate. All he wanted to do, he claimed, was put down on paper the hallucinations he had experienced. Here is the poem.

> In Xanadu did Kubla Khan
> A stately pleasure-dome decree;
> Where Alph, the sacred river, ran
> Through caverns measureless to man
> Down to a sunless sea.
> So twice five miles of fertile ground
> With walls and towers were girdled round;
> And there were gardens bright with sinuous rills
> Where blossomed many an incense-bearing tree;
> And here were forests ancient as the hills,
> Enfolding sunny spots of greenery.
>
> But O, that deep romantic chasm which slanted
> Down the green hill athwart a cedarn cover!
> A savage place; as holy and enchanted
> As e'er beneath a waning moon was haunted
> By woman wailing for her demon-lover!
> And from this chasm, with ceaseless turmoil seething,
> As if this earth in fast thick pants were breathing,
> A mighty fountain momently was forced;
> Amid whose swift, half-intermitted burst

Huge fragments vaulted like rebounding hail,
Or chaffy grain beneath the thresher's flail.
And 'mid these dancing rocks at once and ever
It flung up momently the sacred river.
Five miles meandering with a mazy motion
Through wood and dale the sacred river ran,
Then reached the caverns measureless to man,
And sank in tumult to a lifeless ocean;
And 'mid this tumult Kubla heard from far
Ancestral voices prophesying war!

　The shadow of the dome of pleasure
　　Floated midway on the waves;
　Where was heard the mingled measure
　　From the fountain and the caves.
It was a miracle of rare device,
A sunny pleasure-dome with caves of ice!

　A damsel with a dulcimer
　　In a vision once I saw.
　It was an Abyssinian maid,
　　And on her dulcimer she played,
　Singing of Mount Abora.
　Could I revive within me
　　Her symphony and song,
To such a deep delight 'twould win me
That with music loud and long,
I would build that dome in air,
That sunny dome! those caves of ice!
And all who heard should see them there,
And all should cry, Beware! Beware!
His flashing eyes, his floating hair!
Weave a circle round him thrice,
　And close your eyes with holy dread.
　For he on honey-dew hath fed,
And drunk the milk of Paradise.

Today's use of "pot" and "acid" may belong to the great tradition of man versus time. (Other factors enter into such use, to be sure, but they are far too complex for our present concern.) One hears a great deal of talk nowadays about "mind-expanding" experiences, and it sounds like an echo from De Quincey and Coleridge. Here's how one student defended an indulgence in pot.

There isn't any point in writing about how many college students of today use pot and other things to turn themselves on. More than half of them do, and that's just a fact of life which must be accepted. All the TV shows in the world telling us about the dangers of addiction won't change the facts. The illegality of pot doesn't make it any more or less exciting. The users can get hold of it whenever they want it, and they don't think they are doing something sinful. I think it's much more important to talk about *why* they use it.

I'm not speaking of LSD or "acid," as it is called. I don't happen to go with a crowd that has ever had much use for it. My friends and I sometimes smoke pot because it opens up our senses. It slows things down for us. We see little things that usually go unnoticed because when you're not turned on you're always thinking of other things and never look at what's right in front of you. Pot puts you right in touch with reality—tables and chairs and people's faces and musical sounds and even smells.

A "trip" is something different. That's what you get from acid, and what it does is take you away from reality. That's strictly for people—I call them losers—who don't know what reality is, who have never been in touch with it. It isn't the pot that turns you on, it's the real things you start seeing. When you're on acid you see things that aren't there, and you don't even know it's you having these hallucinations.

The assignment which drew forth the above response was specifically: "Catch yourself in the act of being within the moment. Do you capture it? How? Or are you content to let it go and bide your time, waiting for the important events to take place?" The student writer I have just quoted wrote *about* living in time, but he didn't actually capture a moment on paper.

The following paper does exactly that. It was an answer to the very same assignment but represents an extremely sophisticated and very talented, I think, capturing of the Now in words. As such, it sheds some light on what Coleridge may have been doing and what you yourself can do by way of using language, rather than artificial aids, to expand the moment. Coleridge scholars have long debated whether the poet wasn't turned on just by the words of his poem. Many have advanced the theory that "Kubla Khan" exhibits too much mastery of the medium itself to have been produced "under the influence." My student writer admitted he was using nothing except imagination, and this elicited a wry comment from a classmate: "If it gets around, they'll make *that* illegal too."

The title of this paper is "Mary Jane," which tells us the writer was looking for a prose equivalent of a "high." The images and hallucinations, like those in "Kubla Khan," have an undeniable effect on the reader, and they *do* seem to help the reader lose track of time. As the writer pointed out, most stories go from point to point and therefore still happen within time. His story, he hoped, doesn't work that way. See what you think about this kind of writing as a safe and legal means of expanding the moment. (Maybe that's what a good deal of art is all about anyway.) [1]

A portent staid glassy sage projects the thrill 'round
about
    soothing the beggar who coughs up stale bread.
    Our father who art dead risen once
    Mary reigns, trips through with fairy elves.
    Still voices quake, the dead awake and all the bloody days slip into night.
    (Why to die)?
    Sorry to kill,
        the words from puppet's dreams.
When gadflys drive their carts over swallows in the sky
    slip to me darling children hidden from the hairy clowns
    The silvery scales puffed-up and contracted with each
of the sucking motions made by the lips of the stranded
Jewfish.
    White heat shimmered, cracking great rips in the dried crust
of the river bed. Near the shore stood an ancient wooden shack
supported by stilts.
    Smelling dead roses in Buddha's stomach, I was about to
burst.
    . . . piss . . .
    Down the steps, amid a flood of ducks; the water was warm,
but the air was salty.
    (your generals spraying poison gas)
       & [all this killing can't go on]
    In a mess of sea weed between the water and the sand,
lay a stranded man-of-war. Running over to him, going to
pop his bag; when he hollered, "Don'tcha!" (cause he wasn't
playing tag.)

[1] "Mary Jane" is printed here by permission of the author, Charles R. Lyman.

At the end of the beach, there was an ebony junk. It was connected to the shore by gray manila ropes and a weather beaten gang plank.

In the cockpit, under a canvas awning, sat an old man. He was completely white, except for a stripe near the handle of his cane and his dark pair of sunglasses.

Drops of perspiration formed on his face. The old man leaned forward balanced on his cane and removed his hat. His bald head was pink intermingled with blotches of flakey white skin and brown spots.

"Damn flies," he shouted. I told him it was me. He asked, "Do you play piano?" I answered, "and the guitar."

He led me down the hatch into a velvet covered room. In the corner stood a stage, with some room for a bar. The roof was cracked plaster, adorned with tiny stars surrounding a rusty drain. Purple smoke from a huge white dove covered the floor.

On closer inspection, the bird was made of marble with a glued-on plastic nose.

After playing twenty sets to the dove in the dark, the old man whispered to me, "you should play in the park."

He told me, it was flight time and to hurry out the back.

I turned to tell him "roger" then was nothing 'cept the black.

Next I remember, I was sitting on a bus, looking at a drawing of some bent spread legs. Out between the bars rode a slender nude negress, on a burly white steed; leading three polaroid bedecked wisemen, who saluted with a bird.

I jumped out the exit door and landed on some tracks.

An indian picked me up, said the buffalos were back.

(Bleeding just above the hairline, while walking in the park.) Two youths were sitting outstretched beneath the root of a leafless tree. One was lightly tapping a tambourine with a steely hook, while the other mumbled, "the Lord is risen indeed."

Music and voices came from beyond the thickets on the opposite side of the asphalt paved road.

Two indians, one buffalo hunter, and a black-bearded priest (later told me he was John) were playing on a makeshift stage toward the rear of the clearing fitted with joyous children. In the center of the pasture, hidden in a tree, sat the old blind man with his huge white dove.

During the collection, the dove got pushed out of the tree and was beset by a throne of the flower laden children.

They showered him with fragrant garlands and annointed him with wine. They said he was their chosen master and rejoicing made the sign.

When they placed him on the stage, the dove suddenly came alive and cooed three times. Then the youngest child stabbed him as the priest mixed up some wine.

The priest tore apart his body and whispered to all the crowd, "Take eat, for this is my body"; . . . and they all ate, except for a guru, who said he didn't eat meat. Ran into a garden, filled with luscious fruit, Picked a golden apple, and was startled by a snake. He asked me who it was, I answered, "Jesus Christ." Then a panther ate his body, and an angel picked his eyes.

The old man with the cane was standing next to a bulletin board (filled with dirt and dust; a faint trace of blood; and, four spots of rust). He opened a satchel and sorted out a poster, a hammer, and four nails. He drove in the first nail and started on the second; abruptly a shot rang out penetrating him in the back. He glanced upward to a faint scrawl, "POSTED—NO SIGNS!" A blue coated policeman crowed out, "he ain't in line!" The old one turned, moaned, "God bless you"; then he fell. Cry,
> the fragile fawn
> devoured.

Fly,
> a trilling swallow
> falls.

Lie,
> in jasmine
> coals embellished.

Silly geese with wicked tunes
Air now for pumping dreams.

CHARLES R. LYMAN

EXERCISES

1. Without necessarily confessing to your own habits, take a stand on the "pot question." Do you personally believe it can be a positive good? or at least that it is not a positive harm? Or do you think those who use pot and argue that it expands their sense of immediate reality are only kidding themselves? If they are, why do you think they indulge in it? Do you believe it should be legalized on the grounds that a) people get hold of it anyway, or b) it is not dangerous, or c) it is a violation of civil rights to deny people

the chance to avail themselves of pleasure, or d) it is less harmful in the long run than alcohol?

Of course, the subject has been done to death in the media, and I suspect there are few original thoughts for your paper. One conceivably could be borrowed from Aldous Huxley's *Brave New World*, a 1932 novel with a frightening prophecy about a computerized police state of the future. Among the artificial resources relied upon by the inhabitants of this state are the Soma pills handed out every Friday night by the government to the workers. The capsules permit the user to take a weekend "trip" without having to leave his home. The government encourages such "Soma holidays" in order to keep the people from thinking for themselves, for, Huxley contends, independent thought is always the enemy of the superstate.

Regardless of what Huxley himself has said about mind-expanding drugs in other writings, in *Brave New World* he seems to be pointing to a time when reliance on drugs would take the place of free thought and individualism.

This point of view gives rise to an intriguing question you may want to consider in your paper on drugs, and that is: may the frequent use of drugs be incompatible with the cause of individualism? It's worth considering, because drug users are often those who take part in or at least strongly support all protest movements carried on in the name of individual rights. Does Huxley have a point when he sees drugs as enemies of individualism? Can one be truly himself when he is continually turning on and dropping out of society? Is there some point at which the drug habit becomes an escape from a chance to encounter yourself and others with clarity and understanding?

Perhaps you agree with Huxley about "hard stuff" or with my student about the "beneficial" effects of pot, and would like to make a distinction between the dangers of one and the joys of the other.

Perhaps you believe that Huxley's state of the future is practically upon us already and that the "Soma holiday" is the last desperate search for escape. Can you make out a convincing case for such a belief? one that your readers won't suspect is just another excuse for self-indulgence?

2. Here are some suggested ways of making a stronger contact with the reality of the moment than any of us normally has time for:

a) Have the teacher dismiss the class for, say, fifteen or twenty minutes. Each of you will then take a walk about the campus or just around the building in which the class meets. *Remove all thoughts from your mind.* If at all possible, refrain from any communication with others. Take each object and each face as it comes and as you find it. Look at it. See it as something unique, something in and for itself. Then go back to class when the time is up and, while the experiences are still fresh in your mind, write down exactly what you saw.

b) Without leaving your seat in the class, experience the room and the people in it. No one is to speak. Let all activity cease for about fifteen minutes as each of you looks intensely at the objects and faces in the room. In this exercise, even the teacher becomes an experience, a part of the moment. Try to divorce him from his normal appearance to you as an authority figure. Try to see him in an altogether new light. At the conclusion of the time allotted for the contact-session, write your paper, describing exactly what you saw.

c) If the assignment is an out-of-class one, try lying down on the floor. Close your eyes for several minutes, letting your head roll around as it will. Pretend the floor is not hard but cushioned. Sink into it. Go as limp as possible (but don't fall asleep). Then slowly open your eyes; look at the ceiling; don't attempt contact with any other object until your eyes have explored the ceiling completely. Now take the next object you come to—perhaps a part of the wall—and so on, until you fully experience the entire room. Some people take hours for this exercise. It depends on how long your conscience will allow you to stay suspended between the past and the future. At any rate, go as long as you can. When you have completed your examination of the room, you should find that you have never truly experienced this room before. Now, while the sensations are still fresh, go and write your paper, describing everything in the room with which you made contact.

3. Perhaps you started one of the above exercises and found yourself getting bogged down because of the difficulty of transferring your sensations exactly into words. The reason is that language is often too general and the intense experience of reality too particular and personal. Suppose, for instance, you had many interesting touch sensations you wanted to record? Suppose you felt the rug on which you were lying and wished to find an adjective that would *really* express what the material felt like? Would you give up and call the rug rough? tufted? worn? thin? meager? thick? Or would you go the limit and try for a new word (I just this minute tried

it with my own rug and came up with "mossy"—because I found myself associating the touch sensation with the way I think moss would feel to my fingers if I were lying on a rock).

Perhaps the teacher will take some time in class to allow the group as a whole to experiment with language in this connection. Take familiar objects and see what various people can name them. I did it with one of my classes, and here are a few interesting and odd results:

a) the blackboard—a gathering storm

b) the wastebasket—an orphan flowerpot

c) the ceiling—an abandoned switchboard

d) the whole room—"Where have all the flowers gone?"

e) me—lonesome sentry

We didn't analyze any of these responses. The fact that they were spontaneous was enough to give them some validity. Of course, whether you could do a whole paper like this and communicate to anyone is something else, but you might try it!

4. If you tried the experiment with turned-on language, perhaps you are ready to go one step further and imitate what Charles Lyman tried to do with prose: that is, dart inside a moment in time and lose all sense of any other reality.

One way to prepare for such a bizarre exercise is to try lying down on the floor, as you may have done for the preceding assignment; or, if the paper is to be written in class, just sit there quietly in your chair. In either case, let your mind "go limp." Concentrate on absolutely nothing, until your imagination begins weaving strange little designs and acting out weird scenes in your mind's eye.

Some students who have tried this argue that it's impossible to remember the experiences long enough to write them down. Others say it is possible to sit and hallucinate for a given length of time and then stare at the paper, hoping for a second wave of imaginings. I have known students who wrote papers in class in this manner and seemed almost to have hypnotized themselves. It's a fascinating experience even if what you write makes no sense at all.

Rainy-Day People

Perhaps the majority feel closer to the Boggs family, not the Twills. They go to school or work or else stay home and keep house without worrying about how many pleasures to cram into the space of a single day. It is for them that the term "silent majority" has been coined. They are never included in any talk of "our neurotic society."

Still, these are the people who often fall into disrepute because artists, philosophers, and poets shake accusing fingers at them and point out how miserable their lives must be. In Chapter 2 we talked about Thoreau in relation to nonconformity. Here was one of the most outspoken critics of these rainy-day people. It was Thoreau who made the famous statement that, as far as he could tell, most men lived in "quiet desperation," not even knowing how badly off they were. They devoted their lives to material prosperity, hauling out their bankbooks every night to stare at the mounting figures, justifying a barren present by a vague anticipation of a "secure" future. In *Walden*, Thoreau asks:

> Why should we live with such hurry and waste of life? We are de-termined to be starved before we are hungry. Men say that a stitch in time saves nine, and so they take a thousand stitches to-day to save nine tomorrow.

The uncompromising hedonism of Aristippus and his theory that pleasure must be something actually physical, like a tingling of the spine, was sharply opposed by Aristotle. For him, the goal of life was happiness, but he made it clear that happiness and pleasure were not at all the same thing. Happiness, he said, is "the quality of an entire human life." It is never to be found on a day-to-day basis. A happy life is one that has been "made perfect by the possession of all good things." By "good things" Aristotle meant health, sufficient means, virtue, and knowledge.

Unlike Thoreau, who considered a day wasted if one found no joys in it, Aristotle was not concerned with the character of the moment or the pleasure or displeasure one took in it. When a man reached old age and was ready for death, then and only then could he look back and evaluate his life, deciding whether it had been on the whole a good life or a bad one. If he saw that he had been generally in good health and had not been unduly distracted by the need for money; if his conscience was not bothering him, because he knew that he had achieved a good moral character and made a good name in his community and that he had improved his mind whenever possible, then he could declare: "Yes, my life has been a happy one."

In Aristotle's theory of happiness, you spend all your time planning for the final evaluation. Whenever you are faced with a choice—for example, you win some money and have to decide whether to give it to somebody who needs it more than you or buy an expensive luxury you never expected to own—you make the choice you think you will be most proud of when you look back at your life.

An interesting idea, isn't it? You always know what to do because you see yourself as an old man or old woman, and you look upon your decision as already a memory. Will it be a memory to be ashamed of? If the answer is yes, then don't do it, no matter how much immediate pleasure it may seem to promise.

The frequent objection raised by the hedonist, "Yes, but after all, I may be dead tomorrow," is unacceptable in Aristotle's theory. As a matter of fact, it scarcely matters *when* you die so long as you have fashioned a life that is as good as you know how to make it. The number of joys experienced along the way is not significant, nor the number you may have missed. Building a happy life means that you are thinking of the whole, of the broad outlines. You have a different attitude toward time and the individual moment. You can stand boredom or disappointment. You can stand anything just so long as you are satisfied that you have made the right choices, the ones that will make your life something that *was* good.

Although the average citizen probably knows little or nothing about Aristotle's concept of happiness, he tends nonetheless to be a Tomorrowist. You may say he doesn't *know* how to take advantage of the moment, or you may talk about "maturity" and "responsibility" as qualities that he possesses and that are more important *in the long run* than living moment by moment. Either way, the average citizen is less concerned about time's passing and less bothered by wasting time than the dedicated hedonist.

It is possible to see the youth revolution, in which you yourself and certainly many of your classmates may be engaged, as a rejection of Tomorrowism in favor of Todayism. Its battle cry is not Aristotle's theory of happiness but, rather, Thoreau's continual advice:

> Let us spend one day as deliberately as Nature, and not be thrown off the track by every nutshell and mosquito's wing that falls on the rails. Let us rise early and fast, or break fast, gently and without perturbation; let company come and let company go, let the bells ring and the children cry,—determined to make a day of it.

EXERCISES

1. Who gets your vote—Thoreau or Aristotle? Does it make sense to you to devote each day to making provisions for a tomorrow that may never come? Do the people who keep planning ahead ever,

in your opinion, really find the time to enjoy themselves? Or is it a measure of compensation to think of oneself as very old and looking back with satisfaction on a good life? When you are old, would you rather look back on a life that left no pleasure untried? Or are virtue and knowledge more important than moment-by-moment pleasure?

Here's something to think about. For all that Thoreau is famous for his nonconformity and his celebration of the passing moment, especially spent in observing the beauties of nature, he was a supremely well-educated man (a Harvard graduate) and a prose stylist of great skill. You don't accumulate his knowledge or way with words without a lot of self-discipline and study. So that if you, for example, decided you wanted to be a drop-out and devote your entire life to the pleasures of the moment, you might reasonably expect never to have Thoreau's ability to express yourself or tell others about it. You might even not be intelligent enough to be aware of your life while you were in the process of living it unless you had spent some time intellectually preparing yourself for it.

Write a paper attacking or defending Tomorrowism as a way of life.

2. Back in 1940 Thornton Wilder wrote a play called *Our Town*, probably the most poetic attempt anyone has yet made to point out the ordinary pleasures of ordinary life that are available each day, even for the tomorrow-oriented solid citizen, whom Wilder believes is the real backbone of American society. The trouble is, however (at least according to the play), that rainy-day people are often blind to these pleasures and miss out on many things that could intensify their lives. In the last act of the play, the heroine, Emily, dies and is permitted to go back and relive one of her days on earth. She selects an ordinary, seemingly uneventful day and is surprised to find how beautiful it really was and appalled that she never noticed it when she was alive.

Does Emily's discovery apply to the majority of good people who must think more of tomorrow than they do of today and consequently don't get as much from the simple things as they should? Do they overlook what is actually there for them to take pleasure in if only they would? What about family life itself? the raising of and caring for children, and daily incidents? daily crises? even the arguments that, unpleasant as they may seem, also indicate love and togetherness and people caring enough about each other to argue?

Write a paper in which you pretend that, like Emily, you have returned to some day in your past. Relive it and see what was there that you did not experience at the time.

Of course, nobody wants to force you to find the simple joys of life if you don't believe in such things. If you wish, use the "return visit" as a way of reminding yourself of the drab, unhappy experiences you *were* conscious of and are happy you have escaped from (if you have).

3. Maybe I have been making too much of a case for Tomorrowism and trying too hard to point out the positive advantages of being an ordinary citizen. We surely don't want to forget the frequent description of our American way of life as a "rat race," nor do we want to overlook the fact that frightening statistics show that men die long before women do, mainly from heart attacks (which mean overexertion and straining to the breaking point to get ahead). In other words, have we gone too far? Would even Aristotle urge us to slow down, catch our breaths, and take time out for a sunset or two?

Without necessarily going all out for the hedonist's cause, write a serious paper, pointing out some of the dangers of Tomorrowism as an American "addiction." Even if you approve of settling down, going to work, raising a family, and planning for the future, you must have certain reservations or be conscious of certain pitfalls.

This may well be the most important paper you will ever write, especially if you consider yourself serious, adult, and ready for mature responsibility.

4. There must be many features of contemporary American life that, in your opinion, make it difficult for the rainy-day people, even those most willing to overlook many inconveniences, those who do not require more than a minimum of daily enjoyments. If you had unlimited control over the future, aren't there many changes you'd like to make, to provide daily living with a bit more pleasure? Write a paper suggesting some of these.

Some possibilities:

a) a change in the transportation system so as to do away with hurtling subways, long bus rides, hot, dusty commuter trains, and so on

b) a shorter work week (already on the drawing board, but how about the economics of it?)

c) free health care for all (to prolong everyone's life, including the father's)

d) government price and wage controls (to stop the inflationary spiral and ease the pressure of having to earn more and more money)

e) meaningful urban renewal (tearing down of the ghettos and the building in their place of model cities controlled by blacks)

f) conservation and antipollution ordinances (be specific and also indicate how to enforce them!)

A SENSE OF THE PAST

So far our deliberations in this chapter have concerned the choice each of us may make between living richly and intensely in the present moment with less care about tomorrow or having fewer momentary pleasures in exchange for more security in the future. No matter which lane you take or whether you try to walk the narrow line in the middle of the road, you represent at any given moment an accumulation of all that you have been before. I don't have a future, sang Rose of Washington Square in the old song, but "oh what a past!" No doubt you've heard the old joke: "He has a great future behind him." The past hovers over our heads like the raven in Poe's poem; try to forget it if you will, but you can't stop it from croaking in your ear from time to time.

Many of the Now people (perhaps you are one yourself) argue that there is only the reality of the moment. Time, they say, is a fiction, a human myth, a purely subjective, inner experience. True, the things we do leave their mark on our memories, but memory, they add, is not really happening. If one wishes, he can ignore his memories. Or he can take pleasure in the happy ones, or else he can be miserable, always comparing the inadequate present with the infinitely better yesterdays he sees in a dim haze. Whatever attitude toward the past he may have, he can in no way alter the fact that it doesn't truly exist.

Still, a counterargument is that the past is known by its consequences, and these are frequently a very real part of the present. Suppose, for example, that an ex-music student attends a concert at Carnegie Hall. On stage sits an internationally celebrated pianist. He lifts his hands and then begins to play a Chopin sonata, his thin, agile fingers moving with incredible speed and lightness over the keyboard. The audience sits enraptured by the sounds—all, that is, except the student, who has studied piano *in the past*, failed to make the grade *in the past*, thrown up a stout defense mechanism, and now *in the present* hears totally different sounds coming from the stage. Because

of the accumulation of complexes on the subject of piano performances, it is now all but impossible for the student to enjoy a
great virtuoso performance. He has conditioned himself to disapprove
of the work of even the greatest pianist. He may tell himself the past
is not real and he must live only in the present, but he cannot tell this
to his entire personality, which has been shaped and molded by the
events of yesterday.

But, you argue, what does it matter that the music student was a
past failure? He is at present a member of an audience, and, if he
cannot enjoy the concert, it is his fault. Bondage to the past, a sense
of history, you may say, is not a necessity. It is a neurosis.

Professional historians and philosophers of history would disagree.
History was invented by Herodotus, a Greek who said he wanted to
keep a record of the deeds of his people, especially of their wars with
the barbarians and the causes of them. From Herodotus on, the
traditional view of history has been that it is an awareness of cause
and effect. It could be said, for example, that the music student's
inability to respond to the concert was caused by his bad experiences
in music. It is foolish to deny these experiences. The sense of history
makes us understand the phenomenon of the student.

To say that history is meaningless or unimportant is, for historians,
to say that things or events should not be understood. *History makes
sense out of what happens.* The contemporary historian R. G. Collingwood notes:

> But everything has a past; everything has somehow come to be what
> it is; and therefore the historical aspect of things is a universal and
> necessary part of them. Hence, too, anyone who is interested in any-
> thing at all is interested in something that has an historical aspect,
> and if he is really interested in the thing he must be to some extent
> interested in this aspect of it.[2]

Collingwood sees history as an actual dimension of something or
someone. There is the thing itself, as something to be experienced
for whatever it is, but there are also the forces that went into the
making of the thing. Not to understand these is not to experience the
thing as a whole.

This means each of us carries around his past in the sense of
being the result of a whole lot of forces that worked on him. And
if the history of each of us is real, perhaps history itself—the sum
total of all the causes that have led to the present moment—has to be

[2] *Essays in the Philosophy of History* (Austin, Texas: University of Texas Press,
1965), p. 124.

thought of as real. If this is so, the rituals and commemorations of the past in which people indulge may have a legitimate place and purpose. Even your own ethnic and regional traditions, as shapers of your identity, may have to be given their due. Perhaps it is not, after all, possible to live only in the present and cut yourself off from what has been.

Rituals, Memorials, and Symbols

Not long ago there was a popular ballad which mournfully and sentimentally commemorated the good old days when "we'd live the life we choose; we'd fight and never lose." If it were not for nostalgia for the past, we might even have to give up about half of all the songs we sing.

But human beings do more than indulge in occasional bursts of sweet sorrow over yesterday. They spend a great deal of time and millions of dollars in commemorating its splendid accomplishments. If you live in a part of the country that is "rich in history," then you no doubt grew up accustomed to seeing monuments and plaques everywhere proclaiming that a glorious event occurred on "this very spot." Such a background may have made you extremely reverential toward the past, or it may have given you even further cause to join the Now movement.

My own youth was spent in New England. If you have ever visited Massachusetts, Vermont, Connecticut, or the other New England states, you no doubt recall having run into a commemorative marker on virtually every street corner. "Here stood brave Isaac Dawson on March 8, 1624, and warded off an ambush of sixteen Indians, slaying all but three, who fled into the hills."

Sometimes the present and the past mix it up uncomfortably in New England. I remember that the old swimmin' hole for most of us was Thoreau's own Walden Pond, because the Atlantic Ocean was too far away and you could never find a parking spot at the beach anyway. On hot summer afternoons we would pile into somebody's jalopy and head for the woods. Not that Walden Pond wasn't pretty crowded too. From the dirty bathhouse or the mustard-splattered hot dog stand, you could hear the sound of Thoreau rolling around angrily in his grave.

Now there's even a housing development on the very spot that, for thousands of visitors, used to symbolize the American dream of freedom and dignity for the individual. The local historical society fought long and hard to stop it, but I suppose they were told "you can't block progress." Some old-timers around Lincoln or Concord will never get over all the things that have happened to what they believe should have remained a sacred national shrine.

Worse indignities have been inflicted on the old Concord Bridge nearby. Even if you never visited Concord, you have probably read Emerson's famous poem, the opening lines of which are inscribed on a memorial plaque:

> By the rude bridge that arched the flood,
>   Their flag to April's breeze unfurled,
> Here once the embattled farmers stood
>   And fired the shot heard round the world.

Located behind Hawthorne's Old Manse, the old bridge is particularly charming because it remains essentially what it has always been, a simple wooden means of getting from one side of the river to the other. When you cross it, you don't feel like a gaping tourist. It's part of the useful present and doesn't put on pretentious airs like *some* historical monuments. The citizens of Concord come and go on it, and it seems content to serve them without needing a whole lot of attention.

At the same time, whenever I *do* cross the Concord River on it, I cannot help feeling a surge of sentiment for the past. Yesterday starts feeling good. I stop and look down into the quiet waters of the sluggish old river, which is hardly more than a stream at this point. I suddenly forget the present moment and enjoy the recognition that I belong to something bigger. I have roots; I come from an old tradition. (Imagine thinking like this with a name like mine!) I take visitors there ("foreigners" who have never been to New England) and show off this spot with a certain amount of snobbish pride.

During my last visit I found that a section of the bridge was missing and the whole area blocked off. It seems a band of young militants had decided to launch a new revolution at the identical spot where the first one was born, and they had planted a bomb under one of the planks. The sight of the damage filled me with resentment. "Have they no feeling for the past?" I thought.

Now I admit people have been known to go too far in glorifying the past. There are people who can't let go of yesterday. They buy antiques, rare books, and old wine decanters (though they don't drink). I've been in their houses, and the rooms smell musty and moldy because the windows are never opened. I've been to annual "observance" days and seen men and women wearing seventeenth-century clothes. When I was very young, I used to stand for hours on April 18, waiting for some man dressed like Paul Revere to come galloping down Main Street screaming "The British are coming!"

But I can't think why anyone would want to blow up the old wooden bridge over the Concord River. In the first place, the bridge has stood for all these years as a symbol of freedom. It was here that the Concord farmers scored a great victory in driving the British back. Whoever planted the bomb must never have read the rest of Emerson's poem:

> On this green bank, by this soft stream,
>   We set to-day a votive stone;
> That memory may their deed reform,
>   When, like our sires, our sons are gone.
>
> Spirit, that made those heroes dare
>   To die, and leave their children free,
> Bid Time and Nature gently spare
>   The shaft we raise to them and thee.

The planters of the bomb were some of those children Emerson was talking about.

The symbolic bombing was also a backhanded tribute to the past, a recognition of the importance of the bridge and the tradition it represented. But why such disrespect? Is it possible that the militants walked away feeling proud of what they had done? Can they themselves get along without a normal amount of reverence for history, or is this my New England sentimentality showing?

EXERCISES

1. Even if you don't live in a place that is steeped in history, you can't fail to run across the past continually in a variety of ways. Write a paper on rituals and commemorations of the past that you have experienced or taken part in. Tell how you feel about them: that is, are you glad they exist, or have you decided too much time is devoted to glorifying the good old days?

    Here's a list of rituals you could use, as a start:

    a) your high school graduation as ritual (describe the symbols, the pomp, and the circumstance)

    b) other festivals and observances from your earlier school days (for example, when I was in grade school, we always dressed up in Pilgrim costumes around Thanksgiving time, and created a crepe-paper turkey dinner)

    c) local civic observances (like Ground Hog day)

    d) saluting and pledging allegiance to the flag

e) college rituals you may already have observed or participated
   in (fraternity or sorority initiations, freshman hazing, and "in"
   jokes, like spray-painting the statue of the college founder on
   the eve of the big football game)

f) college sports themselves as rituals (spirited rivalries and various other traditions associated with sports)

Try to be as honest as you can in analyzing and evaluating such
tributes to the past. How do rituals play upon the emotions? Did
you get a lump in your throat when they played the Alma Mater?
Were you bored and unaffected by the pageantry of your high
school graduation? If you have to confess to having been touched
—at least now and then—by rituals, then you must take their
emotional appeal into account. You should seek to determine
whether the positive value of ritual balances or even outweighs the
harm that too much looking backward can do.

On the other hand, your analysis may indicate that it *is* important for people to observe the past; you may find yourself becoming critical of those who say they have no feeling for it.

2. The Concord Bridge bombing is only one of hundreds of such incidents involving disrespect for tradition and its symbols that we
read about continually in the papers. The flag has been a particular
target. Protestors and demonstrators have pulled it down and sometimes burned it to show how much scorn they have for America's
past and present.

If you had been me and been raised close to Concord, would *you*
have felt outraged by the damaging of the bridge? When you hear
of somebody burning the American flag, do you feel angered?
Why? Or why not? Tearing, hauling down, or burning the flag is,
of course, a federal offense, but I imagine most people wouldn't
do violence to it even if it were not. Are they just dull, middle-class
conformists with no imagination, or do you think it is important
for people to have such symbols?

Another symbol that has been questioned is standing during the
playing of the national anthem. Of late there have been cases of
people refusing to do this and then claiming that their rights have
been violated when they were arrested. Is this true? Or does society have the privilege of expecting such observances to be treated
as sacred?

If you legitimately feel you have a cause and if this includes the
right to ignore the symbols and rituals associated with America
and her traditions, you should have the courage and integrity to

make a case for your attitude. By the same token, you have the right to censure verbally those whose disrespect for America and her traditions you cannot approve of. Your position on this very sensitive subject should be the basis for one of the semester's liveliest writing projects.

3. The Now generation, of which you must be either a practicing member or an interested observer, has many rituals and observances of its own. Here is a partial list to which I am certain you can add:

a) rock festivals

b) cult and ingroup procedures, such as significant adornments on the body (love beads, body painting, and so forth), special handshakes, and special positions for sitting around a room

c) particular ways of group indulgence in "stimulation aids," such as smoking the peace pipe

d) making use of Oriental rituals, such as the Japanese tea-drinking ceremony or Zen Buddhist methods of contemplation

The purpose of such ritual is, presumably, to glorify and enhance the present moment; yet may it not be argued that any excessive and ceremonial use of symbolism means giving up a certain measure of one's individuality and indulging in precisely the sort of thing we have noted in connection with the celebration of the past? Or is there a difference?

Write a paper in which you defend or question the popular rituals of the Now people; or write a paper indicating why you believe *all* rituals should be honored, whether they celebrate the present or the past. Your essay should include your own definition of ritual and your own analysis of how one evolves.

4. In an article published in the *Village Voice* (April 18, 1968) film critic Andrew Sarris censured the Hollywood Academy Award ceremonies for glorifying certain old movies like *Gone with the Wind*. Sarris maintained that we can no longer afford any sort of nostalgia for the American past. "To love any aspect of America's past is to acknowledge complicity in America's racism, and Hollywood is hardly the only sinner in this regard." Write a paper analyzing the general subject of *whether our national rituals and memorial observances of the past are white-oriented or whether all citizens should be able to relate to national traditions.* Sarris' observation about nostalgia for *Gone with the Wind* is probably a well-taken point. If you have ever seen the film, you will remember the treat-

ment given the blacks (Mammy adoring and worshipping "Miz" Scarlett, for example). But over and above a dated sort of white supremacy one finds in all the old movies from the thirties and at least part of the forties, there is the fact that *Gone with the Wind* is a ritual celebration, this time of the Old South. The film romanticizes an era in our history the way annual ante-bellum observances in Mississippi and Louisiana do. These, surely, are targets of Sarris' citicism, for they strongly suggest "complicity" in the racism of the past. But in a larger sense, it may well be that Sarris is right and that *all* commemorations—whether they are specifically "Old South" or not—are racist at heart unless they pointedly symbolize an important black contribution to our national heritage, such as the spontaneous, mostly unofficial observance of Martin Luther King Day that sprang up in all parts of the country in 1969. Write a paper giving your opinion on this delicate subject. Do you think black people have a right to feel excluded from most national rituals? (I'm not referring to graduation exercises and the like, but there have been incidents in which black students have refused to salute the flag or stand during the national anthem. Were they justified?) Or do you say that the national heritage belongs to everyone? A case could be made for the fact that this heritage is generally a celebration of freedom and that even though the blacks are just now beginning to win a significant measure of freedom, the tradition itself applies to them as well as to white people (many of whom have also been victims of discrimination in the past).

5. *Gone with the Wind* may offer a somewhat dated and highly questionable picture of the Old South, but it is a novel. It does not pretend to be a history book, and therefore, if the reader objects to its lack of total accuracy, it can be argued tht novels are not required to be true.

A nonfiction, purely historical account of the past, however, promises the reader a far greater measure of the truth. How do you feel about the treatment of American history, in whole or in part, as you have experienced it from school books (or, for that matter, from classroom lectures you have had)?

For example, I grew up with a strong reverence for our earliest settlers, the Pilgrims, inspired by reading in school and by the reverent attitude the teachers brought to this subject. We were taught to think of the Pilgrims as a gallant, noble, courageous, and self-sacrificing band, but for whose bravery and fortitude this country would never have been founded.

Perhaps the historians themselves were influenced by the way in which the Pilgrim fathers sometimes wrote about their experiences. Here's how William Bradford, the second governor of the Plymouth colony, described the famous landing of the Pilgrims:

> Being thus arived in a good harbor and brought safe to land, they fell upon their knees and blessed the God of heaven, who had brought them over the vast and furious ocean, and delivered them from all the periles and miseries thereof, againe to set their feete on the firme and stable earth, their proper elemente. . . .
>
> But I cannot but stay and make a pause, and stand half amazed at this poore peoples presente condition; and so I thinke will the reader too, when he well considers the same. Being thus passed the vast ocean, and a sea of troubles before in their preparation (as may be remembered by that which wente before), they had now no friends to wellcome them, no inns to entertaine or refresh their weatherbeaten bodys, no houses or much less townes to repaire too, to seeke for succoure. It is recorded in scripture as a mercie to the apostle and his shipwraked company, that the barbarians shewed them no smale kindness in refreshing them, but these savage barbarians, when they mette with them (as after will appeare) were readier to fill their sids full of arrows then other wise. And for the season it was winter, and they that know the winters of that cuntrie know them to be sharp and violent, and subjecte to cruell and feirce stormes, deangerous to travill to known places, much more to serch an unknown coast. Besids, what could they see but a hidious and desolate wildernes, full of wild beasts and willd men?

Honestly, we practically wept in class when we heard such accounts of those early hardships. And how we hated those villainous Indians! (The cowboy movies we watched on Saturday afternoons —which are still to be seen on television—did nothing to alter our overwhelming prejudice against the red man.)

Subsequent reading and research have opened my eyes about many historical subjects. I learned, for example, that the Puritans, many of whom became the American Pilgrims, were considered subversive, dangerous people in some European quarters. Moreover, though they may have sailed to these shores seeking religious freedom, they immediately set up a theocratic state that was just about the most intolerant ever known! And what about the Indians? What do you suppose they thought when a bunch of strange people suddenly descended on their lands?

Without being irreverent, isn't it possible for one to hold a sane course between an unquestioning glorification of a past that never was and a cynical denial of history and a refusal to take part in *any* observances of our national heritage?

Write a paper describing some of your own experiences with historical misconceptions, your own awakenings or disillusionments, and what you have learned as a result about the proper approach to history.

Your paper could take the form of the history curriculum you would set up if you were the chairman of a high school department of history.

Looking Homeward

Do you enjoy going to a party at a strange apartment, ignorant of the host and not sure whether anyone you know will be there? Do you stride into the room with utmost confidence? Or do you wait to see how it all goes, knowing you can always slip out the back door? It is the rare soul who is totally self-confident and equal to any occasion. That is why it helps to carry around at least a little bit of your past, your own heritage. No matter how you may feel about national history and the rituals that commemorate it, it helps to think of *yourself* as the important end result of a certain sequence of events: if you will, a tradition. If you say to yourself, "After all, I'm a Winkler, and a Winkler doesn't care what people say about him," you will find it easier to take giant steps when you enter a room.

Like the commemoration of history in general, however, your own private tradition can be something less than a joy forever. People can be suffocated by their pasts. ("Remember, son, you're a Winkler, and that means you don't associate with people like that, you don't marry a girl from that class of society, and you don't ever vote for a liberal candidate.") Or they can be penalized for things that took place before they were born. ("All I know is you're from Mississippi and I'm black, so how do you expect me to trust you?") They can be labeled and typed because of the national origins of their family tree. ("Your parents were born in Sicily, and so you must have a leaning toward organized crime.")

Responsibilities thrust on one for family, nationality, and ethnic reasons can be both unpleasant and unfair. One's father ran up debts with everyone in town; therefore can one never borrow money? Worse, is one expected to spend his life paying the debtors off? If my ancestors were Italian, must I feel a personal need to apologize for the Mafia? If I am black and black militants burned a library down, must I avoid eye contact with white acquaintances, as if to say, "I know how you must feel about what my people did"?

Families themselves have a way of demanding that offspring never forget who and what they are, and young people are often herded along a one-way street before they're old enough to think for themselves. Think back to your own childhood. Try to go as far into the past as your memory will take you. At the precise point when you can begin to recall yourself as a person, weren't you already a number of things? A Presbyterian perhaps? poor white trash from the bad side of the railroad tracks? a tiny aristocrat crawling around on a tiled back porch? a black "second-class" baby citizen, already being taught to "keep your place"? a girl with a high I.Q. already earmarked for future domesticity by a mother with grandmotherly aspirations? a high school teacher's son with his dormitory assignment at Dad's school already selected and his major already determined?

Parents can be the initial cause of rebellion in the home, without realizing that when they insist, "We never tried to interfere," they started doing it long before either they or their children knew about it. As a result many children are forced by circumstances and their own inevitable struggle for personal identity to cut themselves off from their own past, a heritage none of us can afford to be wholly without.

It is probably better in the interest of your identity to look homeward before trying to look ahead and to do it with all the fondness, love, and sentiment you can muster. Sure, there must be plenty of bitter memories, but more than likely, you'll find at the very least a dual attitude. You can't completely despise what your life has been in the past because that is to despise a little of what you are now. Moreover, not to have a moderate amount of nostalgia for the past is to shut the door on the effort to understand yourself. Rebelling totally and hating every moment of the past is for many people just as bad as loving everything about it and being critical of nothing.

Reading the powerful *Autobiography of Malcolm X,* I was much struck by one of nostalgia's most beneficial uses. In the throes of great bitterness the author, who prophesied that he would be assassinated before his book was ever published, sometimes falls upon a cool, pleasant oasis in his memories and pauses briefly to savor a remembrance. In the following passage Malcolm X finds comfort and relief from pain in revisiting one of the few places where he was happy as a child.

> Not only did we have our big garden, but we raised chickens. My father would buy some baby chicks and my mother would raise them. We all loved chicken. That was one dish there was no argument with my father about. One thing in particular that I remember made me feel grateful toward my mother was that one day I went and asked her for my own garden, and she did let me have my own little plot. I loved it and took care of it well. I loved especially to grow peas. I was proud when we had them on our table. I would pull out the grass in my garden by hand when the first little blades came up. I would patrol the rows on my hands and knees for any worms and bugs, and I would kill and bury them. And sometimes when I had

everything straight and clean for my things to grow, I would lie down on my back between two rows, and I would gaze up in the blue sky at the clouds and think all kinds of things.[3]

EXERCISES

1. Concentrate for a time on either one of your parents. Realizing that a dual attitude is both usual and probably inevitable, make a list of the pleasant, nostalgic things you remember and of the hard times as well. You are not trying to stack the cards in either direction. Rather, you are owning up to your past, and you want to see it as accurately as possible. This is the way to begin: that is, by isolating one figure after another and putting the chips on the table.

   Your lists might look something like this:

FATHER

Sweet	*Sour*
Gave me money out of his own allowance so Mother wouldn't find out I had lost mine in poker game.	Often punished me unmercifully and without cause—just to prove to Mother he was head of family.
Tried, awkwardly, to take care of my sex education, even to point of making embarrassing confession about some of his boyhood misadventures.	Once took my license and tore it into shreds after I'd had a slight accident with family car.
Gave up fishing trip with his buddies to go on Father-Son Boy Scout weekend with me.	Sometimes reminded me, angrily, of weekend he once gave up for me.

   The longer you contemplate, the longer your lists will grow. From them you will get the material for a paper reminiscing over your happy and sad memories of an important person in your past.

2. The Roman emperor Marcus Aurelius begins his famous *Meditations* by giving proper credit to his family predecessors for various aspects of his character. Everything he says is favorable, and his show of respect stands as an all-time model. Times, of course, have changed, and no one expects you to believe that your parents, grandparents, and other relatives were perfect or, indeed, that you yourself are! Instead, write a paper in which you either trace some

---

[3] *The Autobiography of Malcolm X*, with the assistance of Alex Haley. Copyright © 1964 by Alex Haley and Malcolm X. Copyright © 1965 by Alex Haley and Betty Shabazz. Published by and reprinted by permission of Grove Press, Inc.

of your most pronounced characteristics to their source in your background or indicate to what extent you find yourself quite different in some respects from your predecessors and why you believe this is so.

Some considerations:

a) Are you overly emotional, easily given to anger or shows of affection? Was this a quality of either parent? Or are you this way (or its opposite) because your parents were not?

b) Are you relatively free of prejudice toward others? Or do you honestly find yourself guilty of discrimination? If the answer is yes, do you remember prejudice in your family background? If you are free of prejudice, is it that you have rebelled against your parents' ways or that they helped you to become tolerant and broadminded?

c) Are you naïve when it comes to sex? Are your parents to blame? If you think they are, do you believe they were sophisticated about it?

d) Are you a good student because your parents forced you to study? because they made you believe high grades were important status symbols? despite the indifference of your parents to your educational achievements?

e) Are you a bad student because your parents drove you too hard? because they never seemed to care, and so why should you have cared? because they were both intelligent and you always felt inadequate? because they never seemed to set good examples for you or make you believe scholastic achievement was important?

3. Go back and reread the passage about Malcolm X's garden. Think back over your own past and find some private, precious little spot that meant a great deal to you. Describe this place as simply and eloquently as you can, trying consciously to imitate the effective "quiet" of Malcolm X's style. Include an account of how you came to be attached to the place. What finally happened? Did you move away? Was the place demolished? Did you just grow up and lose interest?

Try to give your place some special kind of significance. If you are at all familiar with the story of Malcolm X, you can see at once that his garden memory means more to him than just a passing chance to indulge in some nostalgia. The garden really represents what he was looking for throughout his life: a sense of identity, a sense of belonging.

Many writers are haunted by such memories, which come to symbolize something beautiful that has been lost or even the fulfillment of their whole search in life, though they cannot explain why. Thomas Wolfe, for example, in *Look Homeward, Angel* and *Of Time and the River*, epic novels of his own youth and search for identity, keeps mentioning "a stone, a leaf, an unfound door": glimpses or flashes of memory, things that meant so much to him long ago; he knows he will be all right if he can just find them again.

Maybe you have a place, or even some lost objects, whose location you don't exactly remember, but, like Thomas Wolfe, somehow you know you have been searching for them. Was the place a front stoop somewhere? a hill overlooking a pond? an abandoned mill? a covered bridge? Were the objects jackknives? library books? pressed flowers?

Many years ago the actor Orson Welles and a group called the Mercury Theatre produced a now classic film called *Citizen Kane*, alleged to have been a fictionalized account of the life of William Randolph Hearst, a giant in American journalism. For all his wealth and material possessions, Kane keeps searching for the meaning of the term "Rosebud," which has haunted him throughout his life and which he knows is somehow a symbol of everything that has real meaning and value, everything he has missed owning. Kane dies without ever finding the object of his desires, but the audience is shown a closeup of a child's sled on which is painted "Rosebud."

Perhaps you know of such a thing in your own life, a thing that represents what you hope some day to find or what you feel you have lost or what will never be found.

If you select a place for this paper, it may be that you associate it with particular experiences or a whole part of your life that you have lost. Was it, for example, a classroom in a school you once attended? How do you feel about the learning you experienced there? Perhaps you have never really learned as much anywhere again.

Or suppose your place is a church in which much of your childhood was spent. How do you feel about religion now? If you are less religious than you were as a child, do you find something missing in your life?

Ethnic and Regional Customs

The consideration of the past and its importance as a shaper of your present identity properly concludes with ethnic and regional influences, two of the most evident ways in which any of us becomes whatever he is. By "ethnic" influences I refer, of course, to race, color, or nationality: super-forces that often outweigh family traditions or at least largely determine, for many families, what these traditions are to be. "Regional" influences are the native traditions and attitudes that are strong in the part of the country in which you spent most of your past. If you hail from Mississippi, you probably cannot, for example, enter a discussion of race relations without *some* twinges. If you came from the hills of North Carolina or Kentucky, you may still know a good recipe for moonshine, though you may not dare admit it. I've already mentioned my own memories of Paul Revere's ride on April 18, but an observance of the famous event is limited to Massachusetts, where schools legally close to honor the occasion. If I were going to do the regional exercise at the conclusion of this section, I should probably decide that Patriot's Day wasn't an important influence on my development, but the general New England custom of spending so much time celebrating the long-ago certainly was.

Nowadays ethnic consciousness is coming back into its own. This wasn't always the case, at least openly. My own parents, second-generation Italians, were, like a good many of their contemporaries, acutely conscious of trying to "act American" and minimize the ethnic customs. We had spaghetti often enough, of course, but that has long since become as American a dish as, say, chop suey. We lived near other Italians, without seeking out their company, especially if they spoke broken English and didn't seem to be making any effort to Americanize themselves. I remember an old aunt of mine, who finally made it to these shores very late in life. She was scarcely off the boat when she enrolled herself in a night school course that prepared one for naturalization. How proud she was when she got her "papers," and I shall always remember her self-righteous Americanism. She would look at some of the neighborhood "peasants" and say, "I got no use for uncitizenship people!"

My aunt's attitude was a sly form of prejudice, and I guess in those days we were prejudiced without knowing it. My family thought it was one hundred percent American, but what did *that* mean except that we were imitating white Anglo-Saxon Protestant society and pretending we were descendants of the Mayflower voyagers? Some of our Italian friends had already changed their names: from "Iacobucci" to "Jackson," for example. In school I began to meet Jewish kids with names like "Flanders" or "Gainsborough" and Polish kids with names like "Dawson" or "Montgomery." The more English it sounded, the more American it was supposed to be.

There were so few blacks in our town that their whole nature and ethnic identity were mysteries to me. I'm not sure they were very con-

scious of being ethnically unique. In school they were apparently accepted—at least to the degree that we Italians, Jews, and Poles were.
None of us was really Anglo-Saxon, and the kids from the real New
England families knew it. But all of us played the game of being something indefinable called "pure" Americans.

Whether all of us knew it or not, however, the white kids probably
were acting "racist" to the blacks, just as the real Anglo-Saxons observed a strict distance between themselves and the pretenders. The
ethnic differences were there, all right; it's just that nobody made a
point of them. We all stood and sang "America the Beautiful," and
those of us with more exotic backgrounds than others stood half in
shadows and hoped people wouldn't notice skin color, length of
the nose, color of the hair, or the slight trace of a foreign accent that
some of the kids picked up from their parents.

Now that I think back on those early days, I can't help feeling
what a shame it was we didn't do more with our backgrounds and
even share them with each other. Ethnic differences were the subject
of distasteful jokes, which we whispered into the "right" ears: jokes
mainly about blacks, Jews, Poles, Italians, and Irish; or else jokes
about Catholics and Protestants.

Today, with black people leading the way, there is a revival of
ethnicity. Or perhaps this is something quite new and unprecedented
in American life. "Afro" hair styles and "Afro" clothes proclaim not
only that *black* is beautiful but that the unique and distinctive are to
be exploited and gloried in. The Afro movement has for its underlying
theme the importance of differences. The old "melting pot" idea of
American society—which meant that out of a variety of backgrounds
emerged one new and unified nation—has been supplanted by the
premise that America implies a collection of unique ethnic backgrounds.

Each of us has an ethnic past of which he ought to be aware. Read
how the poet Carl Sandburg, in his autobiography, enjoys recollections of his "Swedish childhood" in Illinois. Note how he lovingly
includes little details, like what he ate, foreign expressions, and family
routine. He seems unconcerned about how interesting any of this will
be to his reader: this is *his* past, and that's what counts.

> After the wash was hung three or four children would climb on
> the kitchen table. Mama threw soapy water on the floor and scrubbed
> and mopped while we played we were on an island or on a housetop
> floating down a river. After supper or the next morning I would go
> out and pile the frozen clothes high into a basket and bring them
> into the house. The noon dinner and the evening supper on Monday,
> never failing for years, were boiled herring and boiled potatoes, *sill*

och patatis, for generations a simple classic menu of which they said with straight faces, "This is what make the Swedes so strong."

On the highest shelf of the pantry Mama kept her latest bake of cookies or freshly fried doughnuts. On her leaving the room to be gone five or ten minutes, we would climb a chair and with a long reach get our fingers on cookies or doughnuts or the little bag of sugar lumps and run to the cellar or some other room for sweet eating. She usually saw later that there had been thieves in her pantry and she called us thieves and tried to be stern with a severe face, but generally a half-smile broke through. She was not a natural scold. . . .

Mama saw to it when we had been too long without a bath she half filled a washtub with warm water, gave us soap, and told us to scrub. There would be the months we boys went swimming and didn't need the home baths. There would be the winter weeks of bitter cold when a bath once a month might be considered right. The three sisters would clear out of the kitchen while Mart and I took our washtub bath. Then we would go to bed and the girls would take over.

Mama watched carefully the cellar corner where the cabbage heads were piled in October so that in part of the winter there would be slaw and boiled cabbage. About early-frost time she would buy several bushels of green tomatoes at ten cents a bushel and put up preserves for bread spread and jars of chowchow and piccalilli. If we forgot, she reminded Mart and me in February of the garden and frozen ground where we could pound, dig, and rassle out one or two bushels of parsnips. She saw us peeling raw turnips, enjoying them, and said, "They are good for you." For fun we ate raw potatoes to show her we could do it and she said they would be better fried or boiled. We told her that on the way to school we had scraped grains from the floor of a railroad wheat car and had fun chewing and tasting raw wheat. She said the wheat might not be clean and having done it once, that was enough.[4]

How much of this is ethnic-oriented you'd probably never realize unless you made a specific point of it. What about the references to "the" sisters, for example, instead of "my" sisters? Piling cabbage heads in the cellar to make slaw? "Bread spread"? Even the type of relationship existing between the mother and the children is significantly ethnic. Apparently it was a large family. From reading just this excerpt, one notes that Swedish families are probably closely knit. The mother apparently had time to be playful with the children. (This doesn't, of course, say that other kinds of families aren't close or that *all* Swedish families have to be!)

Not all ethnic memories are as pleasant as those in the passages from Sandburg. They can be extremely bitter or intensely dramatic, like this moving recollection by Malcolm X of the last time he saw his father:

[4] From *Always the Young Strangers,* copyright 1952, 1953 by Carl Sandburg. Reprinted by permission of Harcourt Brace Jovanovich, Inc.

One afternoon in 1931 when Wilfred, Hilda, Philbert, and I came home, my mother and father were having one of their arguments. There had lately been a lot of tension around the house because of Black Legion threats. Anyway, my father had taken one of the rabbits which we were raising, and ordered my mother to cook it. We raised rabbits, but sold them to whites. My father had taken a rabbit from the rabbit pen. He had pulled off the rabbit's head. He was so strong, he needed no knife to behead chickens or rabbits. With one twist of his big black hands he simply twisted off the head and threw the bleeding-necked thing back at my mother's feet.

My mother was crying. She started to skin the rabbit, preparatory to cooking it. But my father was so angry he slammed on out of the front door and started walking up the road toward town.

It was then that my mother had this vision. She had always been a strange woman in this sense, and had always had a strong intuition of things about to happen. And most of her children are the same way, I think. When something is about to happen, I can feel something, sense something. I never have known something to happen that has caught me completely off guard—except once. And that was when, years later, I discovered facts I couldn't believe about a man who, up until that discovery, I would gladly have given my life for.

My father was well up the road when my mother ran screaming out onto the porch. "Early! Early!" She screamed his name. She clutched up her apron in one hand, and ran down across the yard and into the road. My father turned around. He saw her. For some reason, considering how angry he had been when he left, he waved at her. But he kept on going.

She told me later, my mother did, that she had a vision of my father's end. All the rest of the afternoon, she was not herself, crying and nervous and upset. She finished cooking the rabbit and put the whole thing in the warmer part of the black stove. When my father was not back home by our bedtime, my mother hugged and clutched us, and we felt strange, not knowing what to do, because she had never acted like that.

I remember waking up to the sound of my mother's screaming again. When I scrambled out, I saw the police in the living room; they were trying to calm her down. She had snatched on her clothes to go with them. And all of us children who were staring knew without anyone have to say it that something terrible had happened to our father.[5]

Not only the superstitions, the sense of clairvoyance, and the kitchen routine are ethnic factors; much more important, it was the whole unbridgeable gulf between black and white America that was responsible for the father's death in the first place.

Both regional and ethnic characteristics are evident in the following

[5] *The Autobiography of Malcolm X*, with the assistance of Alex Haley. Copyright © 1964 by Alex Haley and Malcolm X. Copyright © 1965 by Alex Haley and Betty Shabazz. Published by and reprinted by permission of Grove Press, Inc.

story written by one of my own students, a black woman with three small children of her own, who started remembering her past in the deep South and came up with this simple and touching account of the parting of two playmates.[6]

The Last Summer

He sat on the lowest limb in the peach tree and watched the path below. A bird on the limb above him made loud noises as if to run him out of her house. Robert looked up at the bird a while and then at the path below the tree.

Suddenly he heard a familiar whistle and the snap of a twig. "Bo-do-do."

"Zo-zo-zo," came the answer. It was their code language.

"What took you so long?" he asked as he pulled his friend up on the limb with him.

"I had to wait for her to leave."

"How long will she be gone?"

"Oh, about five hours."

"Good, then we have a long time."

"Not too long. I have to be back before her. She'll kill me if she finds out I'm with you."

"But why can't we play together anymore?"

"Cause she said we can't."

"But why? We've always played together."

"I know."

"Did she say why we shouldn't?"

"Yea."

"Why?"

"Cause you're a nigger."

"Oh."

Robert turned away, not wanting to look at his friend right then. He let one foot hang down off the limb and leaned back on the tree. Billy, his friend, seemed restless. He moved so in the tree until the limb started to crack a little.

"Better watch it, or we'll end up on the path down there, bottom first." They both laughed.

They jumped down from the tree and headed for the creek. Neither one said anything for a while. Robert was the first to break the silence.

[6] Printed by permission of the author, Beatrice Hines.

"Wonder why God made me black and you white?"

"Don't ask me. Ma said it's a cuss or something."

"What kind of cuss?"

"Oh, some bad word or something like bad luck."

"Oh."

Robert leaned back on the soft grass, pushing the old baseball cap off his head over his eyes to keep the sun out.

"My Ma said it's God's will, cause we must suffer to go to heaven."

"Ain't no black people in heaven, is there?"

"I dunno. My Ma's always talking 'bout when we git there."

"Well, Ma says you got a cuss on you and ain't no cussing in heaven."

"Billy."

"Yea."

"Do you believe in God and heaven and all that stuff?"

"Sometimes."

"When?"

"Well, I gets real scared when it's lightning."

"Is that how you believe?"

"Yea."

Billy sat, throwing little rocks in the water. Robert got up, straightened his hat on his head and looked up at the sky.

"Getting late, Billy—you better go. Your Ma'll be looking for you after a while."

"I know."

Billy got up, stretched and pushed his hands way down, deep inside his pockets. He started down the path toward his house and Robert followed close behind. They didn't say anything for a while.

Robert stopped to pick up a yellow leaf beside the path. Billy looked down at him as he stooped.

"What's that?"

"Nothing."

"What did you pick up?"

"A leaf."

"Why?"

"I dunno. It's pretty, that's all. It's yellow and summer's almost over and soon that old tree won't have no more leaves."

"That's right silly talk, Robert."

"I know."

They came to the end of the path where it divided, forming

a fork. Billy stopped and looked at Robert. He still held the yellow leaf in his hand.

"Good-bye, Robert."

"Bye." Robert looked down at his black toes. He didn't want to look at Billy.

Billy turned and walked away, leaving Robert standing there looking at the yellow leaf. Summer was over. Suddenly, Robert could feel the chill in the air, and it hurt him real hard.

BEATRICE HINES

Like ethnicity, regionalism has not enjoyed a history of uninterrupted popularity. Its heyday in American literature was nearly a century ago. After the Civil War, after the union seemed saved and strengthened, writers felt it was safe to start showing off regional differences and stacking the customs of one region up against those of another, as if to say "We're all Americans, but let's not be afraid to be Dakotans or Californians or Vermonters too."

After the turn of the century, with the mass migration to the big cities, regionalism started to die out. But now, with renewed interest in the proud display of ethnic peculiarities, it may well be that regional celebrations will come back into their own. The cities are spilling over their sides, and we find a stepped-up tempo of migration back to the country, so that we could be in for a rediscovery of the quaint and unusual customs nineteenth-century writers were so fond of depicting.

An example of a possible trend can be found in the recent reprinting of a fascinating volume titled *Unwritten Literature of Hawaii: The Sacred Songs of the Hula,* originally published many years ago as a bulletin of the Smithsonian Institution. The fact that Dr. Nathaniel B. Emerson's anthropological studies of hula dancing should suddenly be resurrected suggests that we may look forward in the future to both old and new looks at regional differences among blacks, Indian lore from various parts of the country, and the influence exerted by the heavy colonization of immigrants in specific locations, such as Scandinavians in Minnesota, Chinese in California, Mexicans in Texas, and Cuban exiles in Miami.

For most of us who have never been to Hawaii, the hula has no doubt seemed nothing more than a tourist attraction. But Dr. Emerson's study makes us see that it is a symbolic dance of sacred origin and a highly complex way of telling ancient myths by means of hip movements and hand gestures, each of which has a particular significance.

I'd be willing to bet you never expected to read about hula dancing in terms like these:

> The hula was a religious service, in which poetry, music, pantomime, and the dance lent themselves, under the forms of dramatic art, to the refreshment of men's minds. Its view of life was idyllic, and it gave itself to the celebration of those mythical times when gods and goddesses moved on the earth as men and women and when men and women were as gods. As to subject-matter, its warp was spun largely from the bowels of the old-time mythology into cords through which the race maintained vital connection with its mysterious past. Interwoven with these, forming the woof, were threads of a thousand hues and of many fabrics, representing the imaginations of the poet, the speculations of the philosopher, the aspirations of many a thirsty soul, as well as the ravings and flame-colored pictures of the sensualist, the mutterings and incantations of the *kahuna*, the mysteries and paraphernalia of the Polynesian mythology, the annals of the nation's history—the material, in fact, which in another nation and under different circumstances would have gone to the making of its poetry, its drama, its opera, its literature.[7]

EXERCISES

1. If you belong to what I have termed the Afro movement, you are no doubt already practicing the celebration of your ethnic past. Why not write a paper explaining the meaning and purpose of the movement as you see it?

   Some aspects to consider:

   a) the history of the Afro hair style

   b) the different clothing styles and their symbolism and significance

   c) the changing attitudes among black people toward black skin (there *was* a time when the lighter one was, the more status he had, and, although this feeling persists in some quarters, leaders of the Afro movement are doing their best to discourage it)

   d) the meaning of the concept of "brother"

   e) the meaning of "soul" (including soul music and soul food)

   f) the adaptation of African dance patterns to American styles

   g) Is the Afro movement limited to clothes, songs, dances, and so

[7] Nathaniel B. Emerson, *Unwritten Literature of Hawaii: The Sacred Songs of the Hula* (Rutland, Vt., Charles E. Tuttle Company, Inc., 1965), pp. 11–12.

forth, or is it the same thing as what is sometimes called "Black Nationalism"? If so, does it represent the establishment of a truly separate black nation, not to be confused with America, or do you see it as a trend toward the enrichment of American life through the fuller expression of ethnic difference?

2. Whatever your family's ethnic background may be, write a paper in which you exploit it as fully as you can. Describe what you most vividly remember from your growing-up years that can be legitimately called ethnic, such as

a) foreign words and phrases

b) peculiar idioms or unusual ways of using English (remember my aunt and her "uncitizenship people"?)

c) ethnic dishes: how they were prepared, how they looked on the table, how they tasted; possibly an incident in which a visitor had a hard time adjusting to an ethnic meal

d) songs and dances you remember

e) ethnic-oriented games you may have played (perhaps you remember attending a Norwegian or Irish or Italian field day in which the old sports were preserved)

f) church services (hand-clapping, hymn-singing revival meetings; the silent gatherings at Quaker meeting houses)

Your paper need not have much structure. The emphasis should be on recollection, nostalgia, and interesting the reader through including all the details you can. Above all, enjoy yourself.

3. It is understood that not every ethnic memory is a sunny and joyous one. No matter how justly proud you may be of your background, there must be many incidents you can remember in which you were made painfully aware of being different. Such things leave scars, and it probably does little good to try to forget or ignore them. In fact, it will probably help a great deal to make a list of some of the most vividly unhappy memories and then choose one to develop into a full paper. (Go back and read Malcolm X's account of his mother's premonitions and his father's violent end.)

Possibilities, to get you started:

a) Were you black and had to give up a white friendship, as in Beatrice Hines' story? Or white and had to give up a black friendship?

b) Are you from a family of Cuban exiles? Was it difficult settling in a strange country and winning acceptance from the people?

c) Are you of Japanese descent, and did the shadow of World War II hang over your family when you were small?

d) Children can be cruel; did you have any unfortunate encounters in school because of your ethnic difference?

e) Did you ever experience one completely shattering moment in your childhood when, for the first time, the meaning of discrimination hit home?

4. As I indicated in the text, the explanation of various unique regional customs will probably keep appearing in books and magazines as the "Different is Beautiful" movement continues to gain momentum. In any event, since this entire chapter has been devoted to an analysis of the various influences that have gone into the shaping of your identity in time, it wouldn't be right to overlook the role played by regional customs, such as:

a) Indian craft and Indian lore (there is scarcely a region that isn't rich in the history of some tribe or group of tribes)

b) Mexican architecture, food, songs, and dances: impact of the "mixing" problem between Americans and Mexicans in the Southwest

c) Louisiana Creole food and language, not to mention the deep-rooted social distinctions between the Creoles and people of French descent

d) the distinctive Chinese atmosphere, without which San Francisco would be a different city

e) the springing up of Cuban restaurants, shops, nightclubs, and theaters that in a decade have altered the entire cultural climate of Miami

f) black culture in rural areas of the Deep South

g) the big-city ghetto; its language, its recreation, its religion (Note: there are plenty of people who in all sincerity deplore the existence of the ghetto without really knowing what it is like to live in one; many have never been close to a ghetto; even the sociologists and human relations teams who come with the determination to help may not see all sides of ghetto life; if *you* live inside a ghetto, it is important to be able to describe your life fully and accurately; who knows? yours may be the description that will get results.)

There are hundreds of other possibilities, and I hope the reader will not feel that his region and its distinctive features have been slighted. Do you come from New England with its constant reminders of the Revolution? or those parts of New York that still echo the customs of the early Dutch settlers? or the Amish country of Pennsylvania with its own Dutch flavors? or the Spanish moss or live oak country—the ante-bellum South with its old battle-fields, cemeteries, and stately columned plantation homes? The list could take us to the end of the book.

Once you have decided on the particular regional customs you want to use, write your paper as though for a reader unfamiliar with the region. In many cases your classmates will share your regional background, but you'll find that each will probably find some aspects of the subject that everyone else forgot to include.

Perhaps you are a student from a foreign country? In that case your paper describing the native customs and rituals that played an important part in your development will be of special interest to your classmates.

"We couldn't call them 'mass' if there weren't so many of them and they weren't so profusely available. . . ."

4

THE SELF

AND THE MEDIA

Next to the past, the forces that probably influence our lives most in a hundred different ways, some obvious and beneficial, some treacherously subtle, are the mass media of communication. Attempts are being made by sociologists, anthropologists, and psychologists to measure the extent of this effect and the degree to which your entire identity is shaped by the impact of the media. Returns are not yet in, but you are probably safe in concluding that you would be considerably different if you had grown up in an environment without television, movies, radio, and the press.

On the positive side, it seems pretty clear you would have been less well informed about a good many things. From your earliest exposure to children's television shows you probably picked up more knowledge and skills than most entering first graders had in the days before television. With clowns and puppets flipping blocks around, with animated arithmetic and lectures on the habits of all sorts of animals—to mention only a few familiar components of children's TV—you may have been ready for school much earlier than used to be the case. (Of course, this readiness can have been the cause of many problems, perhaps causing boredom when a teacher took two hours to explain some geographical phenomenon you had learned about three years earlier!)

You were probably more sophisticated when you entered school than your parents were. Television shrinks the world and brings it closer to the understanding. You can't have failed to see programs about native customs in remote corners of the globe or programs on space, the atmosphere, and the composition of the earth.

You probably sneaked out of bed sometimes, tiptoed into the living room, and stood peering over your parent's shoulders at the grown-up shows. From them you probably got a head start in sex education, not to mention making the discovery at an early age that the nation has a drug problem, that prisoners in jail cells are in perpetual danger of homosexual attacks, that the rate of illegitimate births keeps going up, and that it's hard to walk through Central Park at night without getting mugged. If, after television had done its job on you for the day, your mother tried to lull you back to sleep with *Winnie the Pooh*, you may even have had to humor her and pretend to be *un*sophisticated in order not to worry her.

Understand: I'm not condemning such quick sophistication. I'd even suggest that it may be one of the reasons that people will grow up with their eyes open and with a fair degree of awareness of what's going on in the world. But there *is* a negative side to the media question, and you can't proceed much further with your search for identity without owning up to it and investigating its effects.

What I'm talking about is the hypnotic quality of the media. We couldn't call them "mass" if they weren't so profusely available everywhere and at every moment of the day. It's nearly impossible to sit quietly in a corner and take a deep breath and try to compose yourself without still being susceptible to their influence. In this sense, the media are like the radioactive fallout after the bomb. Their effects are all over the place, but unseen—working on you without your knowledge or consent.

Sometimes the quantity of the media can seriously offset and sometimes entirely outweigh quality. It's hard to back off from the media long enough to absorb what just came across. While you're trying to think about one television show, another one is beginning. While you're trying to assimilate and sort out the things you learned yesterday from the media, you're already starting a new day. The set is on, the morning paper is propped up against the toaster, and perhaps an invisible radio somewhere in the house is urging you, by means of bouncy jingles, to go out and buy Vita-Fluff Cake Mixes.

Do you seek escape? How about a night on the town to get away from it all? Let's stroll along Times Square at about eleven P.M. If you have never had this experience, you haven't felt the full impact of the media all bearing down upon your withering sensibilities at exactly the same time. Don't get me wrong. It can be an exhilarating experience too. You really feel like a citizen of a modern, fast-moving, electro-powered, exploding world. You'll never be bored again. All you have to do is close your eyes and remember what it was like to see those ten-story-high ads, the lights blinking on and off, the blare of the music coming from the all-night record shops, and, everywhere, huge, brilliant W O R D S urging you to see this film, buy that suntan oil, drink that bourbon, and, of course, keep smoking those cigarettes.

Too much for you? How about a nice quiet visit to the neighborhood psychiatrist for a weekly checkup to see how sane you still are? While you're sitting in the outer office, you can calm your throbbing nerves by looking through the latest issue of *Peep*—only quickly, quickly now—you don't have that much time. *Thumb* through it. Hold it in your hands just long enough to catch subliminal flashes of quick, zippy headlines:

NUCLEAR TREATY VIOLATED: WILL THIS MEAN WAR?

THE PILL: HOW SAFE ARE YOU?

CRIME IN THE STREETS: DO YOU DARE WALK DOWNTOWN?

Maybe it's the price we all have to pay for being well informed. It's a sure bet that the information media—television, radio, and the press—feel the need to make use of fast, attention-getting devices. They know how rushed everybody always is, and they also know how willing most people are not to be forced to read fine print. They know they have to become expert in making the quick impact. It's part of the trade, and it's a distinct, even admirable, skill. The only trouble is, for too many people the quick impact is enough. They go from impact to impact, and it soon becomes difficult to tell where *they* leave off and the media begin.

Television and films are not derelict either when it comes to an awareness of the audience they must reach and the way they must do it. Networks vie with one another every hour of the day and night for the biggest share of the viewing public. The heartbeats of the television executives fluctuate with every variation of a percentage point in the sacred "ratings." Specialists are paid millions of dollars a year to hold the public's pulse and take X-rays of its mind. Hollywood producers, with fortunes at stake in cinema enterprises, are necessarily interested in getting their money back and making more. Dramatic excellence notwithstanding, the box office inevitably becomes a telling factor.

Therefore all these media—those of information and those of entertainment—are trying to *do* something to you; they are trying to capture and hold your attention, and despite the vast amount of benefit you derive from them (knowledge, sophistication, aesthetic pleasure), you also stand to be shaped and molded *to an as yet immeasurable extent* by what they do. In fact, "shaped" and "molded" may well be mild terms. Perhaps "besieged" and "battered" may come closer to defining what is actually going on.

The exercises in this chapter are necessarily inconclusive. It would take many volumes larger than this one, all devoted to an analysis of the media, to approach the heart of the problem. But you *can* make a start and at least catch a glimpse of what some of the media are doing to you some of the time.

Since we are limited in time as well as space, it seems logical for us to focus our attention on the media we are likely to encounter each day. Accordingly, let's limit our investigation to the information, advertising, and entertainment media.

THE INFORMATION MEDIA

When we say we are well informed and keep up with what is going on, we generally mean that we make substantial contact every day with the news coverage and editorials in the daily press and with news programming and analysis on television. By "daily press" I refer to the papers you can purchase pretty readily at the newsstands of almost any city or have delivered to your front door. I exclude such publications as *The Christian Science Monitor* or *The Wall Street Journal*, because, though these may be popular in some parts of the country and with a faithful readership, they do not reach a large enough audience to be included with the mass media.

Our analysis of the shaping power of the media properly begins here, because we are far less likely to suppose we are being influenced by information than by either advertising or entertainment. Nevertheless we are, perhaps to an alarming degree.

Front Page Anyone?

What a bargain the daily paper is when you stop to think about it. Just see how much you get for a dime or a quarter. It usually comes in sections so that you can be influenced by more than one kind of force. Many people pass over the news section altogether and with deftly trained fingers slide out the comics, the sports section, the amusement pages, or the television listings. Or else they rely on television for their daily ration of news, and for many the more limited the quantity of news to which they expose themselves every day, the better they like it. This very refusal to bother with the news pages, however, may in a sense constitute an "effect" of the media.

Let us assume that most people do make some contact with information during the course of a single day by holding in their hands the daily paper and at least scanning the front pages. There was a time when the city in which you lived determined to a great extent the degree and the kind of influence exerted by the news in the press. In New York, for example, the widest range of choices was possible: from the conservative erudition of *The New York Times* to the blatant sensationalism of the *Daily Mirror*. The shrinking of this range may be taken as an ominous sign indeed. Except for the *Times*, the popular press in the big city looks suspiciously like the popular press anywhere in the country—perhaps a bit flashier and a bit more obvious but probably no more obsessed with blood and gore than any other metropolitan press. One of my students aptly described the American newspaper as "one big ad—with a generous portion of sex thrown in to break up the monotony."

Like most of the population of the United States, the residents of New York seem to prefer quick, zippy headlines and, at that, mainly the ones that give promise of something sensational. Public taste being what it is, the power behind the press sees to it that no sex or crime story goes unrecorded. There was a time when New Yorkers could make a clear, sharp distinction between the so-called "tabloids"— specializing in huge headlines like NUN ASSAULTED IN SUBWAY and plenty of gory pictures—and a number of snob-appeal papers with the news in terribly fine print and almost no way of quickly discovering what was important. In the battle for readership (or viewingship?) the tabloid approach has proved its mettle.

So let's say that, except for the *Times* and a few other papers of its kind and quality throughout the country, the average resident of the average American city is likely to open the news section and find:

1) relatively large and zippy headlines
2) a generous number of pictures, usually showing action or the immediate results of action, such as a head-on collision or a plane crash
3) an emphasis on sensational happenings (these often thought of as synonymous with "news")

4) a high percentage of space devoted to extremely weird, sometimes trivial happenings (the novel also being defined as "news"), such as a story of a woman who not only raised but suckled a baby chimp, or the story of someone who cooked a breakfast of scrambled eggs, bacon, and french fries on a Third Avenue sidewalk during a heat wave

5) an enormous number of advertisements, with the front pages tending to feature the expensive stores and the "food bargains" tending to be found further back

All right, you may say, suppose the front pages *are* more or less like this? What does it prove? Why must I believe I am being "shaped" and "molded" by something so lifeless as a page full of print? To get some idea of the extent to which you are being influenced, try to imagine yourself as having just dropped out of the sky from another planet. You don't know the first thing about the earth or its habits (though you can, like so many of the "invaders" in the films and television shows, read our language). All you can tell is what you see in the daily paper. *What would be your impressions of a typical day in a typical American city?* Absurd as the comparison may seem, many of us know little more about what is going on in the national or local scene than we are given to know by the daily paper.

It's a matter of selection, isn't it? The things we read about in the news pages did happen and often exactly as they are described. (This is called "responsible journalism," and often even the most sensational tabloid does more distorting in the headlines than in the actual stories.) But editors have to exercise their power of choice. They have to worry about the "layout." They have to work around the ads that pay many of the expenses of the whole operation. They have to think about the reader and what he is likely to be interested in. Thus some items get left out altogether. Others are lengthened because of probable appeal (a nice juicy trial, involving scandalous goings-on in a well-known family is bound to be given more space than the account of a scientific experiment that may have far-reaching significance for mankind). Still others are shortened out of all proportion to their immediate or eventual importance.

One way to test out this journalistic inconsistency is to take note of a scare headline in a late afternoon paper and then try to find the same story the next morning. More often than not, you'll find it buried somewhere at the back, pushed into oblivion by something more attention-getting that has turned up.

Besides, news editors are human beings and are subject to extreme pressures. Many times a day are they forced to make split-second decisions about what to include and what to exclude. Usually they do the best they can. We needn't assume they are *always* looking for sex and violence and *deliberately* squelching less sensational stories. Most likely they are conditioned by the profession itself and are not fully aware of why they select what they do. However, this means that we, their readers, are *highly* dependent on the whole selection process and simply cannot assume that even the news section is presenting us with the "real" reality. We are getting, at best, a small, filtered piece of it.

It may be safe to conclude that if one had all the time in the world and could read the prestige papers from end to end every day of his life, he would be in contact with a greater degree of the daily reality than he otherwise would be, but even the prestige press has its drawbacks. Which seems "realer" to you? A small-print, conservative, hence prestigious headline like

ATTEMPT AT NUCLEAR NON–PROLIFERATION TREATY FAILS

or the typical tabloid handling of it.

WORLD ON BRINK OF WAR

It could be argued that the conservative approach of the fine-print papers might make the reader less apprehensive. But there are things, like nuclear nonproliferation, that are no doubt *worth* a good deal of concern. It could also be argued that scare headlines about crime and violence are more effective in bringing about prompt action than wordier and more analytical treatments of those subjects.

The reader who takes the time to go carefully through the news section is also likely to turn to the editorial pages and read at least one or two columns each day. The advantage of following some colmnists is evident. The top-notch news analysts like Joseph Kraft and economic experts like Sylvia Porter partly compensate for the selectivity exercised by the news editors. They have more time to think about what is happening than the rest of us do, and as a result, we stand to gain a clearer perspective than if we had to try to decide for ourselves which news is most important and what lies behind it.

The disadvantage is equally obvious. One is absorbing more than the results of an editor's selectivity. He is absorbing somebody's opinion, and unless he continually reminds himself of that, he runs the risk of confusing opinion with fact. For example, this very morning I open my paper to the editorial page, and I see that Joseph Kraft is telling me something about Laos and the United States involvement there. Since the threat of a new war is hanging over our heads on this bright day, I read with avid interest:

For it shows the real difficulty in Laos is not that the Nixon Administration has refused to come clean. The real difficulty is that the administration has no good plan for making peace in Southeast Asia.

Now, unless I am very, very careful, I can easily pass over this before I have made the formal distinction between attitude and truth. Who knows? I may even get into a discussion later in the day and find myself saying: "Yes, but everybody knows the Administration hasn't any plan at all for peace in Asia."

This may or may not be the case. How can I know? How can I know that Mr. Kraft knows? Maybe it does no harm for me to pass along such "information," but, on the other hand, it can add to my overall state of apprehension. If I am already concerned about the Asian situation, must I not feel insecure in the knowledge that the Administration doesn't know what it's doing? For all I know, there may be a peace plan already in the works, being kept secret until the proper time. In so crucial an area of concern, it is perhaps better for everyone to keep an open mind and not be automatically swayed by editorial comments. At any rate, it is desperately important for readers to remind themselves that "refuse to come clean" is not an objective, impartial statement of fact.

EXERCISES

1. Take the news section of your daily paper on any given day and subject it to an analysis from the standpoint of discovering the kind of reality about which it offers information. If this is the major source of your knowledge of what is going on in your city or the country or the world on this particular day, how much do you think you know and how profoundly do you think you know it?

   Some guidelines:

   a) Count the number of separate news stories and then compute the percentage devoted to war, crime, sex, drugs, and "novelties."

   b) If you want to be more scientific in this "quantitative analysis" of the types of news stories, you should, if possible, compare two daily papers for the same day and determine which stories they printed in common and which were unique to each. This comparison will give you some idea of how important a particular story seemed to both editors.

   c) To be scientific, you can also compute relative percentages for a number of days running. Thus, if the news on the day you choose for the assignment seems to be top-heavy with crime items, your statistics can help to determine whether *your* paper leans toward the gory and the violent.

d) Look closely at some of the items that, in your opinion, *appear* to be significant. Sometimes, it's true, you have to rely on your instincts. But suppose, for example, you find a tiny little story tucked away on page 16, as I did this morning, which has staggering implications but has been given only a few lines of space? The story I saw began like this: "The urgent appeal on the nation's largest military contractor for up to $641.2 million in federal funds exposes a breakdown in Pentagon policies that could bring the collapse of the defense industry, Sen. William Proxmire says." Admittedly, the news editor is dealing with an Associated Press item, but he still can exercise a choice in its placement, assuming even that the original story was reprinted in its entirety (which doesn't always happen). In the same issue of the daily paper I noted that on page 5 a story on numbers rackets was given three times the space as the one about Sen. Proxmire. Such analysis is an interesting yardstick of the way reality is cut up and parceled out to readers by the press.

e) Look carefully at the language in those items that pretend to be nothing except objective, unbiased reporting. Is it free of slanting, in your opinion? In nearly every case you'll find that somebody is being quoted on something, so that the identity of the reporter all but slips out of the picture. But don't allow this to deceive you. Keep looking. Every so often you'll run across a statement that begins like this: "Foor, who has run unsuccessfully for half a dozen offices, including governor . . ." Now the term "unsuccessfully" is a slanted one, for there can be a host of reasons why someone might run for a political office and be successful in fulfilling his objectives even if he doesn't win. "Unsuccessfully" strongly implies that the person in question is a political failure, and this implication casts a shadow on the rest of the report. In this instance the person named Foor had apparently made allegations about political intrigue in the state of Florida. Without the reporter's having to say anything directly about the source of the allegations, Mr. Foor was made to seem prejudiced in his actions. Normally I should have passed over the item without much thought, but, considering it carefully as I have just done, I see that my opinion of Mr. Foor could easily have been set (maybe for life!) by one seemingly harmless word.

f) Now consider several editorials as sources of information. Give some examples of the subjects involved and the opinions expressed.

How thoroughly did you find the subjects analyzed? How many unsupported opinions were stated? How would you evaluate the kind of editorial language as to degree of fairness? (For example, I would consider Joseph Kraft's statement that the Nixon Administration has "refused to come clean" as being very strong indeed.)

After you have put your findings together, you should be ready to do a fairly comprehensive analysis of the news coverage in the daily paper on a typical day.

2. Most schools have newspapers, and they can provide an even better opportunity for you to study the relationship between reality and the press coverage of it, especially if you feel you know what is going on around your campus. For this assignment take the latest issue of the school paper and analyze it.
Some considerations:

a) Which news items were given the most weight and importance?

b) Do you agree that they should have been?

c) What of significance happened on campus during the week that you think is either ignored altogether or passed over lightly?

d) If you believe the paper accurately reflected the important news, does this mean it can stand no improvement? (Don't be afraid to say so. Analysis doesn't have to imply negation.)

e) If, however, you believe the paper does not fully—or at all— bring the reader into contact with "campus reality," why do you think this is so? Who runs the paper? A certain political group? Profraternity students? Antifraternity students? Is the news filtered through a conservative or liberal screen exclusively?

f) What about editorials? Are all student viewpoints welcomed and published? Or is a high degree of selectivity observed by the staff?

g) Is the school administration, in your opinion, to blame for the way the news and editorials are handled? Does it exercise powers of censorship? Do you know this for a fact, or do you just suppose it to be the case? Give some specific instances you know about in which a news story or a student column was deliberately suppressed or at least substantially altered.

h) It seems to come with the territory for Americans to be against censorship—at least I gain that impression from talking to students. However, if one wishes to be completely fair in appraising campus journalism, he must recognize that many administrations are wary of giving the campus papers a free hand. Most colleges grant students freedom of the press so long as they maintain the standards of "responsible" journalism. It is also true that almost everyone has his own ideas about what constitutes responsibilty in journalism. Would an administration, for example, believe that a no-holds-barred attack on its own policies by a student editorialist is "responsible" and consistent with the ideal of press freedom? What about an editorial urging students to join in a movement to overthrow the United States government? or to burn down the college's administration building?

Students opposed to unlimited freedom in school journalism frequently argue that such freedom always means that the student left moves in and uses the paper as a propaganda device. Do you agree with this view? Are you aware of instances on your own campus of the propagandistic use of the paper by the left? Or perhaps, by the right?

In your analysis of the school paper, you should consider the editorial policy carefully and decide whether it is suffering from administrative restraints (with examples) or abusing the privilege of unlimited freedom (with examples). If this phase of the subject gets too big to handle, put it aside and do a separate paper. It is a crucial area of concern.

3. The aim of this paper is to deliver a report on the newspaper habits of a member of your family, your family as a whole, or your roommate(s). You can accomplish the task by observing first-hand how the press does or doesn't affect someone. By getting your observations down on paper, you may also come a little closer to understanding how this medium may be working on you. Sometimes it is easier to see the truth when you are not trying to observe *yourself* directly.

Make it your business to be up and functioning when the person you have chosen for the study is maintaining the height of his relationship with the daily press. Presumably this will be in the morning.

Without being overly obvious about it, make notes.

a) Does he (or she) go immediately for the news pages? If not these, what section?

b) Does he ever get around to the news at all?

c) If he does come to the news, how thoroughly does he read it?

d) Ask him which items most interested him and why.

e) Does he make any comments while looking at the news section? What is their nature? That is, does he seem to be making observations on the basis of careful reading? Or does he seem to be reacting hastily to zippy headlines and photographs?

f) Does his reading of the news produce responses that, in your opinion, sound like those of an informed citizen? Or do they appear to be biased, snap judgments based on hasty and incomplete scanning?

g) Does he spend much time on the editorial page? If he does not, what reason can you advance? (Such as: "He already has his mind made up before he gets to the editorials.") If he does spend time there, does he start making sage observations immediately afterward, indicating that he gets his "informed" opinions prepackaged?

Put your notes together, and you are ready to write a portrait of a "morning American." Of course, if your subject ignores the news altogether, you ought to ask his reasons. These will provide you with the foundation for your paper. How close are your own newspaper habits to those of your subject?

Has your study of this person opened your eyes about these habits and suggested any improvements to make in your relationship with the press? What are these? Thinking over your subject's habits and your own, can you make some concluding remarks about how you think one should relate to the information reaching him from the press? Did the foregoing exercise prove impractical, and, if so, was it because you couldn't find anyone who had any time to spend with the morning paper? I seem to recall a survey several years ago indicating that suburbanites commuting to their work or school in large metropolitan centers comprise the greater percentage of daily newspaper readers. Most Americans who drive to work or school tend not to do much reading in the mornings at all, particularly of the front page. This doesn't, of course, rule out the possibility that many may save the morning paper as an early evening treat, though chances are that television's news coverage can easily lure them away from print. ("I've had

such a hard day at work . . .") What I'm getting at is the prospect
of discovering a nation that on a per capita basis doesn't relate very
carefully to any newspaper. Whether this trait is bad you can decide for yourself.

"Good Night, David"

"Television is not the only villain . . . but anyone who suggests
that it has no power to influence the actions of people is either danger-
ously obtuse or deliberately evasive."

SENATOR CLAIBORNE PELL

"If anything is poisoning our lives and weakening our society, it
is reality—and not the fabrications of television writers and producers."

PROFESSOR MARTIN MOLONEY

The appeal of the visual experience offered by television hardly
needs analysis. The reader has only to look into his own conscience,
and he may discover how easy it is to relax before the television screen
and how much more taxing it is to read carefully many columns of
relatively fine print. Ever since we were children, haven't we been intrigued by motion and action? But the nature and extent of the
influence exerted by television are still being questioned and investigated academically and politically. Vice President Spiro T. Agnew, on
November 12, 1969, made the most frontal assault on the news media
—*especially* the television commentators and analysts—in the history
of American politics. Accusing the media of distorting the news in
an effort to control the thinking of the vast majority of Americans,
Agnew ignited a controversy that may go on for years.

No matter how one may feel about political interference in the
media, which have always prided themselves on their freedom from
all obligation except to tell the truth, one has to admit that the
powers behind television *can* control the material that comes across
on the screen. Let's say you switch on the six o'clock news while
gulping down a TV dinner. Whatever you see, you see. You can
only watch one channel at a time, and so it is difficult to compare the
information coming through all the channels to see whether you are
getting your "fair share" or some news editor's pet choices. Even if
the major stories of the day are being treated, how can you tell
whether you are getting a total or a partial or even a strongly slanted
view?

I have personally been involved in incidents that both attracted
and apparently bored TV people, for reasons that seemed highly apparent. To give one striking example: at the end of 1969, a nation-

wide moratorium was called to protest the war in Vietnam, the killing
of thousands of civilians, and the conscription of young American
men. At my college, as at many others, there were observances of
all kinds, ranging from out-and-out riots to fairly well-disciplined
discussions, speeches, lectures, and day-and-night reading of the
names of the American war dead. The first moratorium, which took
place in November, was widely publicized in advance, and naturally
this publicity made the administration and the public very nervous.
Television news units were, as you might expect, on our campus
virtually at the crack of dawn.

I made it my business to observe the habits of the newsmen and
found that they possessed an uncanny ability to scent possible eruptions before they took place. They always seemed to be right there
when anything remotely resembling violence was in danger of
breaking out. On one occasion a band of supporters of the Administration's war policies marched into the midst of an antidraft rally. In
a split second a couple of fistfights had broken out, and the TV
cameras seemed to be everywhere, capturing every blow as it was
struck.

But how many fistfights have occurred on how many campuses
since time immemorial? No *riot* ever exploded on this day. The
skirmishes all proved minor. It all looked to me like healthy, normal
student expression and infinitely preferable to the apathy that is
education's deadliest enemy. Nonetheless, the coverage of the events
of the day by the evening news shows was greatly sensationalized and
exaggerated. By means of skillful editing, it was made to appear that
the campus had been "jumping" all day long, trembling under the
continual threat of ugly violence; it was further implied that "next
month's moratorium" might bring even graver dangers. But the second
moratorium came and went without any incidents at all, and the
television news programs found they had better things to show.

It was a shame, too, because student leaders of all factions had
made up their minds in advance that the second moratorium day
would be exemplary. They were going to show the community and
the faculty and the administration that they were mature and deserved
the right of free speech and peaceful protest that they so often had
claimed. They had come to the conclusion that to be violent in up-
holding nonviolence or to be violent in protest against the violence
of the nonviolent was to invite derision and scorn. I strolled about the
campus all day, going from speaker to speaker, and feeling quite
proud of the student body. I kept thinking to myself: "The newsmen
should be here, taking films of American young men and women
practicing their birthright of free speech and open discussion."

Using the three criteria for evaluating television news coverage mentioned earlier in this section, we can interpret the silence of the local channels in any of the following ways:

1) They found out all was peaceful on the campus and decided that free discussion is not newsworthy because it lacks action, especially of a "dangerous" nature.

2) The nonviolence on the campus might suggest, to the viewing public, a waning of student interest in the antiwar movement, and such a suggestion would be contrary to the personal interests of the news commentators or the programmers.

3) The sponsors might not consider a filmed report of peaceful campus activity—*no matter what its significance might be*—as "entertainment" in any sense.

Sometimes the answer to the question of why television stays away or else comes on like the Baltimore Colts is bound up with the complex question of what is meant by "news." That is, the concept of "news" probably involves sensational action, and/or significance (and who is to decide what the significance should be if not those who decide what goes on the screen?), and entertainment value.

No harm done, so long as the implication of "news" is fully understood. But over and above news itself is the role—the tremendous role —played by the news analyst on television. Men like Walter Cronkite, Frank Reynolds, David Brinkley, Howard K. Smith, and Eric Sevareid are enormously powerful figures, who have, at some point or other, influenced you and me in the forming of an opinion. A good deal of their function is to provide their faithful viewers with opinions. These viewers know it and deliberately seek them out, preferring to be guided in their thinking by experts who keep up with events as no private citizen has the time or the facilities to do.

The indictment of the news by Spiro T. Agnew brought the problem into sharp focus and made many people more conscious of the round-the-clock influence of the commentators than they had been before. Specifically, Agnew insisted that the responsibility of the analysts is to subject the news to impartial scrutiny, to make it available so that the listeners can make up their own minds, and to keep their editorial opinions clearly and sharply distinct from pure information. Agnew charged the newscasters with distorting information and, particularly, with having only one kind of opinion—liberal.

The reader is no doubt familiar with a pattern that has become standard on television. Live coverage is given to an important event, such as a Presidential nominating convention or an address to the nation by the President himself. During the convention or immediately after the address, the analysts appear and begin an instantaneous commentary, long before the ordinary viewer has had a chance to sort out the facts and decide anything for himself.

The specific occasion that aroused the wrath of Vice President Agnew was the treatment given by the analysts to a speech on American involvement in Southeast Asia by President Nixon. The address, which coincided with the approaching moratorium observances, had been eagerly awaited. There were rumors that the country would hear a dramatic change in administration policy regarding Asia, that the President was about to announce a virtual pull-out of American troops and a speedy end to America's part in the Vietnamese war. But the President merely indicated that there would be a gradual "Vietnamization" of the war. The fighting would gradually be turned over to the native army, with America withdrawing her support as the circumstances made it possible to do so.

Clearly the address proved a big disappointment to the "doves" and their followers—politicians sharply opposed to American involvement in the war—to college students still facing a military draft, to black leaders hoping the end of the war might mean that federal funds would be available for urban renewal projects, and, apparently, to some of the news analysts themselves. Commentaries began with remarks something like, "Well, the President's speech has come and gone and obviously nothing very much is about to change in Asia." Mr. Agnew felt that the news media (of course, he meant mainly television) had a demoralizing effect on the country at a time when the President deserved the full support of everybody. But the critics of Mr. Agnew condemned his censure on the grounds that he was making a politically motivated attack on all who held views contrary to his own. They charged that he would have had no objection to the "propagandistic" use of news media if the newscasters were pro-Administration in their influence. They also charged that the alternative to freedom of the media is government control.

Adding to the controversy, Howard K. Smith, one of the nation's leading analysts, came out in partial defense of the Vice President. On ABC-TV Mr. Smith stated:

> Political cartoonists have that in common with lemmings, that once a line is set, most of them follow it, though it leads to perdition. The current cliché shared by them and many columnists is that Spiro Agnew is putting his foot in his mouth [and] making irredeemable errors. . . . Well, . . . I doubt that party line. . . . There is a possibility it is not Mr. Agnew who is making mistakes. It is the cartoonists.[1]

[1] Quoted by Edith Efron in *TV Guide*, February 28, 1970, p. 7.

What Smith was saying is that the prominent newscasters were just as political as Vice President Agnew and tended to use the thinking of the left to evaluate everything "though it lead to perdition." Such a profound precommitment, in his opinion, makes it impossible for most analysts to subject the news to truly impartial scrutiny before making up their own minds.

Smith was more than broadly philosphical in his case against his fellow newscasters. He pointed out a number of specific areas of concern and indicated how television analysts tended to handle them. Race was a prime example, for "the newsmen are not interested in the Negro who succeeds—they're interested in the one who fails and makes a loud noise." [2]

A second charge made by Smith was that newscasters automatically condemn conservatives no matter what the issue may be. A third was the scorn shown for middle-class Americans. A fourth was the treatment of the war in Vietnam. Smith pointed out that American casualties were always recorded accurately, but the figures on Viet Cong dead or wounded, which sometimes were a hundred times greater than ours, were not. Finally, Smith charged the newscasters with despising the President of the United States to the point of irrationality. He blamed the "negative attitude" of the news media for the political destruction of Lyndon Johnson.

As one might expect, other commentators have jumped into the ring. Smith has been criticized almost as much as Agnew was in the beginning. Some have denied all the charges and insisted that no network bias exists in the handling of news. Others say there is nothing wrong with the news media in a free country exercising the right of freedom of thought and expression.

But perhaps this position assumes a greater concern for the truth than the average citizen may have. Perhaps, on the contrary, he is quite willing to let someone else do his thinking for him. Perhaps the commentators feel they must save this man from confusion.

It's a painful and crucial issue, however one looks at it. "Meddling with the media" has traditionally been a no-no in our society. Still, when you think of Howard K. Smith's claim that the news analysts despise the middle class for its lack of reflection and the ability to come up with its own informed opinions, you are tempted to wonder whether we have a hen-and-egg problem here. Are many middle-class citizens complacent and nonreflective about current events because the news media keep them that way? Or are the newscasters taking it upon themselves to impose ideas because this is the only way, in their opinion, that society will ever advance?

[2] Quoted by Edith Efron in *TV Guide*, February 28, 1970, p. 7.

You have grown up with television. To what extent has your thinking been "prodded along" by the people who absolutely dominate America from six to seven-thirty in the evening?

EXERCISES

1. Many of the opinions expressed by television newscasters are ones which I hold myself, and doubtless you too hear many echoes of your own thoughts coming from the television screen. But neither of us should be afraid to consider how profoundly or superficially the news is handled through America's dominant medium of communication. We all have room for improvement, right? Whether you agree or disagree with a commentator's position on any given issue, you must surely want it to be a solid one, backed up by as much real information as possible.

   Your primary assignment in connection with television news coverage is, therefore, to come up with a paper describing the habits of one particular commentator to whom you will tune in for several nights running. Try to avoid the local newsmen, because the issues about which they might try to influence your thinking are often not major or national ones at all. Probably Cronkite, Reynolds, Brinkley—or yes—Smith would be the best choices. Listen to them carefully, trying to keep count of opinions expressed in the form of facts. Example: "For the fifth week in a row American casualty figures are misleading." Every time an admitted opinion is voiced, make a checkmark and, next to it, jot down the general subject matter. Example: "$\sqrt{}$—need for national lottery to subsidize public housing programs."

   When the top commentators present an opinion, they usually elaborate on it at some length and give many reasons for holding it. As you listen to the case presented, jot down notes on the way the commentator seems to support his opinion. Does he give any facts? Or does he break down the opinion into other opinions, such as, "Since there is an alarming apathy in Congress over public housing, one assumes the reason is the cost of such programs. A national lottery is the only sensible way to underwrite a public housing program, without further taxing the already weary taxpayer." True or not, such statements contain not one grain of fact. After you have listened to your man for several nights in a row, you should have quite a list of opinions that are frankly opinions and opinions that are supposed to be facts. Study the list and decide whether the analyst seems to be trying to manipulate the viewer's thinking or whether he makes no claim to be doing anything other than offering one man's opinions. Study his style and method of handling the news in general. For example, does he mainly talk? Or does he show pictures to accompany his statements? (What persuasive effect do the pictures have?) Put your notes together and write a paper evaluating your newscaster. Here are some suggested criteria:

a) If his opinions seem worth taking as your own, is it that he presents many facts or that his thinking seems clear and logical?

b) Is he going overboard in an attempt to mold public opinion? Is he too obvious in his message-sending?

c) Is he overly subtle in slipping his opinions in among a whole lot of facts?

d) Do you personally admire such subtlety, or do you consider it dangerous?

e) Compare, if possible, your man's treatment of a given news item or two with that found in the daily paper for the same day. Since the news section of the paper usually includes more information than the television commentators need to give or are more matter-of-fact than the commentators feel they have to be, you should be able to get some idea of how extensive the newscaster's presentation of the material was, or how he may have distorted the information in order to send his particular message. For example, suppose the newspaper reported that the President was spending the weekend in the "Florida White House . . . for reasons, so his physicians report, of further recuperation from a recent attack of influenza." Suppose you then tuned into your newscaster and heard this comment: "The President will take the weekend off and relax at the Florida White House, while hoping to kick the flu bug." It sounds innocent, and under ordinary circumstances, when you weren't listening carefully, you might have accepted the statement as just another fact. But "will take the weekend off and relax" is still slanted language. It says far more than the matter-of-fact physician's report quoted in the paper. When you hear a word like "relax," an image of somebody leaning back in a comfortable easy chair or a lounge by a pool comes to mind. There could be the further implication that the chief executive is goldbricking while working-class people have to go on punching the clock for their salaries.

f) If you ultimately reject this newscaster, do you do so because he presents opinions at all? seems to have no opinions to offer?

sends out opinions that are contrary to your own? sends out opinions with which you agree, but you still cannot approve of the idea-forming powers held by such a person?

2. Possibly the most intense news media controversy in history erupted on the heels of one staggering event that all kinds of people will no doubt still be studying a generation from now: the Chicago riots that took place in the summer of 1968 during the Democratic Presidential nominating convention. It was widely known in advance that there would be extensive television coverage of this occasion, and massive groups of antiwar and antidiscrimination demonstrators converged on the city of Chicago with the announced intention of stealing some of the spotlight from the political activities and attracting worldwide attention to their various causes.

Television cameras seemed to be everywhere in Chicago once the convention proceedings began. Gatherings of protestors were covered; the well-publicized marches were covered; and, on the climactic night of the convention, when the marchers planned to assemble en masse at the very doors of the convention site, the Chicago police and the National Guard were waiting for them. The riots that ensued and the apparent violence and brutality practiced by the police were captured "live and in person" by all three major television networks, while millions of enthralled and horrified viewers sat glued to their sets. Not only were the riots and the beatings of demonstrators by police shown in vivid detail and lurid closeup, but the coverage was so well coordinated and executed that cameras were picking up street action and convention-hall activities simultaneously. Network directors were able to push buttons and flash from convention floor to street to newscasters sitting in their booths and interpreting the events.

For hours the fantastic show continued. There were numberless closeups of Chicago's Mayor Daley in conference with his staff, shots of all sorts of people being dragged from the convention hall by police, even an NBC closeup of one of its own newsmen being roughed up and thrown to the floor by angry cops. Outside, the protestors, recognizing that this was their greatest chance to plead their case, further aroused the wrath of the police by chanting the now famous line, "The whole world is watching!" Throughout the long evening the networks kept showing not only the live action on the streets of Chicago but videotape replays of earlier confrontations between rioters and police. It was virtually impossible for the viewer to distinguish the live from the taped action in every instance. The effects were often artistic and reminiscent of advanced techniques in some of the better films, in that shots of young people being beaten over the head with nightsticks were sometimes flashed in directly on top of rhetorical and empty-sounding speeches by old-line party politicians.

A foreigner visiting America and unacquainted with the internal crises of the summer of 1968 might indeed have supposed from the network coverage of the Chicago convention that civil war was breaking out, as though some final straw had just tried to break the back of the protest movement and the movement was now screaming out in full fury. One saw what looked like the brutal tactics of which American police were capable, contrasted with the bloated indifference of professional politicians, in turn contrasted with the crashing defeat of the idealistic attempt of younger "new breed" politicians to win control of the party and change the whole face of America.

The result? Criticism of the convention, criticism of the Chicago police, investigations, and further protests erupting all over the country, none of which proved to be just what the doctor ordered for the Democratic party, already sagging from the weight of the accumulated protests that had been heaped on it from antiwar and antipoverty crusaders. The Democrats lost the election, and the Republicans, whose own convention in Miami Beach had been marred by only one outbreak of violence—a racial incident in Liberty City miles away—won it.

Many of those who had never been in favor of the Asian and domestic policies of the outgoing Administration questioned the extraordinary performance of television on that memorable night and began to wonder whether indeed the newscasters and those who pushed the magic buttons were not possessed of powers never before suspected to be available to the mass media.

This summary of the happenings on a summer night in Chicago is not intended to suggest any particular interpretation of the role played by television: that is, beyond the fact that *some* interpretations seems to be warranted. Your mission (should you decide to accept it) is to come to a conclusion of your own. I have made a great deal of the whole phenomenon because it brought into dramatic relief a fact that many had suspected before without being able to bring into sharp focus—namely, the *possibilities* within the medium's grasp. If you witnessed the television coverage of the Chicago convention, you no doubt have vivid memories of what you saw. If you did not, there is plenty of material available in the magazines throughout the fall of 1968 and into the winter and spring of 1969.

As you attempt to sort out the many complex strands of fact and fancy that have become tangled together, you might keep a number of questions in mind:

a) Do you think the networks had advance information about some of the happenings?

b) Do you think some of the newscasters arrived in Chicago, suspecting what was coming and predisposed to treat the events in such a manner as to influence public opinion?

c) Do you know whether some newscasters did more influencing than others? How?

d) Is it true that television people were restricted to certain areas? If so, does this sound as if an attempt was made to control the coverage?

Does it look to you as if the fancy button work that went on behind the scenes, whereby the viewer was transported magically from the convention hall to the street fighting, was motivated by a "commercial" desire on the part of the networks to entertain their viewers or by a politically oriented desire to send messages?

e) Since the coverage of the Democratic convention may have been a strong factor in the eventual defeat of the Democratic party in 1968 and since Spiro T. Agnew later charged the news media with slanting and distorting the news and swaying public opinion in an unethical manner, does it seem possible that the media automatically began to attack the party in power? If so, do you regard this policy as healthy or dangerous? Why?

f) Another view is possible: namely, to support Mr. Agnew's charge that the media are dominated by far left interests. This would explain the desire to discredit the outgoing Democratic Administration, frequently criticized for being "hawkish" in its Asian policies. It would also explain the criticism of the Republican Administration that followed. In other words, are most of the major newscasters liberal "doves"? Do they tend to be the spokesmen for all the protest movements? (But if this is the case, do they always show the youth rebellion and the Black Power movements in the best light?)

3. An alternate to the above "marathon" exercise is to analyze the television coverage of a more recent happening, one that may have occurred since this book was published. If you do, you may want to use some or all of the guidelines set up for the Chicago assignment. Perhaps, however, you will need to create some new

ones. It is possible that the controversy that raged for many months after Chicago has led to some significant changes in network handling of important events. Knowing that the whole world is indeed watching their techniques, news analysts may have already ushered in a new era of reporting and editorializing on television. Or maybe nothing has changed.

MYTHS IN ADVERTISING AND ENTERTAINMENT

By now the reader may be wondering whether there is anything about the media that is not really operating on the self; anything that is just sort of fun, that one can sit back and enjoy, without running the risk of being "molded" or "battered" by it. The answer is: by all means. In fact, all aspects of the media can be enjoyable and not the least bit dangerous so long as you know what is going on, so long as you can intercept whatever messages there are before they ever reach your subconscious mind, evaluate them honestly, and decide which ones are useful to you and which are not.

At the same time, you can't let down your guard when you seek entertainment instead of information from the media. You can't sink down into your easy chair merely because the six o'clock news is over and the evening's variety shows, westerns, and situation comedies are about to parade their lighthearted way before you. You can't assume that, because you are at the drive-in movie instead of in front of the TV set, you are free from being influenced.

This is a book in which you seek out your identity, not a handbook for *enjoying* Ed Sullivan or *Gunsmoke* or "Lucy" reruns. If there are ways in which the "harmless" side of the media can influence you, don't you want to look into that matter too? When you do, you are bound to discover the prevalence throughout the entertainment media of *myths*.

Mythology isn't something that belongs to the long-ago world of the Greeks and Romans, but, if you think back that far, you get some clue about its meaning and its effect. Originally myth and fact were considered the same thing. Early peoples wove stories to account for strange phenomena they couldn't understand, because they couldn't bear to be helpless victims in a dark, mysterious world whose powers were beyond their control. *So to build up their sense of security* they invented "suitable" explanations of those powers, making certain that they were humanized or at least turned into things the human imagination could handle. It was fear that probably prompted the earliest mythology.

The early Greeks explained thunder—which, without a myth,

would have remained a mysterious, threatening force—as the voice of Zeus, king of the gods. The lightning bolts were his personal weapons, and he could hurl them earthwards with superhuman accuracy. But so overpowering a myth figure as a god is itself a source of fear, to overcome which the Greeks added other myths. They humanized Zeus. They saw him as a hen-pecked married man with a nagging and shrewish wife and a perfectly human desire to cheat on her whenever the opportunity arose. (To show you how mythology exaggerates, Zeus was alleged to have been responsible for some fifty thousand illegitimate children!)

The three basic fears of early man in his mythmaking days appear to have been these: the sexual mysteries (puberty, excitation, intercourse, pregnancy, and birth); natural phenomena (thunder, whirlwinds, floods); and the cyclical process that seemed to govern all things, including human life (the alternation of the seasons, for example, or the progression from youth to age to death). To account for them, fabulous stories were invented with man as a crucial figure. To ease the fears, to turn them into hopes, the myths attributed to man extraordinary powers. Mythical men, for example, sought and sometimes found the secret of eternal youth. Death was transcended in myths about another world or the achievement of immortality in this one. Some of the Greek myths deal with transfiguration, a magical process whereby a person is transformed by an act of the gods into something else; thus was the maiden Daphne, pursued by Apollo, turned into a tree.

But, though mythology often gave man a sense of importance and a sense of hope, it was also capable of creating new fears. You can't create a Zeus with all his fancy powers without dwarfing human life, no matter how mortal the stories made him seem. Other myths, created to explain the fact of human misery and suffering, probably did more harm than good. The Greeks, for all their pride and individualism, were fatalists, trapped by some of their own stories, which they could not, after centuries, entirely control. A well-known myth personified fate as three sisters; one of them spun the thread of life, another drew it out, and the third arbitrarily cut it with a pair of shears. But the cycle kept going. If fear created fate, fate in turn could lead to renewed hope. The same sisters who could destroy you might also make nice things happen to you. After all, the whole point of mythmaking isn't to strangle in your fears, but to find a way to carry on.

Mythology is still indispensable. You hear remarks like, "It's too bad he had to die, but when your number comes up, there's not much you can do." The three sisters are still there, pulling and snipping that thread. Forces we don't quite comprehend, like economic cycles, are sometimes converted into human beings—the mysterious "they" we hear so much about: "They want to keep the war going because they're getting rich on it." All the old fears are still around: sex, nature, age, and death; and with them, the old hopes: eternal youth, immortality, and human strength and power in general.

Nobody understands these hopes and fears as well as the value of mythology better than the modern myth-weavers: the ad men on Madison Avenue and the dream vendors responsible for popular entertainment in movies and on television. That's not to say that advertising and popular entertainment involve nothing but mythology, but it is important to your search for identity that you be able to detect the manner in which these media can play on your fears and revitalize your hopes.

How the Ads Work on You

Let us pretend for a moment that we are ancient Greeks, living at a period when mythology is a living force, not just an oral tradition. This means that we are beset with fears and really depend upon our myths to restore our sense of security. Let us also pretend that there exists a Greek version of Madison Avenue, inhabited by ad men with sharp psychological insight into some of our fears.

A man might unroll his morning newspaper and come upon a full-page ad, showing the new chariots for 675 B.C. There is a picture, capturing a superdeluxe model (in color) with its gleaming silver carriage, pulled by four magnificent white steeds in perfect alignment, their hooves off the ground, muscles and sinews straining and bulging; in the carriage behind them, holding a whip, stands a muscular specimen of a man, resembling the statues of Zeus himself, his head framed against the cloud-streaked sky. Below, the caption reads: BE A GOD IN YOUR NEW THUNDERBOLT CHARIOT.

Now what is there about the typical Greek reader that the ad men know? First, he enjoys sex. Second, he can never be sure he is potent enough. (Down at the YMGA he hears the fellas boasting of their incredible exploits.) Third, no matter how confident he may feel, he is continually plagued by recurrent fears of losing his potency someday.

The ad men know that this man needs reassurance. He needs the security of identifying himself with a source of unlimited sexual power. What better symbol than a man who resembles Zeus? And they know that the reader will transfer the mythical identification with the god to the product associated with the figure. He will, *he must* buy that chariot. Possessing the chariot will mean a miraculous resurgence of his powers. (See him now driving proudly along the freeways, passing everyone, maneuvering his way through the traffic with splendid and majestic authority. He truly has become a god.)

In soothing one man's fears about loss of virility, the ad indirectly arouses fears in another reader. Its symbolism plants the suggestion that, if he isn't worried about his manhood now, he really ought to be. The ad says to him: "Look, it's your duty to remain in your prime: strong, vigorous, powerful. How old are you now, hmm? Forty, fifty? Getting up there! Isn't it time you redid yourself and restored your vitality? Buy this chariot." The ad makes sexual power seem to be life's most important quality.

Now zoom in your time machine to the present. Open any magazine and look at an automobile ad. Isn't it still saying pretty much the same thing? Chances are the target is still the male reader, because the ad men know that the wives tend to be more practical when it comes to cars. They know how much easier it is to convince the husband that he can't live without the new models, with their stronger horsepower, bigger engines, and super powers of acceleration. (But women aren't exempt. Women like to look and stay young, and a new car every year can symbolize eternal youth.)

Consider now the popularity of a certain imported compact car that is about a quarter the size of the "Greek God" automobiles. Its success in this country cannot be attributed to economy alone. Its advertising campaign has been sensationally brilliant. Does it too address itself to human fears? To human hopes? Whose? How?

The main approach this car's promoters have used is to reverse everything: to make it appear that the prospective buyer is too intelligent to be taken in by such mythical poppycock as the higher-priced competition employs. The car's lines hardly suggest sexual exploits. Nor is there an obvious attempt to appeal to the buyer's hope of cheating the aging process. The ads promise durability, and they play up the fact that the styling of this car never changes at all. Nonetheless, in reversing the appeals, they are getting at the same kind of fears. The durability becomes a substitute symbol for eternal youth and unending hope. (This car will always be in style!) And the very lack of sexual symbolism in the design of the car can have a strong appeal for the thinking man who feels he is superior to the temptations that keep coming out of Madison Avenue. ("Besides, I am still so virile I don't *have* to rely on symbolism!")

The hope of eternal youth makes the cosmetic industry a multi-billion-dollar enterprise. What about all those hair coloring ads that one finds in all the leading magazines, on busses and subways, and on roadside billboards? One of these tells you that blondes have more fun than anyone else. The woman chosen to model the dyed hair is always young, radiant, and sexy, with an ecstatic look on her face. The ad tells women that it may be later than they think. What else is there in life but fun, and have they had their full share of it before age begins to creep in on them? By tampering with the color of the hair, one is somehow tampering with nature itself (remember that fear of nature has been listed as one of the basic fears to which mythology relates). After all, one *can* change her hair color at will, and thus one can "control" the natural process of aging.

The fear of pain, illness, and finally, death itself, is, of course, a deep-rooted part of our lives. The ad men know this too. That's what makes it fairly easy to convince people they need aspirin, pain relievers, tranquilizers, cold medicines, and laxatives. In fact, if you consider the total volume of such ads you may get the idea we are a bunch of positive neurotics on the subject of health.

Many ads are dedicated to the task of selling products which in themselves can be dangerous to health and even speed up the process of aging and death. Cigarettes and liquor, of course, head this list, but they also rake in fortunes for their companies. Many brand names of cigarettes are life-oriented. (What would happen if they called cigarettes by names like Crypt? Tombstone? Wreath?) Remember the old television commercials, showing young, vigorous, intensely alive men and women smoking their cigarettes in healthy, outdoorsy, and nonpolluted settings such as mountaintops? Liquor ads promise distinction, respectability, and success in business and love, not the effects that alcohol frequently has and for which many people drink. Cigarette and liquor mythology helps to bury the guilt, ease the fears, and intensify the same hopes for eternal youth and human strength that underlie many other forms of advertising.

Another deep-rooted fear in our society is that of failure, and many ads take advantage of it. Many products guarantee or are at least associated with economic success. Clothing ads for high-priced fashion houses, ads for expensive apartment houses and homes, even ads for luxury cruises in the Caribbean cause the average reader to wonder why he should not live as the people who can afford such things apparently do. So he is conned into spending money he doesn't have to buy things he doesn't need. (I know a couple who borrowed $5,000 to go around the world about ten years ago. They haven't been anywhere since, and they still owe some of the money.) The ads for expensive items and stores are intended to pull in those who really have no business thinking about them. The legitimately wealthy usually don't require such appeals.

Whether the fear of not "making it" financially is tied in with the fear of losing sexual potency (for men) and being sexually unattractive (for women) is debatable, and the reader can decide only by giving some thought to the people he knows who seem to be most susceptible to overspending. The fear of aging and death may also be involved. After all, if one doesn't take that Caribbean cruise today, who knows whether he'll be around tomorrow to do it?

EXERCISES

1. Much of what I have said in this section may not relate to you directly—at least at the moment. You may not be financially independent. On the other hand, since you and your contemporaries comprise a huge percentage of the population (isn't it nearly half by now?), you are bound to be a source of concern for the ad men. Fashionable clothes, cars, motorcycles, cigarettes, and liquor are all products you may buy—either from your own earnings or by persuading your parents.

   Do a study of some ads in newspapers and magazines that seem to be aimed at your generation, with an eye to discovering the hidden mythology. What fears do you think the ad men are trying to stir up? How will the products advertised ease those fears? How are you threatened if you decide you will not use the product?

   A very obvious example is medication for skin blemishes. Youthful models are always employed, sometimes in a before-and-after situation. The copy in the ads usually indicates that you can expect to be a wallflower until you have removed or at least covered up the blemishes. But, as soon as you do, fun will immediately enter your life. It may not be age or death that you fear, but certainly lack of popularity is made to seem a genuine reason for alarm. Also, isn't sexual potency or attractiveness tied in with the possession or removal of skin blemishes? As you comb through the ads that seem especially directed at you and your contemporaries, make a note of any special fears that I haven't mentioned in this section at all. Perhaps the anxieties of this age have given rise to new fears. If so, we can usually count on the Madison Avenue men to be tuned in.

   Make note, too, of the hidden references to pot, LSD, and other "turn on" devices. Psychedelic lettering and colors could also be included here. Are genuine fears being reached, or do you consider many of these ads the labor of dirty old men with childlike minds? Do such ads turn you off rather than on? The ad men are conscious of the generation gap, and you can bet they're staying up nights trying to think of ways to reach you. But sometimes one gets the feeling they are trying a little too hard, as the Reverend Billy Graham did recently while addressing a Sunday morning audience at a rock festival. He kept making statements like, "Why don't you drop out of sin and turn on to God?" From the rather bored expressions on the faces of the listeners, I gathered that the Reverend wasn't having much luck.

If you want, you can include in your paper some advice to the ad men about the appeals they are using to influence you—that is, unless you think they are all super-successful.

2. If you want to have a little fun at the expense of Madison Avenue, make up your own ads; only, since no profit is at stake, do nothing but tell the truth. That is, show what the ads are really saying.

Here are some examples, but you can no doubt think of much cleverer ones. Anyway, this will give you the idea:

a) "Let's face it, honey, you're over the hill. You've got skin like a leather purse that's been left out in the sun. You've got hair that could scrub pots and pans. No man would be caught dead within twenty feet of you. But you can't live without illusions, can you? Why not dye your hair with Lady Scareall? You'll probably look even more ridiculous, but you've got nothing left except to kid yourself anyway."

b) "Man, you are way past your prime, and you know it. You can hardly keep your eyes open after eight o'clock, and when you hit that sack, you're out for the night. Your woman keeps up the pretense, but can you imagine what she's thinking to herself? You know you feel guilty. Man, you know you are inadequate! But buy the new Hammer of Thor, the road's biggest power machine, and, even if you don't deceive your woman, you can take out your aggression by running everyone off the highway."

3. Do a serious study of mythology in advertising, using some of the basic myths I have considered in this section and adding some of your own. Do a pasteup of the most striking and original ads and turn this in with the paper. Or else do a collage of ads, designed to give one or two dominant impressions about the general nature of the advertising mythology today. For example, is sex the main theme? money? age? death? loss of approval?

4. One product I haven't specifically mentioned is soap. If it weren't for soap advertising, Madison Avenue would probably have to shut down. For this assignment you can use television commercials, though I have avoided mentioning them for the principal

reason that it is easier to do an analysis of advertising mythology when you have the ads right in front of you. However, you have no doubt seen so many soap commercials on television that you could probably analyze them in your sleep.

Now, granted that soap is important and necessary, does it not seem a bit excessive, the way Americans are obsessed with cleaning everything? If it is true that ads, like myths, strike out at hidden fears, do people share a terror of dirt? Why? Do they associate dirty hands and dirty clothes with disease? nasty, filthy sex? unclean minority groups from the other side of the tracks?

What about guilt? Psychiatrists tell us we are all suffering from horrendous guilt complexes, accumulated from past sins that have been buried deep inside us the way people push their dirty clothes into hampers. If the subject intrigues you, take soap advertising as the subject for your paper, and try to find all the mythology in it you can.

5. When you walk up and down the aisles of a supermarket, you find a bewildering array of brand names. Something makes you pick this toothpaste rather than that one. Obviously the continual barrage of advertising contributes to your decisions. Not that it necessarily matters. That is, it doesn't make sense to spend a lot of time reading labels and comparing brands for yourself. In most cases one brand is about the same as another.

Still, you can tell to what extent a person has become permanently hypnotized by the ad men through a study of his buying habits. (A case can be made for the fact that something is always influencing every decision we make. A woman with radical political views once told me that, whenever she found herself lost in a strange part of town, she invariably turned *left* while trying to find her way.) If you think the effort will be rewarding, make a study of your mother's or father's buying habits. You could make out a questionnaire and ask them for some honest answers.

Here are some possible questions for your father:

a) (If he smokes) Why do you use that particular brand?

b) Why do you drive that car?

c) Drink that beer (or hard liquor)?

d) In what price range are your clothes? That is, do you look for bargains? Fashion?

e) What are your motives in dressing? Self-image? Esteem of others?

For your mother:

a) Why that brand of soap? lipstick? perfume?

b) Do you use a hair coloring? Which one? Why?

c) Same dress questions as for your father.

From the answers to these and other questions of your own invention, decide whether your parents are masters or slaves of the ad men. Decide whether they are highly susceptible, moderately so, or not at all susceptible to the mythology. (In case you're wondering what such an assignment has to do with your own search for identity, you can get a better idea of the way advertising affects you by studying somebody else.)

6. Americans have been called anti-intellectual by many cultural historians and anthropologists. Advertising suggests that the charge may be well founded. Do famous philosophers, poets, and novelists ever get asked to endorse a product? Isn't it usually an athlete or a movie star or some intensely *physical* person?

Make a study of a number of ads which, in your opinion, appeal to the fear of intellectualism and encourage mental mediocrity. For a far-out example: what about all the sleep aids and tranquilizers that suggest how terrible it is to have to lie awake? (Look how many great ideas have been born during a sleepless night.) The television ads for these products usually show a man or woman tossing wretchedly in bed and then, after taking the appropriate pill, falling instantly asleep. Certainly relaxation and sleep cannot be considered very intellectual.

See how many ads you can find that offer products promising any kind of intellectual pleasure. Nearly always, pleasure itself is defined in purely physical terms. Don't just show an ad and comment "This is anti-intellectual." Explain why as thoroughly as you can. Try to locate the "myth of mediocrity" in unobvious places (for example, all the products that promise to make housework or carpentry or painting "easier").

7. To show that you have become a master, not a slave, of Madison Avenue and that you can apply its techniques yourself by now, construct an advertising campaign to promote an absolutely ridiculous product, one that nobody has ever heard of and can't possibly use. A guest on a recent TV talk show exhibited a mechanical gadget that did nothing whatever and was about to go on the market for $25! Use mythical appeals, of course, in order to make your useless product seem indispensable. See whether you can corner the whole market: adults and young people of both sexes.

TV: The Mythology of Reassurance

The commercial is over. An anonymous voice announces, "And now back to *The World We Live In*." There is a blurry fuzz over the screen, and then a crisp, clear image. We are inside a doctor's office. There is a couch in one corner, so he must be a psychiatrist. An anxious looking middle-aged woman is sitting across from a handsome man making notes on a pad. "My son, doctor," she is saying. "What will become of him? He's—he's taking LSD." A booming chord from an organ underlines the statement. The camera zeroes in on the woman's face as she begins to describe her "nightmare." And in millions of American homes housewives are watching the painful scene. "Oh, oh," they are thinking, "LSD. It's an awful thing. But it's the truth. We're facing the reality. We've all got to face the reality."

But why? the doctor wants to know. Is John unhappy at home? Oh, doctor, how could he be? He has everything. But does he have love, my dear? What's that, doctor? Perhaps he needs love. Perhaps you have rejected him. Oh yes, yes, doctor. That is surely it. I have rejected my son. My husband and I live in our own world. We drink and go to parties and the theater and we never seem to have any time for him. Oh my darling, darling boy. I'm going to make it all up to you. (More organ music. Then another commercial.) Mrs. Plotz runs back to her ironing. There's a hole in her husband's shorts. But that's a small price to pay for such an intense encounter with the world we live in.

Mrs. Plotz really believes there's a difference between the ads and the story. She doesn't think how both are working on her. She doesn't notice that the story is there to sell the products that the commercials describe. She doesn't know that the story is setting her up for the ads. If she doesn't buy the products, the story will disappear from the screen. So the job of the story is to create good will toward the products. The secret, still, is mythology.

But is there a difference between the story mythology and the ad mythology? The product, after all, has to make itself seem absolutely necessary. This soap is better than that soap, and, if you don't use it, your wash will look dirty when you hang it up and you'll be the shame of the neighborhood. If you have bad breath, you'll be disgraced. If you don't dye your hair, your mate may stop loving you. Over and over, the product stimulates fear and then offers hope. The function of the entertainment that comes over television is primarily to *reassure:* not to arouse fear, but to whisper a message of comfort. All is well. Your values will prevail. Don't worry about the world.

Just worry about your personal problems. Our products will take care of *those*.

From *The World We Live In* Mrs. Plotz finds out that young people are taking LSD. *Reassurance #1:* You were right all the time, lovey. The young kids of today are going nuts. A source of unending concern. *Them*—not you!

Mrs. Plotz also finds out that the problem is being competently handled. The handsome actor playing the doctor is *so* professional and *so* concerned. *Reassurance #2:* Things are being taken care of. You don't have to worry. Somebody is doing something. You don't have to do a thing.

Mrs. Plotz agrees that the mother in the story is part of the problem. She doesn't give her son enough love. *Reassurance #3:* I was right all the time. A good home environment is the answer. Thank heaven my husband and I are providing such an environment for *our* kids. If they stray, if they turn to drugs, it's certainly not my fault.

But the harmless-looking set in the corner is by no means through for the day. There are still the husband and the children to work on. Mr. Plotz will watch *Gunsmoke* and *Bonanza*. The children may look at *Mod Squad* and *Mannix*—and so may their parents. Mr. and Mrs. Plotz may demand to watch *My Three Sons*. The children will then go off to watch *Laugh-In* with its quick-witted "in" flashes and psychedelic effects. The Plotzes also give some time to current social problems (even as Mrs. Plotz had done with LSD earlier in the day), and they watch *Julia* and think to themselves, "My goodness, we certainly wouldn't mind having a black neighbor if she were like Diahann Carroll." They feel proud of having seen the light and wish there weren't so many prejudiced Americans.

The references I have made are to TV shows popular as this book goes to press. By next season the trends may all have changed. Television executives are paid enormous salaries to compute the results of continual surveys and keep one jump ahead of the public. The 1969–1970 season, for example, has tended to stress nonviolence, wholesome family relationships, and a "better" image of teachers and policemen. Whatever the public at large—and this means primarily the stable bulk of the population, the people both under and over thirty who go to work, pay bills, and buy products—seems jumpy and ill at ease about, television must be comforting about.

The main point is that no matter what the trends are at the moment, there will always *be* trends in commercial television in this country. This means that except in a few rare instances (such as the CBS Playhouse series), television VIP's are not willing to take chances on "arty" material that may prove popular with the discriminating few, who probably pay less attention to the ads, but will not be reassuring to the majority.

An example of what can happen when a television show aims too high in its goals is the aftermath of a program that proved to be a fiasco as measured by the ratings. In 1968 NBC laid over $100,000 on the line to purchase a script called *Flesh and Blood*, which had been earmarked for Broadway. When it made the deal, the network announced that it wanted to upgrade its productions and offer the public more highbrow entertainment, even if this meant departing from formula and proven appeal. The play, by William Hanley, offered an extremely cynical view of life and as wretched a collection of characters as the medium has ever assembled on one show. The public reaction was instantaneous—and overwhelmingly negative.

Edith Efron, a *TV Guide* columnist, describes the consequences of the disaster:

> A few days later the official announcement came: NBC was scuttling the status-misery school. The network had signed with Prudential Insurance Company of America to do five original "upbeat" dramas next season—the project to be supervised by specials vice president Alvin Cooperman.
>
> "We need contemporary drama about contemporary issues and problems, that is exciting, hopeful and affirmative," declares Cooperman. "The new plays will all be 'upbeat' in the sense that the protagonist is a heroic type who fights for moral issues. This doesn't preclude comedy or suspense melodrama, but it's all going to be *affirmative*. The protagonist will have *spine* and will fight against *odds*. That's what life is all about! We've been told too long by writers that life is sickness and negation." [3]

A recognition of the mythology of reassurance, which the TV industry fosters, is not to deny the possibility of being genuinely entertained by any given show. Producers and sponsors must rely on trained professionals, and a good many artistic and imaginative people are among them. This creative "underground movement" is likely to keep generating a little hope among the cynical viewers. But the hope seldom lasts very long, especially when it comes to a series. If word gets around that the familiar reassurance formula has been forsaken, out comes the network ax.

Such censorship (for it *is* a form of censorship to have one's entertainment and the values it embodies screened in advance) has been known to extend to shows that don't depend upon sponsors. In Chicago recently there was an abortive attempt to have a soap opera dealing with real issues in the black community: problems such as

---

[3] *TV Guide*, May 25, 1968, p. 34.

contract buying, eviction without notice, and, of course, poverty. The show was subsidized by a foundation grant but lasted for only about ten episodes. Why? Nobody knows for sure, but a good bet is that the network itself intervened and acted in response to strong viewer objections. A soap opera on poverty? No reassurance = no air time, no matter *who* pays the bills.

The shows that endure from one season to the next (*Bonanza, Mannix, Mission: Impossible*, for example) must do so because they offend almost nobody and reassure almost everybody. Let's consider their mythology.

1) *Bonanza:*   the family is an indestructible unit
the old Western ethical code still prevails, and good always overcomes evil

2) *Mannix:*   the proper use of violence is for enforcing the law, not defying it

3) *Mission Impossible:*   the age of computers still requires human ingenuity
the black man figures prominently in this age of ingenuity

I selected these three examples because nearly everyone, regardless of age or skin color or degree of wealth or poverty, can probably find reassurance from at least one of these shows. If *Bonanza* turns off a large percentage of young and poor people and intellectuals, *Mission: Impossible* is likely to turn them on. If not, then there are always re-runs of *Star Trek*, a show that had distinct appeal on college campuses and ran for three seasons.

Other reassurances to be found currently on television:

1) Integration is working smoothly (*Julia, Room 222*).
2) We're not really in the middle of a revolution; even the most hopeless dropout can be brought back into the fold (*Mod Squad*).
3) There's no true crisis in education (*Room 222*).
4) War is not evil; in fact, it can be downright fun (*Hogan's Heroes*).
5) The police can be suave, charming, intelligent, and super-cool (*Mannix, Hawaii Five-O*).
6) There's no generation gap (*My Three Sons*).

A natural question to ask is "What *should* television be doing? What is its function in our society?" The answer lies in the numerous advantages it can and does offer, such as instant news coverage, on-the-spot stories which alert an entire nation to what's going on, interviews with important and controversial figures, not to mention the old films, some of them excellent, and the occasional original dramas of quality and significance. When TV is good—like the little girl in the old nursery rhyme—it is very, very good. It has immediacy, and its cameras can zero in on a haunting face or a trembling hand, heightening dramatic moments in a way that rivals the art of the movies.

Even when it does nothing but reassure, it doesn't necessarily lack value. Everyone needs to be reassured from time to time. As long as the viewer knows he may be playing a game with himself for an hour or so, he can't get hurt too much. The danger from television doesn't lie in the fact that it is reassuring, but rather in one's lack of awareness that reassurance is primarily what television is offering him. The trouble begins when myth is mistaken for reality.

EXERCISES

1. I have been deliberately one-sided in treating popular television entertainment, in order to make and underscore the point. That is, I have no doubt excluded from consideration some show that you personally consider more honest and truthful and less "mythological" than some of those I have singled out. If so, write an analysis of it, pointing out:

   a) its format—how does it depart from the usual mythological appeals?

   b) some of its basic ingredients—more honest treatment of young people? sex? problems of poverty? war? political intrigue?

   c) the target of its appeal—who comprises its probable public? how large is it? how long do you think the show will last?

2. Take some show that you personally liked and that didn't last very long. (In recent years there were, for example, the *Leslie Uggams Show*, which featured an ongoing comedy series about a relatively poor black family; and *My World and Welcome to It*, which used an artistic personality as its central character.) Analyze your reasons for enjoying the show, using the three guidelines in the exercise above and any others you can think of. Then present your opinion of why it was cancelled.

3. Perhaps you couldn't do either of the first two suggested exercises because in all honesty you weren't able to think of any shows that personally appeal (or appealed) to you enough to be singled out. If you are one of those who can't turn on the TV set without being appalled by its flagrant distortions of reality, write a paper setting forth some reassurances you note in some of the popular shows and indicating why these do not reassure you at all.

In this paper you should also consider this important fact: if TV absolutely turns you off, then, by computer standards, you are in the minority and your opinion has to be discounted. By the same token, you can draw a pretty competent picture of the majority, at least as the TV industry sees it. Do a profile of a "typical" American viewer, drawn from the mythology of reassurance you have detected from your own analytical viewing.

4. There is no better way to show that you fully understand the society in which you live than by being able to supply its necessary reassurances. If you want to have some fun, do a paper that offers a suggested outline for next year's TV season. Pretend, if you want, that you are a highly paid idea man for the industry. Every TV season is different, as you well know. As this year's ratings go, so goes next year's mythology. For example, the 1968–1969 season was rife with violence, sex, drugs, and kindred topics. But audience reaction began to be negative. Letters poured into the networks by the thousands. Consequently the 1969–1970 season was considerably deviolenced, desexed, and dedrugged.

Think about the season that is currently upon us. Ask yourself these questions:

a) What seem to be the most popular shows?

b) What reassurances do they offer?

c) Which ones seem least popular and in danger of getting the ax?

d) What can you learn about the current climate of majority opinion from this television season?

From your answers to these (or other) questions, derive your list of possible TV offerings for next season. Be specific. Make up names, stories; indicate what the appeal will be in each case.

5. It is not, of course, accurate to say that *any* TV season is totally devoid of violence. Some of the most enduring successes have violence built into their very formulas: *Bonanza, Gunsmoke, The Virginian, Mannix, Hawaii Five-O,* to name but a few. Still, if our concept of the mythology of reassurance is at all well founded, the kind and use of violence on these shows must somehow not seem threatening to the average viewer.

Do a paper investigating and analyzing "approved" or "safe" violence. Here are some sample considerations to get you started:

a) Who are the violent? What do they represent?

b) Are different standards applied to different types of action? That is, does violence destroy the "bad" violent and work for the good of society in the hands of the "good" violent?

    c) Do you detect any dishonesty? Do you believe, for example, that people secretly enjoy violence and only need to have it justified?

    d) Does the idea of violence seem less threatening when it belongs to a TV fantasy world than it does in the real world?

    e) Are certain characters who can be violent, like Mannix, deliberately aimed at an audience of women who want men to be men, and of men who fear they're not?

6. An analysis of most TV seasons generally confirms one's suspicion that the "typical" viewer is a middle-class white, past twenty-five, moderate to slightly to the right in his political and social thinking, and usually undisposed to consider any change in the status quo.

This means that TV seldom aims its appeals at the anti-Establishment young and those black Americans who reject white middle-class values and who don't want assimilation, at least at this time.

If you place yourself in the category of the "unappealed-to" viewer, how about drawing up a prospectus for a TV season you'd *like* to see? Be very specific about the shows. Name them. Describe their formats. Indicate what values they would need to embody to win your approval.

Optional consideration: would these values be reassurances? Or would the shows be telling it like it is? Explain your position.

Movies: The Mythology of Identification

Though motion pictures have to be considered as mass media, a happy fact is that the cinema in our time has become one of the reigning art forms, rivaling and often eclipsing live theater. It is possible today for dedicated artists to do their thing via the movies and not only get away wth it but actually make money. Mike Nichols' *The Graduate* is a notable example. Filmed in 1967 on a relatively modest budget, because it was supposed to be a little arty, it went on to become one of the box-office champs of all time.

A movie today can be both popular entertainment and artistic triumph, whereas an ongoing television series seldom can be. A number of reasons spring to mind:

    1) The success or failure of a film depends upon gross box-office receipts, and these can only be guessed in advance. There is no sure thing until the returns are in. It is easier for a film director to take a risk on his hunch than it is for a TV director to do so.

Bad ratings can lead to doom before the latter's show is given a full chance, but poor reviews and poor business when a movie first appears doesn't always mean it will ultimately fail. Stanley Kubrick's *2001: A Space Odyssey* (1968) got off to a trickling start, then was discovered by young people all over the world and turned into a financial gusher. With examples like this before them, Hollywood producers simply cannot afford to close their minds to creative new talents.

2) A movie is so much longer and more involved than the average TV show that imaginative directors have more scope to express their ideas than TV directors have. For example, though X-rated films stressing a frank display of nudity and sex have a good chance to reap liberal box-office harvests, a director can combine art and sensationalism without the general public's always noticing it. The shockeroo success of the late sixties was *I Am Curious (Yellow)*, but many found a serious message and complex symbolism underlying the more obvious appeals of the film.

3) The film industry cannot always guide itself by TV ratings because it realizes that many diehard TV fans stay home in front of their sets and that thousands upon thousands of people who are disenchanted with television comprise a potentially rewarding audience for its good products.

4) The social and political sensibilities of young people today have greatly added to an audience for serious, thought-provoking films that may once have been limited to their more intellectual elders.

These reasons help to explain the extraordinary number of superior films that have come along during the past decade.

At the same time, while movies can serve the interests of the more discriminating so long as it is profitable to do so, they remain committed to the needs of the general public as well. Motion pictures today offer a wide variety of appeals, and mythology is involved. With the cinema, it seems to be a mythology of identification: the attempt of the film industry to keep nearly everyone's trust by assuring him that he and his cause are important.

Like any form of dramatic art, a movie has to generate empathy within its audience, the projection of oneself into the action. One has to *care* about the central character, usually by identifying with him and his cause. Of course, some films succeed because of sex alone; others, like *Space Odyssey*, because of an overwhelming appeal to both the senses and the intellect. But most of the time there are a character or set of characters and a viewpoint that the filmmaker is betting will strike a responsive chord with some segment of the population. A really brilliant filmmaker can create more than one source of identification within the same movie.

There appear to be two basic and quite different kinds of identification that can take place within an audience, and the division helps us to understand why both *The Graduate* and the Doris Day-Julie Andrews epics made money during the same decade.

First, we have one-to-one identification, whereby the viewer feels that he is personally very much like the character on the screen, has the same problems, and would respond in very much the same manner. Thus did young America identify with Benjamin Braddock, the hero of *The Graduate*, a sensitive young man who finds himself with an A.B., a proud, affluent, insensitive family, no real sense of belonging to the Establishment, and no true direction in life.

Second, we have wish-fulfillment identification, whereby the viewer pretends he is like the character on the screen but secretly knows he isn't. For years Doris Day has been America's box-office queen. The older she gets, the more conventional and standardized her material becomes. Appearing more blonde and youthful-looking as film succeeds film, she is always the epitome of respectability and wholesome American values. She is always fairly affluent, vaguely religious, not noticeably prejudiced or intelligent but, especially, a symbol of unending youth. She represents to millions of Americans a victory over anarchy, atheism, intellectualism, poverty, and the aging process. Much the same can be said for the wholesome appeal of Julie Andrews, especially after *The Sound of Music* (1965) became the biggest moneymaker in the history of American films.

The Graduate was a phenomenon because it achieved a multi-leveled appeal. Discontented youth related easily to Benjamin, as I have said. But in the character of Mrs. Robinson, the middle-aged, frustrated friend of Benjamin's mother, millions of housewives might have seen their own unsatisfied sexuality. It was probably possible for millions of husbands to identify with Benjamin, reminding themselves of how fortunate their own wives were to be married to such altogether satisfying mates. Both husbands and wives, in turn, probably collaborated in identifying sympathetically with the young lovers of the film, complimenting themselves on being such understanding parents. America as a whole could gang up on the Beverly Hills affluence of the Robinsons and the Braddocks, glad not to have become *that* decadent.

Of course, alienation from both characters and viewpoints is not an impossible reaction to a film. It is a valuable experience to see a movie whose story and people turn you off personally but make you glad to have achieved the insight. One could be fascinated, for example, by a movie that expertly depicted the inner workings of the Mafia, enjoying the enlightenment without necessarily caring about the characters.

In 1968 Peter Fonda and Dennis Hopper collaborated on *Easy Rider,* a powerful film about two motorcycle-riding hippies who go on a bike tour of America and are eventually shot to death by a couple of brutal "rednecks." Not only do the central characters smoke pot in nearly every scene, not only do they and some prostitutes take an LSD trip, but the boys finance their tour by smuggling cocaine from Mexico and selling it in this country. The movie was enormously popular, but not every restless anti-Establishment youth necessarily went so far as to identify with the motorcyclists and approve of their activities and means of self-support.

One of my students, in a review of *Easy Rider,* praised the music, photography, and directing techniques of the movie. She discussed the theme:

> In one scene George sums up the theme of the movie. Billy and he are discussing why people are afraid of the long-haired men with their "funny" clothes. George says that people are afraid of what these men represent: freedom. People, he says, think they are free, but they are actually complete slaves of society. If you try to tell them they're not really free, or if they see someone who is truly free, their fear and rage turn them into dangerous beings who destroy.

The writer went on to say that this is an important theme, one that every American needs to take to heart. But, when all is said and done, she added:

> I found *Easy Rider* a very depressing film. I didn't like the fact that they resorted to drugs all the time, but I suppose this was part of their search and their escape. I didn't enjoy the cruelty with which they were treated either. It was horrible, but I guess it's true.

The writer is a girl who knows what's going on, though she claims the right not to be a part of the rebellion. Her review represents a kind of "reverse" identification but illustrates in a perfectly valid way how movies can be used as an index of the current state of direction of one's thinking.

Over and above the art itself of the cinema, then, we can say that movies offer further guides toward self-realization. By knowing what characters, causes, and viewpoints you identify with (or, in some cases, are alienated from) you get to know a little bit more about who you are.

EXERCISES

1. Write a review of a film that you have recently seen, preferably one that has excited a lot of commentary both pro and con—as op-

posed to, say, a super-spectacle or musical that is generally accepted as good entertainment alone. It doesn't have to be a movie that you particularly liked.

A good review usually contains at least three basic sections:

a) *content analysis.* Talk about the theme, the subject, the message; the substance of the movie, as you see it (this doesn't mean retelling the story); indicate what the events and the characters relate to.

b) *technical analysis.* Talk about photography, music, acting, and any other interesting aspect of the director's art that may be involved; you don't need particular training for this; just say what you noticed.

c) *feeling analysis.* Get down to business here; what are your emotions about the film? Be as honest as you can; you may, for example, admire certain things about the director's technique (skillful editing, slow motion, speeded-up action, frozen shots, distortions, and so on) but find that the subject matter turned you off and the characters alienated you. You may think the film's theme is an important one but have reservations about an excessive display of nudity, an apparently sympathetic handling of drug users, a dangerous attitude toward the law, or a glorification of The Establishment.

You needn't, of course, give equal attention to all three parts of the review. You may simply not feel competent to talk much (or at all) about the technical aspects. In this case, don't. Put the emphasis on content or your personal feelings. Put the emphasis where you seem to have the most to say.

The reason for learning how to divide a review into these various parts is that it gives you practice in separating objective analysis from personal emotions. It is important, I believe, to do this whenever you make any evaluation. Understand: the personal reactions may seem to you to be much more worth noting than interpreting the theme or looking at the technique. If a film really outrages you, you should claim the right to let off steam about it. This too is an act of self-realization. If you wish, be *only* emotional in your review.

One of my students, for example, simply hated the movie *Alice's Restaurant* and used the review as a chance to express her personal feelings about a lot of things. Her paper is perfectly valid because it doesn't pretend to be an objective analysis at all.

ON ALICE'S RESTAURANT

"Alice's Restaurant" is an endless film centered around a hippie's attempts to dodge the draft, and spiced by a few side-shows, including his entanglement with a small town's Chief of Police (for littering, no less), his father dying of Huntington's Chorea, and the assorted sex-ins Alice (the restaurant's owner) undertakes to console herself of a wandering husband (who only wandered to keep those poor, lonely, sad, and otherwise frustrated and inhibited flower children happy).

A rather humorous sequence where mockery of the law is particularly pointed takes place when Arlo (the hippie) gets arrested for littering the countryside. The Chief of Police, realizing that this is probably the biggest crime ever to be committed in Stockbridge, collects enough evidence to make Dick Tracy and Perry Mason turn green with envy (all this, of course, after Arlo and his friends have confessed to the "crime"), only to find that the case is to be tried before a judge, who being blind could not only not see the evidence, but could not see Arlo's thoroughly hippie appearance.

Another funny (in the most general sense of the word) incident develops when Arlo is dumped into a room with a father-killer, a mother-rapist, a father-rapist, and other assorted weirdos at his draft physical. The sequence, of course, is of no relevance to the plot (whatever it may be) of the film, except possibly making sure the viewer realizes the evils of the draft.

The only time Arlo stops long enough to think is when he visits his dying father. His father's inability to talk presents him with a golden opportunity to give vent to his thoughts. These are times when he sees the futility of his life, but still, consciously or subconsciously, refuses to change, going back to his natural habitat among the flower children.

In "Alice's Restaurant" you could also find some insight into the tragedies of drugs and a young man's dependence on them, interwoven with some marital problems. Early in the film, Arlo gets involved with Alice and her husband Ray, who both want to get a new start, a beautiful one among the flower children. They open a restaurant, "The Back Room," which at first is a fantastic success, but because of Ray's growing carelessness goes to pot. After Ray's despondence to the business develops, Alice gets involved with Shel, a flower child recently released from a reformatory where he had supposedly kicked the drugs. But, alas, Alice and Ray make up, and poor Shel is left all alone, unable to cope with the fact that he was only one of Alice's toys, and so he goes back to drugs, smashing himself to bits on the expressway on his motorbike.

There isn't much to be said for the photography, acting or even the music.

The photography is very pretty, very colorful, very realistic, and as far as the acting goes, neither Guthrie nor any other member of the cast could act. They wandered around the set, muttering lines that they had committed to memory.

As for the music, I suppose it is part of the generation (or is it degeneration) gap that exists today, but to make a long story short, it was bleah!

I have used many clichés (flower children, wandering husband, sex-in, etc.) in my analysis of the contents of "Alice's Restaurant," but only with one purpose in mind: To present the film as the series of clichés that, even though recent in age, have become so well-worn by now they bore the viewer. I consider "Alice's Restaurant" to be one of the most boring films I have ever seen, comparable only to *Can Hieronymus Merkin Ever Forget Mercy Humppe and Find True Happiness?* and possibly *Inga*. Although "Alice" had less sex, the plotless plot was still there, making the whole affair an insult to the viewers' intelligence.

2. Though the cinema has reached a stage at which it can be successful both financially and artistically, not all producers will go out on a limb and take a chance on a director whose way-out tendencies could bankrupt them. Along with *The Graduate, Space Odyssey,* and other notable achievements of the past decade, we still get the formula film.

What is a formula film? Does it belong, like the enduring TV shows, to the mythology of reassurance? Along with identification, doesn't it also offer certain stereotyped ideas designed to relax the viewer and make him feel better about his world and his times?

Formula films revise the formula every so often to keep up with the country's tensions. During the Depression years of the thirties, for example, a typical formula film dealt with a wealthy heiress who runs away from a sterile marriage to a titled Englishman and has a lot of fun with a struggling newspaper reporter. Moral: love is more important than money.

During the years of World War II a typical formula film showed all Japanese and all Germans to be cruel and sadistic, whereas "our boys" were always sympathetic. Let's say we have Humphrey Bogart and a buddy playing American soldiers who have just cleaned out a German village. They are smoking a cigarette in a farmhouse when they suddenly hear ominous footsteps outside. Peering through the window, they spy a tattered uniform and an unruly shock of bright blond hair. "It's a Kraut," says the buddy. "Yeah," say Bogart. "But look," says the buddy, "he can't be more than sixteen." Bogart aims and fires; there's the sound of a body hitting the ground. "He'll never be seventeen," smiles Bogart. The audience cheers.

The formula film of the fifties began, cautiously, to explore the theme of sex. Enter Doris Day and Rock Hudson. ("What kind of a girl do you think I am?") In the early sixties the faintest suspicion of a generation gap began to creep in, though it was likely to be confined to *Gidget Goes Hawaiian* and to a bold statement like, "A girl ought to be allowed to go surfing with a bunch of boys if she wants to." The teenage world was a campfire on Muscle Beach, with Annette Funicello and Frankie Avalon singing duets while the other couples huddled platonically under their blankets.

What about the late sixties? the early seventies? What are the current formula films? How do they reassure the young about the old and the old about the young? How do they reassure about race problems? continuing warfare? the moral revolution? Do formula films have X ratings? If so, are they made to appeal to that very "middle" America that supposedly wants tougher moral standards? How do you explain the inconsistency, if there is one?

3. Write a paper about a film that proved to be a box-office failure and that you liked intensely. First, explain what you liked about the movie and why you were glad it was made. Second, explain why you think it failed. Was it because it departed too radically from a formula? created too much alienation? told it like it is and managed to turn off both the Establishment and the anti-Establishment?

4. One of my students, an older man, brought in a photograph taken of a group of young adults, all of whom were smoking pot. According to him, this group was willing to pose for the picture by way of warning others of the morally undermining effects of certain films. In their case the film was *Easy Rider*, and they claimed it had led them to marijuana. This photograph incited a lively

discussion in class of the moral influence of movies. Some class members expressed the belief that films, like any art, should be exempt from any moral responsibility toward the public. Others disagreed and pointed out that children and impressionable young people *could* be harmed by some movies, despite the rating system (which they said isn't properly enforced anyway).

Write a paper setting forth your personal opinion about sex and violence on the screen and the possibility of "moral damage" that can come from exploiting certain themes. (Food for thought: during the popularity of Arthur Penn's *Bonnie and Clyde* in 1967 there was a rash of bank robberies and auto thefts perpetrated by groups patterning themselves after the Barrows gang of the movie.) What about sexual excitement offered by films? Do you feel that your own sexual desires were in any way prematurely aroused by an early exposure to certain movies?

Should there be any form of censorship, as there used to be? (MGM supposedly had to pay a million-dollar fine back in 1939 when it permitted Clark Gable to say "damn" in *Gone with the Wind*.) If so, where should it come from? Does censorship impede the civil rights of filmmakers? Or does the moral good of the people outweigh the danger of imposing restrictions?

PART TWO

THE
SELF
AND
THE
OTHERS

"It is difficult for anyone to be critical of himself. It is entirely human to want to preserve the interior *status quo*."

5

THE SMOG
OF IDENTITY

Suppose you fly off somewhere and then come back; you look down
from the plane and are appalled to find your home town absolutely
hidden under an opaque layer of thick smoke and grime. You suddenly wonder how you could have existed for even ten minutes in
such an atmosphere. If you could learn how to stand back and look
at yourself with the same sudden objectivity, you might wonder how
you could possibly have gone along for so many years without seeing
the haze all around you; a haze I like to call the Smog of Identity.
There's no industry to blame for it, no oversized automobiles with
their exhaust fumes. This dense mist is caused by the mysterious
nature of the human personality itself and the problems of getting
along with others.

Before you can take the first step toward making more realistic
contact with the world and the people surrounding you, it is necessary
first to recognize the Smog of Identity and the obstacles to vision that
go to make it up. If it were as evident as the sooty blanket that
cradles so many of our urban centers, it would pose less of a problem.
But alas! we are near-sighted without knowing it, and often our view

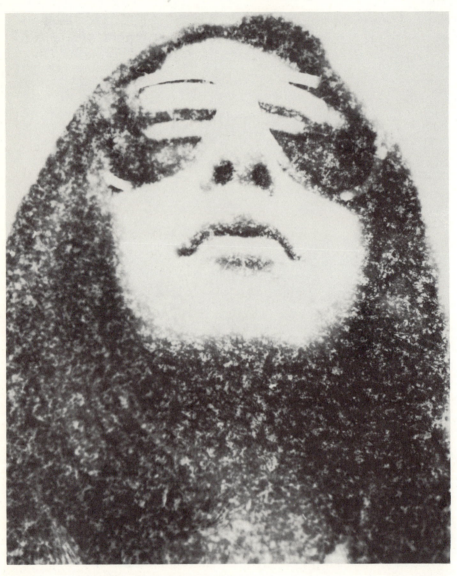

"This dense mist is caused by the mysterious nature of the human personality itself. . . ." (Photo by Gary Tepper)

of the world seems to us as free of pollution as a glass of tap water held before the naked eye.

THE CINEMA GAME

If you wear glasses, you have undoubtedly had the experience of looking desperately around the house for them and at last giving up in despair, convinced that they were lost forever. Then somebody looked at you and snickered, and you realized you'd had them on all the time. If you're accustomed to the glass, you can easily forget you're looking through it.

But now suppose each of us is wearing a plastic veil that completely covers his face. It is so clear and unwrinkled as to be invisible. In itself it is no obstacle to clear vision, right? Yet suppose further that the mind inside our heads is capable, like a movie projector, of casting images through our eyes, images that appear and disappear on the invisible veil that hangs before us. Not always being conscious of the veil, would we not think that the movie images belong to the world outside us? Would they not appear to be coming toward us rather than *from* us?

This illusion whereby we lose a sense of the direction from which things come is prevalent throughout our lives. The ventriloquist counts on it. He causes us to look at the dummy's mouth and make us believe sound is truly coming from it. At the drive-in movie we fail to notice that the voices of the characters are inside the tiny box right next to our ear. We delude ourselves that they are coming from the screen miles away from us.

You are walking along a crowded street. Face after face drifts by. Each looks like the other for all you know. But then out of the crowd there appears what is called a "familiar" face. It is that of an old friend, perhaps even of someone much closer than that. You see this face quite differently from the others. It is in sharp focus, whereas the other faces get blurred. What you see, however, is your own emotions projected outward. You see friendship; you see love coming toward you.

A bit further down the street, from out of the blur of faces, there emerges another, again in sharp focus, but this time it is the face of an enemy. It is an ugly face, a mean face, a threatening face. Its eyes are flashing hatred. You look at the face of your friend or loved one for comfort, and you suddenly see its warmth and reassurance.

It is beautiful to see love and reassurance, of course. But let's not ever forget that the world keeps moving by, and it doesn't see love and hate in the same places. No one sees the screen of your movie but you. If you want to know where the mind keeps its films, take a quick trip downstairs into the storeroom, and you'll find them on shelves marked "My Loved One's Virtues" and "My Enemy's Faults." There are also drawers labeled "Black Traits" or "Polish Habits" or "Liberal Nonsense" or "Conservative Folly." Guard these films well, for taken all in all, they provide all of us with the potential for changing the nature and appearance of the entire world.

If the mind didn't *need* them, it wouldn't provide them. They serve an extremely valuable purpose; without them our very survival could be in doubt. We use these films to doctor up reality until it conforms to the specifications it has to have in order for us to feel secure in it. Without them reality might seem a strange and unfamiliar place. We would have to keep learning about it and trying hard to adjust to it. Especially, we would seem less important in it.

The kinds of film we project vary with the personality of each of us, that is, with the particular needs each of us develops in the course of living. Circumstances and human relationships determine what these needs will be, for as we struggle to keep our balance, we soon learn what we have to believe, see, and hear in order to stay upright. But you can bet that self-interest is at the bottom of it all.

Perhaps self-preservation is the fundamental kind of film. We will believe anything that keeps the general image of the self in tip-top condition. We will see the friendly faces and hear the approving voices. We will believe the ideas that work to our benefit, as the American philosopher James Harvey Robinson so accurately described:

> We are incredibly heedless in the formation of our beliefs, but find ourselves filled with an illicit passion for them when anyone proposes to rob us of their companionship. It is obviously not the ideas themselves that are dear to us, but our self-esteem, which is threatened. We are by nature stubbornly pledged to defend our own from attack, whether it be our person, our family, our property, or our opinion.[1]

From self-preservation, by extension, we go to the preservation of next of kin, then nationality background, ethnic origin, country or cause, religion, and so on. But I guess we're most adept when it comes to "home movies," when we're interpreting everything for the good of ourselves and a few chosen people we let in on the secret, which is that all of nature rings with the joyous sound of our names.

I remember the times when I would get sick, and my mother—as

[1] From *The Mind in the Making* (New York: Harper & Row, 1921), p. 41.

militant a nonbeliever in medical science as you'll find—used to be great at making up explanations for my illnesses and improvising her own cures. If a midwinter cold suddenly made my temperature shoot way up, she would say, "The fever is a good sign. Your body is burning up all its poisons. It mean's you'll be all right tomorrow." To assist my body in its all-out fight, she would administer to me the juice of three lemons. (To this day I still have a mystic regard for the healing power of lemons.) If I ate something that upset my stomach, she would smile approvingly and explain, "It's a good sign. It shows that your system runs so well from the good food you usually eat that it won't stand for any other kind." Not only the lemon juice would cure me, but also, especially, the pride I would take in knowing I had a "special" system, one so perfectly crafted and finely honed that my stomach aches and nausea were like merit awards, justly earned and even boasted of.

My mother was a firm believer in the indestructibility of good old "peasant stock." I'm certain now that all the talk about my marvelous system was tied in with her active participation in the labor movement of the thirties. She was always highly critical of the bosses for whom she worked, particularly their diet, bad complexions, watery eyes, and constant illnesses, which, in their case, were not at all good signs but indications for all the world to see of the unwholesome lives they led.

The other side of the story is to consider what would have happened to me if, when I got sick, my mother had stood in the doorway with an emotionless face and declared, "You have picked up a virus that may or may not be dangerous. There isn't a thing you can do but ride it out." The insecurity might not have helped my temperature. My aunt had an old family doctor who believed in being brutally frank and scientific about his diagnoses. Never mind a "stiff upper lip" about sickness. He believed in laying on the line every possibility in the world. Once when my aunt was injured (or so we thought) in an auto accident, he told her, "You've got one of three things, and two of them, I'm sorry to say, are fatal." The third turned out to have been a case of nerves, and that's what she had. But it's a wonder she ever lived to find out.

Kidding ourselves has its place. What about the people for whom nothing ever quite goes together right? The following paper was written by a student to show the pathetic necessity for self-deception under which some people must live.[2]

[2] Printed by permission of the author, Alice Lee.

JOANNE

Everyone says that Joanne could be a beautiful girl. Could be—not so poignant as might have been; nor bitter as used to be; or sweet as shall someday be; just plain, flat, leaden, take-it-or-leave-it could be—beautiful that is.

Reason why? Simply, she has no sense of vanity. Apparently never looks into a mirror, or why the unplanned hair? As shiny black as reflected night, but totally unplanned. It falls in cascading terraces—a crown and collar and cape, all in one. And skin—completely uncosmeticed.

No planning there. Just lucky-accident close pored and white. Such innocent wrapping for the unexploited structure beneath. And her face—high, wide and handsome cheekbones—could resemble those old pictures of Hedy Lamarr. Instead, plain-jane Joanne, unplanned and unaware.

Consider those eyes of hers, curved widely round and tilting to her temples, with the startled state of a frightened colt. Undisciplined, that look of hers. No mascared veil or polka dotted lids. Just naked eyes that say indiscreet things.

And not even the sense to wrap herself in fashion. The vulnerable shoulders are either bare, or carelessly shawled, or sleeved in undistinguished black; but always hopelessly lacking in chic. Or, follow that to a bosom, small and high, and always hinted at—but never stated with the emphasis, say of a Marilyn Monroe (remember her?)

Well, who would look at such delicacy, with all there is to see today?!!

Surely, there's no suggestion of style in that narrow skirted look, is there? Well, she may think so, but after all, whose style? Certainly not mine or yours, or even *theirs*. Just hers—Joanne's—and what does *that* mean?

Tiny little thing, like a big-eyed bird. With those little boy hips she *could* be a Twiggy. But no, her skirt's too long. Now there's a point for you . . . free-souled and free-loving, but her skirt's too long. And her legs are too long. And her nose is too short, and her ankles, too thin, and her chin's too sharp, and her mouth's too . . . too . . . too something!

Well, can't you see, she just doesn't try to do anything with herself, so why do you prefer her to me?

ALICE LEE

Related to self-preservation, as are all forms of the cinema game we play, the projection involved in this monolog is more accurately labeled *buckpassing*. We ward off the horror of self-recognition by taking a deep-rooted, secret knowledge of what is wrong with us and pushing it outward, locating it once more as a fault in others. We become, like the speaker in the monolog, "objective" observers of the poor wretched creatures who need help in the worst way.

In addition to self-preservation and buckpassing, we play the Cinema Game for some additional reasons:

1) *Pleasure.* Everyone likes to feel good and not bad, and so it is an old trick to project an image of white smoke to cover up ugly realities we don't want to see. (This sometimes passes for idealism, as when the inspired parttime social worker gushes with excitement over the flower pushing its way up through the crack in the ghetto sidewalk—but doesn't notice the ghetto.)

2) *Desire.* This is very close to the principle number 1: we want to see something so badly we project it into existence. (Thus when one sees his beloved walking toward him on the street he may be seeing warmth and reassurance when he *should* be noticing bored indifference, a prelude to breaking up.)

3) *Fads.* We may project the labels "acceptable" or "unacceptable" onto styles and actions that are "in" or "out," respectively. (When I was growing up, the crewcut was considered manly and highly attractive to women; boys wore it proudly. Now, the "in" crowd would find it laughable, possibly even indicative of the wearer's overdone attempt to proclaim his masculinity.)

4) *Morality.* Early upbringing and training as well as the thinking of the groups we later join cause us to store up moral labels, which we project onto people and events. (I'm not trying to suggest that morality doesn't truly exist, but all of us need to be acutely aware of the personal factors that underlie a good many moral judgments.)

5) *Language.* We grow so accustomed to certain words that we make the mistake of thinking they refer to external realities when they actually point to internal attitudes. (People swear up and down that a certain kind of event happened, but they'll use terms that can't possibly have any objectivity. They'll say they saw "this suspicious looking man" or "this brassy blonde—ya know the type—bottomofthebarrel." Then there's the famous story about the defendant on the witness stand, who, after listening to the judge's long lecture on the importance of leaving slanted and evaluative terms out of a court of law, nodded as if with understanding and said, "Yeah, but the guy really did double-cross me!")

6) *Empathy.* You may identify so completely with someone that you project yourself right into the person's shoes. (Sex movies

would have no public at all if it weren't for this phenomenon, and what about the millions of young women who are annually crowned Miss America? or the movie fans who win the Oscars? "May I have the envelope, please? And the winner is. . . .")

7) *Habitual Lying*. This isn't so much a sign of a moral lapse in people as it is the result of mental laziness. There are times when all of us just don't take the time to get all the facts, and we make up the ones we aren't sure of. But the habitual liar is someone who has discovered how easy it is to be lazy and careless about the truth and how uncritical most listeners are. After a while he automatically turns on the projector and describes vividly a whole flock of things that he truly believes happened. He is likely to become hopeless if ever he gets into a spot where his uncanny ability to lie saves his skin.

8) *Glittering ideals*. As I indicated above, people often mistake the pleasure motive for idealism, but there is a considerable difference. The idealist, in this sense of the term, isn't so much concerned about his own immediate pleasures as he is about affirming the truth of his ideals. He will even give up some pleasure as long as he doesn't have to denounce an ideal, which can be defined as a highly abstract concept to which one maintains a stubborn loyalty. (Some mothers nurture the concept of the "nice girl" for a daughter and experience much anguish when the reality doesn't seem to measure up to the ideal. But all such ideals make *advance demands* on reality in an all-or-nothing way. Also in this category are high-sounding, noble-minded concepts like Americanism, brotherhood, and progress.)

The following is a most perceptive short story, again by a student, written in response to an assignment calling for any treatment of the subject of the games played by glittering idealists.[3]

MURDER IN CENTRAL PARK

"Harry Scher."
"Present."
"George Wolperto."
"Here."
"Abe Garfinkel."
"Present."
"That's fine boys, 8 A.M. and all fifteen present and accounted for. Now line up in formation over there by the wall and we'll do a quick inspection of your gear."
Frank West looked old. His six-foot frame was slightly off

[3] Printed by permission of the author, A. E. Rosenthal.

center and he grimaced as he forced his shoulders to a more soldierly stature. His scoutmaster's uniform was clean and freshly ironed but the edges of his bulky pockets were badly frayed. His shoes were brightly polished but viewed from the rear showed heels worn to a curve.

"I want each of you boys to take out your check list and go over each item and see that you have everything with you. If you have forgotten something or were unable to get it, let me know before we start. Even though we are going to spend our jamboree in Central Park this year doesn't mean you can get careless with your camping gear. I want every scout here to be just as prepared for any emergency as if he were going off up in the mountains like we did in previous years. Remember, it took a lot of talking and hard work to get Mayor Lindsay to give us his OK to camp in Central Park. The police have even roped off a spot for us where we will be out of sight of the city and as far as the jamboree is concerned we will have just as much fun and learn just as much as the kids who camped in the mountains.

"Everything checked OK? Now what's the matter with you, George? What did you forget?"

"Toilet paper, sir."

"It's too late to run home now. You'll have to manage without toilet paper somehow. OK, Pinky, you can loan George part of your roll when he needs it. Now, up with your gear, sling it over your shoulders and off we go!"

"Come on, George, don't try walking the curb, just fall in with the other boys and keep in formation."

The streets of Williamsburg were hot and dusty but the boys marched smartly along, following their scoutmaster in his every move.

"Now, listen closely," Mr. West was saying. "I'm going to pass out a nickel to each of you. Stick together, put your own coin in the turnstile and line up on the platform and wait there for me. I don't want any of you getting on the wrong train like George did last year." A loud roll of laughter passed along the line. George shrank a little lower into his oversized scout uniform.

"O.K., this is our train," Mr. West yelled above the din of the halting train. "Get aboard, get aboard!"

The B.M.T. seemed cool and dank and the boys enjoyed their respite from the punishing heat of Williamsburg. At 59th and Fifth Mr. West gathered his flock and soon had them marching parade fashion right up the shady side of the Avenue. Turning left into the park they marched and marched until Mr. West made an abrupt turn and they found themselves facing a small lake.

"We'll pitch our pup tents right here," Mr. West said. "Then I want each and everyone of you to turn in and get a little rest before we start our activities. We'll take the rest of the morning to get our camp shipshape, then we'll have chow. This afternoon I'm going to give you a lecture on how to become an American. I mean a 100% American MAN. And I want you boys to listen to every word I say. Because when I'm thru you will know what it means to be an upright, honest, truthful and loyal citizen of these great United States."

Mr. West's lecture was longer than the boys had anticipated. Their restlessness began to annoy him and he showed it with frowns and scowls that managed, somehow to keep the boys in check.

"I think we are going to have a storm this afternoon," he went on. "Look at those heavy black clouds piling up over there in the west."

Thunder and lightning took over where Mr. West left off.

"Come on," he yelled, "I don't want anyone in their pup tents in this downpour. We've got a good place to stay dry over there under that rock ledge. Just follow me."

The boys gathered around their idol and pressed as hard as they could against the face of the rock that had been hollowed out until it almost presented a cave-like entrance.

"Remember what I told you out there," Mr. West shouted above the din of the thunder, "Americans are brave and no one shivers because of a thunderstorm. But this is really quite a blow. Can hardly see the lake out there any more."

At this point the boys saw a tiny figure pass almost in front of their hiding place. It was swathed in black tatters and little rivers of rain spouted from every torn shred.

"What's she doing out in this storm? She'll die or something," said George.

The boys stared with astonishment as the tiny woman eased her way down the slope to the water's edge. She knelt down as though in prayer. From the inner recesses of her drenched shroud she brought forth a sopping bundle of newspapers which she slowly unrolled. Carefully she scooped up a handful of breadcrumbs and tossed them into the water.

Wheeling in a precision maneuver, a flock of ducks and geese headed for their afternoon meal. "There," Mr. West shouted to his scouts, "there is an example of true Americanism. This little woman braves the dangers of the storm to bring food and nourishment to her little feathered friends. I want you boys to always remember this scene. This is a fine example of what I have been preaching to you at every meeting and at every jamboree."

The ducks were swimming closer to shore. The next offering was tossed right at the lake edge. A skinny hand shot from the ragged sleeve, it dipped for a second and returned to view with the neck of a slithering pintail envised in its fingers. With a deft twist of the other hand the duck's head snapped and it hung limp.

Mr. West said nothing.

A. E. Rosenthal

EXERCISES

1. Analyze your own tendencies to project yourself out into the world—to play the Cinema Game—and not recognize that you are at those times seeing and responding not to reality but to yourself. Use the nine different sources of projection that were cited in the text (adding any others that you may think of). You can probably get a paper out of any of them.

   Some possibilities:

   a) *Self-preservation* or *self-interest*. Illustrate how your background or current orientation determine many evaluations you make; doesn't a poor person, for example, interpret a wealthy person's apparent refusal to contribute to a certain cause as a sign of "indifference"? may not a wealthy person interpret the growing numbers on welfare rolls as a sign of "laziness" and "lack of ambition"?

   b) *Buckpassing*. Read Alice Lee's "Joanne" and then think of a particular person whose "faults" you can analyze as efficiently, "faults" that you fear are your own but that you don't want to admit to.

   c) *Pleasure*. Think of a time when your love of well-being caused you to interpret an action in only one way. I know a lady of considerable academic achievement and esteem who plays the part of Pollyanna whenever possible; she interpreted the riots during the Democratic convention in Chicago in 1968 as "glorious signs of the democratic process at work."

d) *Desire.* Describe an incident that shows that you wanted something to happen so badly that somehow it did. Have you ever lost somebody very close to you, a parent, a relative, or friend, and seen him somewhere again so clearly you could have sworn it was not an hallucination? or wished, for some reason, to find proper grounds to support an instinctive dislike for somebody else and "miraculously" discovered you could?

e) *Fads.* Think of some things you currently consider "in"—such as wearing "freaked-out" clothes or using almost exclusively a vocabulary of fashionable phrases such as "freaked-out"—and some things you consider "out"—such as terms that the far-out crowd no longer considers in—and decide which ones you value mainly because of the importance of group approval.

f) *Morality.* This is one of the most difficult of all "projection areas" to be truly honest about. Try, anyway, to take one of your strongest moral convictions, such as having reservations about birth control or endorsing liberalized abortion legislation, and see whether you can trace it to a source in your early upbringing or the general thinking of a group to which you currently belong and that tends to influence your moral evaluations. You may even find wheels within wheels (if you are in favor of legalized abortion, the reason may actually be a rejection of the morality of your parents). This isn't to suggest that moral labels are not yours to bestow as you please, but don't you want to know why you respond in some cases as you do?

g) *Language.* Think of one or two occasions on which you got into a hassle only to discover in retrospect that language was the cause of it all (the extreme example I know of is the one where a man shot his best friend to death because the latter called the man's dog a "mutt"). Your illustrations should teach the reader how important it is to make a clear separation between words that most can agree represent objective reality and those that state only personal opinions. (What do you do, for example, when someone says "Bring me the pretty chair"?) Describe an incident or two in which your confusion about the direction of language reference got you into trouble and taught you the lesson you now want to communicate to the reader.

h) *Empathy.* Think of a specific incident in which you identified so completely with someone else that you weren't really seeing another person but were, instead, really responding to yourself; an incident in which you may have gotten your ears flattened by assuming certain things about this person. Someone with a minority-group background may, for example, interpret another's behavior in terms of his own cultural heritage—and may be disastrously misinterpreting him.

i) *Habitual lying.* Offer a couple of actual situations that, as you look back now, were responsible for your later career in lying or "mental laziness." Did you ever, for example, try to brighten up a drab, dull day by "improving" upon a certain happening and adding things that never happened at all? Did you ever discover when you were in a spot (like being called on the carpet for excessive absences) that a slight bending of the truth saved you? Indicate how you feel about lying now, especially when, in your opinion, it does little harm? (*Optional:* reverse the subject and do a paper on the difficulties you have encountered from telling the truth on occasions when a lie might have saved you. Are you glad now that you did? or do you believe you were foolish? Try to go from the particular instance to a generalization about the role of honesty and consistent truth-telling in day-to-day life.)

j) *Glittering ideals.* Narrate some incident in which your clinging to a high-minded principle caused you to completely misread someone or some event. How about an occasion when your idealistic views got you into trouble, such as finding out that what you thought was a beautiful gathering of beautiful people had "become" a pot party or a sex orgy? or an occasion when you suddenly found that a close friend didn't really represent a beautiful principle at all? or an occasion when you yourself committed some harm to someone else unwittingly, by acting in accordance with an idealistic motive? An example of the latter might be the excessively right-minded white person who always makes black people feel uncomfortable by singling them out and making them appear "special," or the son or daughter who tries out of love for his parents to bridge the generation gap and explain his attitudes only to have the effort seem like open rebellion and bring about even deeper wounds. This last possibility could yield big results in a paper, for much family strife undoubtedly stems from idealism, on both sides of the gap.

An interesting variation of this exercise would be to take one event you experienced that involved some strong reactions on your part—such as a demonstration or counter-demonstration or family fight—and run it through as many of the ten projection sources listed above as you can. This is valuable to do because very often more than one motive is involved. In a family fight, for example, one may be concerned with self-interest; he may pass the buck in order to preserve his image; he may be following a fad; he usually gets enmashed in a web of language; and, certainly, the quarrel may involve idealism.

2. Select some individual whose characteristic way of thinking and reacting to events is familiar to you. Think about this person for a while, jotting down as many examples as you can find of how he or she uses projection. Use the ten sources of projection as basic guidelines. Write your paper, trying, if possible, to make some generalizations about the person's natural "style" of projecting. Does he or she make many moral projections? Does he or she get confused about language? Is this person mainly concerned about his own pleasure or his own self-interest without realizing it? Try to make an interesting case for the reader. Try to choose a subject who doesn't recognize the frequency with which he projects, preferably a subject who actually believes he is a clear-headed, objective thinker.

Optional: use two people as your subjects. Write a paper describing a specific incident or a number of specific incidents in which they got into a hassle over some point and never knew that they were "cross-projecting."

Some possibilities here:

a) a mother projecting her moral code onto her child; the child projecting his own idealism onto the mother

b) a couple breaking up, and each one passing the buck to the other

c) a parent who wants to bridge the generations by empathizing with a hippie son or daughter; the latter widening the gap by projection from fads. You could make the paper really interesting by showing that both sides are working from self-interest and even the motive of pleasure.

3. Glittering idealism as a source of projection offers so many exciting possibilities for writing that it deserves an exercise all to itself. Possibly no kind of projecting is more dramatic or heartbreaking than this, because the idealist sees himself as being so noble and inspired that it sometimes becomes all but impossible ever to reach

him and make him understand the effects his noble actions are having.

One student, during a class discussion of the subject, related the story of how, when he was five years old, his father had insisted he learn to face reality and stop believing in Santa Claus. All night long before Christmas morning the father made him stay awake to see for himself that no Santa Claus would appear. He forced the boy to sit in a chair and watch while he himself unwrapped the Christmas toys and placed them under the tree. "I work hard for my money," the father patiently explained, "and it isn't fair that you should give the credit for these presents to a creature that doesn't exist." The next morning the boy sat at breakfast, listless and uninterested in either breakfast or the Christmas tree. The mother suggested to the father that the boy had had enough and should be allowed to play "like all normal children on Christmas day." But the idealistic father insisted the boy could not be excused from the table until he had satisfactorily completed the sentence, "There is no . . ." The boy did not seem to understand at first, but the father kept pounding on the table with the palm of his hand and threatening to keep the boy there until he gave the correct answer. After the father had screamed, "There is no . . ." for possibly a hundred times, the boy in weary desperation finally whispered, "There is no father."

Undoubtedly you have a storehouse of memories of the misguided actions of glittering idealists. If you have one that is powerful enough, turn it into a really dramatic situation, like the one I have summarized above.

4. When Lenin was acting as the architect of the Communist Revolution of 1917 in Russia, he made a statement, now famous, to explain the rationale of achieving social progress through violence: "The ends justify the means." Could this statement be applied to any cause that, in your opinion, may be motivated by the self-interest of a group but that will lead to the results they hope to achieve, especially when they assume such results will benefit humanity as a whole? Here are a few questions that may start you thinking on this subject and lead to an interesting paper:

   a) Do you know enough about a particular movement to say that it started from self-interest but proved to be of value to the whole world? Does the Black Power movement belong in this category? Campus revolutions? The Women's Liberation movement?

   b) Are you yourself committed to a specific cause? Can you define it precisely? (Stopping war; integration; black nationalism; student rights; and so forth) Can you describe its goals and objectives accurately? Are these narrow or broad in the final analysis? That is, would eventual success, or even partial success, profit only some groups, or all of humanity?

c) Have any acts of violence already been committed in the interest of the cause you support? What are some of them? Were they inevitable: that is, could they have been avoided? Are you sorry or glad they happened?

d) Do you personally believe it is all right to blow up a bridge or a building as a strong act of protest if you are convinced there is no other way to advance your cause?

e) Do people who advocate such violence have the right to decide what changes should be made?

f) Assuming that violence can often be a dynamic agent of change, does the fact that change has been forced in this manner indicate that there would have been no other way to bring it about?

g) If a violent act is committed in the interest of a cause that was fundamentally good, does the violence indicate that something has gone wrong? Or, to put the matter another way: do you believe deeds of violence can set off a chain reaction that can't be controlled and can't possibly guarantee the success of any cause?

h) Is such a thing as "controlled violence" possible?

i) Would you hijack a plane or take control of a ship on the high seas if you were an agent of a foreign government and the action might benefit your country?

j) What about the United States' policy of continuing to rush to the defense of smaller nations that seem to be in danger of being taken over by Communist regimes? The preservation of United States prestige and the security of its military position in the world are the usual defenses of policy. But just see what continuing warfare has done at home to undermine morale. Is this a case of the end justifying the means? Or is there no end that can justify *these* means? (Additional thought for a paper on this subject: is the United States actually trying to impose her own system of government on the entire world? Is this end desirable or not? What about the belief that freedom is not simply one out of many possible systems but the humane condition under which all mankind should live? Do you think "all mankind" can handle freedom? What about the loss of freedom created by the desire to preserve freedom? the draft? the fact that the President has the right to send troops into a foreign country without getting a mandate from the governed?)

You can easily get a paper out of any one of these questions, or even a portion of one.

HANGUPS

The word hangup is a fairly new one, but the condition it describes is as old as man's dawning self-awareness. We've already talked about Greek mythology (Chapter 4, in relation to the advertising and entertainment media), and what were the ancient myths but stories about some hung-up people? Hera, queen of the gods, was so endlessly jealous of her husband's earthly philandering that she spent most of her time figuring out ways of getting even. Aphrodite, goddess of love, was more than a little hung up on the joys of getting together with men, and this obsession with physical encounters proved to be her undoing on more than one occasion. The Greek tragedies represent a procession of catastrophes brought on by hangups. In fact, when you stop to think about it, what do most writers find to write about but this very subject?

As its label implies, a hangup is something that preoccupies us: a loved one, a new car, a house, a trip to Europe, a new fad, a game we love to play, even a routine we like to follow. For one reason or another, it grips our fancy, and seizes our imagination; it directs our thinking to the extent that we find rational ways to justify it. It is like a newborn infant, thinking itself to be the most important thing in all the world. It demands our full attention, and, when we don't give in, it may scream and carry on until we do.

The hangup, like projection, is not necessarily a bad thing. What is a great artist but someone who gets hung up in the extreme on a certain project and will give himself no rest until he has finished it? Wasn't Michelangelo's ambition to do the Sistine Chapel a mighty hangup for which all of us are the richer? Great achievements in science are also the results of certain hangups, nagging convictions about something that lesser men and women might have renounced, especially after early setbacks. Pierre and Eve Curie offer a notable example. Radium might never have been discovered had these two scientists not persisted in their attempts to find a radioactive element they were convinced existed, despite the ridicule of many of their colleagues. Would Stanley have found Livingston if he hadn't been hung up on the notion that the great benefactor was still alive somewhere in the heart of an unexplored continent?

But the hangup can be treacherous too. It can become a security blanket we cling to, and, when we cover our heads with it to hide ourselves from the world, it can blind us to reality. When someone becomes firmly convinced he is right—like the policeman who sees himself as a great protector of society or the protestor who sees himself as a glorious martyr in the cause of freedom and justice—he can cling so tenaciously to his views that he starts seeing only what he wants to see and hearing only what feeds and nurtures his hangup. He becomes frozen and rigid; he becomes a walking stereotype. To such a policeman, all protestors and rioters may be no-good punks and degenerates. To such a protestor, all policemen may be pigs.

The reason we all get hung up—some more than others, but no one is exempt—is that human nature is basically conservative (not in the political sense of the term). It is difficult for anyone to be critical of himself. It is entirely human to want to preserve the interior status quo. "How can I possibly be a better person?" each says to himself. "It is obviously the world that is wrong, not me." It is easier for the alcoholic to suppose he alone is sober and the rest of the world is drunk. It is easier for the obsessive-compulsive person to suppose the rest of the world is lazy and shiftless. It is easier for the acquisitive materialist to believe others would sell him down the river for a nickel and that, to defend himself, it is necessary to make as much money as possible, than it is to believe he may be a victim of an insatiable need for luxury. It is easier for the person who engages in violence to claim he is only "getting the others before they get me" than it is to consider the possibility that he may really *enjoy* being violent.

Your hangup is the thing you know how to explain and defend. It is the thing you would not like to give up or see changed. When it leads to creative results, when it yields rich dividends that profit not only you but others as well, it can be a blessing. When it creates continual friction between you and the rest of the world, generating tension, sometimes even violent eruptions, then it may be something less than a blessing. It's not always easy to tell. It takes persistent and determined effort to keep looking closely at the premises upon which we base our activities, to see whether we are not in fact getting hung up on something that may eventually prove to be a mistake.

Very dynamic people, those who make their presence felt and exert great influence, sometimes get trapped in a whole complex of hangups. It becomes all but impossible for them to reverse the direction of their lives or see clearly where they may be going sour and heading for trouble. Sometimes they know something is wrong, but they know they are accomplishing much good and so they lack the determination to make any drastic alterations in their life styles. The result? The hangups compound themselves, and these people become increasingly rigid and one-tracked in their outlook and purposes. Let's examine an actual case.

The Story of Helen Farnsbee

Helen Farnsbee lives in a small but historic town north of Boston. It was founded in sixteen-something or other, boasts not one but three antiquarian societies, and has a plaque every few feet advising the visitor that on this very spot Isaac Gebney unsuccessfully tried to ward off an Indian ambush. In this town the leaves change color on September 15 at exactly high noon, the snow falls early in the morning every December 22, and spring arrives precisely three and a half weeks late. You can't buy land here until one of the three historical associations has investigated your family background; you can't build a house until the bank has decided you are a healthy economic risk; and you practically incur the death penalty if you decide your dwelling place will have a modern look.

Helen Farnsbee not only lives here, she is positively central to the town's functioning. To my knowledge she is the only townswoman to have been elected to all three historical societies. She is the chairman of the Town Beautiful Association and the Library Board of Trustees. She is a member of the hospital board, the school board, the law enforcement board, and the censorship board. Aside from all this, she is married to the town's only Congregational minister, and the Congregationalists here outnumber all other denominations by a considerable margin. As a result, Helen is virtually central to the town's religious life.

The meteoric success of Congregationalism is largely Helen's doing. Before she returned from ten years of education and agreed to marry her childhood sweetheart, now a minister, she was aware that the town had been dominated by the Presbyterians from time immemorial. But college had so liberalized Helen (who admits to having been narrow-minded before going away) that she decided to change the whole atmosphere of her town or live elsewhere. She and her husband set to work making converts, and within two years after her marriage, Helen could point with pride to the Herculean accomplishment of having overturned several centuries of tradition in, relatively speaking, a few minutes. If you have the idea that Helen was a dynamo set loose on a defenseless community, you are absolutely right.

But that was years ago. Helen's dynamism at this early stage of her career was nothing more than a slight breeze compared with the typhoons she has been generating ever since. The one thing Helen fears is becoming a typical minister's wife, and she has dedicated herself to scrubbing off the slightest trace of stereotype every time it appears. "No one is in a better position to hang loose," she once remarked. "After all, I don't have a doctorate in psychology for nothing. I haven't worked four years in a clinic to learn how to bake cookies for a Sunday School picnic."

Not that Helen can't bake with the best of them. Some of her recipes have won prizes at fairs, and among her publications she is justly proud of her *Old New England Cookbook*. But, she argues, almost anyone can bake successfully if she sets her mind to it. Almost anyone can write a cookbook if she forces herself to the typewriter. *She* has much to say not only to her town, but to all of American society. She has opinions on the generation gap, the use of drugs, sex education in the schools, the meaningful preservation of law and order, neuroses and psychoses, how to lead a happy and useful life after forty, and how to raise a large family on a minister's salary.

Oh yes, Helen believes in babies and prides herself on the ease with which she can bring healthy and strong children into this world. She has given birth to six of her own babies and adopted three others, one of whom is black as a signal to her town that she will not desist until she has totally eradicated every last vestige of prejudice and discrimination.

Helen Farnsbee is now forty-two years old. Her life adheres to the most efficient and beautiful schedule ever devised by the human brain. She cooks for her family, bakes bread for church socials, changes diapers, works at her numerous professional jobs, and proves loving and affectionate to the parson (after hours) with breathtaking skill and even enthusiasm. She has even managed to become part-time director of a free mental health clinic by deciding that her figure, understandably grown ample, can do without its lunch quite nicely, and this affords her two more hours in the day which she can now devote to straightening out the hangups of other people.

Helen is perhaps as knowledgeable about hangups as anyone has been since Freud. As you might have guessed, she is a compulsive reader. After her hour and a quarter of spontaneous love-making with the parson, who promptly falls asleep, she switches on a specially designed night lamp over the large double bed (Helen believes twin beds will wreck a marriage faster than anything else) and devours the journals of psychology and psychiatry for all the latest theories and methods.

I met Helen during a two-week Human Relations Laboratory conducted by a university not far from her home town. The purpose of the lab was to see whether sixty people, representing a cross-section of the population, could become an ideal society through a certain kind of training. This is sometimes called "sensitivity training," and it means that you sit around for hours at a time, talking together: at first superficially, with everyone being as phony and defensive as possible, and then, ideally, more honestly, with people one by one coming out of their shells and leveling with the group. The theory behind this training is that people will get along better if they understand each other completely. Ignorance is the source of distrust.

At the outset Helen assumed the position of leader of the training group (or T-Group) to which I had been assigned. She pointed out the nature of the experiment and warned everyone of the dangerous consequences of turning a T-Group meeting into a therapy session. As a professional psychologist, she announced, she would not sit idly by and allow nonprofessionals to conduct a workshop that might lead to nervous breakdowns and other forms of mental illness. Her own purpose in being there, she avowed, was to observe clinically how people behaved in groups. When our group trainer, a mild-mannered Japanese who hardly ever said a word but who kept watching Helen with fascination, asked whether she herself might have a hangup or two she'd like to get rid of, she merely smiled condescendingly, as if to say that it's not possible to have a hangup when you work as diligently at living as she had done.

One night our trainer said we would try something nonverbal. All each of us had to do was stand up in the center of the group, close his eyes, and fall backward. The purpose of this exercise is to see whether you really trust people. It's really against nature to relax and let yourself just go kerplunk without looking to make sure you won't dash your brains out on some piano leg. Nonetheless, all of us managed to summon up the courage and found—amazingly!—that people won't let you kill yourself. That is, everyone but Helen. She refused to take part in the game. Her first reason was that she thought her weight might prove troublesome. Her second was that unconscious destructive impulses sometimes came to the surface during games. Her third was that actual participation would violate her own decision to be an objective observer. But I realized for the first time that Helen basically didn't trust anybody. Did she even *like* anybody?

Why had she come to the lab? Was it really to observe? Or was she hoping someone would pull the masks off, layer by layer, and uncover the frightened, lonely woman underneath? With the clue she had given us, our T-Group got to work on Helen and found that her chief hangup was a total inability to believe others were as capable as she of getting any job done. Her ridiculously high I.Q. had been her worst enemy since her youth. It had been a demon, driving her on to accomplish one task after another, not really for the sake of the task itself, but for the sake of proving to herself that nothing, *nothing* was impossible for her.

Yes, we tried to show her, she loved people and wanted sincerely to help them. But on her terms, not on theirs. Sometimes that isn't the way to do it. Sometimes you have to hang back and let people help themselves. Helen's household was what they call a "tight ship," but was the crew really trusted? Didn't the captain have to be in on every crisis and play the major role in making every decision?

Helen finally recognized in herself a compulsion to do everything for people. But this, she argued, only meant that she was a born leader and born leaders had to carry heavier burdens than others. Where would the community and her family be without her? Would she consider changing? Heavens, no! Change??? From what to what? To what avail? Helen finally went home from the training lab, convinced that she had learned a great deal about people and would immediately update some of the methods she used at her clinic. She was convinced her experience had been a great success.

"Locked In"

Helen Farnsbee kept getting deeper and deeper into her life system until she became its prisoner. Her extraordinarily complex routine became her lord and master—not her husband, not even her own enthusiasm for living. You can find out to what degree this is true of you by thinking over the life routine you follow and trying to decide which elements in it you couldn't imagine giving up, which parts of your life you couldn't bear to live differently.

People who have had military service for any length of time are likely to exist within a whole complex of hangups without recognizing the fact. They have operated with a routine for so long they have become the routine. They have exchanged their identities for the system itself. Does not the routine-bound office worker run the same risk? the telephone operator? the professor who has specialized in one subject for forty-three years, rides a bicycle to the campus at eight-thirty every morning, walks to the same lecture hall, and opens his notebook to read from stiffened, yellowed pages? even the groovy student who says "Hey, man!" nine thousand times a day, meets the same friends in the same corner of the Student Union, plays the same records on the jukebox, and indulges in the same round of anti-Establishment complaints?

If you work, can you imagine taking a different job? If you hang out at the Student Union, can you imagine a different circle of friends? a different mode of dress? expressing different sentiments about the Establishment? Can you imagine changing your major? your girl-friend or boyfriend? adopting a new set of parents? living in a different part of the country? changing the color of your skin? (If you're proud of being black, could you bear to be white? If you're white but sympathize or even work for the Black Power movement, can you think of yourself as black?) What about changing your religion? changing your moral code? Could you become a nudist?

Go up to a child and ask, "Can two and two ever be five? Can a dog be a cat? Can mommy be a tree in the back yard?" and you will receive a giggle for your troubles, as well as a curious stare that questions your sanity. Children are hung-up people in one sense. They cling to the few little things they're sure of.

But in another respect they have wild imaginations and can teach us a great deal about how to hang loose. Every day they transform their environment as it pleases them to. They assign new roles to their friends: "I died yesterday; you have to get killed today." They can even break relationships with a matter-of-factness that appalls their elders: "I hate Jimmy now. I don't play with him anymore."

When we grow up, we get mired in certain ruts. Sometimes we know it is happening, and we think we will change the patterns when we get around to it. But that old human fear of trying something different holds us fast, and the rut gets deeper every day. Before we know it, years have gone by. We have become total strangers to ourselves without realizing what has happened. We are locked in.

EXERCISES

1. Use Helen Farnsbee as a typical example of a person caught in a stifling network of hangups and so far gone that he believes his life to be nearly perfect. (Remember: the whole idea behind the hangup is that one can't imagine giving it up or living life in any other manner.) Think about someone who is very much like Helen, though his life style may be totally different. Think about this person very carefully for a couple of days. Get to know him in your mind. Whenever you think of an interesting and revealing fact or anecdote about him, jot it down, until you have enough material to do a stimulating portrait of him on paper. Use any form you wish: fiction, article, poem, short play. Your aim is to hold the reader's attention with a study of a man or woman who appears to have everything or thinks he has everything but who is perhaps missing a good deal.

A suggestion: work your paper up to a conclusion in which the character you have chosen either recognizes what is wrong with his life or else completely misses the point, remaining blind to his hangups.

2. Observe someone you know very well, such as your mother, father, brother, sister, or roommate. Study this person for a period of several days with an eye to making note of what his hangups are and *how he reveals them*. The emphasis in this assignment is on the methods by which hangups make themselves known.

Some sample notes you may jot down:

a) *Sister*   CLOTHES: fads—bizarre outfits—doesn't seem comfortable in them but probably can't escape conformity to her group. APPEARANCE: tons of makeup—weird sometimes—phony eyelashes—wigs—green eyeshadow, and so forth—always changing hair color—wonder what she really looks like now—spends half her life in front of bathroom mirror. WEIGHT: black coffee for breakfast—cottage cheese for lunch—a few bites for supper—constantly going into bathroom to weigh herself—is underweight anyway, as far as I can see—pretends weight is no concern when asked about it pointblank—must associate being thin with something desirable (perhaps belonging to the upper classes?)—even her boyfriend tells her she's skinny.

b) *Father*   SMOKING: does so constantly—always coughing and getting hoarse—*terribly worried* about what he might be doing to himself but can't stop—laughs it off—says "We've all got to go someday."
DEATH: I can see it's on his mind—terrible fear—won't use the word (says people "pass away")—won't discuss such practical matters as what will happen to the family after he "passes away"—has yet to make a will—says it's bad luck—but enjoys going to funerals of other people—I guess it makes him feel superior or lucky.
WEIGHT: getting paunchy and it bothers him—constantly going on diets "tomorrow"—has millions of books outlining fad and crash diets, but they're all phonies, telling you how to lose weight without giving up food and drink.
MASCULINITY: says he means to join a gym one of these days and start lifting weights "again"—when I was younger, he pushed me into the Boy Scouts, Little League baseball, and so on—constantly alluded to the good old days when he hit them out of the neighborhood park.

Since in this exercise you'll be talking about the how as well as the what of hangups, your paper should be quite vivid, full of actions and incidents, perhaps even fragments of conversations (if the subject reveals his hangups through what he says as well as what he does). If you wish, you may try to pull your observations together and come up with some conclusions about the *general character* of this person's hangups. For example, if your notes on your father were something like the sample ones, you might decide that the problems are all interrelated: that is, your father is caught between his love of lazy, "good" living and the terrific guilt complex so many American males develop when they think the penalty they are paying for the good life is flab, loss of masculinity, and bad health. A typical middle-aged American male in every respect, your father wants to play the game both ways: he wants to indulge himself and cling to his youth and his physique at the same time. The fear of death is probably tied in with the intensive materialism of the good life as well as the idea that death is the final insult to someone's masculine physique and youthful appearance.

Optional: This exercise could really yield big results. Don't stop here if you find yourself getting enthusiastic and eager to find out more and more about people from this viewpoint. Perhaps you will want to study your parents and their friends and do a Hangup Profile of their generation as typified in several special cases.

Perhaps you think of yourself as someone who tries at least to hang loose, but you're aware of some of your contemporaries who are hung up: for example, on pot, acid, sex, rock festivals, rock music, hair, and so on. If you wish, do a Hangup Profile of a certain segment of your own generation.

3. One way of approaching the truth of your hangups in a roundabout and less threatening manner is to play a little game in which you imagine yourself as having been convicted of a crime and told that your punishment is to be injected with a wonder drug that will turn you into a different person, with a whole new character and personality. (The drug was invented by a humanitarian chemist opposed to capital punishment.) Now: as you lie in your cell awaiting the fateful injection, you begin to think about those aspects of yourself that you will never, never know again.

You make a mental list of the habits and characteristics you won't mind saying "good riddance" to, such as waking up to a new day and not feeling ambitious or enthusiastic about it; not feeling concerned about your future, even if it means dropping out of school; losing your temper easily at other drivers on the road; gambling on anything, from a Presidential election to the number of hummingbirds in a tree. Incidentally, you'll discover that it's not easy to make up such a list. Most people are more than content with their own characters and find that, for some unaccountable reason, it's always the others who fail to make the grade.

Now undertake the much easier task of making a mental list of all the things about yourself you'd rather not see changed: the color of your hair and eyes; the color of your skin; the dimple on your cheek; your perfect weight; the way clothes look on you; your I.Q.; your cooking ability; your exquisite taste in members of the opposite sex; your musical ability. Make a list of the particular people you can't bear the thought of not recognizing anymore. Make a list of the activities you may never want to indulge in again once you become someone else, like reading, riding a motorcycle, dancing, going to parties, skindiving, or joining in protest marches.

From these lists you should be able to make a pretty accurate survey of your biggest hangups. Now, again, the fact that they are hangups doesn't mean they are necessarily bad. All great creative work, all social progress, all scientific advances were no doubt the result of somebody's hangups. But you can't have a grip on your identity without knowing what the hangups are.

Your paper can be imaginatively done: that is, you can pretend you are really lying in a jail cell awaiting the transformation, and the hangups are the thoughts that go through your mind.

Or you can do it "straight"; you can discuss your major hangups and, if you can, trace them to their probable source. Here's what one student wrote: "I find that for as long as I can remember I have been intrigued by strong authority figures and drawn to them only to rebel at the last minute. In school I tried to become the favorite if the teacher ruled the class with a firm hand, but, if the teacher was permissive and had poor discipline, I was the one that always thought of the tricks to play. With strong teachers I played along and was a perfect angel until the day came when I would decide that the teacher's discipline was too strict and the time had come for some real cutting up. I believe I must have been like this because I wanted my own father to be more of an authority figure in the house and he wasn't, but at the same time I was glad he wasn't; it meant I had freedom some of my friends were denied. Still, I envied them. Maybe I secretly thought somebody cared about them more."

4. Try, instead, a more lighthearted paper, aimed at providing the teacher and the class with a few chuckles. Think of a hangup that you know is silly and you'd love to get rid of but can't. Superstitions of all kinds fall into this category: refusing to walk under a ladder; throwing salt over your shoulder; running back half a block to take the same side of the lamppost your companion did. Base your paper on some actual incident in which your hangup got you into all sorts of amusing difficulties. Example: a person believes

in knocking on wood every time he "tempts fate." He is boarding an airplane after the "last call" announcement has been given. There is a little old lady next to him who voices fears about the plane's safety. The man finds himself saying "Don't be silly. There's no chance this plane can crash." When he realizes what he has said, he panics. He looks around wildly for some wood. Finding none, he turns around and all but knocks the other passengers down in his desperate haste. The stewardesses and maintenance crew look on in disbelief as the man goes frantically through the baggage on the cart for some wooden surface. He has scattered many pieces all over the ground before anyone gets to him, but he himself eludes capture. Instead he makes for the airport building and continues his frenzied search.

Perhaps the example is a trifle exaggerated, but I have known people who caused almost as much disruption for a similar reason. I myself have driven all over town for a certain ice cream flavor after a mad craving had taken hold of me. And I mean *all* over town. I spent hours; ruined a perfectly good evening. I kept going even after the craving had left me, probably because the elusiveness of the flavor had become a personal affront to my intelligence and stature. I was determined to prove that I was the flavor's master. I suppose such extreme actions belong under the heading of temporary insanity, and I suppose the hangup is where it all starts. At any rate, find the hangup that drove you to the nuttiest lengths and try to recapture the whole experience.

5. Quite a few years ago an American playwright who hadn't scored any really tremendous success in the theater visited his maiden aunts, and, on the way home, he allowed his imagination to have a little fun by trying to link the sweet old ladies to the most bizarre and outrageous behavior he could invent. His game provided him with the basis for *Arsenic and Old Lace*, an indestructible farce about two charming and genteel souls who "benefit" lonely old men by poisoning them and putting them out of their misery.

It is a perfectly healthy exercise for each of us to try to hang loose by imagining scandalous departures from our own life styles and patterns. Are you pretty square? That is, are you a well-organized person who does the work expected of him in school; helps around the house, serves on committees at the church, and so on? Is your hair neat and in place at all times; your clothes tidy; your feet planted firmly on the ground?

Well, why not, just for fun, break loose in your imagination? Surely there must be times when even the most satisfying routine gets to be a drag and you feel you would like, if only for a single day, to live a totally different manner. How would you do it?

a) The alarm clock goes off at precisely seven-fifteen, and you throw it promptly out the window.

b) Your mother comes to your room to remind you of an important exam in geology for which you had stayed up very late studying. You inform her groggily that you want to miss the test even though you know you can pass it easily.

c) You make it down to breakfast, dressed in a totally new style. (Make up something weird.) Your mother is horrified, but you quickly cause her to forget your clothes as you launch into a long speech in which you detail her every fault.

d) Eventually you climb onto your flashy new Honda and take off in a squeal of tires for a little tour of the neighborhood.

Take it from here. Your imagination can have a field day. Do you scrawl little mottoes on the windshield of the minister's car? Do you go back to your high school for a visit with your old teachers, so they can see how well you have turned out? While you're there, do you point out a few outmoded and decaying things in their educational system? Do you eventually make it to the college campus in time to lead a sit-in, a strike against classes, a burning-of-the-books ritual?

If nothing else, such an exercise is good "soul therapy." It's good to think now and then about being completely different. It *can* prevent some hangups from getting a strong hold on you.

Optional: Do a variation of the above exercise by making yourself into an imaginary character who decides to alter his behavior without warning. Describe some encounters he has with various establishments that have rigid expectations of his behavior: the mother, the minister, the professor, the coach, the employer. Perhaps his attempt to break away fails because the establishments won't let it happen. Perhaps the mother goes on treating him with gushy indulgence even though he is wearing weird clothes and behaving strangely. Wouldn't that be frustrating? Can't you hear the mother now? "Now, dear, if you want to go to school in the nude, why you just go ahead and do it. You're my baby, and whatever you do is all right with me." "But mother, I despise your indulgence. I despise you as a matter of fact." "That's perfectly normal, my dear. It says so in the Child Guide Book."

MASK-WEARING

> All the world's a stage,
> And all the men and women merely players,
> They have their exits and their entrances.
> And one man in his time plays many parts.

Since the very beginning, men have indulged in theatrics. They have confused reality by play-acting and the wearing of masks. They have painted their bodies and worn strange adornments. They have delighted in exchanging their everyday selves for fantasy characters, as when primitive peoples played hunting games and some dressed up like animals and were symbolically killed or when they performed human sacrifices and perhaps got rid of the blood guilt by putting on masks and pretending "other people" were doing it all.

Whatever the reasons for putting off one self and assuming another, human beings appear to come by the skill naturally and with the greatest of ease. That's why, when we talk about hangups and the possibility of imagining oneself as leading a different life, we mustn't forget that there's no such creature as *the* self, which must be changed or left alone. In reality each of us is made up of many selves, assumed for a great variety of reasons. In fact, when we speak of mask-wearing, we probably shouldn't think of ourselves as putting one mask after another over a "real" face. It may be closer to the truth to think of peeling masks off endlessly and never reaching the point where we can say, "And now will the real Mr. or Miss *Me* please rise?" Maybe our identities are equal to our collection of masks. It's a thought anyway.

The Big Put-On

We come now to the most embarrassing and possibly painful section of the entire book. I tried to be as clever as possible and slip it in without a great deal of fanfare, but I might as well confess at the outset that the reader is about to come face to face with the question to end all questions: WHO ARE YOU ANYWAY?

Let's face it: we all play the identity game. Perhaps this very book is doing just that. We cry out that we want to be "the real us," and we talk endlessly about integrity, as though the self were the fundamental, universal, indivisible unit of reality; a truth beyond which it is impossible to go. But maybe we're really talking about *selves*.

In the space of a single day everyone has enough selves to cast a dramatic production of major proportions. If you are a student living at home, you "enjoy" a certain kind of relationship with your mother, father, brothers and sisters, next-door neighbors, close and distant relatives, strangers on the street, classmates, teachers, deans, shopkeepers, policemen, and, above all, your very closest and confidential friends.

Each of us is like Thespis, the ancient Greek said to have been the world's first actor. Thespis played all the parts in the plays he wrote by the simple expedient of changing masks. The difference is that he probably limited himself to a couple of personalities, whereas each of us carries around a whole trunkful of masks.

To try to list every possible reason for the mask-wearing we do almost every waking moment of our lives would be impossible, but there are four that strike me as being universal. The first is that *honesty is not the best policy*. It is easier to say or do what will create the least amount of trouble than to pursue a completely honest course. We put people on because we don't believe it pays to do anything else.

Very few people want or can stand the truth as a regular diet, and all of us know that instinctively. "How do you like my new furniture?" asks the host who has graciously invited us to dinner. What can one say? "It looks like you hit the clearance sales at the state penitentiary"?

The great short story writer H. H. Munro, who used the penname of Saki, wrote a tale called "Tobermory" about a cat that learns how to talk without learning all the complex intrigue involved in human relationships. Tobermory thinks it's all a simple matter of telling people the complete and exact truth. The humans of the story are charmed and delighted at first by this novelty without quite realizing all the private things a cat knows about everyone. They soon find out. Tobermory tells everyone what everybody else says about him behind his back. In his candor he reveals all the adultery, shady deals, and hypocrisy of which the world is capable. It is disarming honesty, and Tobermory is assassinated in order to preserve that world. Without fraud and deceit human society cannot function, so the author tells us.

The second reason for mask-wearing lies in *the very way society functions*. None of us can exist alone. The groups to which we belong determine to a great extent the various roles we play, the various masks we wear. Before we know what is happening to us, we are born into a family group. Then we belong to neighborhood and school gangs, often to more than one, with each making claims upon us and causing us to behave in ways acceptable to its traditions. In later life our marriage is one grouping; our office associations form another; outside circles of friends, still others; not to mention the old family group that may still see us as children. (Everyone must know at least one person over thirty who is still called Sonny or Junior or Patsy Ann.)

The group constitutes a whole that is greater than the sum of its individual members. It develops a character and nature of its own through the mysterious laws of group chemistry, and these in turn influence and shape the thinking and behavior of each member to a greater or lesser degree, depending upon the amount of time he spends with the group, the relative importance to him of being accepted by the group, and the attraction held for him by rival groups. But even a minor group—such as "the fellas" down at the "Y" with whom John T. Bixterhoff lifts weights once a month—will supply him with yet another mask to add to his collection. At least once a month he will swagger, swear, tell dirty jokes, and afterwards put away a few quarts of beer with his "buddies." Then it's off to home and the resumption of his duties as model husband, father, and citizen of the community.

A Day in the Life of Bob Winslow

A third explanation for the mask-wearing habits of us human beings is *expediency*, the demands made by circumstances themselves. We can try to walk a straight line, try to plan each day so that it can be lived consistently and with integrity, but as sure as the sun must rise, things will happen to force us to put on and take off any number of masks.

Let us imagine the case of Bob Winslow, aged eighteen, a freshman at Brently College, and, with his parents, a resident of an upper-middle-class suburban community called Pinewood Heights. Bob is good-looking, well groomed, popular, a B student at school, polite, and well mannered—a product of what is called "good breeding." He ought to grow into a man of some stature and means and will probably marry a charming and poised woman; together they will raise two or three handsome and well-behaved children and become well known in Pinewood Heights as a couple to be admired, respected, and counted on to help in community affairs. Bob will become the "very picture of respectability" and "the soul of honesty." And it will all be true, except that he will be the wearer of many masks.

On this crisp October morning he awakens to the first day of the week and lies in bed, collecting his thoughts and remembering what has to be done that day. The first order of business, of course, is to find Diane, a girl he's been dating for several months, and tell her frankly that it's over. He's met Barbara, who turns him on in a way that Diane doesn't, and he might as well be completely honest about it.

Then there's the matter of the fraternity that's been rushing him. Got to tell them it's no deal. Too much homework, and that must come first. Besides, Barbara isn't impressed by frats, and she's right. Bunch of snobs. Practice discrimination, something he'd always been taught was wrong. If the frat wants to know why, he means to tell them the truth.

Finally, there's the matter of Dr. Williams, his sociology prof, who gave him a B+ on a research paper but wrote on it, "Very interesting, but it sounds as if you may have used one or two sources you haven't given proper credit to. See me." Well, today Bob means to see him and straighten it all out. Yes, he had gotten the main idea from that master's thesis he'd run across in the card catalog, but, for one thing, he wasn't at all sure anyone was supposed to use footnotes for unpublished work. He'd meant to ask Dr. Williams but never got around to it. True, Bob's conscience is a little embarrassed about the whole bit, but he intends to tell the truth and give the credit to the thesis. Just a little oversight, Bob; nothing serious; your grade still stands; thanks for coming in.

Bob sits having breakfast. His mother and father exchange glances uncomfortably. Nobody speaks until finally the mother breaks the silence. "By the way, Bob, while I was cleaning your room yesterday, I happened to see a paper on your desk, one you'd written for . . ." Oh, that. Nothing, mother, really. Just a misunderstanding on my part. (*What right does she have to read what's on my desk anyway?*) Did he do what? STEAL A PAPER??? "Mother, I'm insulted you'd even ask me such a question." (*Do they think I'll risk losing their good opinion of their darling boy at this point? Never happen.*)

Bob catches sight of Diane waiting for him outside Greenway Hall. She smiles and waves. (*Now why does she have to look so glad to see me?*) Sure, she's pretty and all, so well dressed, always so in fashion without ever being extreme about it. But she's square. She's a typical WASP (white Anglo-Saxon protestant) and there's nothing she can do about it. He means to tell her right now and get *that* off his mind. (*Look here, Diane, you might as well know it, I'm going out with Barbara now. She swings, you know what I mean?*) "Bob, I've been frantic, why haven't you . . . ?" "I meant to, Diane, I really did. Been busy—the frat and all." "I understand, and I'm so proud of you for making Kappa Phi. It's just the *in* frat." She kisses him on the cheek, and he senses the delicate fragrance of one of those rare, expensive perfumes Diane's mother buys her in Paris. Before he knows it, he is making a date for Friday night.

"But Bob, I thought we had tickets for the rock festival Friday night." Barbara's lips turn downwards into a pout. He has, of course, forgotten the festival. It's important that he go, that he be seen there, especially with Barbara, the loner, the strange, brooding girl who plays a mysterious guitar and sings hypnotic, mystic songs of her own devising. He *must* be the one to take Barbara to the festival, if only to redeem himself for copping out on that protest march. (*But I was worried about Kappa Phi then.*) "You never told me you had an aunt coming in at the airport, Bob."

That settles it. The frat must go. He means to go there right now and scratch his name from the pledge list. High time too. All that humiliating subservience and running errands. Decadent, outmoded, meaningless tradition! "Glad to see you and Diane getting back together, Bob, old boy. I saw you from the stairs." "Oh, well, that was just . . ." "If you don't mind my saying so, that Barbara's a psycho. Dating her wasn't helping your image with the guys." (*Can you really think I give two cents for what the guys think?*) Hand-shaking all around. Congratulations, Bob, old man. You made the right choice. (*It wasn't for Diane, though! But Dad deserves something. He's paying for all this.*)

What's happening? The day that started off so well and so confidently is turning sour. Why, why? At least there's Dr. Williams and the thesis bit. He means to go there right now and get it over with. (*Barbara will understand. She'll smile.*) "Oh Bob, how are you? I hear you're thinking of pledging Kappa Phi. That's my fraternity, you know." Hand-shaking. (*Now how was I supposed to know he's a Kap?*) "About that paper, Bob, I may have been a little hasty. After all, I had nothing to go on, just a hunch we teachers sometimes get." (*What a switch! Now HE'S copping out because of the frat bit. Well, two can play the cop-out game.*) "I quite understand, sir." "I hope no offense was taken." Hand-shaking. Dr. Williams is put at ease and made to feel better about having made a somewhat reckless accusation.

He sits at the supper table and drains off the last delicious drops of wine. The father and mother exchange smiles. Their boy is growing into a man. He notes the interchange. Not much escapes Bob. He smiles inwardly. It's good to be loved, and it's good to make them proud. The wine has warmed him, and he climbs the stairs to his room. What a pleasant feeling. What a pleasant day it has been.

He puts a record on the stereo and lies back on the bed, his head cushioned on his folded hands. He is totally at peace as he listens to Simon and Garfunkel.

Compensation and Mask-Wearing

The motives behind our mask-wearing are not clear and distinct; they criss-cross and overlap. Bob Winslow, for example, responded to expediency and circumstances, but he was also guided by the knowledge that honesty is not always the best policy in human relationships. At the same time the groups to which he belonged—his family, the campus community as a whole, Kappa Phi, the "Diane Set," and the "Barbara Set"—all tried to cast him in a certain image and provide masks for him.

When he returned home and was at last back where he started, in the safe privacy of his own room, his spirits lightened by the wine, he donned yet one more mask: *that of the self-image.* Sometimes this is known as "the real me," and it is possible that sometimes the label is justified. But it is also possible that "the real me" can be a dream-self created in compensation for the guilt one feels for wearing the other masks.

In *Henry IV, Part I* Shakespeare uses the soliloquy, as he does in other plays, to allow the central character to objectify his thoughts to the audience and make known the true self that the actions of the plot don't always reveal. This literary myth—that people have inside them a hard, irreducible core of being—has been woven by writers for centuries now, and avid readers can grow up believing it's all true.

The main character of *Henry IV* is Prince Hal, who would, Shakespeare's audiences knew, eventually become Henry V, the great leader who finally conquered the French; he was a figure revered and glorified by the English as we do Abraham Lincoln. But in *Henry IV* Shakespeare chronicles the early life of the Prince, which centered around some pretty rowdy companions with whom Hal frequented the taverns and lived it up in high style. At one point, however, Shakespeare has the Prince stand alone on the stage and speak of his relationship with the gang.

> I know you all, and will a while uphold
> The unyok'd humour of your idleness.
> Yet herein will I imitate the sun,
> Who doth permit the base contagious clouds
> To smother up his beauty from the world . . .

In the language of today, one might be tempted to observe that the Prince is putting himself on, playing a little game with himself in order to justify his roustabout behavior.

It is also possible that Shakespeare recognized this game as something fundamental to human nature. A good many of our great writers have observed how men have worn masks even to themselves and have practiced self-deceit in order to compensate, either for guilt (like Prince Hal) or for the hardships inflicted on them by the world. Who has not known what it was like to be snubbed by his contemporaries and then tell himself: "I'll show them."

One of the classic stories on this theme is *Counterparts* by James Joyce, in which the hero Farrington is at first intimidated by his boss, who threatens "You impertinent ruffian! You impertinent ruffian! I'll make short work of you! Wait till you see!" Cowed by the verbal lashing, Farrington takes refuge in the local pub, where he drinks himself into delusions of grandeur and challenges a muscular marvel to an elbow-wrestling match.

> The trial began again. The veins stood out on Farrington's forehead, and the pallor of Weathers' complexion changed to peony. Their hands and arms trembled under the stress. After a long struggle Weathers again brought his opponent's hand slowly on to the table. There was a murmur of applause from the spectators.

Pushed into humiliating defeat twice in one day, Farrington staggers his way home, finds his little son all alone in the house, and at length finds someone he can bully and persecute. He beats his son unmercifully for having allowed the fire to go out.

> The boy uttered a squeal of pain as the stick cut his thigh. He clasped his hands together in the air and his voice shook with fright.
> "O, pa!" he cried. "Don't beat me, pa! And I'll . . . I'll say a Hail Mary for you . . . I'll say a Hail Mary for you, pa, if you don't beat me. . . . I'll say a Hail Mary. . . ."

The mask is snugly in place. Farrington, like Bob Winslow and Prince Hal, has come home.

EXERCISES

1. An interesting prelude to this writing assignment is to play the Listing Game. First, compile a list of all the people to whom you might for any reason wish to send a Christmas card next year (or a Channukah card or a Buddha's Birthday card or whatever). The point is to compile a master chart of all your acquaintances, and a card list appears to be the best bet, since you are unlikely to leave anyone out as long as you know that all these people will be connected only by the mails. That is to say, as long as Aunt Hattie Belle will never meet Suzy Sex face to face, as long as Aunt Hattie Belle nurtures a fond memory of you as her special favorite ("Such a nice child. I never heard a foul word escape your lips!") you won't feel intimidated by including her on the same list with Suzy and the hundred-odd friends you may have (and how odd are they?) If you were making up a list of close friends to invite to a party, however, you couldn't possibly allow the card-list people to be the same as the party people. From your card list select the names of a number of persons who have different impressions of you. Next to their names put down as much information as possible, such as:

Name	Relationship	Where met	Person's concept of me
Edith Doppelfinger	Mother	Around the house	Occasionally rebellious Often considerate Perhaps aware of the facts of life; hopefully no
Hattie Belle Doppelfinger	Aunt	Her home in Baltimore	Never grows older Never did, never will learn the facts of life Never drinks, smokes, or swears Probably just needs a haircut
Jed Bascomb	Buddy	High school gym class	Locker room braggart Always broke, looking for a touch Holds the record for most beers consumed in a single night Knows the best dirty jokes in town Generally regarded as the prime informant and confidant to all the gangs in matters of sexual conquest.
H. Wellington Cosgrove	Professor	Philosophy class	Asks a barrage of questions Probably on the verge of important awakening Highly original ideas Can't be impressed by established "names," no matter how great he is told they are

Now pretend that you have decided to give a party and a friend has offered to address the invitations but picks up your card list by mistake, so that everyone on it is invited and shows up at the affair. Write an imaginary account of what the party is like. Think of your predicament! Who would you be? Wouldn't you get all your masks mixed up?

What happens when Aunt Hattie Belle meets Jed Bascomb and his locker room stories? What happens when Uncle Sid finds out you have already spent the inheritance he has promised you and he isn't even dead yet? What happens when Professor Cosgrove, who looks upon you as a liberal and free thinker, discovers the local parish priest and find out you go to church? What happens when a liberal and a conservative get together and find out you have commitments to both political parties? Or when two persons meet and discover you are engaged to both of them? Or when Mother finds out you know more about life than she and Dad?

Will you come to some realization about mask-wearing? Will you decide you are a fraud? (But what is the real you?) Will you create a new mask to meet the occasion? Will you decide that these multiple identities give life its spice and excitement?

2. Using the day in the life of Bob Winslow as your model, make a study of your own mask-wearing traits during the course of a single day. To prepare for the assignment, select one specific day for your experiment and then jot down a note every time you believe you assume or change a mask. Indicate as honestly as you can the reason you do so. From this material put your paper together.

Use as your guide the four major motives for wearing masks that were discussed in this section: namely, the policy of dishonesty, group patterns, expediency, and compensation.

Person	Situation	Mask	Motive
Lady next door	Carried her bundles in from car	Polite concern for her health and interests	Dishonesty, perhaps, though at the time I thought I was being genuine
Young black girl, hired to teach French	Met her in student-faculty joint Senate meeting	The big sympathizer with cause of black power	Group patterns; I always think blacks expect me to come on strong (but they probably don't)
Close friend	Needed to borrow ten bucks for overdue traffic ticket	Pretended to be flat broke	Expediency; wanted to keep the money for a date but didn't want to hurt his feelings
Myself	Made a C in an exam which I thought I had aced	Convinced myself I hadn't really studied (but had)	Compensation

Your aim is not to discover or confess that you are being phony most of the time, but rather to face honestly this phenomenon of changing selves continually as the circumstances and the human relationships of each day dictate.

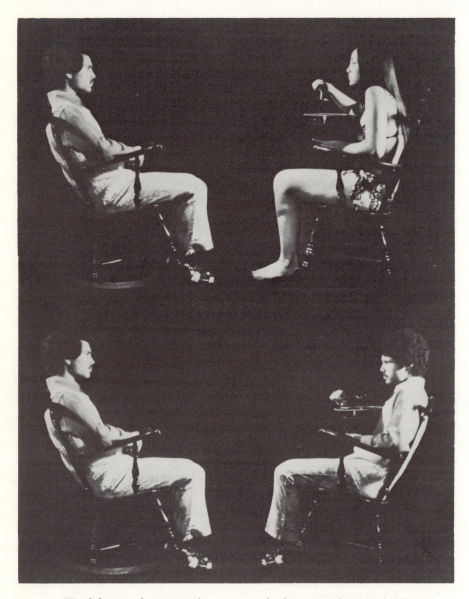

"Real human beings with names and phone numbers and four dollars and eleven cents in their pockets are what go to make up the world."

6

GETTING

OUTSIDE

YOURSELF

Now I will do nothing but listen,
To accrue what I hear into this song, to let
   sounds contribute to it.

WALT WHITMAN

Learning to catch glimpses of yourself in action, in the world of
space and time and human relationships, is just about the most difficult task in the world. For many, the very existence of this task remains unknown. They suppose identity is strictly a matter of getting
into things about themselves. Do they love? Do they find their
family, teachers, friends, and contemporaries easy or difficult to live
with? How do they feel about the police, the governor, the President?
How do the media influence them?

Even the material of the preceding chapter—projection, hangups,
and mask-wearing—can offer still more chances to dwell on your own
internal life, though that was not the reason for including it in this
book. (Don't be like the egotist who made an attempt to transcend
his preoccupation with himself by announcing "Well, we've been
talking about me all evening. What do *you* think of my problems?")
If your analysis of the Cinema Game or the innumerable masks worn
during the course of a single day has given you some further insights
into your own nature without letting you peer cautiously over the
top of the circle that surrounds you, then we must now try to push
our investigations into this (for most of us) unfamiliar landscape.

Instead of being concerned mainly with the effect the world and its people are having on you, let's reverse the procedure and take a stab at finding out what effect you are having on them. When you commit a certain action, for example, and then you forget about it, turning your attention to other matters, you can't believe others may not continue to feel the consequences of what you've done. And when you are observing or reacting to the others, you may see and hear them in a certain way, but how do you think you are coming across to them? Loud and clear? Or muffled and indistinct? There's a very good chance that if you knew how to gauge the feelings of others and the effects of your actions, you could risk a good deal more honesty and consistency in your behavior and lay aside at least some of your masks.

THE EVALUATION OF ACTION

The first step is to see your actions in an altogether new light. Try to think of them as tangible products, manufactured by you, but existing out there where they can be seen or used by all. Even statements such as, "The trouble with Tom is that you can't really trust him"—which may sound, when it escapes your lips, like a perfectly harmless passing comment—should be thought of as having assumed three-dimensionality. It hangs there like a swinging sign and it announces DON'T TRUST TOM for all the world to observe.

Did I do something really enormous? Did I invent the automobile? Well then, I must not ignore what my deed has been doing all these years. Has it been a marvelous advance for the human race? Perhaps. Or perhaps the thousands who have died because of it may modify the verdict.

Once an action has happened, it enters the world of time and space; it becomes part of human society and must be reckoned with. You can be run over by the very automobile you invented. Your actions need to be interpreted by you in the same manner they are open to interpretation by anybody else. It is the blind mother who sees only "her baby" and nothing of the things her grown-up child has done (like blowing up a building or hijacking a plane).

All our actions have three aspects: what one believes he is doing; what is done; and the way others are affected by it. In between them probably lies that phantom we have called "the reality." We may never be able to reach a knowledge of this, at least consistently and for any length of time, but it is important to make the effort to do so. If nothing else, we stand to recognize how far from this reality we normally operate.

Telling It Like It Is

It is easier to talk about "it" than to describe "it." When we accuse someone else of not telling it like it is, we generally mean he is obviously hedging, or we suspect he is lying. Can we indicate in one-two-three order just what "it" is that he is supposed to be telling it like?

Let me offer a simple, yet at the same time complex, example of the problem. I recently taught a course in which I decided to experiment with a group-process approach. That is to say, I divided a class of sixteen into four groups, each of which was charged with the task of writing, memorizing, and performing a dialogue-debate on any subject. The aim was to make use of a method of reasoning whereby one party, attacked by the other three, not only defended his own position but ended up by totally dismantling the arguments of his opponents. It's a risky exercise at best, because it depends upon the cooperation of four people.

One of the groups experienced no end of trouble working up the assignment. First this member would fail to show up for meetings; then that one would be out sick. I could see the team effort disintegrating. While the other groups would be sitting in their circles, enthusiastically exchanging ideas and methods, the "sick" group—as many of them as would be present for that day—would just be sitting, staring vacantly at each other or else scoffing quietly at the others.

Finally a spokesman for this group came to my office and asked to drop the course. He had had it "up to here, sir." Nobody would cooperate. Nobody cared. The whole exercise was pointless anyway. As far as that went, college itself and the whole stupid Establishment were pointless. I offered no resistance but gave him the necessary forms, which he immediately tore up. "Never mind," he said and left.

The next day in class, after the other three groups had performed their dialogues with reasonable proficiency, the course-dropper and one other member of the sick group came to the front. "We have a dialogue to present," they said. Here's what they did. They pretended they were meeting somewhere outside of class. The course-dropper announced he was going to drop the course because of the absurdity of the current assignment. What value did it have anyway, this dialogue business? "It helps you to think, I guess," said the other. The course-dropper then proceeded to dismantle the friend's reasoning in wishing to complete the assignment, not to mention the professor's reasoning in having made it in the first place. He offered a fifteen-minute careful analysis of the fallacy of logical thinking in general and of classroom "mental gymnastics" in particular. When it was over, the rest of the class applauded heartily and commended the pair for their originality and daring.

"Huh," snorted the course-dropper. "That's what I'm talking about. The whole educational system is wrong if you think we did anything worth applauding. Don't you understand? We just copped out, and you were had."

I sat there, looking as mysterious as possible. Fortunately the bell rang, and I didn't have to give an opinion there and then. For hours afterward I pondered the problem. *Had* we been "had," as he put it? Or had these two unintentionally done the clever thing the class wanted to commend by applauding?

Writers have long been fascinated by the subject of the difference between things-in-themselves and things-as-we-view-them. What about Don Quixote and those windmills? Don Quixote falling on his knees and worshipping some fat peasant woman in rags and seeing her as a beautiful maiden in gorgeous raiment? What about Hamlet, who accidentally murders his girlfriend's father and considers it "one of those things"—certainly not a dreadful deed of violence?

More recently, a number of stories, plays, and novels have appeared dealing with this elusive question of reality and where it's at. Lionel Trilling's short story "Of This Time, Of That Place" has made a notable contribution to the literary exploration of the problem.

The hero, Joseph Howe, is an English teacher at a fashionable liberal arts college. One day a peculiar young man named Tertan is added to his class. With unkempt hair and nervous mannerisms, with a vocabulary so extraordinarily advanced for college freshmen as to be almost ridiculous, and with the habit of making statements about life and art that almost, but not quite, make sense, Tertan becomes a campus mystery, a class joke, and the source of much perplexity for his teacher. Is the boy, for example, a genius, so far above everyone's head that they must ridicule him, as the world ridicules all of its superior minds? Or is he—as the college administration fears—out of his mind? Howe finds himself unable to decide whether Tertan's difficult, sometimes almost unreadable papers are the work of a profound and misunderstood intellect or of a diseased mind.

The administration, like Howe, is perplexed, for it is hard to say yes or no on the question of insanity. After all, where does one draw the line? Howe himself evades the problem by giving Tertan a grade of A—. ("But really only a mark of M for Mad would serve.") At length the administration seeks medical opinion, and the decision is that Tertan must be dismissed.

In one of the most poignant and beautifully executed moments in modern fiction, Tertan, unaware of his impending dismissal, visits Howe in his office carrying a membership form for the campus literary club.

> "Even the spirit who lives gregariously, above the herd, must have its relations with the fellowman," Tertan declared. He laid the document on Howe's desk. It was headed "Quill and Scroll Society of Dwight College. Application for Membership."
>
> "In most ways these are crass minds," Tertan said, touching the paper. "Yet as a whole, bound together in their common love of letters, they transcend their intellectual lacks since it is not a paradox that the whole is greater than the sum of its parts."
>
> "When are the elections?" Howe asked.
>
> "They take place tomorrow."
>
> "I certainly hope you will be successful."
>
> "Thank you. Would you wish to implement that hope?" A rather dirty finger pointed to the bottom of the sheet. "A faculty recommender is necessary," Tertan said stiffly, and waited.
>
> "And you wish me to recommend you?"
>
> "It would be an honor."
>
> "You may use my name."
>
> Tertan's finger pointed again. "It must be a written sponsorship, signed by the sponsor." There was a large blank space on the form under the heading, "Opinion of Faculty Sponsor."
>
> This was almost another thing and Howe hesitated. Yet there was nothing else to do and he took out his fountain pen. He wrote, "Mr. Ferdinand Tertan is marked by his intense devotion to letters and by his exceptional love of all things of the mind." To this he signed his name, which looked bold and assertive on the white page. It disturbed him, this strange affirming power of a name. With a businesslike air, Tertan whipped up the paper, folding it with decision, and put it into his pocket. He bowed and took his departure, leaving Howe with the sense of having done something oddly momentous.[1]

Even without the context of the entire story, this brief scene sheds much light on the problem we are presently considering. If we think of Howe's signing his name as the crucial action, we can see the interrelationship of the three aspects of any committed deed: namely, what one believes he is doing; what is done; and the effect it has on others.

First, what does Howe believe he is doing here? No doubt his mind is entertaining two interpretations of the recommending action. One is that it is a last act of kindness to a boy he may have helped to dismiss by not defending him. The other is that it is an act of

[1] From "Of This Time, Of That Place" by Lionel Trilling. Copyright 1943 by Lionel Trilling. Originally appeared in Partisan Review. Reprinted by permission of The Viking Press, Inc.

cowardice, a cruel stroke applied to one who is about to suffer, and wrought out of the inability to be honest.

If Tertan is indeed mad, we can have no true idea of how he may view the action. On the other hand, if he is lucid, he may see it as a beautiful, symbolic gesture, a supreme act of intellectual bondage between a teacher and a student. Surely it has a beneficial effect on him, and, if he is eventually whisked off to a mental institution, he will never know that his English teacher had any motives other than the desire to express his admiration for a gifted student.

The question we may ask about this scene, then, is: what *does* constitute the reality of Howe's action. Was it cruelty? kindness? friendship? admiration? Could it somehow be a mixture of all these things? And doesn't it bear a suspicious resemblance, in its complexity, to the dialogue performed by my two world-weary students who thought they had deceived both an entire class and a world-weary professor?

EXERCISES

1. The foregoing analysis of the incident from Lionel Trilling's story has given us a three-step process for telling something like it is. It should be clear that very few people ever get far enough away from their own interpretation of an action to do this with total frankness, honesty, and objectivity. But here's an opportunity to practice. Once again, the three steps:

   a) When the action was occurring, what did you believe was happening?

   b) What was actually happening? (That is, in reality—apart from your feelings and interpretations. You have to describe this with no adjectives or adverbs that evaluate the action for a reader or listener.)

   c) What was happening to other people involved? (Here you have to try to put yourself in their place and ask, "How would I have felt if I had been this person and that action were taking place?")

   The assignment is to take some incident that recently took place and in which you were substantially involved. At least one other person must also have been involved. (For the first crack at this kind of analysis you would do better to deal with no more than one other participant in the action.)

   Begin with a brief but clear description of the incident as a means of identifying the thing as to time, place, and participants.

Try to avoid making value judgments—evaluative statements—at the outset that would prejudice the reader. Here's an example of the wrong way to start:

> Last night I decided to have it out with a boy I had been dating for the past two months. I was sick and tired of always playing second fiddle to the rest of his harem, and, though I still had strong feelings for him, I told myself the time had come to put an end to his deceptions and lies.

Do you think you can ever achieve any degree of objectivity after such a beginning? The reader is all set to hiss the villain as soon as he shows up.

A better opening (at least for the purposes of this assignment):

> Last night I had a final date with a boy I'd been going with for several months. We weren't supposed to have gone out, but I telephoned him earlier in the day and told him it was absolutely necessary to see him. At first he said he was unable to get together with me. (As opposed to "He made many excuses" or "At first he tried to get out of the date," both of which would be value judgments, prejudicing the reader.) Finally he agreed, and we met at a spot along the beach where we'd gone the first night we ever went out.

The incident has been set up in the reader's mind, but even though he knows this will be a parting of the ways for two people, he isn't reading in terms of innocent girl vs. cruel boyfriend.

Next take the first step of the three-step process listed above. Here the girl author of our hypothetical paper could allow her own emotions to come out, as long as it was clear that this is how *she* viewed the incident.

> As soon as I saw him, I wanted to cry. I thought to myself, "How could anyone so kind and considerate-looking be so cruel?" But I controlled myself because I didn't want him to go away believing I'd been just another one of his victims. I could even see him studying me and looking for a sign that I was about to come apart. Probably he was hoping that I would, so he could say, "Don't you think it's better if we just call it quits?" He wasn't at ease. I could see I bored him and he couldn't wait to get back to whatever chick he was currently giving the business to. But I told myself I'd be damned if I'd let him make a fool of me. *He* wasn't going to be the one to break the whole thing off. So I pulled myself together and told him I was through.

Sound familiar? It should. This is the usual way people tell other people what happened to them. That is, they include in their

descriptions built-in, predigested evaluations of the other participants as well as the very nature of an action. If all you had to go
on was this account of a couple about to break up, how would you
tend to relate it to someone else?

a) A proud girl gave a smooth-talking con artist of a boy the
   gate before he could tell her to get lost.

b) A girl who'd been humiliated and deceived salvaged her dignity
   by being the one to terminate a bad relationship.

Okay, now comes the hard part. You have to indicate what was
actually happening. You have to concentrate on the incident as it
really occurred, as if you were photographing the whole thing
for a movie company. Don't worry how flat it sounds. Switch
to the third person if it seems easier. Thus:

> The girl looked out at the ocean for a few minutes, saying nothing.
> The boy kept looking toward her, also saying nothing. Now and
> then she would glance quickly in his direction and then quickly
> away again. He lit a cigarette and drummed with his fingers on the
> bench. She kept making sniffing noises as if trying to hold back some
> tears, or else she was having some trouble breathing. She opened her
> purse and took out a handkerchief. He looked toward her sharply.
> She turned her face away from him and used the handkerchief in some
> manner he could not see. Then she put it back in her purse. There
> were a few more moments of silence during which the girl made
> circles in the sand on the sidewalk with the tip of her shoe. Suddenly
> the girl looked over at him and said: "I'm not going out with you
> any more."

Naturally this could be expanded so as to capture the full
scope of the incident, but you have the idea. Reading *this* section
of the paper, one would not be able to say for sure who was more
nervous, the boy or the girl, or who may have been responsible
for the break-up, or whether indeed both shared the responsibility.

The final stage of the process is for the writer to identify with
the other party. Since this is extremely difficult, it is sometimes
necessary to supply a number of possible versions of the other
person's feelings. Thus:

> VERSION #1 OF THE BOY'S VIEWPOINT. I wish she'd hurry up and say
> what's on her mind. I don't want to have to be the one to break it
> off because then it'll get around what a louse I am and that'll be bad
> for business. Oh, oh, there she goes. Whew! She said it. I'm off the
> hook. Too bad, chick, but wasn't it nice while it lasted?

> VERSION #2. I hope she isn't going to cry. I feel pretty rotten. Now
> that I look at her, I can see why I was attracted to her in the first

place. I want to keep this thing going. I mean, I *really* do. But how the hell do I open my mouth and say anything? I can guess what she's been hearing about me and the other chicks. How can I explain? How can I make her understand that I could go out with them and still like her a lot and want to see her?

VERSION #3. I have an idea she's building up to telling me to get lost. I can see from the way she's avoiding my eyes. I guess those stories I heard about her are true. I mean, she's been seeing a lot of other guys. That's why I've been keeping away. I thought she might start missing me a little. Maybe she's already engaged. Well, she socked it to me pretty good there. I've had it. Okay, chick, if that's the way you feel, I'll just find me someone else.

The last possibility may prove too generous for most people to even consider including. But if there are no tangible reasons for believing the worst of other people, it might prove a novelty to give such an alternative a try. The paper you finally write will not be a smooth and logical one. It will seem disconnected, perhaps even incoherent, but maybe this is one way of getting closer to "like it is."

2. If you want to try something really imaginative, create a hypothetical court trial in which the guilt or innocence of the defendant hinges on the interpretation of a certain action.

a) Describe the action, as it would appear in a police report. (If it was murder, just indicate who and where and what evidence was found.)

b) Present the prosecution's case against whoever the defendant is, explaining why this person appears to be guilty.

c) Present the defendant's version of what happened.

d) Show how each of the following people are responding to the case: a biased member of the jury; an impartial member of the jury; the defendant's mother; the victim's wife; the judge.

You need come to no conclusion. If you offer enough conflicting viewpoints and interpretations, the reader will get a very powerful message.

3. But, you may object, one can go on forever seeking out possible interpretations of any event; it is entirely human and necessary to respond to actions in ways that benefit the responder. Therefore one has to draw a line at some point and say, "I choose to see this event in this manner." In order to take your stand, however, with greater authority and with more profound reasoning behind it, write a paper about some recent event (such as getting thrown

out of a class for creating a disturbance, or losing your car-owning privilege after your father and mother decided you were not a competent driver), an event you have frequently described negatively to others and continue to feel negative about. Do the following things in this paper:

a) Relate the incident as you normally tell it to sympathetic listeners.

b) Tell what happened, without using evaluative adjectives and adverbs.

c) Try to talk objectively about the feelings and motives of the others involved.

d) Explain why you still claim the right to feel negative *even though it is possible to see other viewpoints.*

e) Generalize about people's rights to view an action in terms of their private needs and benefits or losses.

f) Indicate, if you can, what you have learned from doing this assignment about the prospects for better understanding among people.

g) Indicate what you think would have to be done to promote better understanding.

h) Indicate whether you would be prepared to take the first step or would wait for others to do it.

4. Lionel Trilling's story, "Of This Time, Of That Place," also focuses on what is for many teachers the embarrassing subject of grading and the difficulty of being totally objective in evaluating a student's performance in a course. With unrelieved honesty in leveling with the reader about the way teachers arrive at grades, Trilling shows how the English teacher decided to give Tertan a grade of A minus, which, in some grimly humorous fashion, symbolized for him a twilight zone between sanity and insanity. He reasoned he couldn't flunk a student who might well have genius, nor could he give him a "pure" A, for that would confuse his status with that of another student "with his beautiful and clear, if still arrogant, mind."

No doubt you have some personal misgivings about the way some teachers have arrived at their grades. Write a paper airing your observations about a particular teacher's method or about the whole questionable process. To stir up your imagination, ask yourself whether you have ever

a) had a teacher who was obviously biased in grading you or any other member of the class (be specific)

b) asked a teacher for an explanation of a grade and been turned out in the cold

c) had a teacher who used a revised grading system that you think made sense (explain what it was)

d) failed to experience any satisfaction whatever in connection with any grading system (explain what you think is wrong, then, with the whole idea of grading)

e) argued that you should have received a minimum passing grade "for effort" and been turned down. What was the teacher's reason? What reasons can you give for believing effort alone should be rewarded? What reasons can you think of for arguing against such an idea?

f) developed your own grading method (if so, here's your chance to explain it to the world)

Motive-Effect Analysis

It may seem impersonal and heartless to suggest that one can come closer to "telling it like it is" by using a diagram method, but this does have its advantages. For one thing, if you can actually sit down and put on paper the pros and cons of anticipated actions *before* they are committed, you are a little less likely to do anything in a highly emotional state. Perhaps the crime rate might drop sharply if prospective murderers or thieves took the time to work out an analysis of what they wanted to do, why they wanted to do it, and what effects it would probably have on those involved. If nothing else, confronting an action before it happens can be a sobering experience.

You can gain experience in analyzing your own projected deeds by using historical models first. Select some event that occurred or some invention somebody put on the market and construct a diagram that will show:

1) the event or product in the center, signifying the neutrality of the thing-in-itself apart from the motives of the person responsible for it or the influence it has had on other people

2) arrows directed toward the center, signifying probable motives, and arrows leading away from the center, signifying known effects; position these arrows so that they go from "Good" at the left to "Touch and Go" in the middle to "Bad" at the right

For an example, let's go back to the automobile: marvelous advance or instrument of air pollution and death? If you had invented it, would you be entitled to lean back contentedly or should your conscience be bothering you? How can one tell? The diagram method will at least help.

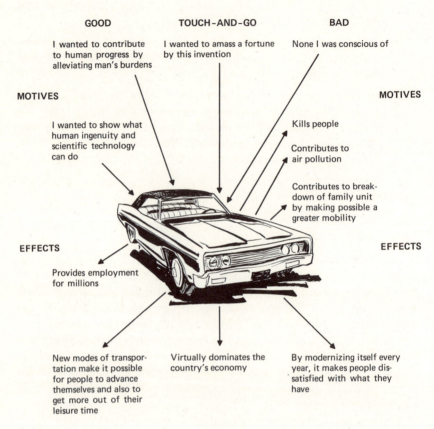

GOOD   TOUCH-AND-GO   BAD

I wanted to contribute to human progress by alleviating man's burdens

I wanted to amass a fortune by this invention

None I was conscious of

MOTIVES   MOTIVES

I wanted to show what human ingenuity and scientific technology can do

Kills people

Contributes to air pollution

Contributes to breakdown of family unit by making possible a greater mobility

EFFECTS   EFFECTS

Provides employment for millions

New modes of transportation make it possible for people to advance themselves and also to get more out of their leisure time

Virtually dominates the country's economy

By modernizing itself every year, it makes people dissatisfied with what they have

EFFECTS

The use of historical models can put us into the habit of trying to see more clearly all sides of a problem created by a specific event or product. One can even apply this method of analysis to current events, thus coming still closer to one's own time and concerns. What about a nationwide strike?

Possible Good Motives: Workers haven't been allowed to keep up with rising living costs.

Standard of living of the workers has thus been forced down.

Others have been allowed to better themselves. (Perhaps the strikers are forbidden by law to call a work halt; perhaps they work for the federal government.)

	Strikers love their families and wish to provide for them as well as they can.
Touch-and-Go Motive:	Strikers wish to show that the monetary needs of working people are more important than the welfare of the entire population, bound to be adversely affected by a nation-wide work stoppage in some vital area (postal service, railroads, airlines, telephone and electric utilities, and so on).
Possible Bad Motives:	If it's a strike against the federal government, perhaps the strikers want to "get even" with the President for trying to balance the nation's economy at what they consider to be their expense.
	Perhaps the strikers have been subject to the outside influence of radical and anarchic groups who sense a golden opportunity to disrupt the country.
Possible Good Effects:	Workers' salaries go up.
	Their standard of living—temporarily, at least—goes up.
	Their families profit.
Touch-and-Go Effect:	Workers in vital areas have served notice that they are indispensable to the normal operations of the country.
Possible Bad Effects:	The image of the Presidential office is badly tarnished.
	Radical groups have achieved another milestone in their project to totally disrupt the affairs of the country.
	Taxes will have to go up to cover the pay increase; prices also go up; the strikers eventually find themselves back where they started from.

When you do an analysis of a past or present event that doesn't involve you as directly as a family crisis would, you gain the habit of climbing on top of a situation, of viewing it dispassionately, without getting hung up on certain aspects of it. The aim of the analysis or the diagram certainly isn't to persuade yourself that the bad effects outweigh the good ones. It is to help you see things with a somewhat sharper perspective.

You should be ready now to do the same thing for an action you are thinking about committing or a product you are planning to buy or a movement you may be preparing to join. Suppose, for instance, you are the son or daughter in an average family, and you are planning to leave home. You can no longer endure what you consider the unreasonable restrictions placed upon your actions by your parents. You've thought the matter over and have decided you can make it on your own from now on. Using the same diagrammatic principle as we did for the analysis of the automobile, we can arrange the good, touch-and-go, and bad motives and effects accordingly:

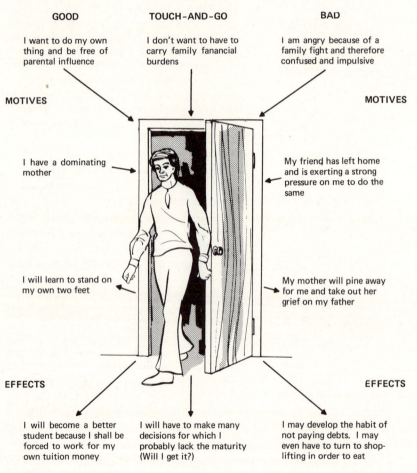

GOOD   TOUCH-AND-GO   BAD

I want to do my own thing and be free of parental influence

I don't want to have to carry family fanancial burdens

I am angry because of a family fight and therefore confused and impulsive

MOTIVES   MOTIVES

I have a dominating mother

My friend has left home and is exerting a strong pressure on me to do the same

I will learn to stand on my own two feet

My mother will pine away for me and take out her grief on my father

EFFECTS   EFFECTS

I will become a better student because I shall be forced to work for my own tuition money

I will have to make many decisions for which I probably lack the maturity (Will I get it?)

I may develop the habit of not paying debts. I may even have to turn to shoplifting in order to eat

EFFECTS

One's immediate family does not, however, constitute the only group of people likely to be affected by a projected action. It takes a superior effort of will to force oneself to think about the behavior, happiness, or unhappiness of all the possible groups that might be concerned, but if one does so, he is bound to gain additional perspective. Thus, our young man who feels he must leave home would, using this group-effect method, begin by listing the various groups likely to be involved.

Immediate	Family
	Circle of friends
	Neighborhood softball team
	College swimming team
	Fraternity
Less Immediate	Store where employed as part-time clerk
	Customers of that store
	Neighborhood as a whole
	Student body of school
	Faculty and administration of school
Long-range	Area of town
	Town itself
	State
	Country
	Mankind

Don't sit there snickering. People who pretend to be cynical about the extent of their influence may be kidding themselves, using their cynicism as an excuse to evade a feeling of responsibility toward anyone outside of their immediate family and circle of friends. What if everyone in the world decided he didn't matter to the operations of the whole and wanted to end his life? There'd be one loud, universal gunshot—and then everlasting silence.

"Any man's death diminishes me," said poet and minister John Donne long ago in a sermon, "for I am involved in mankind." To demonstrate this very point, somebody made a movie a few years back called *It's a Wonderful Life;* it was about an obscure, simple man who considered himself the most unimportant person ever to live. In a burst of fantasy, the author had an angel come down from heaven to take the man on a tour of the future, in order to see what the lives of the people in his town would be like without him. Needless to say, he changed his mind about himself.

But if one is important, it follows that he can be a force for both bad and good things with respect to many other people. The discontented son, having drawn up his list, could break down the possible effects in this way:

FAMILY EFFECTS

Improvements	*Disruptions*
Mother will learn to get along without son.	Missing son may cause mother's health to deteriorate.

FAMILY EFFECTS

Improvements	*Disruptions*
Mother will transfer affection to father, who needs it.	Mother-father relations will get worse.
Easing of tensions will improve physical and mental health of both parents.	Without son to hold them together, father and mother will get divorce.
If divorce results, it will mean there wasn't much to the marriage anyway.	

FRATERNITY EFFECTS

Power struggle among officers will ease.	The sudden disappearance of a member will be demoralizing.
Sense of brotherhood will become sharper.	Community-oriented project will be set back.

TOWN EFFECTS

Fraternity may "cut up" less without his influence.	If fraternity projects (such as organizing ball team for ghetto children) are shelved, community will be the poorer.
	Since father works as plumber and since his working capacity may be severely curtailed over son's disappearance, community plumbing problems are bound to suffer.

MANKIND EFFECTS

None very obvious.	If community suffers, there are bound to be chain reactions.
	Suppose the ghetto ball team never materializes? It is possible one child who could have been helped will become a criminal.

It is interesting to note that as the imagination takes in a wider and wider horizon of effects, the good results of the son's leaving home tend to shrink, whereas the bad results become increasingly obvious. What about the elderly woman who always singles the young man out to wait on her at the store because he is kind and thoughtful to her? Perhaps the two- or three-minute conversation she has with him is the only conversation she can be sure of having with anyone. What about the neighbors he may help in so many countless ways? What about the benefits the town will lose because he may never settle there and contribute to civic movements or cultural developments? If, further, his leaving home means also dropping out of school, what about the artistic or philosophical talent the entire human race may never get the chance to enjoy? the musical ability? the dramatic flair? the shrewd business mind that might have helped to solve the nation's economic problems?

Of course, these considerations can be balanced or at least somewhat offset by anticipating new groups of people he may join and help to improve. The nation and mankind as a whole may yet benefit from his existence, perhaps far more than they would have if he had stayed home. But subjecting a proposed action to such searching analysis before undertaking it helps one to weigh one probable set of circumstances against another. Are the bad effects of leaving home much surer than one's high hopes for the future? Not that hope is a bad thing to nurture. It's a matter of degree and of being as honest as possible.

EXERCISES

1. Since we have spent a good deal of time on a trial analysis of somebody's moving out of his house and going far off somewhere, why not use it as the basis for an imaginative paper?
   a) Describe the departure; be as documentary as you can.
   b) Then describe how the event is interpreted by the various members of the family: the mother, the father, perhaps a younger brother or sister, and finally the boy or girl in question.
   c) Referring to the motive-effect and the group-effect analyses in this section, evaluate the action, showing that it was the right or wrong course for the person to have taken.
2. Set forth some course of action you yourself plan to take in the near future, such as getting your own apartment, getting married, or buying a motorcycle. It should be, however, some action you are sure will raise a storm of objections from other people, one that is certain to have far-reaching effects. Then:
   a) Indicate first why you intend to do this thing.
   b) Analyze the probable effects on other people.
   c) Analyze the probable effects on the groups to which you belong.
   d) Indicate whether you still intend to carry out your plan, and *why*.

The purpose of this paper is not to get you to change your mind or "sell out." It is to get you to stand more firmly on your own two feet. No proposed action has any integrity if the doer is not prepared to defend it in the face of all the anticipated objections to it or if the doer is unwilling to consider these objections.

If you got ready for an analysis of your own proposed actions by experimenting with historical models or current events, and if you came up with some interesting and enlightening thoughts, do a paper in which you show why a past event (such as the Vietnam War, the Cambodian offensive, or the 1969 Supreme Court confirmation of the unconstitutionality of school segregation) was on the whole a fortunate or an unfortunate thing; or why an event you feel is on the brink of happening (such as government-enforced integration of all neighborhoods and housing facilities or the extension of the Medicare program to people of all ages or the liberalization of drug and abortion laws or the Catholic Church's changing its stand on celibacy) should or shouldn't happen.

Do a diagram like the one used for the automobile and use it as the basis for your written analysis. You need not, of course, reach a final decision if you feel you can't honestly do so. It is enough to show the good, bad, and marginal aspects of the event. However, by all means attempt a positive or negative evaluation if you think you can defend it all the way.

PUTTING YOURSELF IN THE OTHER PERSON'S PLACE

> It is after all the writer's job to empathize, to feel himself into situations he has not experienced, to write more than his own autobiography.
>
> DAN JAFFE

Anybody can say he wants to be objective in evaluating the actions he has committed or plans to commit, but, in order to be completely honest in carrying out the kind of analysis recommended in the preceding section, it is necessary to take a further step, one that is for most people far more drastic than putting their thoughts down in a diagram. That step is trying as far as is humanly possible to enter into the thoughts of another person. It is difficult, but not impossible. Enough common humanity exists between all persons to make such empathy a distinct possibility. ("Empathy" means projecting oneself into the personality and feelings of someone else.)

"Catching On" and Getting the Right Messages

When most people act and react within a group, they are likely to be insensitive to the currents of feeling that ebb and flow beneath the surface. Nor is it a matter of becoming familiar with the group. At times excessive familiarity may prove to be more a hindrance than a help. Consider the family group. The closer the ties, the greater is one's tendency to relax into a deceptive sense of ease within the circle. One develops so *much* security there that he stops looking at the others or really listening to what they say. He becomes almost totally absorbed in his own problems. "Why shouldn't I have the car?" "Who are you to tell me what I should do?" "I refuse to account to anyone for what I do!" But the accusers and questioners, for their part, can be just as self-centered. Thus: "You will never appreciate how I have suffered and slaved to make something of you!" or "Nobody cares how hard I work to make ends meet for this family, and then look at the thanks I get!" Parents want to be thanked; offspring resent parents' attempts to force a sense of gratitude. What ensues is more often than not a battle of wills instead of an intelligent compromise among mature people sensitive to each other's needs.

In all group encounters, especially when we know each other very well, we fail to tune into the thoughts and feelings of the others whenever we concentrate on our personal needs, which is probably most of the time. Even the conditions of a casual get-together, where no hostility is present, can prove a breeding ground for insensitivity.

Did you ever sit around with friends and start exchanging witty stories, dirty jokes, or amusing anecdotes about recent experiences? Did each member of the group listen carefully to whoever was holding the floor, making eye contact with him, absorbing every shade of meaning he wished to communicate? Or do you think each person was mentally leaping ahead to the time when *he* could wrest the floor from the speaker and regale the others with his own stories? Friendly gatherings seldom yield truly direct communication.

Even when two old friends run into each other after a long separation, the bubbling, spontaneous joy of each, the enthusiastic recounting of years of complicated experiences may well be the seizing of an opportunity to show off in front of the other; it may *not* be a true indication of genuine concern. Has such an encounter happened to you recently? Who started the recital of past events? You or your friend? Or did each struggle to win the right to lead off? For how long a time were you able to sustain an honest interest in every detail your friend was describing? Did you find yourself straining with anticipation of what you would say next, as soon as the other person had the decency to keep quiet?

Learning to get the right messages when someone else is speaking or not speaking in your presence is necessary before you can feel empathy for him. While you occupy the floor and are delighting mainly yourself with a wildly funny (to you) experience that involved people your friend has never heard of, are you closely scanning his face for telltale signs of boredom or impatience? Are his eyes casting furtive glances in the direction of his watch? Does he make a few halting efforts to break into the conversation only to be beaten off by your persistence? If so, he's trying to tell you to shut up.

Writers are aware of the insensitivity of people to each other's feelings. Contemporary novelists, dramatists, and short-story writers are particularly fond of showing the tangle of human relationships, whereby people hurt each other without intending to or generally fail to respond to the messages of need and longing that are being sent out continually by everyone. For the past century, literature has tended increasingly to look at good and evil, not as static qualities in individual personalities (heroes and villains), but as the effects people have on each other. It's only in popular television shows and movies and fiction—especially westerns—that we still find a sharp separation of the true-blue-good-from-head-to-toe, and the thoroughly-rotten-to-the-core. The serious modern writer has seen us all for what we are: well-meaning, but blind to each other; locked inside the prison of our own narrow self-interests, and usually misunderstood even when we try to leap over the wall.

Katherine Mansfield is one such writer. Her stories are beautifully perceptive gems of insight into such criss-crossing relationships. Reading her work, one gets the feeling that the greatest moment in a person's life would be the achievement of a total understanding of another person.

"A Dill Pickle" describes how a man and woman meet for lunch after being apart for six years. Each is intellectual and apparently sensitive to what goes on in the world, but as they converse with each other, the reader begins to see that neither is sensitive to what is going on across the table.

The two characters have been lovers once upon a time, and somehow—neither appears to know why—they drifted apart. For some unaccountable reason, they keep saying, a relationship between two gifted and talented personalities, which should have been logical and ideal, couldn't last. Now, after six years, each confesses to the other how lonely he has been, how drab and uninteresting have been all subsequent relationships, how foolish they have been to deny themselves the pleasure of each other's companionship.

Here's a sample of the conversation. You'll see at once that each character is only physically sitting at the table, and you'll be able to tell why their relationship couldn't materialize in the past and never will in the future. The man has spent some time in Russia and is vividly describing his adventures. He looks over at her.

"What a marvelous listener you are. When you look at me with those wild eyes I feel that I could tell you things that I would never breathe to another human being."

Was there just a hint of mockery in his voice, or was it her fancy? She could not be sure.

"Before I met you," he said, "I had never spoken of myself to anybody. How well I remember one night, the night that I brought you the little Christmas tree, telling you all about my childhood. And of how I was so miserable that I ran away and lived under a cart in our yard for two days without being discovered. And you listened, and your eyes shone, and I felt that you had even made the little Christmas tree listen too, as in a fairy story."

But of that evening she had remembered a little pot of caviar. It had cost seven and sixpence. He could not get over it. Think of it—a tiny jar like that costing seven and sixpence. While she ate it he watched her, delighted and shocked.

"No, really, that is eating money. You could not get seven shillings into a little pot that size. Only think of the profit they must make. . . ." And he had begun some immensely complicated calculations. . . . But now good-by to the caviar. The Christmas tree was on the table, and the little boy lay under the cart with his head pillowed on the yard dog.

"The dog was called Bosun," she cried delightedly.

But he did not follow. "Which dog? Had you a dog? I don't remember a dog at all."

"No, no. I mean the yard dog when you were a little boy." He laughed and snapped the cigarette case to.

"Was he? Do you know I had forgotten that. It seems such years ago. . . . I cannot believe that it is only six years. After I had recognized you today—I had to take such a leap—I had to take a leap over my whole life to get back to that time. I was such a kid then." He drummed on the table. "I've often thought how I must have bored you. And now I understand so perfectly why you wrote to me as you did—although at the time that letter nearly finished my life. I found it again the other day, and I couldn't help laughing as I read it. It was so clever—such a true picture of me." He glanced up. "You're not going?" [2]

This very last tells us that, all through the man's self-centered talk of the past and her letter, the woman has been making preparations to leave and that he hasn't noticed how she "had buttoned her collar again and drawn down her veil." If you were talking about yourself and your "listener" was buttoning her collar, would you catch the message?

But just before she goes, hope rises once more within her that their relationship still has a chance. He seems to making some direct contact with her—meaning, of course, that he seems to be interested in *her* feelings.

> "I felt that you were more lonely than anybody else in the world," he went on, "and yet, perhaps, that you were the only person in the world who was really, truly alive. Born out of your time," he murmured, stroking the glove, "fated."
>
> Ah, God! What had she done! How had she dared to throw away her happiness like this. This was the only man who had ever understood her. Was it too late? Could it be too late? *She* was that glove that he held in his fingers. . . .
>
> "And then the fact that you had no friends and never had made friends with people. How I understood that, for neither had I. Is it just the same now?"
>
> "Yes," she breathed. "Just the same. I am as alone as ever."
>
> "So am I," he laughed gently, "just the same."
>
> Suddenly with a quick gesture he handed her back the glove and scraped his chair on the floor. "But what seemed to me so mysterious then is perfectly plain to me now. And to you, too, of course. . . . It simply was that we were such egotists so self-engrossed, so wrapped up in ourselves that we hadn't a corner in our hearts for anybody else. Do you know," he cried, naïve and hearty, and dreadfully like another side of that old self again, "I began studying a Mind System when I was in Russia, and I found that we were not peculiar at all. It's quite a well-known form of . . ."
>
> She had gone. He sat there, thunder-struck, astounded beyond words. . . . And then he asked the waitress for his bill.
>
> "But the cream has not been touched," he said. "Please do not charge me for it." [3]

With remarkable precision, Katherine Mansfield has given us a model for understanding how people fail to receive each other's messages. Neither of these characters is willing to go beyond his own self-interest and try to comprehend the other. Each is willing only to use the other as a "marvelous listener."

From such a story as this we learn that *communication* has more than the two main forms we heard about in school: that is, oral and written. We learn that much, if not most, communication is carried out nonverbally and that it isn't what others are *saying* that often matters, but rather what they are *showing*. No teacher, for example, should fail to understand what it means when the faces in front of him are looking all about the room, not at him, or when students are forcing attentive looks, pretending an interest they don't truly possess, perhaps in hopes of averting a "pop" quiz. Yet how many teachers do read these signs? How many shake their heads when the class is

---

over and tell themselves and their colleagues that the students are "getting worse every day"?

EXERCISES

1. Did the above excerpts from Katherine Mansfield's "A Dill Pickle" awaken any vivid memories of an amorous relationship you have had in the past with someone you *thought* you knew but apparently did not? If you have experienced the breaking up of a romance you believed would go on forever and have been puzzled for a long time over just why it didn't work out, use this exercise to help you come to more definite conclusions. It may well be that a good many such relationships eventually fail because both parties got their signals crossed and missed important nonverbal messages, as Katherine Mansfield's man and woman apparently did every time they met.

   Why not put yourself and the other member of the relationship in an imaginary situation, like the one in the story? That is, pretend the two of you have just met after a long separation, or else that you have decided to have dinner together to talk about the problems you are having in establishing real communication. Even if this never happened, you can jot down beforehand all the messages the other person was sending that you now believe you failed to receive, and all the messages you were sending that your friend seemed to miss. For example:

   a) If you were the boy, did you telegraph messages that said "I have a strong and healthy male ego, which needs to be understood and indulged"? Can you think of anything you did to communicate this idea without success: such as hogging a whole conversation with accounts of your exploits on the basketball court while she was looking bored and impatient?

   b) If you were the girl, did you try to tell him nonverbally that you felt insecure and needed continual confirmation that you were the only one in his life? Or that you too had a strong ego that needed to be indulged? How did you do it? Perhaps by becoming aggressive every time his eyes started wandering about and glancing at the other girls, seizing his hands and drawing him obviously back to the conversation you were having?

   I'm sure you can think back on the relationship and see all too plainly what each of you did. Now write your account of the supposed meeting between the two of you. Put your notes together and pretend that all the missed signals were sent out during the course of this one dinner. (The advantage of working out your problems in prose is that you can take such liberties with time and space.)

One parting word on this assignment: you can, of course, write it up so that you come out the hero and your friend the villain. You can see yourself as having been wronged and misunderstood. But if you are completely honest, you may realize that both parties usually share some of the responsibility for the breaking down of a once close relationship (or one that was thought to have been close).

2. In order to learn better how to get the right messages from others, it helps to become more aware of your own nonverbal signs. Although some of these depend upon circumstances, each of us has a collection of favorite signs, whether he knows it or not.

Write a paper on your own nonverbal habits. If necessary, do a little research on yourself. Ask the others to help you out and tell it like it is about you. Make a list of your most frequent signs, and ask some questions about them. For example:

a) I seldom make eye contact with people (what am I hiding? am I afraid of reality? or of other people? Do I feel inferior?).

b) I make apparent eye contact, but if you watch me closely, you'll realize I seldom really listen to others (am I totally wrapped up in my own problems? Is it that I'm impatient to steer the discussion into channels that concern me? Does my mind run in abstractions, so that it's hard to hold onto the here-and-now?).

c) I make intense eye contact and I listen with full attention; in fact, I "overdo" the directness with which I can relate to others (Am I lonely? Am I trying to tell others this?).

d) While others are speaking, I hold my chin in my hand; sometimes I rub it thoughtfully; sometimes I pull on my ear lobe (Am I insulting them by really saying "I'm a deep thinker and can't be bothered with your trivia"? Am I trying to persuade myself I *am* a deep thinker?).

e) While others are speaking, I find it impossible to sit idle and just look at them and respond to everything they say; so I perform needed tasks, such as sewing, dusting the furniture, making out a shopping list, glancing through my notebook to see whether there are some homework assignments I've forgotten. (Am I informing the constant talkers that they are idlers and shouldn't waste everybody's time, especially mine? Am I actually so self-centered that I pretend to have other things to do in order to disguise my lack of interest in anything the others say?)

f) While others are speaking, I tend to scratch the back of my hands, my arms, my neck, and so on. (Am I trying to cover up my boredom?)

g) While others are speaking, I tend to yawn (no interpretation problem here).

h) I have a tendency to force a smile or a laugh or keep nodding my head at periodic intervals, but sometimes I get caught by laughing when it isn't appropriate or nodding an affirmation when the speaker is really expecting a negation. (Are these friendly gestures on my part? or rudeness?)

You don't have to reach any specific conclusions in this paper. But, if you wish, you may speculate on what your nonverbal signals generally indicate about you, about others, about human relationships.

Possible conclusions:

a) I have a great deal to learn about truly relating to other people.

b) Some of my acquaintances make too many demands on a person's inner life and expect me to devote altogether too much time to them.

c) Looking back on some of my customary ways of not relating to people and realizing that others are doing the same with respect to me, I can't help feeling that human relationships are almost never direct and honest.

You may also want to consider some changes you would like to make in or relative to your nonverbal behavior so as to relate more honestly with others. Do you now propose to

a) listen more carefully?

b) make and hold eye contact?

c) do nothing else while others are speaking?

d) speak your feelings out honestly and tell people when you are bored or impatient to get to work on important tasks?

3. The nonverbal signal is not necessarily a bad thing. Cultivated properly, it can provide each of us with a defense against life, a way of expressing himself silently and (usually) without getting caught, a way of releasing emotions that have to be stifled because of the social and family rituals in which each of us engages every day of his life. Feelings are like steam. If you don't open a valve,

steam will find another escape. Silent messages offer one such escape route for pent-up emotions.

Make a list of familiar encounters that form integral parts of your life routine—especially encounters that involve you in relationships that can't be completely honest or that normally bore you. Next to each jot down some of your characteristic nonverbal signals, which, you realize now, express your feelings *for* you. Sample list:

Encounters	*Signals*
breakfast with parents	eating without pausing glancing casually at paper attacking the toast with butter and knife blowing strongly on coffee gulping down milk noisily
conference with professor over poor grade	snapping open and shutting clasp on briefcase during talk lips up tight; jaw firmly set elbow on desk, hand covering mouth direct, intense eye contact with professor, as if eye were ray gun
polite interchange with secretary at draft board	overdone smile ambiguous tone of voice when saying such things as "you're very kind" or "I really appreciate this" some symbolic way of sitting there to suggest being a slave, such as hugging oneself with one's arms or grasping the back of the chair so as to pin oneself down nonchalantly picking up pencil and holding it like a bayonet, occasionally taking a "stab" at the desk
friendly conversation with annoying guy who won't take no for answer	head held high as a sign that one is not an easy make frequent shaking of head whenever appropriate as apparent response to his statements but actually a way of saying no overdone use of eye contact, hoping he'll see the twinkle constant smiling as a way of laughing at him

If it is too difficult to pin down encounters you have just had, or if you haven't really had any in which you felt the need to use nonverbal signals, make up some encounters that you could have and indicate how you would express yourself nonverbally.

Optional variation of assignment: Perhaps you honestly believe yourself to be a person who tells it like it is and seldom holds back his feelings. Perhaps you find yourself noticing how others use evasive nonverbal methods of expressing themselves and believe that to do so is a coward's way out. If so, write a paper describing some of the typical nonverbal evasions of honesty that you find in people you know and have trouble relating to as directly as you'd like.

Possibly you have a certain acquaintance whom you consider to be really messed up and who continually sends out mixed messages; that is, who says one thing but shows quite another: a girl, perhaps, who pretends an interest in you but constantly combs her hair while you are trying to get serious. Or a boy is too shy to make advances but scrapes his feet around on the floor and gently strokes the back of his neck while discussing abstract and dull things. If so, turn your paper into a character sketch of this one person as an illustration of the "nonverbal cheat."

Role Reversal: Thinking like Another Person

Empathy for another goes beyond getting the right messages. Most people, however, are unprepared to take the bold and adventurous step of trying to project themselves into the mind and feelings of somebody else and to exchange identities with him, if only for a few moments, thereby glimpsing the world from his viewpoint. But it can be done more easily than you might suppose. In fact, if you have done any of the nonverbal message exercises, you may already have discovered how obvious people often are about how they feel or what they are thinking.

Let's begin with a very simple example. You have just spent a weekend fishing from your friend's boat. Many big ones got away, but you did manage to land a pretty impressive catch, say, a sailfish. Someone you know quite casually asks you how you enjoyed your weekend and whether you had any luck. You can't resist the invitation, which, for all you know, was tended to you out of mere courtesy. So you start to describe every detail of the marvelous experience, which exists vividly in your mind but which may or may not be interesting to your casual acquaintance. In the middle of your lengthy monolog, you suddenly become aware that your "listener" is looking not at you, or even vaguely in your direction, but at a piece of lint he has discovered on his shoulder. You continue to describe your dazzling skill in hauling in the fish, but you see that he is picking at the lint and seems quite absorbed in his efforts.

Chances are your initial reaction would be, like that of most people, to feel offended. "Well, really!" you huff and puff. "I hope I'm not boring you." Chances also are that, no matter what your friend may say, you will go on feeling however you felt during your immediate reaction. You will make no effort to enter into his thoughts and try to look at the possibilities:

1) He did indeed notice a spot of lint, and it bothers him.
2) He is trying, as politely as he can, to let you know it is time to yield the floor. Perhaps he was hoping you'd ask about his weekend, and he can't wait to tell you about the $500 he won.
3) He has nothing special to tell you but is not interested in your fishing success either. After all, why should he be?

How can you be sure which one of these comes closest to representing his true state of mind? Was noticing the lint a nonverbal signal, or had it nothing to do with listening to your story? Have you any right to be offended, or do you owe him an apology for imposing on his friendship with a long, dull tale?

One way to find out is to ask him outright. But we seldom get honest feedback. "Tell me what you really think of me" often is interpreted as a sign that you want desperately to be lied to, and friends usually oblige. Even "Have I been boring you?" can set up an immediate defense mechanism. You become the aggressor with such a question, and the response "Heavens, no!" is a way of warding off the attack.

There seems to be no other way than figuring out for yourself what someone may be thinking in such a case. Here are some logical steps:

1) Assume only the fisherman is ever really concerned about the fish.
2) Assume that if your story were fascinating, your friend would tell you in some way, probably by keeping his eye contact with you.
3) Assume that most people would know how impolite it seems to show obvious distraction—*unless* the degree of boredom has momentarily lulled to sleep their tact.

It seems safe to conclude your friend would just as soon have you change the subject or allow him to talk.

If you think you can stand to go a bit further, sit down and make a list of some of the people to whom you reacted recently—say, yesterday. Indicate what they said and did and how you felt about it; that is, what you told yourself about them. Examples:

Mother: As I was leaving for school, she said, "If you don't get a haircut sometime today, don't bother coming home."

Reaction: That suits me just fine. If she doesn't want me, I'll oblige her. What right has she to tell me how to wear my hair?

Policeman: All right, so I was going a little fast. He stops me, stares me up and down suspiciously, then whips out the old citation book.

Reaction: Definitely a case of harassment. The fuzz are always out to get us. We're not far away from a police state.

The Steady: Corners me just before class and demands to know where I was last night.

Reaction: I will *not* be forced to account to anybody for what I do.

In other words, these reactions should represent honest expressions of the role in the relationship you tended characteristically to play: the rebellious son, the outraged victim of "police brutality," or the participant in a romance who stubbornly intends to keep his freedom. They should also serve as indications that you did not attempt to reverse roles and try to gauge the other person's feelings or motives. Yet it is possible in these instances for:

1) the long-haired boy to assume that his mother loves him and wants to spare him society's scorn; or that she is aesthetically offended by long hair; or that she is fearful of having her family talked about by the neighbors

2) the speedster to assume that the policeman flags down fast cars without regard for who is driving them; or that if he does make a point of stopping young people, he is anxious to teach them a lesson that may someday save their lives; or even that he fears that long-haired drivers may be so strongly anti-Establishment that they might go on breaking laws for the sake of doing it

3) the person getting the third degree from his steady date to assume that this person loves him enough to worry about him; or that this person fears *she* is being rejected and needs reassurance; or that his persistent signs of independence can be rightfully interpreted as signs of waning interest in the relationship.

Sometimes one just happens to be in the right place at the wrong time, as it were, and becomes unknowingly the stimulus for provoking a reaction of some sort from another. The reaction may have nothing really to do with him at all, a further possibility to keep in mind when trying to think like someone else. The long-haired son, for example, may not be aware that his mother and father have just had a terrific battle over finances and the sight of the untidy head happened to be the thing to ignite the mother's wrath. Perhaps at other times, when she is not overwrought, the mother may secretly feel proud that her son has an intellectual air about him. Perhaps she was never able to attend college and is happy that her child has such advantages.

In some instances it is entirely possible that people feel nothing much at all about us. We have no reason to react negatively when, for example, we approach a friend just in time to see him yawning in our direction (quite by coincidence) or when we put down our luncheon tray to join a group, all of whom happen to be leaving at precisely that moment.

In still other instances, possibly innocent motives are given sinister interpretations because of some profound insecurities we may be experiencing at the moment: insecurities that have nothing to do with the person whose thoughts we are misreading and distorting. I used to be in the theater as actor, director, and playwright (at different times), and, like many theater people, I was paranoiac about critics. If ever I received a thumbs-down review, I would slink around the back streets, darting furtively into alleyways if I chanced to see an acquaintance coming my way. As far as I knew, the whole town was whispering about my flop and snickering behind my back. Once, however, I bumped into a friend before I could duck away. He greeted me with the broadest grin imaginable and said warmly, "I see you got your name in the papers again." In my state I took this as an insult. I assumed he was thinking of me as an abject failure and was cruelly enjoying my disaster. I avoided his company for months after that, much to his confusion. When finally confronted by my accusation, he was astounded. "Hell," he said, "I just think it's great to be such a celebrity. Nobody takes any kind of notice of what I do."

Mothers and fathers, friends and lovers, policemen and professors are three-dimensional, complicated beings. Too often we regard them as robots who come to life only to taunt and jeer at and hate us, only to nag at us, only to lie in ambush waiting to hurt our feelings again. In this respect we find ourselves being affected by the stereotyped characters that parade their traditional and unchanging wares before us every day on television or in movies. We get into the habit of seeing nagging mothers; turned-on, mixed-up kids; dumb cops; stupid, narrow-minded, small-town southern whites; arrogant and inhuman intellectuals; brassy blonde hustlers; or super-cool private eyes. Our capacity for looking with fresh eyes at every new encounter with other people becomes greatly weakened. "Here comes the cop," we say to ourselves. Or, "That mother of mine is going to start in again."

Popular mythology also adds to the gallery of stereotyped roles, making it difficult for us to put ourselves accurately in anybody else's place. If blacks on television and in movies are usually without faults, the everyday thinking of many whites tells a different story—in the other direction. Thus: "They're not all bad, of course; some of my best friends are . . ." and "The trouble is, when you let one in, you know what happens" and "Not that I mind, but there *are* sanitary problems. . . ."

But neither blacks nor whites are pushy, militant, threatening, cruel, or perfect—to the exclusion of a million other traits. Real human beings with names and phone numbers and $4.11 in their pockets are what go to make up the world. Learning to recognize the stereotyping we do ourselves is thus another important step toward thinking like the other person. And sometimes we must reverse the process and see that the other person is stereotyping us.

Once I asked the blacks in one of my classes to try to think like whites, and the whites to think like blacks. Here is what one black student wrote:

This is the story of a black laborer. A man with two years of college. He stopped school because he had to work and save money to continue his education. During his second year out of school he met and fell in love with a young lady. They were married after dating each other for six months. Because the both of them were ambitious they didn't have any children for three years of their marriage. Working as a secretary, she was salaried at one hundred and fifteen dollars ($115.00) a week. He, as a construction laborer, made about one hundred and seventy five dollars ($175.00) a week. Maintaining a modest apartment from their wedding night they were able to accumulate a sizable amount of money in the bank. They both thought that a house would be a nice investment. Scanning every paper they could get, they finally went to see what they thought was a beautiful home in a pleasant neighborhood. Upon discovering that the neighborhood was "Lily white," and that they were not wanted by the other residents, they went to a government agency to help them buy the home. Upon checking the particulars on the house it was discovered that the $32,000 asked for the house was $12,000.00 more than it would have been if it were sold to a white person. After thinking it over the house was bought, because the couple wanted to live in a nice quiet neighborhood.

When it was discovered by most of the neighbors that a "Negro" black family had moved into their midst, one by one the whites started moving out and selling at tremendous profits. As the whites sold, more and more blacks moved in. Soon the whole neighborhood was black. Once the neighborhood was solid black, garbage collections dropped off, the streets were cleaned less often and trash was left for weeks. Because city officials did not enforce the laws, the neighborhood went down. After 3 or 4 years a government program decided to renew the area. Now the agency placed a value on the houses that was less than the original $20,000.00 cost, proving to the bitter end that "Negroes," "Niggers," or Black folk are a major reason for property value decreasing.

When I read this paper to the class, a vigorous debate ensued over whether the student was stereotyping white thinking or accurately reversing roles with people in a white neighborhood who could be expected to think like this. Sometimes the only way to tell who is guilty of stereotyping is to test out your suspicions and see whether they are confirmed.

Believe it or not, this class actually decided to do just that. We checked out a movie camera from the Audiovisual Department, found someone who was willing to let us use his house for the experiment, and then arrived, some twenty-three strong, in an upper-middle-class white neighborhood. The object of the experiment was to make the residents believe some blacks were moving to their street and to film the spontaneous reactions (neighbors peeking through curtains, curious children coming to the borders of the property but not venturing one step further, and so on) and decide whether white people *probably* would react unfavorably to such a state of affairs. The results, preserved on film, showed us that the closest thing to a positive reaction we could find was that of a jolly little man who thought we were putting him on and who "cut up" for the benefit of the cameras.

In other words, the conclusion this experiment at least appeared to justify was that some upper-middle-class whites live up to the stereotyped role the average black casts him in and that, in this instance, the black student was being realistic in his appraisal. The black student had achieved a degree of empathy with a certain white viewpoint. Of course, we all agreed that it is probably easier for blacks to anticipate white roles than for the reverse to be true, simply because of the cumulative white stereotyping of blacks that has gone on for over a century, abetted by the entertainment media's past and, to some extent, present handling of black culture. The author of the paper I have quoted also made the excellent point that blacks have had to adjust to white thinking in order to survive in white society, whereas whites who didn't want to have not been forced to adjust to black thinking at all.

EXERCISES

1. The observations that have been made about role reversals and the possibility of thinking like someone else may also teach us a good deal about the secret of great and lasting works of fiction and drama. Many of our most important writers, especially those who we say provide "insights into human nature," no doubt possess an extraordinary ability to see into another person's heart and put themselves in the place of different sorts of people, perhaps even people of whom they privately disapprove. Great actors also have this ability; otherwise they would not be able to play convincingly a wide variety of parts.

   The average person, however, gets few opportunities to exchange identities with others so intensely and for such sustained periods as the artists do. In fact, if you were to ask him whether he should enjoy doing this, his reply might very well be, "Why should I? After all, nobody tries to understand *me* that well."

   So we are really back to the familiar problem: *What's in it for me if the others stay the same?* And just as soon as we ask such a question, we're back where we started: projecting our own thoughts into the others. We tell ourselves *they* won't try to think like *us*, but aren't we actually creating them in our own image so we won't have to put ourselves out?

   Still, you can argue that writers and actors get paid for their insights into others, and so you may have a right to demand more down-to-earth and dollars-and-cents motives for worrying about why the other guy is picking lint off his shoulder instead of looking at you. Maybe there aren't many practical gains for us ordinary folk, and maybe there are. Write a paper analyzing the pros and cons of empathy.

   To get started:

   a) On the most personal level, does it offer a means to a more happy life? Why? Is it because the more we are able to think like another, the easier it is to anticipate his actions and thus steer clear of trouble with him?

b) Do we stand a better chance of having a clear conscience if we learn how to avoid harming or insulting somebody? What is conscience anyway? Do you think it's acquired, or do you think it comes naturally to people to worry about what they may have done to others?

c) Is it all a matter of "enlightened self-interest"? That is, do we make out better in life if we get along with others, and is empathy a good way to do this?

d) How long do you think you would be able to empathize with someone who kept kicking you in the shins for your pains? Suppose the "other" is a person without advantages, a person you have felt very sorry for, but one who seems incapable of thinking of anyone but himself? At what point does your patience wear thin? Or is one-sided empathy its own reward? If so, why?

e) Suppose you achieved what you thought was empathy with another and actually overcame a prejudice toward that person, totally dissolving the stereotyped image you had formerly entertained—only to discover through some action he later committed that you were right about him in the beginning and had misread him when you decided to liberalize your approach. Would you say that you had profited anyway by your attempted empathy, or would you believe the incident just proves the foolishness of empathy?

f) If you are white, how do you feel about my student's charge that only blacks are required to practice role reversal? Do you think the time has come when whites cannot afford to stereotype blacks and refuse to enter into their thoughts?

g) Stokely Carmichael and other black militants have said, in so many words, that there are no "good" whites, in the sense that the Black Power movement would lose momentum unless it created a solid and unified target: namely, the white community. If you are black, do you believe it is not to your advantage to feel empathy for whites? (If you are white, could you empathize with a black militant, understanding why he felt the way he did, or would you inevitably refuse to take the first step so long as he refused to compromise?)

h) Do you believe learning to think like another means that you will like him? that hatred and distrust stem from ignorance and misunderstanding? If so, wouldn't this liking be another practical gain to be enjoyed from practicing empathy?

Doubtless there are other considerations that may come to you as you start thinking about this project, but the questions I have listed will give you a push in what I hope is the right direction. Do your paper on three or four of them, or just one, or else some that you have developed. Whatever the material you use, try to deal with specific incidents that offer concrete illustrations of why we should or should not exchange identities with other people.

2. Perhaps the exercise described above strikes you as being too complex and abstract. If so, you can try something in a more imaginative vein that may yield as much meaning. Pretend that a white family moves into an all-black neighborhood. Or pretend the opposite; or that a Cuban family moves into New York's Puerto Rican district (thus suggesting additional struggles from employment priorities); or that a Mexican family moves into a San Antonio suburb. Or any ethnic combination you wish.

Divide the paper into two parts. In the first section show the stereotyping that goes on in the mind of one person, who represents one ethnic group. In the second section, reverse the empathy, so to speak. Show what the other representative is thinking and how he misreads the first one.

You can make this as amusing, or as serious, as you want. But do what you can to be as fair as possible to both sides.

3. How the stereotyping tendency develops is a subject far too complex to try to cope with in a short paper, but you can take one certain *kind* of stereotyping that you think you practice or have practiced with considerable "skill" and trace it to a possible source: group stereotyping, for example. Nearly everyone can point to many instances in his formative years when he heard and then passed on jokes about Jews, Catholics, Protestants, women, blacks, whites, or whatever group may have been the target of ridicule in a given year.

Perhaps your parents or relatives or teachers or close friends or combinations of all of them were in in some way responsible. Can you think of characteristic things they have said or done that, as you look back now, seem to have pointed you toward an ethnic bias (or several of them)? This isn't to say you're bound to find your past filled with outright snobbishness toward minorities. Many of the most deep-rooted discriminatory tendencies can no doubt be traced to the most innocent-sounding remarks. I once asked a class to hand in lists of such remarks that they recalled from their past:

a) *Chinese food:* "We'll go inside for lunch, dear, as long as it's clean."

b) *Integrated schools:* "I'm sure there won't be any problem, but I do hope they keep two school nurses there."

c) *Cuban stores:* "I just love to browse around and look at all those funny brand names."

d) *Lobby of a restricted theater:* "You get away from there. Those white folks don't want you messing their place up."

e) *Seminole Indian Village:* "We'll stop in if it isn't too dark when we get there."

You can get plenty of material for your paper by making your own list of choice items like these.

Role-Playing

Once you've acquired the habit of trying to think like somebody else, you're in a better position to head off trouble. If you can anticipate the characteristic role people will assume in moments of crisis, you can sometimes figure out in advance what can be done to ease tensions or even to improve things. You have no doubt engaged in role-playing many times in the past, perhaps without realizing it. Didn't you get to know how your mother or father would react to, say, your coming home at three in the morning? Didn't you sometimes devise ingenious methods of entering the house undetected, and didn't you have a we-ran-out-of-gas story handy just in case? What I'm talking about now is the same idea, except that you try to be more systematic and extend it beyond the family circle.

To illustrate how to play the game, let's use a dispute over student rights, and we'll see that the roles taken by the various parties involved need to be determined before any progress can be made. As you note, role-playing is akin to "doping out" the race before the horses are on the track. You need to understand the past performances before you can predict the probable finish of each horse entered. Of course, sweeping generalizations are sometimes required, but nonetheless people do have a way of living up to expectations in a critical situation.

Very briefly, here are the circumstances. A year or so ago the American Association of University Professors issued a model bill of rights for students in order to guarantee academic freedom on the other side of the podium. Ever since the controversial document appeared, many student groups throughout the country have adopted it *in toto* or else adapted it to their specific needs. In most cases, however, this was done without the official sanction of the college. To back up their demands, as embodied in the various bills, students have been demonstrating, picketing, sometimes boycotting classes. Sensitive to the growing unrest among student populations, some college staffs have been trying to find a reasonable way to allow students as much freedom as possible without causing a corresponding decline in the freedom of faculties and administrations. Here we have a prime example of an explosive situation in which lines are clearly drawn and responses can readily be predicted. Let us look at typical demands in a typical bill of rights and do some role-playing on all sides.

Demand #1 is that attendance in class be voluntary and that in no case will a student's grade reflect his attendance habits.

Person	Response	Analysis
Accounting teacher	Negative	Business-world background; hence reacts as he would on economic issues; voluntary attendance for students = mounting demands by unions for higher pay; this in turn = intensified inflation, and inflation = bad economy.
Young English teacher	Positive	Idealistic; own background involves personal rejection of pursuit of money; hence reacts liberally, as he would on a political issue. Voluntary student attendance = civil rights, which he advocates since he has no great financial investments to protect.
Militant student	Positive	Rejects any imposed regulations; mandatory attendance = mandatory service in armed forces; war = possible death.
Conservative student	Negative	Voluntary attendance = victory for liberals, radicals, and other undesirable, unsavory drop-out types; since his father has money and a business, he has an advantage that he must protect; being required to attend class = opportunity *to gain further advantage* by willingly bending to discipline.
Dean of students	Positive	Voluntary attendance = lessening of possibility of student demonstrations; this in turn = responsible handling of position and increases likelihood of higher salary, promotions, and other benefits.

Person	Response	Analysis
President of college	Negative	Voluntary attendance = selling out to students = getting chewed out by trustees, who are businessmen and therefore have "retain the advantage" in their blood; this = hold the line wherever possible, unless it is better strategy to compromise a little bit; compromise is all right as long as it doesn't turn off the donors to the college's endowment fund; amount in fund = prestige of trustees = what they vote to pay president.

Demand #2 is that students and student groups be permitted to invite and hear any outside speaker of their own choosing, without prior screening or censorship by faculty or administration.

Person	Response	Analysis
Philosophy teacher	Positive	Freedom of thought and expression is essential if Western civilization is to continue its tradition of speculative philosophy; to deny any person the right to speak and to listen is to open the door for suppression of inquiry and eventually to brainwashing.
Political science teacher (one who has aspirations of becoming a chairman someday)	Negative	Historical patterns show that unlimited freedom of speech is impractical; somewhere lines must be drawn, otherwise anarchy reigns in society; sensible limitations on such freedom, when necessary, are the prerogative of the government, and on the campus, the administration is the government.
Chairman of business department	Negative	We train our students for the business world, and my prestige as an educator is vitally related to good feedback from companies who employ our products; since discipline and the ability to curb one's will are important qualities for the successful businessman, it is bad practice to encourage our students to exercise unlimited freedom of choice in the matter of speakers.
Militant student	Positive	Administrative interference = establishment censorship = right of federal government to declare war and enforce a draft system, and so forth. Once anything of this sort is denied, any kind of suppression of rights is possible.

Person	Response	Analysis
Conservative student	Mixed	I don't want to give up too many of my rights even if I *am* committed to Father's business; the threat of administrative censorship = memories of Father's threats and punishments; however, I can't very well side with the anarchists, for if *they* ran the country, our economy would collapse.
Young English teacher (who has already been in trouble over student magazine and has been warned of peril to job)	Positive	Administrative censorship = threat to security = outrageous denial to me of the security that those who oppose us already have.

A third demand found in the bill of rights has to do with student desire not to have to conform to any code of dress. This demand offers possibilities for a variety of motives.

Person	Response	Analysis
Middle-aged professor (with unattractive, nagging wife)	Positive	The dress fads are often cute, especially among the coeds; tight blue jeans are a most welcome addition to the classroom atmosphere.
Unattractive and unmarried lady professor	Negative	Many of the dress fads allow for a disgusting display of the body = increased chances for these immoral girls to find husbands = more people for me to envy.
Dean of women	Mixed	I enjoy wearing the latest fads myself, but it is also setting a bad precedent to abandon such an important part of school discipline. Relaxation of discipline = questionable need for my job at all! On the other hand, being too strict = possible rebellion = possible violence, and, after all, I'm only a woman in a man's world.

The characteristic positions taken, together with the analysis of each, were purely hypothetical, but the people represent prevalent types on college campuses today. At any rate, they are useful in pointing out the conflicting motives that underlie such disputes, and, especially, the impossibility of anybody's reaching *the truth*. Perhaps you even identified the role you yourself would take should a student rights dispute erupt on your campus. If so, did you look upon it as one possible role among other possible roles, or did you suddenly say, "Oh, but this is the proper outlook"?

Once you gain sufficient skill at role-playing, however, you are less likely to consider your own position to be the only sensible one. You come to realize that others can be just as convinced that theirs is the true and honorable course. After all, is it unlawful for the unmarried lady professor to envy the young girls on campus? Should a middle-aged gentleman professor *not* enjoy the way the coeds dress? May a conservative student not be interested in his future in business? Role-playing doesn't necessarily imply that you must always seek to change the thinking of others—only that you seek to understand it better.

On my own campus the student rights issue was peacefully resolved by a coalition committee of faculty, students, and administration, each of whom indulged in role-playing and strove to appreciate the position of the others. Each came to see the problem in terms of motives, rather than universal truths. When this happens in any case involving bargaining, a meaningful compromise can usually be worked out so that the most precious right of all is preserved: the freedom to choose one's role.

EXERCISES

1. Perhaps your own campus is now or has recently been involved in some kind of unrest. Have there been sit-ins, demonstrations, protest marches? If so, why not practice a little role-playing in retrospect, to see how trouble might have been avoided if positions had been anticipated and compromises had been made? Some guidelines:

   a) What specifically was the issue? A Black Studies program? A student rights bill, as in the example above? The banning of certain kinds of organizations from the campus? co-ed dorms? tuition?

   b) What was the exact nature of the disturbance? (Include an existing state of tension as a disturbance, even if no flareup has taken place.)

   c) Who were the main parties involved? Example: dean of men, dean of women, president of student government, United Black Students members, members of a club composed of war veterans, and so on.

   d) List a typical representative of each viewpoint or role you believe was taken on the issue before the trouble started, using the models given in the text.

e) Then decide how the trouble could have been averted. That is, what compromises should have been made but weren't?

f) Has this analysis given you some additional insights? Or do you still adhere to the position you yourself took at the time (or would have taken if you had been there)? Were you and those who agree with you in the "right"? Even if something called the "right" were possible to define, which is more important: holding to it no matter what the cost, or "bargaining" with other viewpoints?

2. Have you ever been witness to, or deeply involved in, an incident in which trouble *was* averted through advance role-playing? Describe the incident in detail. Show what the various roles were, how they were worked out, and how the knowledge prevented conflict from erupting.

3. In order to practice the skill of role-playing, select a number of crucial issues of the day and a number of possible positions that people might take. Here are some suggested people:

a) Mother

b) Steady date   (Don't forget yourself!)

c) Liberal teacher

d) Conservative teacher

e) A college administrator

f) Local officeholder

g) Your state senator

h) Vice President of the United States

i) President of the United States

j) Secretary-General of the United Nations

Suggested topics:

a) Peaceful protest demonstrations

b) Violent protest

c) Required military service

d) Bussing to achieve integration

e) Legalization of drugs

Whatever list of people you adopt, make sure that you give yourself a chance to analyze a variety of motives and a variety of involvements. Thus: the UN Secretary-General can be expected to be less concerned about the internal affairs of any specific country and more concerned about the outlook for the whole world in reverting to his typical role; but the Vice President of the United States may have to worry, not only about world peace, but about possibly ensuring himself of his boss' endorsement for the top spot on the ticket at the next convention. *You* may be idealistic and think a good deal about the fate of the world, but you also have parents and teachers and military service to consider.

Your paper can be nothing more than these analyses, or you may wish, on the basis of the analyses, to make some observations about the outlook for a better society and a peaceful world, measured against the realities behind the roles people take.

PART THREE

THE
SELF
IN
PROSE

FOREWORD

It is high time we came to some sort of terms with what so-called "literate" or "literary" people have meant for centuries when they referred to prose. So far in this book our principal concern has been with doing one's thing on paper, so to speak: getting it all down before the inspiration cools and the insight vanishes. We've been committed to the general premise that outlines and lessons in "how to get style" delivered *before* the fact are about as valuable as Wendell Willkie for President buttons or a 1943 Arthur Murray Dance Manual.

The intention behind this final section of the book is to see how (or indeed whether) it is possible to do one's prose thing *better*, or at least to explore ways of making one's prose thing seem "respectable" to literate persons. They may have some credits on their side of the ledger. It wouldn't be fair not to give yourself a chance to make more of a literary showing if you have the inclination to do so.

It is apparent that "prose" means two things. One is whatever you manage to get down on paper. It is how you arrange your words, how you translate yourself into sentences and paragraphs. The other meaning has to do with style in your language, with your effectiveness or lack of it in making yourself noticed through what you write. It would be a shame, wouldn't it, to have gone this far, developing ideas and expressing yourself on crucial issues, and *not* know whether you're coming across with any degree of distinction.

Back in the eighteenth century English letters enjoyed a golden age of prose style, but the emphasis was often shifted to the how rather than the what of communication. Writers tried to outdo each other in grace, polish, and finesse. They pored over their sentences for hours at a time until they were exquisitely crafted and finely honed, designed to be quoted by ladies and gentlemen of fashion and breeding. In this respect, prose resembled the dress of the period: full of frills and frequently overdone. Moreover, you could get away with being insincere.

Today, at least, standards have changed. There's still a distinction between prose and *prose*, but the latter isn't the exclusive property of ladies and gentlemen of fashion and breeding. Everyone is entitled to his day in literary court, and you can't be testified against just on the old grounds of being ungrammatical. You can wear bizarre prose styles like bizarre clothes and force people to give you a full measure of attention and respect. You can be fresh, original, and disarming. You can split infinitives, dangle your modifiers, and use prepositions to close your sentences with. But if you don't do these things with *some* kind of style, the world will go right on past your door.

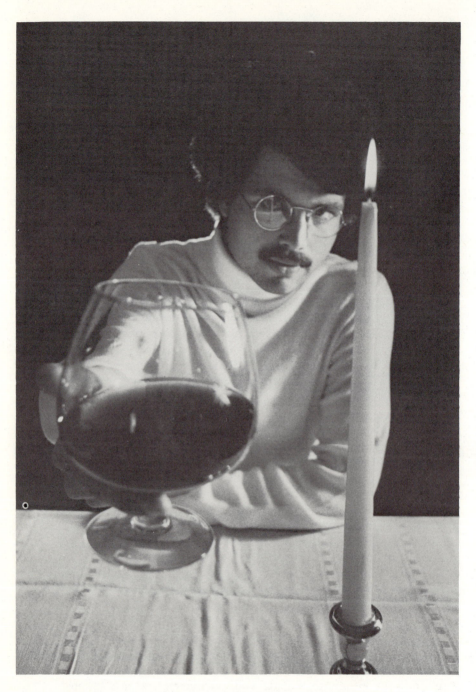

"He has at every moment a clear objective, even if it is only to thoroughly explore the possibilities of a moment that might strike others as being trivial or wasted."

7

PUTTING
SOME STYLE
INTO IT

The X factor in the way things are put is sometimes called style. It goes beyond the ideas themselves, because two people could have identical feelings and express them in different ways: one stylish, the other just a lot of words. Is Shakespeare remembered solely for the content of his plays? for the ideas to be found in abundance in every scene? Memorable as these are, their creator probably would never have made it to the top of the literary list if it hadn't been for the language flair, the special twists, the fantastic originality he brought to the arrangement of words.

Everybody knows "Friends, Romans, countrymen, lend me your ears." Everyone has been quoting it since he learned how to talk. It really doesn't mean very much, though, does it? An unstylish writer could have said the same thing: "Now listen everybody, I got something to say." Shakespeare's first three words even repeat the same idea. Marc Antony isn't asking for the attention of three different groups of people. If he had just said "Countrymen," he'd have gotten his message across, but maybe nobody would be quoting the line today.

I'm not even sure I know *why* the line is so great. If I project it into the present, somehow I don't get the same results: "Friends, Americans, fellow countrymen, listen to me." Shakespeare's effect may have something to do with the way the first three words sound in conjunction with each other. He had an unparalleled ear for verbal sound. His syllables often seem to fall into place as though they had always been like that. I also think "lend me your ears" has tickled the fancy of all those who have quoted the line. If you think about it objectively, it's a positively *mad* thing for anyone to say.

I mentioned the line not to analyze it or even to use it to help define "style," but rather to point out just how evasive yet real the factor of style is. Here's still another example, closer to home this time:

> Eighty-seven years ago the people here then set up a new nation. They were free men when they did it, and their idea was that everybody is equal.
>
> Right now we're fighting a civil war that's going to tell if a free country can last. We're meeting here in a cemetery that's filled with those who have died in this war.

Understand, I'm not trying to be irreverent or to make fun of Lincoln. I'm trying to show that I could say just about the same thing Lincoln said at Gettysburg, but I hope I succeeded in being totally unstylistic about it. I think you'll admit that, if Lincoln had started off the way I just did, he might have lost his audience.

Prose style, moreover, is only one aspect of the total problem of style, and we shall probably gain a better understanding of it if we first look at the X factor in three other areas: your way of dressing, your surroundings, and your general manner of conducting yourself (sometimes referred to as your "life style").

IDENTITY THROUGH CLOTHES AND OTHER CHOICES

Habits and Habitats

Aside from language, people have considerable choice when it comes to finding ways of expressing themselves with what they consider to be distinction or style. But in all modes of self-expression, originality is achieved with the greatest difficulty. When it comes to dress and living quarters, in particular, it is hard to rise above all the influences to which each of us is subjected every day of our lives. There are economic factors to consider. One may lack the funds to dress the way he thinks would really suit him or to live where he wishes or within surroundings of his own creation and design. One may live with parents or relatives or in a college dormitory and feel that his surroundings are anything but a valid expression of him.

Still, these obstacles can be overcome, at least partially, if there is a strong desire; and if the situation appears hopeless—if you can't ever seem to get your outfits to look like much of anything and your living quarters to resemble much besides somebody's attic—you can always turn to language. (I'm secretly hoping for that, I suppose you realize.)

I think it's pretty accurate to say, however, that most people prefer to take a stab at being stylish where it shows the most: in their homes, if possible; or in dressing so as to produce ooh's and aah's from the others. In my own case, verbal style always came easier. I have never spent too much time worrying about clothes, which do little for me, or I for them, I'm not sure which. It's probably a defense mechanism, a consequence of having a too prominent nose (a proud Roman nose, my father always maintained, and a too heavy beard, which once caused a student interviewer from a campus newspaper to write, "His face resembles an unrestored Greek statue." How's that for style?) So I figured clothes would be wasted on a classical relic.

As you might expect, my living quarters reflect someone who is always too busy to tidy up, to put it mildly. There are days when my study looks like the aftermath of a Kansas twister. It's not exactly chaos. That is, I know where everything is but wouldn't if things got put back into their right places. Loved ones and close friends, however, are often appalled and seem to find little to excite their aesthetic senses in my quaint and colorful surroundings. They could say my quarters are so me. They could point to the stacks of books lying around the floor, all opened to certain pages for quick reference, and say "He's hopeless"—which of course I am when it comes to what I consider to be the trivia of house cleaning and running a tight ship.

Not that my living quarters are appalling to me. As far as I'm concerned, they have a certain charm and a certain style because they are the way I want them to be. They are artless and disarranged because I work better when my tools are handy, even if the handiest place happens to be the floor.

Style in dress or surroundings, like style in language, probably has more to do with how you personalize these things than how fashionable you are. Maybe style is overcoming the influence of fashion altogether. In one of my classes, for example, there is a boy who writes long, complex, and profound analyses of current events.

He is especially fond of dismantling the logic of our national figures, as when the President gives a speech on television explaining a certain policy. This student will be able to show that the President used seven non-sequiturs, five verbal paradoxes, and eleven informal fallacies. Logic is strictly a game with him. He can be logical so easily that he has no use for logic and delights in showing that he can explode other people's. His personal taste leans toward the metaphysical and the poetic, possibly even the mystic; so he dresses most illogically all the time. His trousers are incredibly old, never cleaned or pressed; his shirts never match the trousers and seldom stay inside them because he has a habit of not wearing belts (which is dangerous because he is excessively thin). On more than one occasion one sock has been inside out or hasn't resembled the other sock in the least. But if anyone tries to call him a slob, I shall defend him with passionate conviction. This young man has style, and do you know why? Because whatever he wears, he wears deliberately. Intellectually he has shown he knows what's going on. His mode of dress is his defiance of a computerized society in which the rules of living are set forth for people by supremely logical machines (well-planned diets, IBM-matched dates, and all the rest). Ever go into a store and see one of those coordination wheels that tell you what colors go with what colors and what materials cannot be worn with others? My poet isn't worried about the fashion thing.

In striking contrast, I notice the girl in the corner—call her Jackie. This morning she is wearing a suede Buffalo Bill jacket, complete with fringe, a matching leather skirt, and calf-length boots. Around her head is one of those bright-beaded Indian bands. I mentally observe, "Jackie is a suburban hippie." Can't you see her with her mother on the shopping mall, purchasing the components of her highly coordinated Nonconformity Outfit? (Was there a sign in Mlle. D'Arcy's window that said BE A SWINGER IN THIS WILD WEST CREATION BY PIERRE?) Jackie looks as if she's wearing a costume for a play, one that doesn't quite fit. Do I think she's in style? Not on your life, and I'll bet the French Buffalo Bill job cost her plenty.

Written in 1922, Sinclair Lewis' *Babbitt* still has much to say to us about the dress and living habits of the small-town businessman (who also lives in the big town, by the way). That vast bulk of the population now known as the Establishment still needs to be reminded that clean, conservative, and respectable clothes—just so long as one looks like everybody else—seldom make for style.

His first adornment was the sleeveless dimity B.V.D. undershirt, in which he resembled a small boy humorlessly wearing a cheesecloth tabard at a civic pageant. . . . But most wonder-working of all was the donning of his spectacles.

There is character in spectacles—the pretentious tortoiseshell, the meek pince-nez of the school teacher, the twisted silver-framed glasses of the old villager. Babbitt's spectacles had huge, circular, frameless lenses of the very best glass; the ear-pieces were thin bars of gold. In them he was the modern business man; one who gave orders to clerks and drove a car and played occasional golf and was scholarly in regard to Salesmanship. His head suddenly appeared not babyish but weighty, and you noted his heavy, blunt nose, his straight mouth and thick, long upper lip, his chin over-fleshy but strong; with respect you beheld him put on the rest of his uniform as a Solid Citizen.

The gray suit was well cut, well made, and completely undistinguished. It was a standard suit. White piping on the V of the vest added a flavor of law and learning. His shoes were black laced boots, good boots, honest boots, standard boots, extraordinarily uninteresting boots. . . .

A sensational event was changing from the brown suit to the gray the contents of his pockets. He was earnest about these objects. They were of eternal importance, like baseball or the Republican party. They included a fountain pen and a silver pencil (always lacking a supply of new leads) which belonged in the righthand upper vest pocket. Without them he would have felt naked. On his watch-chain were a gold penknife, silver cigar-cutter, seven keys (the use of two of which he had forgotten). . . . Depending from the chain was a large, yellowish elk's-tooth—proclamation of his membership in the brotherly and Protective Order of Elks. Most significant of all was his loose-leaf pocket note-book, that modern and efficient note-book which contained the addresses of people whom he had forgotten, prudent memoranda of postal money-orders which had reached their destinations months ago, stamps which had lost their mucilage, clippings of verses by T. Cholmondeley Frink and of the newspaper editorials from which Babbitt got his opinions and his polysyllables. . . .[1]

Babbitt's surroundings are scarcely more dynamic. He lives in Floral Heights, an exclusive suburb of midwestern Zenith, and there aren't many passages in modern literature than can rival Lewis' description of Babbitt in the bathroom, getting ready for his day's work.

Though the house was not large it had, like all houses on Floral Heights, an altogether royal bathroom of porcelain and glazed tile and metal sleek as silver. The towel-rack was a rod of clear glass set in nickel. The tub was long enough for a Prussian Guard, and above the set bowl was a sensational exhibit of tooth-brush holder, shaving-brush holder, soap-dish, sponge-dish, and medicine-cabinet, so glittering and so ingenious that they resembled an electrical instrument-board. . . .

The bath-mat was wrinkled and the floor was wet. (His daughter Verona eccentrically took baths in the morning, now and then.) He slipped on the mat and slid against the tub. He said "Damn!" Furiously he snatched up his tube of shaving-cream, furiously he lathered, with a belligerent slapping of the unctuous brush, furiously he raked his plump cheeks with a safety razor. It pulled. The blade was dull. . . .

He hunted through the cabinet for a packet of new razor blades (reflecting, as invariably, "Be cheaper to buy one of these dinguses and strop your own blades,") and when he discovered the packet, behind the round box of bicarbonate of soda, he thought ill of his wife for putting it there and very well of himself for not saying "Damn." But he did say it, immediately afterward, when with wet and soap-slippery fingers he tried to remove the horrible little envelope and crisp clinging oiled paper from the new blade.

Then there was the problem, oft-pondered, never solved, of what to do with the old blade, which might imperil the fingers of his young. As usual, he tossed it on top of the medicine-cabinet, with a mental note that some day he must remove the fifty or sixty other blades that were also, temporarily, piled up there. He finished his shaving in a growing testiness increased by his spinning headache and by the emptiness in his stomach. When he was done, his round face smooth and streamy and his eyes stinging from soapy water, he reached for a towel. The family towels were wet, wet and clammy and vile, all of them wet, he found, as he blindly snatched them. . . . Then George F. Babbitt did a dismaying thing. He wiped his face on the guest-towel! It was a pansy-embroidered trifle which always hung there to indicate that the Babbitts were in the best Floral Heights society. No one had ever used it. No guest had ever dared to. Guests secretively took a corner of the nearest regular towel.[2]

True style, in fiction as in life, seems to be the exclusive property of those who are slaves to no tradition or social pressure or even the necessity of conforming to the life standards of nonconformist groups. It is therefore as difficult to find really stylish people on the pages of books as it is on the streets of a real city. Most of the time authors are content with a few brief details—such as "Marta looked positively stunning in her black shift and one simple strand of pearls" or "He looked around at the modernistic furniture and realized how well she had been doing"—and allow their readers to fill in the details from their own imaginations.

Occasionally we catch a glimpse of what some super-cool character is wearing or what his surroundings are like. For richness of imagination few writers can outdo the old master Jules Verne, who had a

---

[2] From *Babbitt* by Sinclair Lewis, copyright, 1922, by Harcourt Brace Jovanovich, Inc.; renewed, 1950, by Sinclair Lewis. Reprinted by permission of the publishers.

special fondness for the unique in people and places. Here's his description of the library of Captain Nemo in *Twenty Thousand Leagues under the Sea*, that rugged individualist who lives at the bottom of the ocean in a marvelous submarine of his own devising (not bad when you consider the year is 1866!).

> High pieces of furniture, of black violet ebony inlaid with brass, supported upon their wide shelves a great number of books uniformly bound. They followed the shape of the room, terminating at the lower part in huge divans, covered with brown leather, which were curved, to afford the greatest comfort. Light movable desks, made to slide in and out at will, allowed one to rest one's book while reading. In the centre stood an immense table, covered with pamphlets, amongst which were some newspapers, already of old date. The electric light flooded everything; it was shed from our unpolished globes half sunk in the volutes of the ceiling. I looked up with real admiration at this room, so ingeniously fitted up, and I could scarcely believe my eyes.
>
> "Captain Nemo," said I to my host, who had just thrown himself on one of the divans, "this is a library which would do honour to more than one of the continental palaces, and I am absolutely astounded when I consider that it can follow you to the bottom of the seas."
>
> "Where could one find greater solitude or silence, Professor?" replied Captain Nemo.

Pretty cool, eh? If you need privacy, what's more natural than inventing the submarine before anybody else had thought of it? And, if you're hard pressed for light at the bottom of the ocean, isn't it a fairly simple matter to invent the electric bulb, even if it is only 1866? I have a hunch Captain Nemo constitutes a myth figure with whom his creator could identify—a loner of epic dimensions conceived long before the anti-Establishment fashion of today.

But dress? That's something else again. Presumably Captain Nemo wears the standard regalia for naval officers of his day. Had Verne written his novel at the current time, it is conceivable that his extraordinary underwater intellectual might have worn a guru's outfit, yet, even at this, he would have been conforming to *somebody's* idea of fashion.

Perhaps we must all be forced to content ourselves with picking those items of clothing that come closest to embodying our image of ourselves. To what extent the fashions themselves force such images upon us, we may never know, except that I'm sure that somewhere at this very moment a respectable white-collar worker is furtively eyeing a psychedelic shirt in "one of those" shops, a shirt that positively glows when you turn out the lights, and wondering if this could possibly be "the real me at long last."

To completely overcome the influence of fashion, you would no doubt need to be a twentieth-century Thoreau and find a still undiscovered Walden Pond where you could build any sort of dwelling you fancied and wear whatever outlandish habits you pleased. The taxes nowadays might run a trifle high, however, so you might have nothing left for clothes at all. But beware of nudity-as-style. Many nudists look distressingly alike.

EXERCISES

1. Write a paper analyzing the problem of achieving style in clothes, using the definition given in the text: "Style is overcoming the influence of fashion altogether." Here are some questions to put to yourself in preparation for writing this assignment. Add any others that occur to you.

   a) How prone are you to conform with the fashions of any group whose approval you seek by dressing as it dictates?

   b) If the answer is *very* prone, explain the nature of the group. (Don't rule out the possibility that a person may have to dress to please a number of different groups.)

   c) What is the general mode of dress of this group (or these groups)?

   d) If you must wear more than one mode, are you comfortable in all of them? Why? Or does one strike you as being "you" more than the others? Why?

   e) If you consciously avoid dressing to please anyone but yourself, are you careless about what you put on? Or do you carefully select each article of dress because it somehow means you?

   f) If your characteristic outfit is, to the best of your knowledge, put together in a manner that above all pleases you, describe it in detail and explain why you feel it is an expression of your identity.

   g) To what extent is this "original" outfit conventional?

   h) If your outfit is a kind of uniform, it may be that you are proud of it and don't at all feel that your individuality is threatened by dressing like a number of other people. Show that you remain the complete master of your wardrobe by explaining the philosophy behind the outfit.

   i) To what extent does the desire to be attractive to the opposite sex enter into your choice of clothes? Does it give you satisfaction to be admired? Can you say that it is the opposite sex that determines what you wear? Is this in any way a threat to your identity? Or a fulfillment of it?

j) How do you feel about older men and women wearing the fashions of your generation? Doubtless you have seen people in their forties clad in serapes, Oriental outfits, and Afro styles. Are they being ridiculous? Do they have a right to do *their* clothes thing? Or do you think they have sold out and have no identity whatsoever? Give some specific examples. Describe the outfits and then venture a guess about what each person is trying to accomplish.

k) Men's fashions seem to be in the midst of an unprecedented boom. When I was going to college, the standard fare was gray flannels, a tweed jacket, white shirt, no tie, and dirty white sneakers. The possibilities for finding a trace of one's own identity in such a limited wardrobe were very few. But nowadays it seems as if there are almost *too many* choices. Do you find it easy to "discover" yourself when you enter the typical campus shop of today? If so, why? If not, what are the problems?

l) Finally, if the fashions, despite their number and variety, leave you cold, if you despair because it seems as if, no matter *what* you wear, you are conforming to some standard other than your own, indicate what kind of outfit would be most completely "you," assuming you had unlimited funds and your own personal tailor or dressmaker. Let your imagination run wild, and, if you wish, do your whole paper on this one item. Don't be hemmed in by any traditions. You don't, for example, have to wear material. You can wear bricks; a stove; a wheelbarrow; a drainage pipe. You can wear nothing and paint your body something different every day. (What? Why?)

2. Your teachers constitute an especially interesting group to study with respect to clothes and identity. For men, there has long been a traditional academic fashion; conservative and highly coordinated. For women, there has been the battle to keep the skirts as decently long as possible and the dresses as loose as possible without becoming altogether unfeminine. This doesn't mean there haven't been many exceptions over the years, but they were clearly understood to be exceptions. (I recall a young woman who taught us French in the chic, sexy fashions of Paris; her contract wasn't renewed.)

Today one notes some radical changes in faculty dress habits. A young art teacher on my campus wears bright lavender shirts, tight bell-bottoms, and sandals. Nobody is especially scandalized. What about your own campus? What are the faculty members wearing? Do you think they have succeeded in throwing off their shackles and making their clothes express them? Or do we have a split between those who conform to the academic fashion and those who conform to the way-out fashion? One of my students, for example, referred to some of his teachers as neo-swingers— implying, I assume, that they were getting a bit on in years to be squeezing into tight pants or skirts. He expressed a definite dislike for faculty members who don't dress the part and try to bridge the gap by imitating student fashion. How do you feel about the neo-swingers on your campus?

For this paper, take one or two of your teachers and analyze their mode of dress. Your aim is to see whether any of them comes close to having style and why; whether any of them can properly be described as a swinger; whether he is, instead, a neo-swinger; and, finally, whether there are still any left who fit the old "absent-minded" stereotype and who dress in undeliberately uncoordinated outfits, the sort that used to denote the extreme intellectual. The more ludicrous his clothes, the more he was admired by the students; does it still hold true?

3. Describe your habitat. If you live with your parents and had no say at all in the decoration of the house or apartment or even of your own room, then write a critical analysis of your surroundings, indicating why you disapprove, or approve, and why you think these surroundings don't (or do) reflect you.

Do your living quarters instead reflect your parents? What can you say about their style or lack of it? Are they terribly other-directed when it comes to the nature and arrangement of their furniture? Or do they seem totally indifferent to these matters? Are they supremely the masters of their surroundings, or the slaves?

Perhaps, within surroundings that you didn't create, you have put together a room or den ("my lair," as one of my students described his room) that you feel is more truly you than the rest of the house. Describe it in detail, and explain why you think your part of the house has style.

Of course, you may live in a dorm, but even dorm quarters can acquire some of the identity of their occupants over a period of time. Has yours? How? Your parents may be too strict or the college regulations may forbid hanging things on walls, and so on, so you may presently be at total odds with your living quarters. If that's the case, close your eyes and imagine what your surroundings would be like if you had all the freedom and money you could possibly need to spend on them. You can do this kind of paper even if you have quarters that are partially "you" and partially what you can afford.

4. Babbitt's bathroom reflects the hapless modern American who has become victimized by all the details in his surroundings: the "crisp clinging oiled paper" that conceals his razor blade; the vile, clammy towels; the forbidden guest towel (Can't you picture it? Doesn't it have one large rose in the center?); the problem of where to throw old blades, and so on. But the novel is a product of 1922. Since that time, the life of the contemporary Babbitt has been made even more complex by all sorts of gadgets: electric can openers, self-cleaning ovens, self-defrosting refrigerators, self-propelling "thinking" vacuum cleaners. Are these always the servants of man? One of my neighbors, for example, complains that her miracle refrigerator sometimes dumps its water all over her kitchen floor, that her toaster burns the toast more than *she* used to do, and that her vacuum cleaner once went on a rampage and broke the glass door of her china closet. If you want to have some fun, do an imaginative account of some modern citizens totally victimized and held prisoner by their marvelous home "conveniences."

The Flair for Living

Too many people have as little genuine style in the personal conduct of their lives as they do in their mode of dress or manner of arranging their living quarters. In the complicated cycle of wheeling and dealing we must face each day of our lives, it is difficult at best to keep one's eyes continually open and be so equal to all occasions that one is never engulfed by a situation the way even the most skillful surfer can be washed out by a giant wave. Indeed, many people have been beached along the shore a long time ago and just lie there, grateful to be able to breathe.

A real life style, at least in my opinion, means that you are one of the rare ones that people point to and say: "He's the person who can handle this. He's the one we need." As in dress and living quarters (and, as we shall soon see, in language too) one can be on top of things or overwhelmed by them. If one's day is disorganized from start to finish, if he's never entirely sure what's happening, but goes from one task to another with sleepy-eyed conditioned reflexes, it may be said that his manner of living truly reflects him; but what kind of "him" is being reflected? A disorganized, sleepy-eyed robot? Right!

So it becomes a question of where you want to be: on top or underneath. The people who hang loose and try to keep their senses and minds continually operating may simply get a bit more out of life than the rest do. They are bound to make their presence felt and win admirers, and this must be a source of great satisfaction. Or, even when they don't aspire to positions of leadership of one sort or another, they make it their business to seek out the leaders *they* choose to follow, rather than be driven from one leader and one fad to another by the throng. The person with a genuine flair for living becomes part of this throng when it suits him and he knows how to escape from it when *that* suits him.

The flair for living announces itself at once. It is as unmistakable as a truly distinctive apartment or a witty line someone delivers that has the stamp of a master on it. The flair person may command attention as soon as he enters a room. He may have a certain way of fixing his eyes, and his remarks seem prefaced with a quiet verbal fanfare that hushes an entire group into fixed expectancy: "Now I am about to tell you something. . . ."

Or he may be quite the opposite. He may enter a room unnoticed, leaving it to the pseudo-flair people to make flashy entrances and dominate the conversation. He may simply be there, calmly in a corner, but even so, you can tell he's a *real* flair person just by the way his manner sits on him. He listens, he watches; he makes his comment, if at all, only when the time seems just right.

The flair person has been dubbed "cool." He is probably not a "swinger," as that term is generally used nowadays (referring to someone who keeps up with all the "in" things) because he likes to keep himself apart from the fads. He can follow them when he pleases, but he can scorn them at will. This way, he has the enviable skill of "going with the action" in order to absorb as much of life's joy as he wishes and of sitting back to study it too. He knows you have to think about it much of the time and not let it overcome you.

The flair person knows how to dress for any occasion. He doesn't have to call people up frantically at the last minute to find out what others are wearing. If his attire is strikingly different from anyone else's, somehow *it* becomes the standard by which the others are judged. How can he do this? By not being self-conscious, of course. By not fumbling around with embarrassed words: "If I had—uh— known this was—uh—going to be informal I'd have—uh . . ." He relaxes into the occasion. He makes eye contact with people. He knows what each of them is talking about. He forces them to forget what he is wearing altogether.

Above all, the flair person is alive. He has at every moment a clear objective, even if it is only to thoroughly explore the possibilities of a moment that might strike others as being trivial or wasted. I had a friend once who was super-cool. He especially enjoyed the chance to teach impatient drivers a lesson. If he was parked at a light that had just turned green and if the guy in back started honking belligerently, he would turn off his ignition, step out of the car, close the door, walk very slowly over to the now-furious driver, and ask pleasantly, "Did you want something?"

Like the stylish dresser, the flair person achieves style in living by overcoming the influence of fashion. At his best he is the wonderful original, and everyone copies him. What did the Beatles have if not flair? They looked, spoke, and played their instruments in a new way. They wore long hair while everyone else was still in a crewcut. They behaved nonchalantly, as if they didn't care if you enjoyed their music or not. They had a way of performing as if they were doing it for themselves, and they made you forget the millions they were raking in. Within a few years they had revived a hair style for men that hadn't been known for centuries, and they still seemed unconcerned about it.

My generation had Humphrey Bogart, liked his personality well enough, but never quite knew what to do with him. Years after his death he was rediscovered by the cool crowd, who made him a hero. At his greatest, Bogart is supremely the master of a situation. The character he plays to perfection—the guy who has been toughened by life and has learned to cope with it by never showing his real feelings—can never be outtalked or outwitted. He always knows when there's somebody waiting to ambush him behind the hotel room door.

In one of the Bogart masterpieces, *The Maltese Falcon* (1939), he plays Sam Spade, Dashiell Hammett's·super-cool detective, who may have started the tradition of the suave tough guy: romantic lover one minute and karate champ the next. In the final scene it is discovered that the murder has been committed by Sam's own girlfriend. Here's the dialogue as I unofficially remember it:

G.F.: What are you going to do now that you know, Sam?
BOGART: (*at telephone*) Only one thing *to* do, baby. (*picks up phone*) Get me the police.
G.F.: (*clutching at him*) Sam, you can't do it. Sam, it's me.
BOGART: Sorry, baby.
(*He informs police where they can pick up the killer, then hangs up.*)
G.F.: Oh, Sam, what's going to happen to me?
BOGART: Oh, I dunno. You'll cross those pretty legs in court and maybe get off with twenty, thirty years. And if you do, I'll be waiting for you, baby.

G.F.:   Oh, Sam, will you? But—Sam! What if, what if I don't
          get off? What if I get the chair?
BOGART: (MATTER-OF-FACT) Then I'll always remember you.

Detective, crime, or spy fiction is where you go to find many of
the classically cool characters of literature. Since people with an
infallible style in living don't abound in real life, the so-called
"serious" writers are more apt to be writing about characters that
resemble you and me in their passions and irrationalities. But it's fun
to take time out from serious problems to seek the companionship
of a character who always knows what's going on and never can be
outmaneuvered.

The popular hero of the classic detective story, like those written
by Edgar Allen Poe or Arthur Conan Doyle, is the super-logician.
M. Dupin, the cool Frenchman, and Sherlock Holmes, the cool Englishman, have fantastic I.Q.s that enable them to solve apparently
perfect crimes, outwitting the world's more accomplished thieves
and murderers. Whereas Holmes' sidekick, the affable but relatively
simple-minded Dr. Watson, always jumps to the wrong conclusion,
Holmes is able to penetrate to the very heart of things. Here he is in
one of his characteristic displays of mental agility. Just see what the
sharp old character is able to tell from a footprint and a few other
clues that would be meaningless to us ordinary mortals.

> There has been murder done, and the murderer was a man. He was
> more than six feet high, was in the prime of life, had small feet for his
> height, wore coarse, square-toed boots and smoked a Trichinopoly
> cigar. He came here with his victim in a four-wheeled cab, which was
> drawn by a horse with three old shoes and one new one on his off
> foreleg. In all probability the murderer had a florid face, and the
> fingernails of his right hand were remarkably long. These are only a
> few indications . . .[3]

The Bogart "tough cool" is one of the many twentieth-century
versions of unbeatable flair that have replaced the intellectual cool
of the earlier detectives. Another, of course, is the pleasure-loving
James Bond of Ian Fleming, who can enjoy the morning like nobody
you ever knew:

> Bond liked to make a good breakfast. After a cold shower, he sat
> at the writing-table in front of the window. He looked out at the
> beautiful day and consumed half a pint of iced orange juice, three
> scrambled eggs and bacon, and a double portion of coffee without
> sugar. He lit his first cigarette, a Balkan and Turkish mixture made
> for him by Morlands of Grosvenor Street, and watched the small

[3] From Sir Arthur Conan Doyle, "A Study in Scarlet," in *A Treasury of Sherlock
Holmes*, Garden City, New York, Hanover House, 1955, p. 24.

waves lick the long seashore and the fishing fleet from Dieppe string out towards the June heat-haze followed by a paper-chase of herring-gulls.[4]

The difference between James Bond and Sherlock Holmes is that Holmes will never waste time watching herring gulls. Holmes always smokes his pipe while tracking down clues. Bond can't be rushed. He takes life at the most leisurely pace possible and is never too busy on a spy mission to pause for a casual affair with a stewardess at the back of the plane. The super-cool of James Bond is his outrageous disregard of all the conventions that hold you and me back from enjoying life to the fullest. Characters like Bond have to do that *for* us.

Television has launched a few cool customers who may turn out to be classics in their own right. At the top of the list I would place Phelps of *Mission: Impossible*. The whole mysterious organization of which he is the key figure has become a modern myth. From the moment he finds the self-destructing tape recorder in an unlikely place (inside a washing machine agitator, under a fire hydrant, concealed in the cap of the left mezzanine usher at Radio City Music Hall) to the supreme moment when we see how the mission has been carried out, Phelps walks an unerring course. His mind (and he is a souped-up version of the logicians of old) seizes at once upon his plan, and the suspense for the viewer consists only in wondering how all of the pieces will fall into place, seldom in fearing Phelps will be caught.

The second-rate detectives and secret agents are those who have to run a little faster (*Hawaii Five-O* or *Mannix*) and shoot a trifle straighter than their opponents. But too much is left to chance. Too much in these and kindred TV series depends upon "our man's" being lucky enough to find a banana crate to hurl in the path of a pursuer or an open window that just happens to look down on an expanse of blue water—perfect for swimming.

Enjoyment for the viewer can also come from the reverse of the flair detective. The person who doesn't quite make the grade as a cool operator seems to me to be almost a perfect comic hero, and I wonder why we don't run into him more often. A few years back Peter Sellers created in two films (*The Pink Panther* and *A Shot in the Dark*) a memorable character, Inspector Clousseau of the French police. This poor creature had an image of himself as a man of the world, a man of impeccable knowhow in the conduct of life and the investigation of crime. But if he attempted to slide with catlike precision from the backseat of an automobile, he would invariably have failed to notice that the car was parked next to a duck pond.

[4] *Casino Royale*, in *Gilt-Edged Bonds* (New York: Macmillan, 1961), p. 29.

286 THE SELF IN PROSE

If he picked up a yardstick in order to point to the exact spot on the
diagram where he was sure the murder had been committed, he would
invariably poke somebody in the eye. If he attempted to shut a drawer
with authoritative finality, he would invariably crush his other hand.
Inspector Clousseau, in short, was the ideal loser, the exact opposite
of the man with a true style for living.

Somewhere between the two extremes, Phelps and Clousseau, stand
you and I with our ups and downs, our wins and our losses. Life
doesn't defeat us continually, nor can we possibly carry it all off
with the style of the masters. But perhaps we can try harder, and
that's why it's fun to have the cool characters for models.

EXERCISES

1. How about creating your own super-cool detective or secret agent?
   Try to make him really clever, not just lucky. If he's a detective,
   decide on his characteristic approach to solving a crime. Will it
   be pure reason like the classic characters Dupin or Holmes?
   Or, if you wish, you can make the solving of the crime secondary
   to your main concern, which is describing the detective's character
   and way of life. Describe his clothes and his apartment. If he is a
   pleasure-lover like James Bond, perhaps he has some unique forms
   of luxury in his house, such as a bar that automatically mixes a
   cocktail by remote control and serves it to you by means of a
   mechanical hand.

   Is he tough-cool like Bogart? If so, put him in the midst of a
   crisis and show his devastating superiority to the situation as well
   as his admirable lack of emotion. Is he an agent like Phelps? If so,
   create some nifty gadgets for him to use as he accomplishes an
   impossible mission.

   You don't have to be all that serious about this assignment.
   The flair person himself usually has his tongue in his cheek.
   Here's how two of my students responded to this assignment.
   Admittedly the super-logician-as-detective is showing his age by
   now, and these students achieved a certain amount of cool in
   having fun with him:

THE MURDER OF HAZEL HAZENFLUCK

Detective first-class Hugo Groove looked the situation over
very carefully. The body of Hazel Hazenfluck was lying nude on
the bed, which was bare of sheets and had been pulled away

from the wall. The room was in disarray as though someone had completely ransacked it in search of something of value. Miss Hazenfluck was known to have in her possession several valuable jewels. Groove pondered things as he looked at the floor covered with face powder from the many opened boxes lying scattered about.

Once before Groove had investigated the theft of one of her gems and found it hidden in a box of powder. He thought to himself that possibly whoever committed the crime must have known about that theft.

He looked toward Pat Picht, who had first called the police and reported that he was an eye witness to the crime.

"Tell me the story again, will you, Mr. Picht?" asked the detective.

"Well, as I said before, I live across the court yard from this apartment. This afternoon I got a new pair of binoculars, and was testing them out," said Picht. "You mean, you were looking into this window from your place?" asked Groove. "That's right," said Pat, "I wasn't snooping. I was just testing my new binoculars."

Pat Picht continued. "I saw this man enter the room. At first he had a mask over his face, but it seemed as though she recognized him anyway, because he pulled the kerchief from his face. I could see him very clearly. I could even see a scar on the right side of his face. He started to go through all the drawers and went all over the room, very systematically. She did not move. She was obviously very frightened as he went about his business. He came over once and slapped her across the face. She gestured as though she did not know where whatever he was looking for, was.

"Anyway, he went back to his search and opened at least ten powder boxes and emptied them as you can see all over the floor. He then took the gun from his pocket and pointed it at her. She laughed at him as though she did not believe he had the nerve to shoot her. This apparently angered him, because he pushed her down on the bed, took careful aim and fired one time. He then wiped the fingerprints from the gun and threw it on the floor. That's when I decided to call you."

"I see," said Detective Groove. He sat staring at the floor, pulling the lobe of his left ear with his right hand. He stared at the powder that was everywhere except for the spot where the gun had lain. He stared at the perfect outline of the gun. From a distance anyone would think it was a real gun.

Then he got up quietly and took his handcuffs out of his

pocket. Turning to Picht, he said calmly, "Sorry, but I'm going to have to arrest you for the murder of Hazel Hazenfluck."

Picht looked surprised. "What tripped me up, Groove?" he asked.

"It's really elementary when you think about it," said Groove. "I'm ashamed of you for being so careless in your story. If it was true that the murderer threw powder all over the floor before using the gun, there could hardly be the bare outline of a gun down there now."

2. An interesting way of doing this assignment is to divide up into groups, as my class did, and have each group collaborate on a presentation. If you solve the "perfect" crime, either singly or in groups, a further twist to the exercise is to present the crime and the clues one day, let the other members of the class wrestle with the solution, and then during the next class have your detective show them how it's done.

3. One way people achieve supercool personalities is by excelling in a complicated game, like bridge or chess. It is maddening to try to beat a game-playing expert. For this assignment, write up an account of any unusual games that you know and that you could share with the rest of the class; games at which each player can learn how to be unbeatable. If possible, make up your own game and show the class what it is, perhaps challenging several people to try to beat you before you reveal the secret.

Here's one invented by one of my students. (Try it out on your friends. Better still, use it as a model for your own inventions.) Take fifteen coins or matchsticks and arrange them in three rows in this manner: 3, 5, 7. Come on very strong when you ask for a challenger. Tell everyone it is impossible to beat you. This will, hopefully, throw the others off guard and give you the psychological advantage. You then explain the object of the game, which is that each player may remove any number of coins or matches from any one row. Both take turns until one player is forced to take the remaining coin or coins. Whoever is forced to do this is declared the loser.

Close the book at this point and try the game with someone else. If you don't know the principle behind it, you can't count on winning every time, can you? All right; here's the secret. You *must* win so long as you manage to keep an arithmetical progression for your opponent. For example, if you move first, take three coins from the bottom row leaving the other player with 3, 5, 4. If he goes first and removes, say, two from the top row, your best move is to take the third coin away from the same row, thus leaving your opponent with a 5, 7 progression. *Never leave him with two even rows.*

(The inventor of this ingenious game came on a bit too strong for another student, who promptly challenged the infallibility of the system. He came to the following class and insisted on going first, removing three coins from the bottom row and eventually defeating the inventor. The challenger said there were many other ways to beat the system. Can you find them?)

4. Write a character sketch of someone you know very well who has achieved what you consider to be a true flair for living. Describe his living quarters, his way of dressing. Describe how he makes his living, who his friends are, the kind of parties he throws, the kind of conversation you hear at these parties. Describe how you think he achieved such distinction, such style.

Of course, you may recognize the flair but not envy this person in the least. One can be happy, presumably, without being the total master of his existence. If you lead a completely different sort of life from this person, describe how you feel about the gap between you. Despite the fact that you are to a certain extent hemmed in by various kinds of obligations (family, school, religion, and so on) you may find that much satisfaction is to be derived from shouldering responsibilities and doing one's duty. May not this be another *form* of mastering one's existence anyway? May not yours be simply a different sort of flair for living?

5. On the other hand, you may deplore the circumstances that hold you back from leading the same kind of life your friend does. Indicate this honestly if it is the case. What, if anything, do you propose to do about your manner of living if it is not to your liking?

6. Inspector Clousseau, as created by Peter Sellers on the screen, was an all-time loser. By the definition of style we have been using— that is, overcoming the influence of fashion—a loser is someone who gets engulfed by the situation. He has a positive genius for making the wrong move and having everything turn out to his disadvantage. But Clousseau was made even more ridiculous by the image he had of himself as a winner. He would look mysteriously at the inhabitants of a room and turn for an abrupt departure, supposedly to astonish them, but invariably he would walk smack into a wall.

Do a character sketch of a genuine loser masquerading as a winner, someone who positively maddens you because of the airs he puts on and perhaps even because he has deceived so many others. Describe some typical mannerisms and expressions, such as the calm look of amused condescension he puts on in your presence or his way of saying, "It hurts me to have to tell you this, but . . ." This is the kind of loser we don't mind criticizing, for his lack of humility tends to turn off any feeling of pity we might have had for him.

Describe some specific incident in which this loser actually lost but somehow missed the point. Did he, for example, announce he was about to put somebody squarely in his place, only to be outrageously insulted by this person without knowing it? perhaps believing he had been successful?

If you wish, you could consider one of your parents or teachers in connection with this assignment. Does this person come on in the image of the great discipliner, the all-seeing, all-knowing wielder of punishments and lessons in living? In your opinion, how does he fail to make the grade? That is, what is it that prevents your being able to admire him? Is there a contradiction between his own behavior and the discipline he exacts from you? Perhaps he achieves partial success in your estimation but fails in some areas. What are they?

7. The stand-up comics of today are identified not only with funny lines or gags but with definite characterizations as well. Often they use the winner or the loser, as we have been defining these terms. Bob Hope and Alan King, for example, are generally on top of things. Their humor comes from the digs they take at everything else. King gives the impression of being the poor harassed citizen, but the fact that he is totally aware of incompetence and inadequacy on all sides makes him something of a flair person. Hope, of course, will never be at a disadvantage so long as his wit holds out.

On the other side are the definitely *unflair* people, like Dick Martin or Tom Smothers, except that both of these comics do a variation of the straight loser. By talking circles around their respective straight men, Dan Rowan and Dick Smothers, they succeed in confusing all issues so much that they have not *clearly* lost. The laughter is directed quite as much at the befuddled straight men as it is the comics themselves.

Then we have a Jackie Vernon, the comic for whom the whole experience of living is just too much. The only thing that saves Vernon is his wry sense of humor in the midst of losing, as when he points his famous poker face directly into the camera and comments, "The one thing that saves me is my ability to laugh," and then creases back his mouth in a quick, subliminal grin that is gone immediately.

Take one of your favorite comics or comedy teams and analyze the nature of their humor. Is he (or they) on the side of winning or losing? What is the basis of your laughter? That is, do you laugh *at* him or *with* him?

Optional: Instead of doing a paper on an actual comic, why not pretend you have an opportunity to break into show business if you come up with a good comedy routine? From our consideration of winners and losers, you should be able to create a character that can evoke laughter from an audience. Describe him. Better still, have your paper take the form of one of his routines, or at least a part of one.

If you study a given comic very carefully, you will find that his material all revolves around a relatively simple basic characterization. Norm Crosby is a comic loser who affects a certain flair only to bungle it consistently by using the wrong words. Example: "I am not only a person of vast indigence and a high Q.E.D. but I'll have you know I possess extra sensible perception." Why not, for example, create a comic who attempts to perform certain actions with great finesse only to fail, such as putting on white gloves with man-of-the-world precision and not seeing they have no tips, or throwing a scarf nonchalantly over his shoulder and nearly strangling himself? *Hint:* Losers are easier to create than winners.

STYLE IN LANGUAGE

Verbal style involves the same knowhow, the same knack, the same flair as style in dress, decor, or living in general. Your language can be, like your outfit, uncoordinated without being planned that way. It can be, like your room, a hodgepodge of unrelated junk. It can even be the height of verbal fashion without having style or distinction. You can write English in the manner of textbooks for the foreign-born and be grammatically perfect—and deadly dull. Or you can use double negatives and even say "ain't" and still be stylish, provided you know what you're doing.

The person whose personality is vague around the edges, who has never quite come to terms with his identity, will have a way of speaking and writing that betrays him constantly. Your style in language is "your own thing" in words. It is your presence as much as your body is, and when it is very, very fine, you can make that presence felt by others even without being around in the flesh. The great writers are supernatural beings. They are capable of being everywhere on earth at once. They can never really die. Read a sonnet by Keats and ask yourself whether his physical death so many years ago has had any real effect on his presence in the world. The death of a great writer only means that his publisher can stop corresponding with him.

You can always gauge the importance of verbal style by groping for it and not finding it. Nothing is so frustrating as the thwarted desire to say something clever. The occasion is so right; all it takes is the killer phrase; you open your mouth, but the phrase isn't there.

Who has not writhed in his chair while watching the finals of the Miss America pageant? "Each of you five girls will be asked a question," says the grinning master of ceremonies. "On your answer will hinge the judges' final choice." Now, I ask you: would any judge in his right mind select a beauty queen on the basis of her *language?* "First, Miss Okefenokee," says the smiling M.C. "What would you do if your parents told you not to enter this contest even if you were sure you'd win?" Miss Okefenokee bats her eyes and smiles the way you might smile if the jury had just failed to recommend mercy. Then comes the answer: "Well, I would feel real bad about it, but I'd realize Mommy and Daddy know what's best for me. They have always brought me up to have confidence in their wisdom. We go to church together every Sunday morning and have prayer service together at night before supper, so I know my parents are wonderful and much smarter than me about everything. We also fly the flag on Washington's birthday." When a Miss America candidate is drowning, all the clichés in her life pass before her eyes. (To add further insult to the viewer's intelligence, Miss Okefenokee wins in a walk. Moral: If you think you've got a chance to be Miss America, you can ignore this part of the chapter.)

An astronaut was interviewed on television just before being sealed inside a lunar spaceship. His main comment is worth noting:

> I don't know what my words will be when I'm up there. I only hope I'll be able to describe what it's really like.

The thrust of man into space has created an increasing interest in verbal style. During the "pioneer" days of lunar orbiting, before the first moon landing was made, a team of astronauts, acutely aware that they were the first men ever to view the earth from the vicinity of the moon, the first men *really* to penetrate the midnight blue heart

This is a student photographer's version of a lunar landscape (actually a shot of a dried-up stream captured at sunset). Imagine yourself an astronaut. What words would you use to describe this scene?

of infinite space, became very language-oriented. They finally resorted to Genesis in order to send back to earth *some* idea of the majesty they were experiencing. Perhaps NASA in the future will be giving vocabulary tests to aspiring spacemen. Nobody wants the first vision of a Martian sunrise to limp back down here in a statement like, "Boy, this is really something."

Granted that verbal style is important unless you want to win beauty pageants, granted there's a difference between "astro haves" and "astro nots" in the matter of language, can skill in verbal expression really be acquired? The obvious answer is that you'll never know unless you try. There are certain systematic ways of doing the verbal thing at least a little better. The ultimate killer phrase, the line that will echo around the globe, may elude our reach, but we can be satisfied, at least in the beginning, with a little less.

In reviewing the problem in my mind, I see four categories of linguistic style:

> definitiveness
> logic plus originality or wit
> rhythm, balance, and simplicity
> metaphor, imagery, and analogy

Let us look at each of these closely and discover how relatively painless it is to practice and improve verbal style when you have a definable objective.

Definitiveness: The Emperor Quality

The definitive utterance is the statement that leaves no room for argument. It appears to sum everything up and leave no door open for further discussion. It is also rare, particularly in conversation. But you *can* come closer to achieving it when you sit down with paper and pen and labor over it for a while.

The most famous line ever written for the theater is also one of the classic examples of a definitive utterance; it is Hamlet's "To be or not to be: that is the question." What more need be said here? When you take away all the words ever spoken or all the arguments ever voiced for and against any issue you can think of, you come down to the final, ultimate, and eternal issue: does life make it or not? Of course, Hamlet's reason for asking such a question was the anguish he was going through. His father's murder, his mother's infidelity, his own need to commit murder to avenge his father: these things drove him to contemplate suicide. But "To be or not to be" has the

universality of all great utterances. It applies to any problem one
might have. It is the appropriate question to ask when the problem
boils down to nothing but the simple alternatives of whether to go
or not go, get married or not, invest in the stock market or save the
money for a house. This one utterance has given all of us a permanent
form for making a crucial decision. When you are able to say, "That
is the question," you know at least where you stand.

A variation of Hamlet's statement can be found in Patrick Henry's
"Give me liberty or give me death." Again we note that a choice
between two alternatives is posed. Such statements gain stunning
power by being so presented, for it looks as though the speaker or
writer had thought of absolutely everything and had at last come
down to making the final decision. The alternatives, moreover, are
also extreme opposites. In selecting one, you are forced to reject the
other. If you don't choose death, you must assuredly have liberty,
or, as in Hamlet's case, if you're not to die you must definitely go
on living. Right now, wherever you are, take your doodling pad and
see how many definitive statements cast in this *alternative form*
you can think of. Such as:

> Pass antipollution laws or pass me a mask.
>
> Let's have some standards of taste in movies, or abandon the pretense
> of rating them altogether.
>
> Legalize pot, or build bigger jails.

For a definitive statement to impress sophisticated listeners, however, it must be the genuine article, not a rhetorical trick couched in
similar language. The difference is often hard to determine. The
examples cited above lie somewhere between true definitiveness and
verbal trickery.

It's hard for many to resist the temptation to see how far they can
go with statements and questions that *sound* as if all the alternatives
had been reduced to two. For example, the Faculty Senate of the
college in which I teach recently experienced a conflict between certain
members who favored total withdrawal from the college community
and the formation of an independent corporation with bargaining
powers similar to those of a labor union, and those members who
wanted to bring about changes in college policy without going outside
the existing system. Those favoring incorporation took polls of their
constituents to see if enough collegewide support for their project
could be encouraged. One pair of senators proudly announced that
the results of their poll proved conclusively that the average faculty
member wanted the Senate to pull out of the college. But, in examining

the results, we learned that the question had been put to the department in question in the following form: "Do you favor the incorporation of your Faculty Senate as an independent body with bargaining powers of its own, or do you want the Senate to continue its present existence as the impotent puppet of the administration?" This kind of either-or business is well known to politicians and debaters. A truly definitive use of the alternative form on the other hand, sets up a choice between believable opposites. In Hamlet's case, one must indeed live or die. In the case of our Faculty Senate, giving in to the administration was not necessarily the opposite of incorporation.

Try writing some pseudo-definitive statements that pose false alternatives. It's not hard, and it makes you more intensely aware of what such utterances may really be up to whenever you find them in newspapers or on television. For example:

> Give me my own key, father, or put me in chains.
>
> Give me an A, or let me fail.
>
> Support your local police, or admit you're a troublemaker.
>
> Are you with us or against us?
>
> If you can't beat 'em, join 'em.

Since the last two are frighteningly familiar, we gain some insight here into the artificial alternatives involved in much thinking. It's the "all or nothing" mentality: "We must have people of one color only in this neighborhood, or we must all face a distressing loss of property value."

In addition to the alternative form, definitive utterances can also be cast in the *exclusive form*, whereby one appears to have covered the possibilities so thoroughly in his mind that any choice becomes impossible. One of the most famous exclusive utterances is that of President Roosevelt, made in reference to the "Depression blues" sweeping the nation in 1933: "The only thing we have to fear is fear itself."

When you try to achieve definitiveness through exclusion, however, you can hardly avoid using some tricks. Probably no such thing as true exclusion exists, but such statements have great value if they can persuade the reader or listener that they contain at least a great deal of truth. Doubtless an American in 1933 could have thought of other things to fear, but by accepting Roosevelt's premise at all, he would have been agreeing not to have any fear. If Roosevelt had said, "The only thing we have to fear is being depressed about everything," a 1933 listener could have shaken his head disapprovingly. He could have listed for openers "hunger, poverty, disease . . ." One evaluates such an utterance in terms of the need it serves and the success it has. When it contains much truth as well as much cleverness of expression, we have a right to say that it has high verbal style.

Without some principle of verbal style, such as the use of "fear" as both verb and noun, an exclusive utterance invites protest because, for one thing, people are just ornery enough to like to take the opposite side whenever you leave yourself wide open for it. In his "Self-Reliance" address, Emerson stated simply but definitively: "Life only avails, not the having lived." This affirmation of the present over the past is breathtakingly persuasive, yet there are many who might question Emerson's sweeping negation of past achievements. "Avails," after all, covers a lot of territory. But Emerson gets away with it because of the grammatical relationship between "life" and "having lived." The latter sounds so final, so *dead*, while the former is so alive that no one feels like taking issue with Emerson. (Why not take some time out to try your hand at some exclusive utterances, trying to gain impact by coming up with some style principle that gives the impression your statement covers the whole field.) Examples:

My professors seem to know everything but knowledge.
What I would like to see in my professors is evidence of learning, not the having learned.

Frequently it isn't the grammatical form of the statement so much as the personality behind it that provides definitiveness. We can say that these utterances are cast in the *powerhouse form*. The speaker's mighty presence is felt behind the words. He sounds so much like an authority that we yield the floor to him. He takes our breath away with his self-announced right to speak with positive finality on all subjects. We don't even pause to examine the statement too closely. We don't check for fraudulence. It is enough that we are bowled over.

It takes a certain kind of magic to accomplish a powerhouse punch with language. If one word falls in the wrong place, all may be lost. If you say too much or too little or the statement is too complex, if you give your audience even a split second to reflect on your right to wield such authority, you have missed your mark.

Jonathan Swift was a master of the bold stroke, the outrageous stance, the imperious pose. He said some of the most devastating things about man anyone ever dreamed up, and still we sing his praises for it. He puts us down continually, and we come back eagerly for more. The stronger his venom, the better we like it. At one point in *Gulliver's Travels* the hero is standing on the palm of the giant

king of Brobdingnag and telling him of how we humans live and
govern ourselves. After listening to Gulliver's story, the king replies
definitively: "But, by what I have gathered from your own relation,
and the answers I have with much pains wringed and extorted from
you; I cannot but conclude the bulk of your natives, to be the most
pernicious race of little odious vermin that nature ever suffered to
crawl upon the surface of the earth."

Swift's famous put-down was a long time ago. In our own age we
find an impressive revival of powerhouse prose, both spoken and
written. The various anti-Establishment movements have been partly
responsible. Leaders like Rap Brown don't win followers just from
the cause they uphold. Brown knows a thing or two about verbal
style, and he knows how to wow an audience. Advocating violence as
the only means of social change, he once expressed this idea in a
powerhouse utterance: "Violence is as American as the Fourth of
July and cherry pie." In addition to the obviously intended shock of
pairing the idea of violence with "harmless" items that call to mind
images of family picnics and foot races, Brown also achieves a sense
of underlying logic by reminding us that the Fourth of July originated
in blood. The subliminal flash of red blood is then picked up by the
use of cherry rather than the traditional apple pie.

When the spirit moves Rap Brown, it is as likely to be the muse of
poetic prose as it is the idea of revolution.

> Black folks don't buy a Cadillac and we don't drink RC Cola. We
> don't do nothing. Just like the history book they've sold to black
> people for years. Everything black is bad. Black cows don't give
> good milk. Black hens don't lay good eggs. You talk about black
> mail and that's bad. Funerals are black, weddings are white. Angel
> food cake is white. Jesus is white, Judas is black. We ain't won
> one yet!

A little later in this same speech Brown paraphrases one of the all-
time masters of the powerhouse utterance and scores a double thrust:
"George Bernard Shaw says of America and its white people that
America is the only country he knows that went directly from barba-
rism to decadence without going through civilization." Not only does
Brown have the use of Shaw's own verbal rapiers, but he applies them
to American racism. He has an authoritative figure speaking *for* him,
in a sense, but he also gives Shaw's remark a specific context it didn't
have originally.

It is hard to specify a rule of thumb for achieving the powerhouse
effect. If you can bowl people over, you've done it. The King of Brobdingnag's put-down gains its effect from its momentum. Anybody that

can put so many syllables together in one sentence must blast us into submission. Shaw's sense of superiority comes through all of his writings, and, when you keep telling people how great you are, they'll have to start believing you. Brown's secret is to combine shock with logic, but there's some other secret ingredient that's hard to determine. Perhaps it's the passionate belief in what he's saying, a dedication to his cause that's so strong he keeps coming at you with more and more. In this respect he shares with Swift an effectiveness gained through momentum. It can be imitated, but you need a lot of syllables at your command.

Logic Plus Originality: Wit

All statements that have style are in one respect "definitive," but there are several other specific methods that can be imitated for the improvement of one's own style, methods that employ approaches not found in the statements we have so far examined. One of these methods is well known to writers famous for their wit. It is to say something that sounds reasonable, even familiar, but to give it a twist that changes the expected meaning and allows the writer or speaker to say something quite different and often more profound. It is the quality of unexpectedness that causes us to laugh or smile when we hear it, but it is the wisdom that gives it distinction.

Oscar Wilde's *The Importance of Being Earnest* (1895) contains one of the world's largest single collections of witty lines, most of them given to Lady Bracknell, the prototype of social lionesses, the grand gorgon of London society, a fierce old warhorse who makes every utterance sound as if it were the final word on that subject. In writing her dialogue, Wilde consistently uses the formula of logic plus originality. Here are some examples:

1) Interviewing Jack Worthing, a young man seeking her daughter's hand in marriage, Lady Bracknell asks whether he smokes. He admits he does. She replies: "I am glad to hear it. A man should always have an occupation of some kind."
(*Analysis:* It is true that a man needs an occupation, but most people would not consider smoking in this category. But the *profundity* of the remark is that Jack, like most of the eligible young bachelors in her social stratum, is idle, uncreative, and totally useless. Thus it is *logical* for smoking to be considered his "occupation.")

2) Having asked Jack whether his parents were living, Lady Bracknell is informed that the young man has lost both his parents. She replies: "Both? . . . That seems like carelessness."
(*Analysis:* Lady Bracknell is not necessarily unfeeling, though she

always refuses to say the obvious and trite things. Most people would say: "Oh I'm sorry" without particularly meaning it. Her "fresh" answer, among sophisticated people, would be preferable to a pretended display of sympathy. Besides, she is hitting back at Jack's own use of the trite sentiment. Like many of us, Jack is afraid to face the reality of death and resorts to the evasive word "lost," thus inviting Lady Bracknell's realistic comeback. The logic of the remark is that you shouldn't evade the issues without being prepared for such a reprisal. If Jack had said "My parents are dead," Lady Bracknell would have had no chance for wit.)

3) In a later scene Lady Bracknell discovers that her nephew plans to marry a wealthy young girl. She warns the bride-to-be that the nephew has "nothing but his debts to depend upon," but hastily adds that it wouldn't be a good idea for a girl to marry only for money. "When I married Lord Bracknell I had no fortune of any kind. But I never dreamed for a moment of allowing that to stand in my way."
(*Analysis:* The logic is evident here. Lady Bracknell is arguing against mercenary marriages, and what she says about her own "unmercenary" intentions appears to follow from the general context. But then you realize that she has shifted gears without warning. In not "allowing that to stand in my way," she has really been the most mercenary of all. As in the first line we analyzed, however, Lady Bracknell is making an indirect comment about the Victorian society in which she lives. She is admitting that marriage has to be mercenary and is therefore approving of her nephew's choice.)

Another Victorian famous for his wit and generally quotable remarks was Benjamin Disraeli, whose prose and oratory carried him to the prime ministership of England. One of his memorable utterances was a parody of a famous line of Alexander Pope that every schoolboy has had drummed into his head by teachers: "A little learning is a dangerous thing." Disraeli's version is, "A little sincerity is a dangerous thing, and a great deal of it is absolutely fatal." The switch is that Pope wants us to learn more: a lot of learning is not dangerous but greatly to be desired. We expect the same conclusion about sincerity but instead find that we should quit while we're ahead with just a little. If Pope's line had not already been in existence, Disraeli's would have meant much less. Pope offers the logical form of the statement, Disraeli the original twist. By providing a climax that is as unexpected as it is also logical itself, Disraeli is able to make a profound commentary about what happens to honest, idealistic people in this world and to make us smile at the same time.

A master of the unexpected but logical *climax*, as indeed he was a master of verbal style in general, was Mark Twain. He had that rare ability to combine a significant *what* with a memorable *how*, unlike other writers who go out of their way to sound clever but really aren't when you start looking carefully at their statements. In the following two sentences, note how Twain builds up the reader step by step to a definite expectation, then totally frustrates this expectation with a striking twist that is not only witty but powerfully sobering. On top of that, Twain forces him to accept the absolute validity of this verbal performance and realize that the original expectation was a foolish and sentimental one:

> Whoever has lived long enough to find out what life is, knows how deep a debt of gratitude we owe to Adam, the first great benefactor of our race. He brought death into the world.

Rhythm, Balance, and Simplicity

Joining the what and the how of your statements becomes a lot easier if you adopt the method of the old Chinese schools: that is, do your work out loud. Many beginning writers could spare themselves the embarrassment of hearing clumsy sentences read back to the class from the teacher's podium if they would anticipate such sessions and say each statement orally during the act of composition itself. All of us have heard enough effective speakers to have our ears attuned to the gratifying sensation of rhythm and balance, as opposed to the grating sensation of words put together without regard for their order.

Teachers can be just as guilty of carelessness. Here is a sentence from an expository essay written for me by a social science instructor who was taking a writing workshop:

> I noticed how uncomfortable some of my fellow teachers became when we discussed the way most times we agree to a new concept and then revert to the comfortable old way of giving facts, numbers, dates, and asking the pupils to memorize things which we teachers would not even know without the answer books right in front of us.

Sentences like this one send writing teachers straight to their analysts. There's nothing really *wrong* with it. Still, when you read an entire paper in prose of this quality, your conscience tells you it isn't worth an A. You know what's basically wrong is that there isn't anything especially right. Had the author paid attention to the principle of rhythm and balance in style, he might have turned in a paper of distinction. The fact that the sentence quoted above has so much to say makes its lack of style even more regrettable.

Another way of developing a sense of rhythm and balance—that is, if you don't trust your ear—is to try it with your feet. Take one of your sentences, get out there in the center of the room, and try to dance to it. Of course you won't do the conventional steps, but you can improvise, can't you? You'll certainly be able to tell the difference between those word arrangements that allow you to glide smoothly and those that suddenly give you two left feet. Try gliding to "the way most times we agree to a new concept and then revert to the comfortable old way of giving facts, numbers, dates, and asking etc. etc."

Some of the most memorable utterances ever made owe their durability to their rhythm and balance. Through this one principle their authors have achieved what is sometimes termed *simplicity*, but which almost never is as simple as it looks. (Simplicity in writing is like gliding on ice skates. It takes plenty of practice, no matter how easy it seems when others do it.)

Here are three statements by Winston Churchill that exhibit the principle almost to perfection:

> Now this is not the end. It is not even the beginning of the end. But it is, perhaps, the end of the beginning. (From a speech to the British people during World War II. British morale during the blitz was in large measure bolstered by Churchill's stirring oratory.)
>
> Death and sorrow will be the companions of our journey; hardship our garment; constancy and valor our only shield. We must be united, we must be undaunted, we must be inflexible.
>
> Never in the field of human conflict was so much owed by so many to so few. (Spoken in the House of Commons as a tribute to the Royal Air Force.)

Or what about this one from Mark Twain, who here combines rhythm and balance with his favorite device, the unexpected but logical climax?

> It is by the goodness of God that in our country we have those three unspeakably precious things: freedom of speech, freedom of conscience, and the prudence never to practice either of them.

Like Churchill, Abraham Lincoln is remembered for his style quite as much as his statesmanship. In fact, the one can hardly be separated from the other. *The Gettysburg Address* in its totality is a marvel of simplicity and is perhaps the most easily memorized single piece ever written. But Lincoln's repertoire is vast. You couldn't ask for a more incisive definition of democracy than:

> As I would not be a *slave,* so I would not be a *master.* This expresses
> my idea of democracy. Whatever differs from this, to the extent of
> the difference, is no democracy.

Note also the concreteness of the contrast between slave and master.
How much more effective than a bunch of abstract words about
democracy.

Here are two versions of the same famous idea:

> If a house be divided against itself, that house cannot stand. (Mark,
> King James Bible, 1611 translation.)
> A house divided against itself cannot stand. (Lincoln)

Lincoln's paraphrase is an improvement on the original mainly
through the elimination of the second "house."

But we needn't look only to the great statesmen for important
comments on national problems. At any moment we can find one that
ought to be famous because it has real style.

> No nation has ever talked so much of religious liberty; no nation has
> had such a strong movement for conservation; no nation has declared
> itself so strongly for freedom as the American Nation. And no people
> in America has had so close an acquaintance with America's failures
> in all these areas as have the American Indians.[5]

The continual repetition of "nation" keeps building up a sense of
American greatness, and this in turn is dashed to the ground by
"failures." The writer of this editorial is using the "Mark Twain
effect" of rhythm plus the unexpected but logical climax.

All of these examples have been widely separated in time and
intent, but one thing they seem to have in common is a certain quiet
conviction, in contrast to the more emotion-packed momentum of
the powerhouse utterance. The following paragraph belongs to the
enduring literature of moving simplicity. It is a direct quotation
from Bartolomeo Vanzetti, who with Nicola Sacco, was executed
in the Charlestown State Prison in Boston on August 22, 1927, for a
payroll robbery murder. Up to the very end they maintained their
innocence. The case made international headlines, and Vanzetti's
statement, given to a reporter in a prison interview, reflects a philosophical calm and clarity that transcend the speaker's lack of formal
education. The rhythm and balance of the prose became the trademark of both men.

[5] From an editorial published in August, 1967, in the *Oracle of Southern California.*

If it had not been for these thing, I might have live out my life talking at street corners to scorning men. I might have die, unmarked, unknown, a failure. Now we are not a failure. This is our career and our triumph. Never in our full life could we hope to do such work for tolerance, for justice, for man's understanding of man as now we do by accident. Our words—our lives—our pains—nothing! The taking of our lives—lives of a good shoemaker and a fish-peddler—all! That last moment belongs to us—that agony is our triumph! [6]

Metaphor, Analogy, and Imagery

If the idea is compelling enough and the language simple and uncluttered, you are bound to have impact on readers or listeners. But there are times when there is no effectively *direct* verbal equivalent to what you are feeling. The poets know what it's like to have a tremendous and beautiful idea to communicate and realize no words have yet been invented to get the job done. At such times it is necessary to create something new.

A metaphor is writing about something in terms of something else. In its less significant sense, it means taking the abstract and making it more concrete. When Longfellow said, "Sail on, O Ship of State!" he was merely giving color and vitality to the concept of American government. He was not exactly using the metaphor of the ship to make accessible to the imagination and the understanding something that would otherwise elude both. He was, in short, just being fancy, and that isn't my idea of metaphor.

At their worst, metaphors are ghastly relics of a rhetorical past. Nineteenth-century writers often employed them for show the way a woman might adorn herself with a glittering necklace, four bracelets, a wristwatch, and three diamond rings. Sure, she attracts attention to herself, but who needs that kind of attention? Here is a specimen of nineteenth-century prose, regrettably written as late as 1925:

> The Constitution is neither, on the one hand, a Gibraltar Rock, which wholly resists the ceaseless washing of time and circumstance, nor is it, on the other hand, a sandy beach, which is slowly destroyed by the erosion of the waves. It is rather to be likened to a floating dock, which, while firmly attached to its moorings, and not therefore at the caprice of the waves, yet rises and falls with the tide of time and circumstance.

Metaphors are doubly dangerous because you can get carried away and apply a number of different comparisons to the same object or

[6] Transcribed by Philip D. Strong and quoted in *The Letters of Sacco and Vanzetti*, ed. Marion Frankfurter and Gardner Jackson (New York: E. P. Dutton & Co., Inc.)

idea, as the high school student did once by defining a virgin forest as a place "where the hand of man has never set foot" or the poet Joyce Kilmer does in his famous "Trees," when he offers us the confusing idea of a tree as a woman wearing a hat which looks like a robin's nest while she is simultaneously holding up her arms in prayer *and* suckling at the sweet flowing breast of Mother Earth. The next time you take gymnastics, see whether you can get into all those positions at once!

The proper use of metaphor is to make the inexpressible available to the understanding through the use of appropriate comparison. In 1946 Winston Churchill summed up what suddenly seemed to be happening all over Europe as the Soviet Union, formerly an ally against Germany and Hitler, began to separate itself from the free world: "An iron curtain has descended over the Continent." The phrase has stuck, and no one today can think of a better way of describing the invisible but no less tangible barrier between Soviet territory and the rest of Europe.

As timely today as it was when he thought of it in 1906 is this definition of prejudice written by Ambrose Bierce for *The Devil's Dictionary:* "a vagrant opinion without visible means of support." As you can see, when metaphor is truly in there swinging, it is not just a stylish decoration. It makes us understand something as we never have done before.

When metaphor is expanded a little further so that it makes use of more than one aspect of the comparison, it becomes *analogy*. We would turn the definition of prejudice into an analogy, for example, by adding another sentence: "One should be careful about picking it up and giving it a free ride."

As you can see, the effect of analogy is likely to be humorous. One reason is that writers are self-conscious of using figurative language for fear of going too far, and analogy is one way of doing just that. But if you want to make a devastating point and get away with it, analogy gets the job done for you. See how novelist Max Shulman opens one chapter of his story about college life, *Barefoot Boy with Cheek:* "St. Paul and Minneapolis extend from the Mississippi River like the legs on a pair of trousers. Where they join is the University of Minnesota."

Ambrose Bierce, also in *The Devil's Dictionary*, describes marriage through an analogy that is grimly funny but also quite serious: "a community consisting of a master, a mistress, and two slaves, making in all, two." Mark Twain, the master of wit, was also the master of analogy. Here is an incisive comment about all of us that has some humor but plenty of grim truth: "Everyone is a moon, and has a dark side which he never shows to anybody." Twain can also be completely serious in using analogy: "Thunder is good, thunder is impressive, but it is lightning that does the work."

Closely allied to analogy is imagery, a device of style whereby the inexpressible is made available to the reader's imagination through words that create a picture in the mind. By seeing the picture, the mind grasps the idea. A lot of writers have talked about the cruelty, unpleasantness, and, often, sorrow of life, but when humorist Tom Lehrer describes existence as "sliding down a razor blade," we get both a ludicrous image *and* the point!

True poets and good songwriters would be out of business without imagery. Whoever saw age better expressed than in this image by William Butler Yeats?

> An aged man is but a paltry thing,
> A tattered coat upon a stick . . .[7]

I don't believe all the books on religion I've ever read or all the sermons I've ever heard have brought closer to me the idea of God than does this famous image by Gerard Manley Hopkins:

> . . . the Holy Ghost over the bent
> world broods with warm breast and with ah!
> bright wings.[8]

Some poetic images are far more complex than even this and offer subliminal, but haunting, glimpses of pictures—things that don't quite stay stable in the mind, but nonetheless we know they have caught hold of realities. The great Welsh poet Dylan Thomas, for example, captures the sense of what Sunday was like to a young boy:

> And the sabbath rang slowly
> In the pebbles of the holy streams.[9]

If my life depended on it, I couldn't analyze this image or tell you why it works, but we both know it somehow does. And so does this haunting way the American poet E. E. Cummings describes the fragile

[7] Reprinted with permission of The Macmillan Company, The Macmillan Co. of Canada, and Mr. M. B. Yeats from "Sailing to Byzantium," *Collected Poems* by William Butler Yeats. Copyright 1928 by The Macmillan Company, renewed 1956 by Georgie Yeats.

[8] From *Poems of Gerard Manley Hopkins* (New York: Oxford University Press, 1967). Reprinted by permission of Oxford University Press.

[9] Dylan Thomas, *The Collected Poems.* Copyright 1946 by New Directions Publishing Corporation. Reprinted by permission of New Directions Publishing Corporation.

beauty of a young girl "Nobody, not even the rain, has such small hands." [10]

These fragments are not intended to represent an exhaustive analysis of imagery in poems. One needs a separate book to handle such a subject. My intention is to make you conscious of the usefulness of vivid pictures in your writing. Like poetry, good prose is filled with images. Here's a random collection:

> The skull of life suddenly showed through its smile.
>
> DOROTHY CANFIELD FISHER
>
> He felt like an insect crawling through the entrails of a horse.
>
> NORMAN MAILER
>
> Now comes the warm smother of night, taking over the streets of once-Peking, now renamed Peiping, no longer capital but Northern Peace, taking over its million people, taking over the great plain of China, and preparing the bed of steadfast night.
>
> HAN SUYIN
>
> The shell in my hand is deserted. It once housed a whelk, a snail-like creature . . . it is simple; it is bare; it is beautiful. Small, only the size of my thumb, its architecture is perfect, down to the finest detail. Its shape, swelling like a pear in the center, winds in a gentle spiral to the pointed apex. Its color, dull gold, is whitened by a wash of salt from the sea. Each whorl, each faint knob, each criss-cross vein in its egg-shell texture is as clearly defined as on the day of creation. . . . My shell is not like this, I think. How untidy it has become! Blurred with moss, knobby with barnacles, its shape is hardly recognizable any more. Surely, it had a shape once.
>
> ANNE MORROW LINDBERGH

You can argue that the last quote is not imagery, but analogy. But I see no point making clearcut distinctions. The labels are conveniences at best. We could say that a metaphor doesn't have to be as visual as an image and that an analogy is more fully developed and explicit than either. Yet nobody is going to be like Miss Prendergast, who spent the entire year hair-splitting about "figures of speech." (Did you ever get ten points off for calling something a metaphor when it was really supposed to be a simile? Or for not knowing your synecdoche from your hyperbole?) The important thing is to do a little experimenting with your writing and try to rev it up with more power and punch than it may now have.

[10] From "Somewhere I Have Never Travelled, Gladly Beyond" by E. E. Cummings. Copyright 1931, 1959 by E. E. Cummings. Reprinted by permission of Harcourt Brace Jovanovich, Inc.

EXERCISES

1. Take a position on some controversial issue of the day, such as
legalization of drugs, the administering of alcohol tolerance tests
to those suspected of drunk driving, forced bussing of pupils to
achieve integration, the resistance to forced bussing, or the United
States involvement in foreign struggles. Think your position
through as carefully as you can. Write your paper. Let it cool for
a day or two. Then come back to it and examine your important
statements. Are they definitive? If you think they are not, using
the criteria for definitiveness set forth in this chapter, work on
them. Try to cast one or two in the alternative form or the exclusive form, and as many as possible in the powerhouse form.
In fact, the entire paper should reflect your confident, powerhouse
personality. It was Ben Franklin who said, "God helps them that
help themselves." You may not, of course, get away with it, but
one way to achieve prose power is to claim it as your due.

    If this assignment is given to the whole class, ask the teacher
to read some of the more provocative papers and have the class
decide which writers state their positions most definitively and
impressively. Discuss how they manage to do it. Ask the teacher
to read some papers by writers whose ideas are strong but whose
way of expressing them doesn't seem definitive. Discuss the reasons.

2. Literary and drama critics alike point with regret to the decline of
distinguished language in fiction and plays of the current age. In
particular, they seek in vain for the wits, though the decline of wit
is surprising in view of the thinking of your generation. That is,
if wit can be defined as giving an unexpected twist to the expected
or the familiar, it could be called *going against the language Establishment.*

    Do a paper on one of the controversial topics, but this time try
to include at least two really witty remarks. If you did the preceding assignment, you could use the same paper, substituting wit
for definitiveness in the key places.

    To illustrate the nature of wit a bit further, here's a random col-
lection of contemporary subject matter (though the authors are not
necessarily living now). You will note that every instance involves
a clash between the expected and the unexpected:

    1) *Pursuit of affluence:*   "Early to rise and early to bed makes
    a man healthy and wealthy and dead."
    (James Thurber)

2) *Emphasis on the physical:* "A sound mind or a sound body— take your choice." (Gene Shepherd's advice to Boy Scouts)

3) *The American Dream:* "Making the world safe for hypocrisy." (Thomas Wolfe)
Examples 4, 5, 6, & 7 use a special trick of building up to an unexpected climax.

4) *Blind faith in people:* "Put all your eggs in the one basket and—WATCH THAT BASKET." (Mark Twain)

5) *You-can't-win department:* "In this world there are only two tragedies. One is not getting what one wants, and the other is getting it." (Oscar Wilde)

6) *American education:* "If I were founding a university I would found first a smoking room; then when I had a little more money in hand I would found a dormitory; then after that, or more probably with it, a decent reading room and library. After that, if I still had more money that I couldn't use, I would hire a professor and get some textbooks." (Stephen Leacock)

7) *Modern folklore:* "If at first you don't succeed— phhhhhhhhhhhh"
"Do unto others, then split."
"A stitch in time means you don't get to buy a new dress." (From a student)

In other words, a relatively painless way to inject wit into your writing is to make a list of subjects you could treat, find some expected things to say on each (such as clichés or old folk sayings), and then throw the old curve at the reader. To get your eventual paper, you could put the remarks that go together into family groupings. For example, suppose you found you'd written four witticisms on the Generation Gap. This would then become your main subject.

Or: you can start off with certain headings, such as

War
Education
Morality
Censorship
The Establishment

Let's say you select the Establishment. You could then make a list under this heading of all the subjects for your clever remarks. Thus:

My mother
My father
Teachers
The old
Politicians
Everyone who

Once you have chosen a likely list of subjects, start sketching out the rest of the sentences. A good idea is to try out different verbs, beginning with "to be" and see where it leads you.

For example, if you wrote down, "My mother is . . ." you could search around for some famous old expression. I just had a brainstorm, and this came to me for whatever it's worth: "My mother is a red, red rose that's newly sprung her mind." If you're not averse to puns, here's another twisted expression: "Teachers should be screened and not hired."

Now try your own. I'm sure you can do much better. Just bear in mind that you'll come up with a great response to this assignment if you get the wit first and the subject later.

3. The Generation Gap has long been one of the most attractive subjects for writers. If anything is universal, it's that some people are older and others younger. The old try to cling to their authority and sometimes become fiendishly clever just to put the young people in their place. The young, for their part, like to retaliate, but on the verbal battlefield it often becomes a matter of experience vs. enthusiasm. When it comes to style, enthusiasm must work very hard to overcome the disadvantage of having less experience.

In a recent interview Noel Coward, one of the most consistently clever gentlemen of the twentieth century, made a comment about the younger generation, couched in his usually confident manner: "The young today act as though they had invented youth." Perhaps you are also familiar with George Bernard Shaw's immortal quip, "Youth is wasted on the young." Long, long ago the epic poet Homer combined definitiveness, cleverness, and rhythm in one sweeping indictment of youth: "Few sons are like their father, most are worse, few better than the father."

But if these and kindred lines arouse your indignation, just remind yourself how quickly time passes and you find yourself facing your own children's angry rebellion against *your* values. The poet Constance Carrier, addressing herself to the problem of this endless cycle of youth vs. age, wrote a poem to a young man named Peter, who at fourteen couldn't pay attention in the classroom to the dead study of Latin. But, Miss Carrier warns the young daydreamer, one day "nature will betray you." Here's the whole poem:

PETER AT FOURTEEN [11]

What do you care for Caesar, who
    yourself
are in three parts divided, and
    must find,
past daydream and rebellion and
    bravado,
the final shape and substance of
    your mind?

What are the Belgae, the Helvetii
to you? I doubt that you will read
    in them
metaphor of your stand against
    dominion,
or see as yours their desperate
    stratagem.

They found their tribal rank, their
    feuds, their freedom,
obliterated, lost beyond return.
It took them years to see that law
    and order
could teach them things that they
    might care to learn.

As fiercely individual, as violent
as they, you clutch your values
    and your views,
fearful that self may not survive
    absorption.
(Who said *to learn* at first is like
    to lose?)

Not courage, no, but nature will
    betray you.
You will stop fighting, finally,
    and your pride,

[11] "Peter at Fourteen" by Constance Carrier from *New Poems by American Poets*, ed. by Rolfe Humphries. Copyright, 1953, by Ballantine Books, Inc. Reprinted by permission of Ballantine Books, Inc.

> that fed so long upon your independence,
> flourish on what convention can
>   provide,
>
> till you may grow more Roman than
>   the Romans,
> contemptuous of pagan broils and
>   brawls,
> and even, mastering your mentors'
>   knowledge,
> go on to build cathedrals, like
>   the Gauls.

Aside from the compelling overall idea behind the poem, the expression "more Roman than the Romans" is likely to live on as the classic way of suggesting the inevitable cycle of youth to age. On the other hand, other writers have recognized the importance and value of youth's fiery enthusiasm and dedication to causes. Robert Louis Stevenson made one of the finest utterances on this subject: "Give me the young man who has brains enough to make a fool of himself." But the number of sage and clever observations about the young written by the mature far exceed the number of sage and clever observations written by the young about the old. It's too bad, for the pen still has mighty powers and can be as effective as demonstrations, campus disruptions, and so forth.

Use this assignment as an occasion for making your own contribution to "generational" literature. Write an essay—or poem, if you wish—about the adult Establishment, trying to be clever as well as profound. Try, for example, to come up with your own version of "Youth is wasted on the young." (Read Constance Carrier's poem a couple of times. Have you any answer to it? That is, try to include in your paper a consideration of her belief that the rebellious youth will eventually turn into the upholder of the Establishment.)

4. The danger with wit is that so often it takes over completely. It puts to sleep one's perspective and sometimes one's taste. Some of the people most renowned for their wit were not above going five miles out of the way to score a verbal *coup* they were certain would be quoted for generations to come. Dramatist Channing Pollock once wrote a play called *The House Beautiful*, which critic Dorothy Parker handled in but one crisp, never-to-be-forgotten statement: "*The House Beautiful* is the play lousy." Funny? Sure. It's a scream. I suppose I even wish I'd said it. But do you realize something? Until I wrote this chapter and decided to run down the precise circumstances of the review, I hadn't even known who

the author of the play was. Perhaps no play could be bad enough to warrant such a scathing attack. Was Dorothy Parker trying to show off?

Then there was George S. Kaufman's acid summary of a flop he had seen: "I saw it under adverse circumstances; the curtain was up." We don't want to practice cleverness at the expense of other, sometimes more solid, stylistic achievements.

This time try to stir and move the reader through rhythm and balance—that is, language of simplicity, but direct and honest feeling. The following paper was written in response to this assignment by one of my students, a young girl who grew up in rural Cuba and is here remembering an event out of her childhood that made a deep impression on her. Note the really exquisite simplicity of the writing, almost suggestive of the slow plucking of a guitar.

DAWN IN FEBRUARY

The flying kite reaches the end of the port. From afar, on top of the highest hill, I contemplate the setting sun behind the ships. A multitude of houses separate the harbor from my eyes. Barefooted, I am standing near the statue: a patriot eight feet tall. I sing in a whisper, "Twenty-fourth of February, sparkling light of splendor . . ." The words encircle the stone man. It is late afternoon of the twenty-third day. The kite is free.

My town has two main avenues; it has a church, a police station, warehouse, bars, a theatre. On the walls facing the streets, the signs of past and future events. One reads: American movie. Another reads: Parade on the Twenty-fourth. Gray façades, green trees. Drowning voices become incoherent as I walk home. My house is pink. Tomato soup is warm on the table. I go to the bathroom and wash hands and feet. I murmur, "Sparkling light of splendor." Clean. Eating slowly, I read a lesson for school, subtract and divide the assignments on my notebook. After finishing arithmetic, I draw patiently on yellow papers. Clouds, boats, stars.

I go to my room and open the window. My sister sleeps. I fall in bed with a sigh. Waiting, waiting through hours awake, I call my sister, "Elena, listen, aren't the musicians going to play?"

"What?" Elena groans.

"The musicians. It is the dawn of the twenty-fourth of February and they play every year in each corner of the town. They're not coming. It is dawn already."

"So what if it is? Leave me alone." Elena moves in bed and soon is snoring. I stay looking at the street. A cool breeze inundates my face. My eyes do not move from the place where the musicians should appear. Rigid. Two, three, five, seven, nine men on the corner. They carry axes in their hands. They walk towards the hill. With quick soundless steps, I leave the house. I follow the men from a distance.

The nine men proceed silently until they reach the summit. There they stop for a moment before the statue. In agreement, they direct their axes to the head of the stone man. Hitting, hitting, I hide and look in frozen astonishment. My head falls to the ground. I run. I tremble in my bed. It is daylight.

"Hurry, finish your breakfast," says Elena, "You'll be late for school and today is the parade."

I comb my hair with lentitude. The starched uniform is stiff.

"Did the musicians play?" asks Elena.

"No, they did not." I reply looking at the floor.

"You never sleep on the twenty-fourth of February. How patriotic! Let's go or we'll be late!"

Elena and I leave the house. When we arrive in school, the children are already in lines. The teacher distributes the roses. One for each boy and girl.

"Miss Martinez, I have to tell you something," I say.

"Not now please," the teacher replies as she gives me a flower, "can't you see I'm busy with the parade?"

From the school building the children move to the street. There are two long rows: the right for the boys, the left for the girls. At the sound of the drums, they begin marching. The flag goes in front. The roses. Walking towards the hill, the children sing, "Twenty-fourth of February, sparkling light of splendor . . ." The drums. The grass under their feet. The voices. Stop.

From the bottom of the hill, they see the headless statue. Silence and stillness. The teacher looks at me for a second. The children murmur between themselves.

"All right," says Miss Martinez, "let's go back to school. Hush, no more talking."

As the children turn, the roses slip through their fingers and fall. I do not move. The sky is blue. Facing the statue, I begin running upwards. I wave the flowers in my hand.

Nearer, closer, nearer, closer. Breathlessly, I place the roses at the foot of the statue. The morning sprinkles my eyes. Quietude. It is the twenty-fourth of February.

5. One notable form of literary expression in which your generation shines is the lyrics to rock, hard-rock, and acid-music. Surely names like John Lennon, Paul McCartney, Leonard Cohen, Bob Dylan, and Paul Simon will be remembered long after the music fads change. If nothing else, they will leave behind them a vivid portrait of the thought and feelings of this age.

Many adults, however, find themselves bewildered by some of the lyrics. They wonder who Leonard Cohen's "Suzanne" is and what she does. Or else they may be scandalized at some of the subject matter: take the Beatles' "Norwegian Wood" as an example, or "A Day in the Life."

As a member of this generation, as a lover of its music can you write a defense of some of these songs? Explain two or three of them (or just one if it's as complicated as "Suzanne"). Explain some of the noteworthy phrases and symbols. If you want to have some fun, dig up some of the lyrics to songs of the late thirties and forties, and make a comparison.

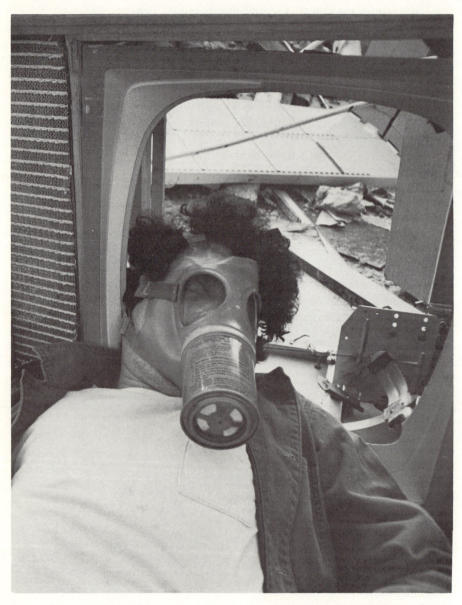

". . . In his defeat, we recognize the eternal story of human frustration."

8

WRITING JOKES, PARODIES, AND SATIRES

THEORY BEHIND HUMOR

Humorous writing—that is, trying to sustain a comic effect for longer than the occasional witty line—is one of the most valuable ways of exploring and getting hold of your identity in prose. Some of man's most profound hopes and fears, some of his most cherished ideals often lurk beneath the surface of a slight joke, and lengthier prose parodies and satires constitute an enduring treasury of great and important literature.

A sense of humor is a sense of the gap that exists between our expectations of life and the actualities we observe. If something is said to be "ridiculous" or "absurd," we mean that it is crooked when measured against the "straight" line of our own attitudes.

Our sense of humor is one of our sturdiest defenses against life's insanities, and by coming to understand what makes us laugh the most, we gain insight into ourselves. Our sense of humor is really the means of confirming ourselves. If we begin to doubt the rightness of our views, we have only to witness another absurdity coming our way and feel that familiar urge to laugh welling up inside, and we are once again reassured about our own values. Humor says to us: "The madness is out there, not in here. It is life that is absurd, not you. Keep your cool."

A sense of humor is one of the most civilized possessions anyone can have. It isn't greater than rationality, for it is virtually identical to it. People so confused they don't know up from down are not likely to be polished laughers. Their sense of humor isn't going to be much different from that of the child in the playpen, who has so little reason that almost anything seems silly to him. You must first be mature and have your feet solidly on the ground before you learn to distinguish what is truly mad around you. This is why the current idioms "It's unreal" or "I don't believe any of this" are right on target as ways of introducing the ridiculous.

You can't have done much thinking about life without having some idea of what it should be all about, some expectations, some ideals—how frustrating life can be! Why was it that my good father had his name in the newspaper only once—his obituary—and they spelled it wrong? Shouldn't I have known it would happen? Incompetence, inadequacy, not to mention actual corruption, knavery, and inhumanity, ring us completely. If it weren't for humor, most of us would be locked away in institutions. Jonathan Swift, the world's greatest satirist, once declared that the only way to be truly happy is to be a "fool among knaves." But if you can't or wouldn't want to be a fool, you can keep your hold on your sanity *by exposing the foolish.*

This, after all, is the primary purpose of all forms of prose humor, from the casual joke to the most complex satires, like Voltaire's *Candide* or Cervantes' *Don Quixote*. By writing down the humor you feel, you are actually discovering what it is that most frustrates your expectations. You are making an indictment against life in the name of reason.

THE JOKE

The big difference between a joke and more ambitious kinds of prose humor, aside from length, is that parodies and satires tend to deal directly with the things that bother their authors, whereas a joke doesn't have to be personal. A joke constitutes a miniature model of *all frustrating experiences*, and so is the appropriate kind of humorous expression for us to begin with.

Making up a good joke is an exercise in living. By imitating the form of a frustrating experience, which is what you do in a joke, you are actually strengthening your belief that you've got life pretty well in hand. You're not waiting for a frustrating thing to happen. You make it happen with words, and in this way you can restore your cool any time you want to.

Basic Structure

A joke, in one classic sense of the word, has to tell a story. Its central character has to represent US. He has to be in action, in some direction, working toward a goal of some kind. He has to be frustrated in a way that strikes us as *maddening but nonethless true*. Thus, in his defeat, we recognize the eternal story of human frustration. Our laughter is a defense against the frustration; our laughter is what strengthens us for the real battles we have to face.

My favorite joke probably belongs to that suspect category generally called the shaggy-dog story. For some this denotes an unfunny story, a joke that didn't make the grade. But for me, shaggy-dog stories at their best illustrate the profound truth that real humor doesn't require an explosion of belly laughs. At any rate, this story has the classic structure, the one most readily imitated:

> While running to catch his eight o'clock bus one morning, Mr. Smith suddenly stopped and asked himself, "What am I doing? Why this senseless rushing to get to a job I detest? Every day, the same routine. Wake, breakfast, rush, bus, job, rush, bus, home, dinner, television. No real contact. I'm through! I will not lead this meaningless existence for one more moment."
>
> With that, Mr. Smith resolved to draw all of his money from his savings account and use it to sustain himself while he would search for some meaning to life. He also resolved to leave home and not return until he could do so as a new man, an enlightened man, a man with a purpose.
>
> With his savings clutched in his hand, Mr. Smith travelled all over the world, wherever he had heard that great intellects were living, in order to question them about the meaning of life. But always he received the same answer: "I'm sorry. I don't know."
>
> With the money dwindling, he finally lucked into a rumor that the High Llama of Tibet, a man over eight hundred years old, was in possession of the elusive truth. Certainly if such a man didn't know the meaning of life, who possibly could?
>
> Near starvation now, in rags, his strength ebbing away from him, Mr. Smith climbed over the Himalayas and crawled into the palace of the High Llama of Tibet. With his voice barely audible, he pleaded with the wise one to tell him the meaning of life before he should die.
>
> "My son," the great man smiled radiantly, "life is a fountain."
>
> Mr. Smith was stunned and nearly died on the spot. But with superhuman force he gathered together his remaining strength and screamed into the old man's face: "You say such a thing to me after I have given up my youth, my vitality, my money, my wife, my job, my

friends, my homeland, all because I wanted to know the meaning of life? I have suffered and starved, I have climbed these mountains in the freezing cold. I have thrown myself at your feet as the last possible hope of wretched humanity because you were supposed to be wise, and now you have the gall to tell me life is a fountain!" Whereupon the High Llama, looking very puzzled indeed, replied, "It isn't a fountain?"

Whether you've heard it before isn't the issue. The story is so beautiful it holds up under repeated tellings, and do you know why? Because it captures *the ultimate frustration.* Everything you've ever suffered at the hands of people, institutions, or the uncontrollable circumstances of life is summed up in the old man's feeble metaphor. If that's the best he could do after eight centuries on this earth, then what hope can anyone have for understanding life?

This joke embodies the very essence of a certain kind of frustration we experience every day of our lives. When I called up the newspaper, angry because it had misspelled my father's name in his obituary, what do you think the girl asked? "What is the correct spelling, sir?" As if that made a difference! When your car's engine falls out on the ninety-first day, all you can get from the manufacturer is, "But the guarantee was for only ninety days, sir." Once I bought a home and discovered, after a severe rainstorm flooded us out so badly we had to move into a motel for two weeks, that the property was eight inches below sea level. "Sorry, sir," announced a man at the courthouse, "that street was put in before the present building code was established." But, good heaven, I wanted to cry, wasn't sea level the same then? In the final analysis, this joke tells us, nobody gives you satisfaction; nobody cares; nobody listens. People just want to get you out of their hair. People want you to go away.

EXERCISES

1. Make a quick list of some jokes that are currently going the rounds. Pick out two or three that in your opinion embody the structure of all frustrating experiences and that have for their central characters people like Mr. Smith; that is, fundamentally human beings with whom it is easy to identify and be sympathetic. Retell them in your own words.

2. Pick out a joke that you think is funny and that doesn't appear to recreate the structure of a frustration. After you tell it, analyze the reason you think it works. In this way you will be discovering other methods of evoking laughter through jokes.

3. Get in practice for writing your own jokes by telling about a memorably frustrating experience you yourself have had. Try to make it as amusing as you can without sacrificing the humanness and believability of the situation. To induce your memory to start working, you might take a look at this list and see whether you can recall being frustrated by an encounter with any of the following:

> A clerk at the draft board
>
> A telephone operator
>
> The clerk who couldn't find your transcript
>
> A policeman who couldn't understand that you weren't breaking any law
>
> Airline baggage department personnel ("Your suitcase has been located in Algiers, sir.")
>
> The insurance claim investigator (Alan King recently did a TV skit about insurance frustration. The investigator denied the claim of a wretched couple whose house had just burned down, saying it wasn't covered by the "Fire and Theft" clause. When the couple wanted to know why not, he informed them that in order for a person to collect, his house had to be both burned *and* stolen at the same time.)
>
> The teacher who couldn't explain the reason for a mediocre grade

The important thing in this paper is for you, the central figure, to represent suffering humanity up against a wall. But the situation must be possible and the incompetence of the others universal enough to encourage reader identification with your plight.

Another joke structure represents the reverse of the frustration story. This kind of joke has for its central character a beaten-down, defeated figure who represents, again, suffering humanity, except that this time the hero has already been frustrated over and over. He is the universal underdog, the Loser. What causes us to laugh is his unexpected victory, rather than the defeat we anticipate.

Such "reverse frustration" tales abound in the folklore and traditional humor of peoples with a long record of being oppressed. Here's a contemporary version which grows out of the black struggle for equal opportunity.

> After several frustrating years of unsuccessful attempts to be hired by the rich and powerful firm of Hinton, Blinton, Witherspoon, and Flitch, Stock Brokers, Lamont Parsons finally was accepted for employment by this most prestigious organization.

No less than Augustus Hinton, the president himself, escorted Lamont on a tour of the facilities. He pointed out the latest electronic equipment, the plush furniture and decor, the all-glass bar for wealthy customers, the private pool, and so on. He pointed with pride to the young, vigorous, and attractive staff.

"But," said Lamont, "I see no other blacks."

"Which goes to prove," replied Hinton, "that we do not always see what is, and what we see may not necessarily be. More may be true than is apparent. The hand is quicker than the eye, and there are more things in heaven and earth, Parsons, that are dreamed of."

"I see," said Lamont, extremely puzzled.

After several weeks, Lamont was still not satisfied that Hinton, Blinton, Witherspoon, and Flitch were not guilty of tokenism when it came to the integration of their staff. Once again he approached President Hinton and one again was answered with the same mysterious double talk.

One day a government agent came into the place. While he was making his rounds, Hinton came up to Lamont and whispered into his ear: "Remember, in case you are asked, that the eye is not always to be trusted. More may be real than is apparent, while less may be evident than is so. In short, my dear Parsons, if you allow this gentleman to believe Hinton, Blinton, Witherspoon, and Flitch are practicing tokenism, you will be suddenly bereft of employment."

With the ominous warning, Hinton stood to one side, while the government agent approached Parsons. "Do you realize, sir," he said, "that you are the first black I have encountered here? Tell me the truth. Is this firm guilty of tokenism?"

"Well," he began and then his eye caught Hinton's, who was pretending to study the board but was avidly listening to every word of the conversation. "We do not always see what is . . ." He looked over and saw Hinton smiling and nodding. "More may be real than is apparent. The eye is not always to be trusted." Hinton smiled more broadly and with strong approval.

"Never mind the double talk," said the exasperated agent. "Is this firm practicing tokenism or not?"

"Of course not," said Lamont. Smiling more broadly than ever, Hinton nodded again. "How can my employers be accused of tokenism when all of us who work here are white?"

Though the underdog appears to have scored a total victory, this particular joke format is somewhat more complex. The triumph is short-lived. As soon as we have laughed or smiled, we realize that welcome as Lamont's ingenuity is, Hinton, Blinton et al. would not, in real life, be so easily exposed. A real Lamont Parsons would most probably never get the chance to make the decisive statement about tokenism. What this type of joke embodies is the universal improbability of the underdog's winding up on top. We are thus laughing at the illogic of our own fond hopes.

This second kind of joke is not really much different from the first.

The story of Mr. Smith exposes universal incompetence, a source of unending frustration. The story of Lamont Parsons exposes the futility of everyone's good wishes for the loser, and, since all of us lose more often than we win, it offers the old frustrations to us once more, in disguised form.

EXERCISES

1. Find some jokes that embody the format of the loser winning and evoke laughter by reversing the expectation of defeat. Analyze them and show that we laugh at the victory because it is improbable.

2. Recreate an incident in which you were a clear underdog, headed for obvious disaster, and were able to seize an unexpected victory by some stroke of cleverness. Perhaps this never happened to you, but shouldn't it? Don't you deserve it? Take compensation by making up such an incident. You will be writing, in effect, a comic tale, using the Lamont Parsons format. Let your persecutor be the embodiment of a force or institution that you wish you could outwit as Lamont did the brokerage firm.

I am not trying to suggest that other structures do not exist or even that all sources of laughter necessarily fall into the "frustration" category. But I'll bet that, if you watch television tonight and concentrate on the comics, you'll find that a good many of the "unanalyzable" laughs stem from facial expressions or vocal tones or the general personality of the comic himself, rather than from some new and mysterious structure or subject. Nor everything Jack Benny or Flip Wilson says, for example, is hilarious in itself, yet the manner in which each stands, looks, reacts, and speaks makes him almost continually amusing.

At any rate, let's use the "frustration structure" as a basic format. The following are some further samples, chosen by subject matter.

The Generation Gap

Parents have always found it hard to reason with rebellious offspring, as is shown by the following story, said to be the very essence of the comic by the great French philosopher Henri Bergson:

> A mother, growing anxious over her son's addiction to gambling, decided to talk with him and point out the evil of this terrible compulsion.

"I am frantic that you spend every night at the casino. You go there in hopes of making an easy fortune," she admonished, "but I assure you it doesn't work out that way. If you win one night, you will surely lose the next."

"You're right, mother," returned the son, much to her relief. "So I shall take your advice and go every *other* night."

This is a classic frustration story no matter which viewpoint you take. The son's ingeniously literal response to her purely figurative statement represents defeat for the older generation. At the same time, you can look upon the son as a Lamont Parsons figure—that is, as an improbable victor. It depends on how things are currently going at home.

The Moral Revolution

This story represents, to the young, an improbable victory for the Establishment viewpoint; to the Establishment, however, it suggests how right they have been all along.

It seems a troupe of television newsmen visited St. Petersburg, Florida, for the purpose of doing a show on senior citizens: what they used to do, how they passed the time now that they were retired, and, particularly, to what they attributed their long life.

They set up their cameras on one of the famous piers and approached one extremely old gentleman.

"What is your age?" asked the interviewer.

"Eighty-eight," came the hoarse reply.

When asked what was his secret, the senior citizen said, "A disciplined, well-regulated life. Early to bed, early to rise. No night life."

The team moved on to another, even older-looking gentleman and asked his age. It was one hundred and three. Marvelling, they eagerly demanded to know *his* secret. It was: "A disciplined, well-regulated life. I never took a drink or smoked a cigarette. And I have never had sexual relations with anyone."

Nodding with understanding and smiling, the newsmen caught sight of the oldest, most withered-looking specimen they had ever seen. "Here, ladies and gentlemen, is surely the oldest man in the world," announced the interviewer.

The microphone had to be placed virtually upon the old man's lips, so difficult was it for him even to whisper. But he appeared to understand the questions, especially the one that asked for his secret. "The wild, free life," he replied, much to the astonishment of the news team. "I have been the lover of over a thousand women, I have smoked four packs of cigarettes a day religiously. I have drunk three fifths of bourbon a day, not to mention the *illegal* stuff I take continually."

"But how amazing," said the interviewer, "And how old *are* you, sir?"

"Twenty-two," was the almost inaudible reply.

Education

The ten-year-old son of Mr. and Mrs. Rubin was an absolute terror. He wasn't allowed anywhere near a public school, and the unhappy parents had just about run out of private schools when a friend suggested St. Polycarp's.

"But that's Catholic," protested the Rubins.

"Yes, but they have the severest discipline," said the friend. "If they can't handle your son, nobody can."

Reluctantly, the parents agreed, and young Rubin was duly enrolled. To their amazement, his first report card showed all A's and a gold star for conduct.

Not believing it could happen, the Rubins journeyed to St. Polycarp's to investigate this wondrous transformation in their previously unmanageable offspring. But it was all true. The child that met them at the gate was the most polite, gentle, and affectionate son any parent could have wanted. Taking their hands, he led them on a tour of the school.

Unable to keep silent any longer, Mrs. Rubin blurted out, "My darling boy, how is it that you have changed so much? Yours is the model of behavior."

"Oh, that," replied the son a little nervously. "Well, I'll show you."

Tiptoeing to the door of one of the classrooms, he opened it noiselessly and beckoned to the parents to peer inside.

"See what's up there on the wall? Well, that's what they *do* to you here if you don't behave."

You may argue that the point of this joke is religion rather than education, yet that's what makes it so fine. It can be viewed in a variety of ways. But it has long been a favorite joke among the people of my profession, no doubt embodying the educator's deep-rooted longing for some effective means of discipline. Others also enjoy it: Catholics for obvious reasons, and non-Catholics perhaps for the pathetic but absurd hope that the educational establishment can reach an "easy" solution of the discipline problems that abound in schools today.

The Army Way

The military establishment is one of the primary targets of all contemporary jokes. Comedians and humorists tend to consider it a continual source of frustration, especially because of what it does to the humane instincts and sensibilities of the men who are taken annually by the thousands and subjected to its rigorous, impersonal discipline.

This story offers a sharp illustration of the way the army might handle a delicate and sensitive problem.

The sergeant was summoned to the office of the C.O., who was so absorbed in paper work that he didn't even bother to look up. Instead, he waved a telegram in the sergeant's direction.

"Jenkins in your outfit?" the C.O. mumbled.

"Yessir."

The sergeant took the telegram and read the news that Jenkins' mother had just died unexpectedly. For all that he was a twenty-year man, for all the unpleasant things he had experienced, the sergeant found himself greatly upset. Jenkins was a nice kid, and it seemed a shame to have to break such news to him. But he thrust out his chin and decided there was nothing for it but to face the task. Out he went.

When the outfit was relaxing in the barracks for a few minutes after mail call, the sergeant decided to get the matter over with. But when he approached Jenkins, the young enlistee smiled at him and held out a box of cookies. "Hey, sarge," he said. "Have one. My mom just sent 'em to me."

The words froze inside the sergeant's throat. He decided to put the disclosure off until that night.

After mess, the outfit was lounging around in the barracks once more. And once again the sergeant approached Jenkins, this time finding the boy deeply absorbed in letter-writing.

"Who's the letter for?" asked the sergeant pleasantly as an opener.

"My mom," came the reply. "I'm writing to thank her for the cookies and tell her she's the greatest mom a guy ever had."

The sergeant decided now was not the appropriate moment for the revelation. For days afterwards the pattern remained the same. Every time the sergeant attempted to bring the subject up, Jenkins would say or do something that would have made telling the truth seem cruel and heartless. Soon a week had passed.

The C.O., happening to pass the sergeant, stopped and asked, "Well? How did that Jenkins boy take the news of his mother's death?"

Embarrassed, the sergeant stammered out a confession that the news had not yet been broken. He tried to explain the circumstances.

"Sergeant!" exclaimed the C.O. angrily. "You will tell Jenkins by tonight or lose your stripes. The army makes men, sergeant. It makes brave and courageous men, equal to any occasion. You can do this efficiently as well as tactfully—the army way! And that's an order!"

After mess that night, while the outfit was laughing it up around the barracks, the sergeant entered and called the men to attention. "All right, you guys," he said. "I'm calling a meeting in the next room for everyone whose mother is still living." There were mumbles, grumbles, the shuffling of feet as most of the men began to move toward the door. "Oh, not you, Jenkins."

The Nonconformist

The nonconformist story embodies the theme of frustration because he lives by his own peculiar standards and always gets the better of us. Creatures of convention that most of us are most of the time, we begin to expect certain kinds of behavior from other people, and we don't know how to handle those who don't behave "normally" except, whenever we can, by laughing at a joke about them.

> Edward was a slob. He lived in a one-room efficiency apartment in a seedy part of town. He was unmarried and had very few friends, but this apparently was the way he liked to live.
> One day Louis, one of Edward's few acquaintances, happened to meet him on the street but was surprised to see him leading an old, gray horse by the reins.
> "Edward," said Louis, "what on earth are you doing with that horse?"
> "I just bought him from a milkman," replied Edward.
> "But where will you keep him?"
> "In my bathtub."
> "Edward, why in God's name would you want a horse in your bathtub?"
> Edward said, "I want him there so that if anybody visits me and goes to the bathroom and comes running out, screaming, 'There's a horse in the bathtub,' I can say, 'Yes, I know.' "

The Knife in the Back

As the jokes we hear day and night tell us, life thwarts our expectations. Reality shatters our ideals. The truth gives the lie to our hopes. But sometimes life can become so frustrating it almost seems as if it were doing it to us deliberately. The knife-in-the-back stories embody not only the usual frustration theme, but a cruel ironic twist that ranges from exasperating, as in the first example, to downright diabolic, as in the second. The first is one of Myron Cohen's favorite tales:

> A CIA agent was being briefed for a very important and very dangerous mission to Istanbul.
> "Listen carefully," said the chief, "because none of this can be written down. You are to proceed to Istanbul. Take a taxi to the Ali Baba Arms. There you will find a certain Mr. Goldberg. Go to his apartment, and when he opens the door, deliver the code message, 'Tomorrow morning the sun will rise.' Now you must get the message exactly right, or it will mean disaster."
> Trembling, the agent repeated the words "Tomorrow morning the sun will rise."

"Moreover," continued the chief, "you must carry with you this cyanide tablet. If you are captured, swallow it. Better death than failure!"

The agent, following his directions to the letter, arrived in Istanbul, proceeded at one to the Ali Baba Arms, but was horrified to discover that not one but two Goldbergs were listed in the directory! Realizing there was nothing for it but to make an arbitrary choice, the agent, clutching his cyanide capsule in his hand, went upstairs to the apartment of one of the Goldbergs. When the man opened the door, the agent, in a hushed, tense voice, said, "Tomorrow morning the sun will rise."

"Oh," came the pleasant response, "You're looking for Goldberg the spy. He lives upstairs."

The second story is so cruel it can't even be a tragedy. Such utter frustration can only make us laugh, or else we must lose our sanity altogether.

George Weatherby began to suffer from excruciating headaches. They became so bad he could no longer work. His wife finally prevailed upon him to seek a physician's advice.

After making a thorough examination, the doctor asked to see George in his private office. "I'll level with you, Mr. Weatherby," he said, "All the signs point to the fact that you're suffering from an extremely rare malady—so rare, in fact, it hasn't even a name. But we do know how to cure it."

"Well, that's a relief," smiled George.

"Mm—yes. However, the cure is hardly a pleasant one."

"I don't mind, doctor, as long as it's a cure. What is it?"

"Mr. Weatherby, are you married?"

"Yes, but I don't see—"

"The fact is you will have to learn to live without the customary joys of married life. You will have to undergo a very—uh—delicate operation."

George understood what the doctor was driving at. A dismal feeling crept over his whole being. Still, what other choice had he? He agreed to submit to the operation.

After he was released from the hospital in an understandably depressed state, George decided to cheer himself up by going on a wild shopping spree. He went to the most expensive men's store in town and ordered a suit of the finest imported silk.

"Excellent choice," said the salesman. "Now, as to size, I would say 40."

"Amazing," said George, "that you should know without measuring."

"My business," smiled the salesman, gratified. "You will need shoes. Shall we say 10C?"

"Amazing! I also need some undershorts."

"To be sure. Shall we say—size 34?"

"Oh, oh," laughed George, "you made a mistake. You're human, after all. I take a 32 in undershorts."

"34," insisted the salesman.

"32," insisted George. "Really, sir, I ought to know."

"Very well," sighed the salesman, "If you insist. But you'll get headaches."

EXERCISES

1. The time has come to stop reading jokes that other people have written and start writing some of your own. Use the categories I have set up, or invent others. You should probably stay with the frustration story until you can do it well. At least here you are operating on sure ground, for the frustrated individual is always bound to attract the sympathies of the reader. Here's a suggested list of losers, in whose company all of us can be found at one time or another:

> the son or daughter
> the father or mother
> the teacher or student
> the tenant
> the poor taxpayer
> the enlisted man
> the girl who doesn't get asked
> the boy who isn't with it

In your joke you can use either "frustration method." That is, your loser can go down to a final, crushing defeat in a "what's-the-use" story. Or he can turn out to be an unexpected, if improbable, winner.

You can work out your joke by developing the fundamental conflict first and then deciding which kind of frustration you want to create. That is, select your character and list the kinds of systems that will either defeat or be outwitted by him.

Suppose, for example, you select "the student." A likely list of institutions would include:

> the teacher
> the administration
> the fraternity or sorority system
> the draft board

You select "the teacher." Now make a list of possible frustrations that students can experience at the hands of teachers:

inability to follow the course
unreasonable assignments
teacher's overpermissiveness
teacher's favoritism
getting off on the wrong foot
cryptic grading standards

Let's choose the last one on the list. I know my own under-graduate career was plagued by some instructors whose methods of grading belonged to the realm of pure mysticism. The very first English composition I ever wrote in college was returned with one four-letter word scrawled across the top. But there was no other comment, not a trace of a constructive suggestion. "How may I improve it, sir?" I asked the instructor. "By doing it better," he retorted. To all such helpful members of the academic establish-ment I fondly dedicate the following sample joke written by one of my own students (hopeful that I wasn't the inspiration!)

It seems John Steinberg could never please his English teacher. Being a conscientious, if somewhat slow, student, John would labor for hours over every assignment, trying to perform it to the letter, but always without success.

One paper would come back with "F. Much too brief."
Another would come back with "F. Too long."
Or "F. Far too general."
Or "F. Gets bogged down in specific details."
Or "F. Too vague and abstract."
Or "F. Too descriptive."

In desperation John decided to copy the published work of a pro-fessional, so he went to the library. Being generally unfamiliar with writers, he was delighted to find a book on a shelf that was written by someone with almost his very own name. John decided that he would hand in a super work that would just *have* to satisfy his highly demanding instructor.

For months John toiled at the loving labor of plagiarism. At long last he came into his English class carrying several thousand hand-written pages and a cover sheet on which he had printed in careful, gold lettering, *The Grapes of Wrath*. But in his excitement he forgot and lettered *by John Steinbeck*.

Several weeks later the English teacher handed back the papers. John's was at the bottom of the huge stack. How his heart pounded as he waited for the unfamiliar experience of success and praise! The teacher threw the manuscript on his desk where it landed with a dull thud. And there, scrawled across the title page, was his grade and a red circle around the author's name:

"F. Now you can't even spell your own name."

There is some question about whether it is the Establishment or his own folly that defeats John Steinberg. But the author insists his intentions were to suggest that the teacher himself didn't know who John Steinbeck was and wouldn't recognize a classic if he saw it. In either case, the joke illustrates very well the frustration structure.

THE PARODY

As your sense of identity becomes stronger, the distance between your standards of what should be and your observations of what unfortunately *is*, tends to become greater. Wit, discussed in the preceding chapter, and jokes, which you have been—I hope—having some fun with, are two ways of relieving your frustrations. But there comes a time when it isn't enough simply to experience relief, for this is strictly private. That is, your relief doesn't change the world, doesn't *do* anything about the causes of your frustration. You want to take more positive action. You want your laughter to be an agent of change.

Ridicule can be more effective in improving things than protest marches or straight say-it-like-it-is confrontations. Ridicule wins support for itself even from among those who are not directly involved and who otherwise couldn't care less about the things that irritate you. Laughter wins friends and influences people, and the two forms of ridicule that do the most damage are *parody* and *satire*.

Parody is the more specialized of the two forms in that it is aimed at a much narrower target. Parody ridicules other writers by impersonating their style and their purposes. The sources of the frustrations that lead you to parody are either the (in your opinion) undeserved success of a particular book, movie, play, or television show, or some irritating literary sins committed by a certain writer, sins you feel bound to expose to the world. The writer of parodies is a literary moralist, as it were, one who does a service to his fellow man by trying to make him conscious of the folly of allowing literary junk to succeed or of letting a writer get away with some characteristics that were always, or have now become, foolish.

When you write parody, you do nothing directly. You're not even critical. You simply write about something else and pretend it's the thing that infuriates you. Parody is one of the most devastating forms of criticism because it concentrates only on the faults and leaves them hanging there for all the world to see.

Not much is sacred for the parodist, though to earn our full respect, he ought to aim his barbs at things we agree *should* be lampooned. Even at that, if one looks, he can find plenty to joke about in the greatest literary or dramatic achievements, including Shakespeare's. In an essay called "Looking Shakespeare Over" the humorist Robert Benchley single out some outmoded and ridiculous elements in Shakespeare that would-be parodists could seize upon with some justification.

> But you can't blame the actor entirely. According to present standards of what constitutes dramatic action, most of Will's little dramas have about as much punch as a reading of a treasurer's report. To be expected to thrill over the dramatic situations incident to a large lady's dressing up as a boy and fooling her own husband, or to follow breathlessly a succession of scenes strung together like magic-lantern slides and each ending with a perfectly corking rhymed couplet, is more than ought to be asked of anyone who has, in the same season seen . . . any one of the real plays now running on Broadway.
> It is hard to ask an actor to make an exit on a line like:

> > I am glad on't: I desire no more delight
> > Than to be under sail and gone tonight

> without sounding like one of the characters in Palmer Cox's Brownies saying:

> > And thus it was the Brownie Band
> > Came tumbling into Slumberland.

> That is why they always have to exit laughingly in a Shakespearean production. The author has provided them with such rotten exits. If they don't do something—laugh, cry, turn a handspring, or something—they are left flat in the middle of the stage with nothing to do but say, "Well, I must be going." [1]

Ridiculing Purpose

It is easier for the parodist to lose sympathy with a writer's (or dramatist's or filmaker's) purpose than with any other single aspect of his work. The tendency to cater shamefully to the public is probably the most ridiculed of all such purposes. Periodicals such as *Mad Magazine* consistently make fun of the mass media of entertainment for giving up artistic integrity in the interest of popular appeal. In recent years the superabundance of violence and sex on the screen has come under fire.

[1] From *The Benchley Roundup*, edited by Nathaniel Benchley (Harper & Row, 1954). Reprinted by permission of Harper & Row, Publisher, Inc.

Of course, at the other end of the spectrum is the "high minded" reaction against these things, and sometimes this also earns the scorn and retaliation of the parodist. Everyone is familiar, in particular, with the incessant experimentation that goes on with elementary school textbooks. These are constantly being changed according to the whims of professional educators, some of whom may never have seen a real live child. The humorist Pierre Berton provides us with the following parody of the well-known Dick and Jane series: [2]

FUN WITH DICK AND JANE AND LITTLE RED RIDINGHOOD

Look! Look! Look!
See the little girl. She is all red. She is Little Red Ridinghood.
She lives in this modern ranch-style bungalow, designed for gracious living. It is in an exclusive district. They call it Rivercrest Heights.
That is because it is built on an old river bottom.
See happy Red Ridinghood. See happy Mummy. See happy brother Dick. See happy sister Jane. See Spot. See Puff. See the wealthy psychiatrists. Where is happy Daddy? Oh. Oh.
Oh, Daddy went away. That is why he is happy. On Sunday afternoons Red Ridinghood visits Daddy. So does Dick. So does Jane. Spot and Puff stay with Mummy. Daddy does not care for Spot or naughty Puff. Daddy does not care much for Mummy either.
Where is Grandmamma? She lives on the other side of Forest Grove. Grandmamma is hungry. That is because she lives on the Old Age Pension. Good, kindly Mummy is making Grandmamma a basket of food. She is making it in the Waring Blender. It is lovely gruel and so nutritious. Perhaps Grandmamma will lace it with a little gin. Clever Grandmamma!
Little Red Ridinghood will take the basket to Grandmamma. She will have to walk through Forest Grove to get there. That is because Dick and Jane are using the Cadillac. Little Red Ridinghood fears Mummy will be lonely. Good, kindly Little Red Ridinghood! But Mummy will be O.K. Nice "Uncle" Max is coming. That is why Little Red Ridinghood is being packed off to Grandmamma's.
See! See! See!

[2] From *My War with the 20th Century* by Pierre Berton. Copyright © 1965 by Pierre Berton. Reprinted by permission of Doubleday & Company, Inc. and the Canadian publishers, McClelland and Stewart Limited, Toronto.

See the pretty tenements! See the quaint children! See the interesting social workers! Oh! Oh! See the lovely wolf! How well-dressed he is in his narrow lapeled, three-button suit hand-crafted by custom tailors. See how nicely he tips his handsome Stetson straw woven of genuine Italian raffia! He has offered to carry Little Red Ridinghood's basket. Polite, gentle wolf!

Now he is asking for her phone number. He asks very politely. Always be polite, children. Little Red Ridinghood kicks him in the groin. The nice wolf is leaving. Good-bye wolf!

Little Red Ridinghood is sorry she kicked the wolf. Little Red Ridinghood dislikes violence. Little Red Ridinghood is lonely. She wishes the wolf would come back. She wishes he would take her to the movies. *The Thing from Outer Scarboro* is playing. Always be kind to wolves, children. In the end it pays off.

Look! Look! Look!

Here is Grandmamma's place. See the peeling wallpaper! See the rusty gas meter! See the worn-out carpet! See the color TV set! See happy Grandmamma watching Peter Gunn!

Grandmamma sees Little Red Ridinghood. Little Red Riding-hood sees Grandmamma. Grandmamma blushes.

Oh! Oh! Oh! See the handsome Stetson straw woven of genuine Italian raffia! What big eyes you have, Little Red Ridinghood! Look! Look! Look! There is someone in the closet. Why, it is the friendly wolf! Hello, wolf. Will you take Red Ridinghood to the pictures? Sorry kid, I don't rob cradles. I prefer the mature type. Clever, discriminating wolf! Good-bye Little Red Ridinghood! Here is a nickel for a *Mad Monster* comic book. Get lost. Good-bye kindly wolf. Good-bye happy Grand-mamma!

See! See! See!

See merry Red Ridinghood skipping home! What a lovely story she will have to tell Dick and Jane. How Mummy will laugh when she tells bout the wolf! How Daddy will laugh, too. Kindly, truthful, non-violent Red Ridinghood! Always tell the truth, children, even when it hurts.

EXERCISES

1. In order to do a "purpose parody" it is necessary first to identify and isolate some special target: a literary or dramatic (stage, film,

or television) atrocity you want to expose. Here's a suggested list from which you might wish to draw:

Soap operas in general

Current tendency to bring soap operas up to date by dealing with sex, drugs, homosexuality, racial matters, and other "controversial" subjects

The ceaseless efforts of television producers to make "the season" acceptable to current tastes

Movie ratings

The best-selling novel

Way-out or avant-garde plays and films that seem to make a great deal of money anyway

Textbooks in general

Movie magazines

2. While the Dick and Jane series is popular, there must be other examples of educational experiments that you think should be parodied. How about, for example, the way history is presented? Is the presentation perfectly objective? Find a specific history book and use it as the basis of your parody. You can use any educational level you wish, but perhaps your parody will be more significant if it is critical of the approach taken at lower grades, for younger students are more likely than older ones to be easily molded.

3. Select some well-known political figure and do a parody of his methods and characteristic approach to any issue. You don't want to choose this topic unless you have some strong purpose for doing so: that is, recognizing some characteristic, however well meaning, that you feel detracts from the figure's effectiveness. Your parody should take the form of a speech, and you should impersonate the kind of promise he makes, his characteristic sayings, and his prejudices or tendency to stay very carefully in the middle.

4. Select a well-known columnist or television personality, one who wields a lot of power and influences the thinking of large numbers of people. It should be someone, obviously, of whom you disapprove. Do a parody of one of his columns or telecasts, exaggerating those elements that you consider most harmful and most needful of correction.

Ridiculing Style

The success of a specific work or a specific body of work often incurs the wrath of the parodist, and his revenge is to write something that pretends to be the identical thing, though it may be thinly disguised with a different title, and so on: that is, either a given book, story, film, or play or else a faithful reproduction of an author's characteristic style. You ridicule a specific work when you think it has won its popularity under false pretenses, or when there is something about it you think its followers have overlooked. You recreate the work *for* them, hoping the exaggeration will discourage or at least dim their enthusiasm for it. You ridicule a body of work when you think its author has taken a good thing and run it into the ground or when the style that made the author famous has foolish elements that should have been eliminated.

Back in 1930 Pearl S. Buck wrote a book called *The Good Earth*, which was hailed as a masterpiece by the critics, made its author a living legend, and was directly responsible for her becoming the only female novelist ever to win the Nobel Prize for literature. Frequently praised was Miss Buck's biblical style and the "simple humanity" of her characters: Wang Lung, a Chinese farmer, and his wife O-lan, who together live a most primitive (and perhaps monotonous) existence, waging what the book jacket tells us is man's "ever-heroic . . . struggle for existence in any age and in any part of the world." But Robert Benchley found himself irritated by Miss Buck's drab style and (to him) laughably overdone simplicity. Here is a sample from the actual book by Pearl S. Buck:

> Spring came with blustering winds and torn clouds of rain and for Wang Lung the half-idle days of winter were plunged into long days of desperate labor over his land. The old man looked after the child now and the woman worked with the man from dawn until sunset flowed over the fields, and when Wang Lung perceived one day that again she was with child, his first thought was of irritation that during the harvest she would be unable to work. He shouted at her, irritable with fatigue.
> "So you have chosen this time to breed again, have you!"
> She answered stoutly, "This time it is nothing. It is only the first that is hard."
> Beyond this nothing was said of the second child from the time he noticed its growth swelling her body until the day came in autumn when she laid down her hoe one morning and crept into the house. He did not go back that day even for his noon meal, for the sky was heavy with thunder clouds and his rice lay dead ripe for gathering into sheaves.

The excessive primitivism and dull earthiness of the book aroused Benchley's scorn. His response was "The Chinese Situation," one of the classic parodies of modern times.

Benchley begins by jumping all over Miss Buck's pretentious biblical style:

WRITING JOKES, PARODIES, AND SATIRES 337

It was the birthday of Whang the Gong. Whang the Gong was the son of Whang the Old Man, and the brother of Whang the rich and of Auld Whang Syne. He was very poor and had only the tops of old Chinese wives to eat, but in his soul he was very proud and in his heart he knew that he was the son of old Whang Lung who had won the Pulitzer Prize for the Hop-Sing-and-Jump.

Now Whang the Gong, although he was known far and wide among the missionaries as a heathen, had read enough of the gospels to know the value of short words and the effectiveness of the use of the word "and." And so Whang the Gong spoke, and it was good. Good for fifty cents a word.

Further on, Benchley parodies the earthiness of the book's subject matter:

Now the winter wore on, and it was still the birthday of Whang the Gong, for Whang the Gong liked birthdays, for birthdays are holidays and holidays are good. And Rum Blossom, his wife, came to him and said, lowering her eyes as she pulled the stump of an old tree and threw it into the wood-box, "I am going to have another baby." And Whang the Gong said, "That is up to you." . . .

So Rum Blossom went into the library and had another baby. And it was a woman, or slave, baby, which in China, is not so hot.

"I will scream your shame to the whole village," said Whang the Gong when he heard of the incident. "Yesterday you had a man child, which was good. Today you have a girl, which is bitterness upon my head and the taste of aloes in my mouth." And he repeated it over and over, such being the biblical style, "I will tell the village— I will tell the village." And Rum Blossom, his wife, said, "All right. Go ahead and tell the village. Only get out of bed, at any rate. And get your old man up out of bed, too. I am sick of seeing him around, doing nothing."

And Whang the Gong got up out of his bed, and got his old man up out of his bed, all of which made but little difference.[3]

Often it happens that a given work, perhaps unobjectionable in its original style and intent, becomes a sensation with a particular ingroup and achieves a notoriety that the parodist thinks is way out of proportion to its actual worth. Such has been the fate of Tolkien's trilogy *The Lord of the Rings*, which was quoted in Chapter One as an example of good fantasy. Many feel that it is unreasonable of the author to expect a sophisticated adult reader to plough through over a thousand pages of fairy tales about hobbits, elves, and gremlins and wonder how it can have attracted so many loyal followers.

To shatter the Tolkien myth, the Harvard Lampoon issued a slender volume entitled *Bored of the Rings*, in which a staff of talented young

[3] From *The Benchley Roundup* edited by Nathaniel Benchley (Harper & Row, 1954). Reprinted by permission of Harper & Row, Publishers, Inc.

humorists rewrote the entire Frodo story (renaming him Frito, by the way, what else?) To refresh your mind, here's a sample of the original. At this point in the story Frodo and his companions are preparing to leave the magic land of the elven queen Galadriel.

> Now Galadriel rose from the grass, and taking a cup from one of her maidens she filled it with white mead and gave it to Celeborn.
> "Now it is time to drink the cup of farewell," she said, "Drink, Lord of the Galadrim! And let not your heart be sad, though night must follow noon, and already our evening draweth nigh."
> Then she brought the cup to each of the Company, and bade them drink and farewell. But when they had drunk she commanded them to sit again on the grass, and chairs were set for her and for Celeborn. Her maidens stood silent about her, and a while she looked upon her guests. At last she spoke again.
> "We have drunk the cup of parting," she said, "and the shadows fall between us. But before you go, I have brought in my ship gifts which the Lord and Lady of the Galadrim now offer you in memory of Lothlorien." Then she called to each in turn.[4]

The Lampoon version ridicules Tolkien's pretentious and archaic style, his incessant word coinages, his long and static cataloging of details, like the list of gifts given by Galadriel to the travelers; his constant use of epigrams, whether they relate to the action or not; his triteness, forgiven by the critics on the grounds that he is writing out of an ancient tradition; the many songs, which frequently retard the action and which infrequently make sense; and, one might say, the whole imposition of the long-winded epic on the reader's time. Here's how the Lampoon treats the same scene from the original:

> In the eastern sky, Velveeta, beloved morning star of the elves and handmaid of the dawn, rose and greeted Noxema, bringer of the flannel tongue, and clanging on her golden garbage pail, bade him make ready the winged rickshaw of Novocaine, herald of the day. Thence came rose-eyeballed Ovaltine, she of the fluffy mouth, and lightly kissed the land east of the Seas. In other words, it was morning.
> The company rose, and after a hurried breakfast of yaws and goiters, Cellophane and Lavalier and their attendants led them through the wood to the banks of the great river Anacin where three small balsa rafts lay.
> "It is the hour of parting," said Lavalier solemnly. "But I have for each of you a small gift to remind you of your stay in Lornadoon in the dark days to come." So saying, she produced a large chest and drew out a handful of wondrous things.
> "For Arrowroot," she said, "crown jewels," and handed the sur-

---

[4] From Tolkien's *The Hobbit*. Reprinted by permission of the publishers, Houghton Mifflin Company and George Allen & Unwin Ltd.

prised king a diamond-shaped pear and a plover's egg the size of an emerald.

"For Frito, a little magic," and the boggie found in his hand a marvelous crystal globe filled with floating snowflakes.

She then gave each of the other members of the company something rich and strange: to Gimlet, a subscription to *Elf Life*, to Legolam, a Mah-Jongg set, to Moxie, a case of Cloverine Brand Salve, to Pepsi, a pair of salad forks, to Bromosel a Schwinn bicycle, and to Spam a can of insect repellent.

The gifts were quickly stowed away in the little boats along with certain other impediments needful for a quest, including ropes; tins of Dinty Moore beef stew; a lot of copra; magic cloaks that blended in with any background, either green grass, green trees, green rocks, or green sky; a copy of *Jane's Dragons and Basilisks of the World*; a box of dog yummies, and a case of Poland water.

"Farewell," said Lavalier, as the company crammed themselves into the boats. "A great journey begins with a single step. No man is an island."

"The early bird gets the worm," said Cellophane.

The rafts slipped out into the river, and Cellophane and Lavalier boarded a great boat-shaped swan and drifted a short distance beside them, and Lavalier sat in the prow and sang an ancient elvish lament to the heart-breaking timbre of steel drums:

> "Dago, Dago, Lassi Lima rintintin
> Yanqui unicycle ramar rotoroot
> Telstar aloha saarinen cloret
> Stassen camaro impala desoto?
> Gardol oleo telephon lumumba!
> Chappaqua havatampa muriel
> U canleada horsta wata, bwana,
> Butyu canna makit drinque!
>
> Comsat melba rubaiyat nirvana
> Garcia y vega hiawatha aloo.
> A mithra, mithra, I fain wud lie doon!
> Valdaree valdera, que sera, sirrah,
> Honi soit la vache qui rit.
> Honi soit la vache qui rit." [5]

EXERCISES

1. Is there a book or author that, in your opinion, is currently making altogether too big a splash in the market? Is the book being praised out of proportion to its worth? Do you think too many people are being taken in by it?

   I don't necessarily want to put any ideas into your head, but

[5] From *Bored of the Rings* by The Harvard Lampoon. Copyright © 1969 by The Harvard Lampoon, Inc. Reprinted by permission of the New American Library, Inc., New York.

there is a certain authoress whose first two novels have sold twenty-five million copies and reaped unpronounceable sums in screen rights. She boasts, among other attributes, two first names and a style of writing that one critic said ran the gamut from "inept" to "imbecilic." What makes her books sell faster than pot at a rock festival is her knack for throwing her characters into bed on every page and for making the mass reading public believe it's getting the "inside story" behind the glamorous worlds of Hollywood or the television industry. She is thus able to satisfy the prurient interests of her public, their desire to identify with wealthy and gorgeous and excitingly decadent people, and at the same time their supposed need for "moral enlightenment." In fact, this unbelievably successful woman has said many times that her work is intended to expose rather than encourage moral decadence.

That parody is not only inevitable but also profitable has been proved by the recent (1969) efforts by a group of twenty-five journalists, who formed a committee to write the worst possible novel they could, directly after the manner of the young lady I have been discussing. The title of the book was *Naked Came the Stranger*, and Penelope Ashe was the pen name the group chose. The lampooning of the sex, drug-taking, and other playtime activities of our authoress's characters has delighted those who have caught on and apparently gone over the heads of the public that creates best sellers, for *Stranger* has sold almost as well as the works it parodies.

Perhaps you are familiar with the lady I mean—or some other current favorite—and would like to try your hand at recreating some memorable moments from specific modern masterpieces.

2. The Dick and Jane books, discussed in the preceding section, remind me of another institution that is continually experimenting and trying to adjust to what it considers to be the needs of the modern world. This, of course, is television, and it is a useful skill to learn how to parody its offerings, if only to keep your sanity.

Specific suggestions are hard to make for parodying TV because of the very obvious fact that each season is different and nowadays doesn't even last for the traditional eight months. It is an annual sacrificial ritual for the leading networks to murder low-rated programs on New Year's Day and make a desperate substitution. It is possible to imagine such a ritual and to list some representative substitutions:

"Tales from Norse Mythology" for "Tales from the Ghetto"
"Black Beauty" for "Lassie"

The continuing story of "Bonnie and Clyde" for "The Greatest Story Ever Told"

"The Travels of John the Baptist" for "Then Came Bronson" or "Route 66"

"The Yoko Ono Hour" for "Bishop Fulton Sheen Speaks"

One interesting assignment in this connection would be to take any current edition of *TV Guide* and go through it painstakingly to determine this season's patterns and then to come out with your own version of the *Guide*. Here's a sample that I received from one student:

7:30 P.M. (CHANNEL 11) *Gunjoke* (COLOR)

Flatt Villain, sheriff of Dodge City, comes back after a weekend fishing trip to find that Twitty, the lovely saloon-hall hostess he has loved platonically for the past twenty-eight years, has disappeared. Rumor has it that the girl has eloped with Cad Kincaid, the Miami Beach Kid, and plans to open a really big gambling emporium on the Las Vegas strip. But Flatt knows that Twitty would never betray him or carry on with another man, especially since he gave her his Boy-scout ring. Following his hunch and keen sense of smell, Flatt tracks Twitty and the Kid to a shootin' showdown before a sellout crowd at the Colosseum (just to prove how fair'n square he really is). We won't give it away who wins. You'd never guess.

3. We are living in the era of the huge, roadshow cinema, with its reserved seat policy, its lengthy intermission, and its formula plot. Perhaps you saw *Khartoum*, *Krakatoa: East of Java*, or the inevitable musicals like *Sweet Charity*, and perhaps you didn't like some or all of what you saw. What better chance to get your revenge than to create your own super-spectacle? If you're clever at artwork, you can even draw the ads for your movie ("The Story of a Peasant Girl Whose Love Defied an Empire!") and present it visually. If not, stay with prose and try to describe the big scenes as vividly as possible.

SATIRE

If one had to choose which was the greatest, noblest, and most important form of humor for the human race, the honor would inevitably go to satire. The reason is that the satirist is frustrated less by specific instances of human folly or by specific books or movies that have achieved an undeserved success than by the *general incompetence* of the world. If the source of humor is the gap that exists between what is and what we think ought to be, the satirist is a person who is painfully sensitive to the difference. The satirist is an idealist. Life keeps rubbing him so much the wrong way that his defense is to keep ridiculing it. The joke-maker adds to the enjoyment of life by giving us occasional things to laugh at; the parodist performs a valuable, but narrow, service for us. The satirist, on the other hand, tries to be a constant island of sanity in the midst of a sea of absurdity.

The General Subject Matter of Satire

Satire is serious criticism, through ridicule, of all that is wrong in human nature, the social, political, economic, relegous, and educational institutions of man, and the dreadful things men do to each other and to themselves. The most trivial satire is ridicule of some passing state of affairs; the most significant satire is ridicule of the follies that have been with the human race from the beginning and show no signs of disappearing. War, for example, has been a constant source of frustration for the satirist, who has been hurling his barbs at man's inhumanity to his own kind ever since Greek youth protested the long-drawn-out war against Sparta.

That satire seldom leads directly to an improvement in things is evidenced by the fact that we are still fighting wars. For all that Aristophanes told us in *Lysistrata* 2500 years ago, or, in our own time, Terry Southern in *Dr. Strangelove*, we are still marching, shooting, bombing, negotiating, marching, shooting, and so on.

On occasion, however, satire has led to reforms, especially the ridiculing of a passing condition, such as an election campaign or the phasing out of some important welfare service that the satirist believes must be continued. A good example of the effectiveness of specific satire occurred recently in one city, where a fifty-cent hot lunch program for the poor had to be discarded because of a loss of tax revenue. This happened at the same time that the governor of the state was given a thousand-dollar-a-plate testimonial dinner. One newspaper columnist observed wryly that the poor ought to be allowed the "privilege" of paying fifty cents for their lunch if other people were granted the "privilege" of paying a thousand dollars for their supper. This comment focused the attention of the citizenry on the poverty problem. Soon afterward a private restaurant chain volunteered to continue the hot lunch program.

Even without being directly responsible for change, however, satire is psychologically valuable for both the satirist and his audience. It allows all those who share a certain viewpoint to know they are not alone. It creates a warm fellowship among people who will probably never meet face to face. It is the enduring underground movement, the resistance taken by the fraternity of the frustrated against a world that is far from perfect. If nothing else, it makes the world somewhat easier to inhabit.

Although the scope of satire is extremely broad and continually being expanded, it is possible to set down some of the recurring themes and to suggest methods of ridicule that you can experiment with. The three most common general targets of satire are *institutions, human types,* and *actions.*

Some of the institutions often satirized for one reason or another are:

> the government and its red tape
>
> politicians in general (promises, promises!)
>
> the law (especially corruption among law enforcers)
>
> organized crime
>
> the legal profession (ambulance-chasing and the like)
>
> education (endless experimentation by people who have never been inside a classroom)
>
> the older generation (rigidity)
>
> the younger generation (fads and fancies)
>
> marriage (they both lived happily ever after?)
>
> the family (Home Sweet What?)
>
> religion (especially hypocrisy: do-as-I-say-not-as-I-do)
>
> undertakers (just leave everything to us, my dear, and we'll bill you later; by the way, how much *was* the insurance?)
>
> entertainment in the mass media

The human types that incur the wrath of the satirist are those whose peculiarities in some way retard the smooth operation of living and the progress society ought to be making. Fair game for satire is the *single-minded personality;* the satirist, as a person of reason, a person who tries to be adjusted to reality in all its complex phases, will not tolerate hung-up, frozen, or rigid mentalities

*especially when the people in question seem happy in their inade-
quacies.* Some of these single-minded types are:

> greedy materialists
> social climbers
> snobs
> hypocrites (on any social level)
> gossipers
> conformists
> conforming nonconformists
> insincere politicians
> teachers clinging to outmoded methods
> teachers using only way-out methods
> overly strict parents
> overly permissive parents
> creeps of all ages and sizes
> prejudiced people
> liberals who protest too much

The list could go on and on for pages, but I have put down a few of
the more obvious satiric types, some of which I think are just coming
into the range of satire. Others, like snobs and hypocrites, have been
around for thousands of years.

Finally, satire can be aimed at kinds of action the satirist feels
are not in the best interest of the health and progress of mankind.
He might, for example, ridicule a Communist takeover of a backward
country on the grounds that the revolutionary leaders were thinking
of their own power, not of the people's needs. He might ridicule a
specific war being fought for senseless reasons or else warfare in
general on the grounds that it is never justifiable for men to destroy
each other. Usually broadly humanitarian in his thinking, the satirist
is opposed to all activities that lead to the death of human rights
and prevent mankind from fully enjoying its brief stay on this earth.
In addition to warfare between nations or revolutions within a nation,
some of the commonly satirized activities are:

> political programs that will profit only a very few
>
> the superimposition of any way of life on the many by the few. A
> recent movie *Wild in the Streets*, for example, had for a premise
> the election of a twenty-four-year-old President, who, with his own
> ingroup, placed everyone over thirty in a concentration camp; near
> the end of the film the President realizes he is being plotted against
> by a group of nine-year-olds.

a certain kind of cause, which, however right-minded it may have sounded in the beginning, becomes inflexible and single-minded. A governor of a state recently came out against the forced bussing of pupils to bring about the integration of schools; when a federal court ordered bussing in a certain county, the governor personally seized control of the schools, fired the entire school board, and then locked himself inside the administration building to avoid arrest!

any deeds that reveal the blindness of people, such as the unquestioning adulation given to any celebrity, whether he's a movie star or a murderer, or the often mysterious logic of the public mind when it comes to elections. A political figure popular in New England, for example, was once convicted of mail fraud and sentenced to prison, where he conducted an entire campaign and actually won an election for an even higher political office.

deeds that reveal the moral hypocrisy of people. Examples include pulling over when there's an auto accident and secretly reveling in the suffering and devastation; gossiping about the "immoral" behavior of others, thereby helping to destroy somebody's reputation; falling all over oneself to be sweet and kind to one's unfortunate brothers and thereby creating as many racial problems as one attempts to correct.

Having a subject, however, doesn't guarantee that your ridicule of it will find sympathetic ears. It helps to adopt a workable method of making satire effective. I have selected three methods for study.

The "Modest Proposal" Method

No question about it, the classic of all satires is the essay "A Modest Proposal" by Jonathan Swift. It is doubtful that anyone will ever think of a more devastating way to make a point or a more memorable premise on which to build. Written in 1729 as an expression of Swift's indignation at the British maltreatment of the Irish and, in fact, at the whole appalling and dismal picture of Irish poverty, the piece, legend has it, was taken seriously by some people but proved a sobering experience for most of its readers. Certainly, if you had been a contemporary of Swift and had encountered this essay, you couldn't possibly have remained indifferent to the conditions that it indirectly exposes. I say "indirectly" because the whole thrust of "A Modest Proposal," and the satiric method I have named in its honor, is the author's pretending to be a part of the very Establishment he seeks to ridicule. Swift adopts the personality and views of a conservative member of the landed gentry, a man who deludes himself into believing he possesses humanitarian instincts, but who is about as concerned for the poor as a medieval feudal lord throwing a partridge to each of his serfs during his annual Christmas tour of the property (without bothering to remove the arrow!).

Swift begins the essay in a tone of high seriousness. The essence of the "Modest Proposal" method of satire is deadpan. Don't let on for one minute that you're anything but serious, for the more you assume the false identity and play it for real, the more completely will you discredit it. Swift's opening statement is that of a concerned, liberal humanitarian:

> It is a melancholy object to those who walk through this great town, or travel in the country, when they see the streets, the roads, and cabin doors crowded with beggars of the female sex followed by three, four, or six children, all in rags and importuning every passenger for alms. These mothers, instead of being to work for their honest livelihood, are forced to employ all their time in strolling, to beg sustenance for their helpless infants, who, as they grow up, either turn thieves for want of work or leave their dear native country to fight for the Pretender in Spain or sell themselves to the Barbadoes.

Then he begins to win the reader's sympathy by assuring him that he has taken the matter of Irish poverty to heart and has at length hit upon the most marvelous plan ever devised and here it is:

> I have been assured by a very knowing American of my acquaintance in London that a young, healthy child well nursed is, at a year old, a most delicious, nourishing, and wholesome food, whether stewed, roasted, baked, or boiled; and I make no doubt that it will equally serve in a fricasse or a ragout.
>
> I do therefore humbly offer it to public consideration that of the hundred and twenty thousand children already computed, twenty thousand may be reserved for breed, whereof only one fourth part to be males, which is more than we allow to sheep, black cattle, or swine; and my reason is that these children are seldom the fruits of marriage, a circumstance not much regarded by our savages; therefore one male will be sufficient to serve four females. That the remaining hundred thousand may, at a year old, be offered in sale to the persons of quality and fortune throughout the kingdom, always advising the mother to let them suck plentifully in the last month, so as to render them plump and fat for a good table. A child will make two dishes at an entertainment for friends; and when the family dines alone, the fore- or hindquarter will make a reasonable dish, and seasoned with a little pepper or salt, will be very good broiled on the fourth day, especially in winter. I have reckoned, upon a medium, that a child just born will weigh twelve pounds, and in a solar year, if tolerably nursed, will increase to twenty-eight pounds.
>
> I grant this food will be somewhat dear, and therefore very proper for the landlords, who, as they have already devoured most of the parents, seem to have the best title to the children.

When you pretend to endorse the Establishment attitude by borrowing its very identity and then suggest cannibalism as a humane solution to the problem, how much defense, how much comeback have you allowed that Establishment?

EXERCISE

1. Imitate Swift's deadpan method by pretending to be a representative of a group whose attitudes or actions strike you as inhuman. Develop your own "modest proposal" for solving a particular problem that this group normally solves in a manner you find unacceptable and deserving of ridicule.

    Here is an example to serve as a guide. It was written by the wife of a prominent professional man in Miami Beach as a protest against the treatment of the many senior citizens who move to Florida and have nothing to live on except social security checks.[6]

    There is no doubt about it, the plight of the aged and infirm of our community presents a problem to challenge the wisdom and ingenuity of a Solomon—famed senior citizen of another era. One has only to view the sufferings of these elderly denizens of the southernmost tip of our city to recognize the hopelessness of their situation—on the one hand kept alive by the latest geriatric discoveries of medical research, and on the other hand, bereft of the strength and vigor to enjoy the few extra years with which medical science has endowed them.

    Daily, we witness the many indignities to which they must submit: herded behind red plush ropes at the bank each month as they wait interminably on snakelike lines to cash their paltry social security checks (soon to be raised by a measly 15 percent); standing for hours outside a movie theatre to make the matinee prices so that they may fill the emptiness of their lives with a few hours of meagre pleasure, under the illusion that they are enjoying themselves (at an additional 50 percent Senior Citizen discount); queued up at a bus stop, the helpless pawns of the capricious scheduling of mass transportation, waiting for the privilege of jostling and squeezing themselves into a bus to go to no place in particular, at Senior Citizen discount fares. And what about the most humiliating degradation of all—

[6] Printed by permission of the author, Alice Lee.

standing in line for a 50¢ hot lunch doled out by economy minded politicians, who would much prefer to use the taxpayers' funds for junkets abroad than soup kitchens at home.

Has your heart never lurched at the electrifying sound of the rescue squad rushing to the aid of some aged crone, struck by a coronary or stroke, or some fragile relic, felled by a crack in the sidewalk, and crippled with a broken hip? And have you never been awakened by the screech of an ambulance siren, heralding the endless task of conveying those ancient husks from bed to bed, and almost always, in the middle of the night?

If you visit one of our smaller, par three golf courses in nice weather, then you have surely seen these doddering sportsmen, struggling gallantly down a fairway, clubs in tow, and swinging valiantly at that elusive little white ball. How frustrated those arthritic athletes must feel, knowing that an empty day stretches endlessly ahead of them, and a line of impatient golfers stretches endlessly behind them.

Surely, these pathetic old beings deserve some relief. For many of them, life is truly over, but they lack the knowledge, technique, and, in some instances, the funds to end it. And, due to the problems of overpopulation, urban crowding, water and air pollution, shrinking food sources, neglectful absentee land-lordism, the rising birthrate, and growing student unrest, the community also needs and deserves some relief! We must find a way, therefore, to put these poor people out of their misery, to sink them, gently, lethewards, and, at the same time, to stem the tide of ancients that has threatened to envelop us since science has begun to work the miracle of longevity.

Of course, one could wish that all our senior citizens were models of Shaw's Superannuated Man, but since they are not, we must dedicate ourselves to finding some humane way of eliminating from society these forgotten and putrefying left-overs of nature. The simplest thing would be to deny them access to the miracle drugs, chemicals and hormones that have been prolonging life beyond the point of pleasure and conven-ience. But, failing that—our idealistic scientists with their self-deluding ethics being what they are, and considering the per-sistent will to live that motivates these stubborn old crones—one must consider other methods. As one who has made a consider-able and even serious study of the subject, I would like to make a modest proposal.

First step in solving the problem of disposing of the aged, a law should be passed—a civil service test for the selection of those senior citizens deemed fit to survive, a sort of social security, in reverse. The patent purpose of this survival test could be to determine which individuals are most in need of government medical aid. Thus the aged and decrepit would not only be quite willing to take the test, but their family and children would urge them to do so in order to qualify for additional free medical care, a gift which such individuals have never been known to refuse.

The actual purpose of this test, however, would be quite different. It would provide a basis upon which we could decide which old people are still able to perform as useful citizens, capable of contributing some constructive service to the community, and which ones are so feeble and senile that they have become parasites—unsightly burdens who are no longer of any use to themselves or to the community which must support them. Of course, children are helpless, too. But they, at least, are investments in the future, while the helplessly, hopelessly aged are nothing more than withered stalks blighting the gardens of a youthful and vigorous society.

The practical aspects of ridding ourselves of these mushrooming pests is a problem to which I have addressed myself at great length and with much energy. Of course, mass extermination of the scope and scale conceived by the late Adolph Eichmann and others of his ilk during the final flowering of the Third Reich would be the fastest and most efficient method, but one naturally feels a certain reluctance to adopt the methods of a nation which proved to be, in the long run, losers. Besides, older people have a tendency to be suspicious, and, in addition, so many of them were so emotionally involved with what they refer to as the "holocaust" of the Nazi Regime, that they would hardly submit quietly to a similar fate. In other words, they might not walk easily and willingly into a gas chamber or crematorium. And even if they did, there is the cost to be considered. Crematoria are initially expensive, and would require extensive maintenance. And besides that, they would surely compound the problem of air pollution. No, a simpler and less expensive method of elimination is needed here. And this is it: prune juice.

Everyone knows that these elderly people cannot subsist (or think they cannot, which, in this case, is just as effective) without a daily purge of prune juice. It seems to have a salutary effect upon their systems, a daily dose having the result of keeping these individuals contented and happy, and in good nature for the rest of the day. They would never, under any circumstances, omit their morning prune juice, the consequences of which would be so dire as to preclude contemplation. And therein lies the solution to the problem of getting rid of these oldsters—*we must poison their prune juice!*

A poison can be selected whose effect would simulate the symptoms of heart attack, or some other such natural but fatal illness. This would satisfy the conscience of the ethical community, and provide a safe, sure, and humanitarian exit from a cruel existence for these pathetic individuals whose souls would then be freed from their decayed and crippled bodies, content in the knowledge that they are no longer a burden to their family, friends, and the state which has provided them with a swift and merciful end.

It is hoped that serious consideration will be given to the above proposal—one which can be so adapted that it could be carried out with the knowledge and tacit approval of all, without causing anyone to feel that he has sinned by being personally responsible for the demise of a beloved parent or grandparent.

The state will provide the final solution and bear the guilt, and the youthful and near-youthful builders of society will then be rid of the unaesthetic and unproductive eyesores that have for too long cluttered our landscape.

Let them quaff a draught of prune juice, and with Socrateslike dignity, slip quietly away.

ALICE LEE

The Trojan Horse Method

After ten futile years of attempting to conquer Troy by direct, frontal assault, the Greeks finally resorted to the method they were better at than they were at fighting: ingenuity. Troy was finally toppled by brains, not brawn. The Greeks knocked at the door, smiled, said they were sorry about the war and why not forget the whole thing, and gave the Trojans a present to show their good intentions. Everybody knows what happened.

The *Trojan Horse satirist* comes on smiling and bearing gifts, but don't trust him. He's just waiting for the prey to open the door wide enough for him to gain entrance, and then ZONK! This method is very much like that of the "close friend" of the Broadway actress, who goes backstage after the opening and cheers her up in this fashion: "Darling, you were magnificent. I argued with everyone in the lobby." You can always keep people paranoiac by saying, "I think it's deplorable what they are saying about you, but I want you to know I don't believe a word of it." Even better: "You have so many friends it just goes to prove how little people really care about physical appearance."

In 1925 Thomas Reed Powell wrote a review for *The New Republic* of a book entitled *The Constitution of the United States*. To my knowledge neither the book nor its author has ever been heard from since. Mr. Powell never said a negative word, however. He even praised the book enthusiastically, except that he used a simpleminded style, thus implying that only the most ignorant reader could possibly find anything good to say about the book. The review begins like this:

> Even before the eighteenth amendment, books about the United States Constitution were apt to be pretty dry. They usually tell what the Supreme Court says in a lot of cases and try to show how what it says in one case will jibe all right with what happens in each case, then they try to forget it and to put all the cases together and make up a set of rules to show what the Supreme Court has been up to and what it is going to do next. That is a very hard thing to do, and it is very hard to read after it has been done. You have to think very hard all the time, and even then you get all mixed up. This kind of book makes you tired because you have to try so hard to think, and so you usually stop trying to read it.
>
> The new book which Mr. Beck has written about the Constitution is a very different kind of book. You can read it without thinking.

A slightly different aspect of the Trojan Horse method is illustrated by the prose style of Alan King, a stand-up comic of considerable distinction, the man who has become solidly identified with the character he always assumes: the middle-class, middle-aged American male, victimized by the female of the species, trapped in that institution from which he believes no release is ever obtainable—the family. Whatever Valhalla Mr. King may privately enjoy with Mrs. King, there is no getting away from the fact that his great popularity stems from the identification almost all married people are able to make with the friction-filled everyday situations King describes. His satire has a knack for striking squarely in the middle of every American living room.

The technique King uses is a variant of the Trojan Horse approach. His words come accompanied by a broad grin, and then his statement will attack your most vulnerable ideals, and you can almost see behind the words that fading sad smile that has become the comic's trademark.

Whether you're already married or are thinking about marriage poetically, you are fair game for Alan King, as witness:

> Has it ever occurred to you that the greatest loves of history and literature had one thing in common? The boy and the girl never got married.

Think it over. Paris and Helen of Troy, Tristan and Isolde, Cyrano and Roxanne, Antony and Cleopatra, Don Jose and Carmen. I could go on.

Not only don't they get married, they virtually never see each other. The lovers are always kept apart by family, society, wars, crusades, the black plague, or they're married to someone else. If you want to read about love and marriage, you've gotta go out and buy two separate books.

Romeo and Juliet, they got married. They spent one night together and the next day he committed suicide. Then she committed suicide. I'm trying to figure out what went on in that bedroom. That's a hell of a way to start a marriage. Can you imagine what this epic romance would have been like if they had to live together like normal people?

"Aren't you going to shave, Romeo?"

"It's Saturday; why should I shave?"

"Because my mother is coming over, that's why."

"Your mother doesn't shave on Saturday, either."

"And on your way out, take the garbage with you."

"Who's going out?"

"You are. My mother wants you to pick her up." How's that for romance? No more of this "Wherefore art thou, Romeo?" jazz. She knows damn well wherefore he art. He's hiding in the garage trying to figure out why he ever got married in the first place.

I think that all these romantic classics do more harm than good, because the kids read them in school, and they grow up with a warped outlook on life. We should be teaching them that marriage has many advantages, too. I can't think of any offhand, but I'm not a teacher. Let 'em do their own research.

Look, I think I can speak from experience. I've been married for eighteen years. That's a fact. Jeanette and I just celebrated our eighteenth wedding anniversary. You know how every anniversary is associated with a material symbol—the fiftieth is golden, the seventh is copper, the tenth is tin. Well, the eighteenth is iron. If you can stay married to my wife for eighteen years, you've got to be made out of iron.

I don't ever remember being single. My wife and I were kids together. I've known her since she was seven years old. We both lived in tenements. We grew up in the same slum together. Of course, to look at my wife today you'd never dream that this was her background—unless you talk to her. Then, right away, you know where she came from.

I remember how much her father was against our marriage. He wanted her to marry a doctor, and, now that I look back on it, he was right. She should have married a doctor. It's the only way I could ever have gotten even with the medical profession. Furthermore, her father didn't want her to get married below her station. Jeanette's station was Fourteenth Street, and I had to get off at Eighth Street. That was six blocks below her station.

Obviously her parents weren't crazy about me. You'd think that marrying their daughter was a great big status symbol. It just so happened that my family had more money than her family, and we were on relief. So you can imagine what a big thrill they were.

The more I think about it the more I think that someone could have written a great novel about the two of us. We had all the elements. Her family opposed the marriage. They sent her on a boat trip around Manhattan Island. Maybe she'd forget about me. Maybe she'd meet another man. But all that happened, we were more in love than ever. We were going to get married, and there was nothing they could do about it.

The smartest thing we could have done was elope, but Jeanette wouldn't hear of that either. "We've got to do it right," she insisted. "Go ask my father for his blessing."

What an experience that was. Getting my father-in-law's blessing to marry his daughter was like getting the Governor of Alabama to give his blessing to a Freedom Bus.

"Your Honor," I said, doing a little curtsy, "your daughter and I are in love and we want to get married."

Right away he started with the wailing. "My little baby; she's going to be married."

It was a very touching performance. "Don't cry, sir. Try to remember you're not losing a daughter; you're gaining a son," I said.

"THAT'S WHAT I'M CRYING ABOUT, YOU BUM!"

He had one more standard question. They've always gotta ask it. It's part of the ritual.

"Will you support my daughter in the manner to which she's accustomed?"

"Sure," I replied, "We're moving in with you." [7]

EXERCISES

1. Select some institution, as Alan King does in the above example, and discuss its characteristics, using the Trojan Horse method. Never say anything bad about it directly. Just come on smiling, building the reader up, and then striking swiftly for the kill.

    If you'd rather not try your hand at being quite so funny, you can imitate this method of satire by using irony or sarcasm throughout. Thus, for example, if you think some of the educational practices at your school are scandalously outdated, you could say things like

    Nothing could be more progressive than the curriculum here at good old ——— College. My only criticism is that they take your breath away a little too quickly with all their far-out ideas. True, we're living in the Space Age, but somebody ought to prepare us for our first encounter with higher education: that course of dazzling complexity and intellectual stimulation: Orientation 101.

[7] From the book *Help! I'm a Prisoner in a Chinese Bakery* by Alan King. Copyright © 1964 by Roband Productions. Reprinted by permission of E. P. Dutton & Co., Inc.

I trust you can take matters from there.

Here's a dandy example of this rather direct use of the indirectness of the Trojan Horse method, written by a student at Girl's Latin School in Boston, one of the most venerable and ivy-covered of all educational institutions:

> Congratulations. You've finally made it. You've gotten into the best school in the city. You enter the hallowed halls, overawed at the Greek statues (evidences of the high cultural level) and proceed to the assembly hall where the headmistress welcomes you and reminds you of the high standards of the school. You work hard for six years, memorizing—it doesn't matter whether you understand it or not, just as long as you can shoot back the answers. You then apply to the college of your choice (Ivy League—of course) and are readily accepted. Enlightened by a Liberal Arts course, you graduate with honors and marry a nice professional man. You move to a nice suburb, bring up nice kids, and send them to that nice school which has undoubtedly improved with age.
> What more could you want? [8]

It is doubtful that any critique of contemporary education in any erudite journal of the specialists, by the specialists, and for the specialists could ever make a more devastating attack than this simple but deadly paper.

2. Write a critique of some book, play, movie, or television show, using the Trojan Horse method employed by Thomas Reed Powell in the review from which I have quoted. Show your utter distaste for the thing by assuming the identity of someone who would, in your opinion, enjoy it.

The Peterian Method

Among the many delights of a recent book called *The Peter Principle* (1969) is the invention by its authors Laurence J. Peter and Raymond Hull of a brand new method of making satiric points. This technique, which I call "Peterian," differs from its predecessors in that it purports to be—and to some extent is—highly scientific. It woos the reader to its side by never being anything but objective and factual in its presentation. It offers countless examples for every point it wants to make, and the reader in each case recognizes that the example is not farfetched, but quite valid and even broadly representative. The Peterian method gains the sense of being scientific by concentrating fiercely and doggedly on a given line of thought, dealing with

[8] From *How Old Will You Be in 1984?* edited by Diane Divorky. Reprinted by permission of Avon Books. Copyright © 1969 by Avon Books.

it so thoroughly that the reader just about forgets that other examples have been excluded that might have seriously weakened the argument. It is science with style; it puts its subject to bed, so to speak, not because it has truly exhausted it—in the laboratory sense—but because its wealth of examples has made the reader share its view. What more does satire have to accomplish?

The Peter Principle, the very title of which makes you think of a scientific law, is subtitled "Why Things Always Go Wrong," and thus at the very outset indicates it is going to explain something rather than attack something. It virtually forces you into accepting the premise "Things always *do* go wrong" without looking too closely at the fact that it means *all* things, not just some. In this way it takes on right away the veneer of a scientific tract.

Hull's introduction sets up the rationale for the book by concentrating on a whole host of things that are always wrong and thus grabs the reader before he has a chance to think about it [9]:

NOTE: *See how he sets himself up as a competent authority?*

As an author and journalist, I have had exceptional opportunities to study the workings of civilized society. I have investigated and written about government, industry, business, education and the arts. I have talked to, and listened carefully to, members of many trades and professions, people of lofty, middling and lowly stations.

But "bungle their affairs" is not a truly scientific phrase.

I have noticed that, with few exceptions, men bungle their affairs. Everywhere I see incompetence rampant, incompetence triumphant.

I have seen a three-quarter-mile-long highway bridge collapse and fall into the sea because, despite checks and double checks, someone had botched the design of a supporting pier.

The examples may or may not offer definitive proof of incompetence. The point is the author makes them seem to be incontestable evidence. Note that names, dates, places are seldom included. The author is talking about general

I have seen town planners supervising the development of a city on the flood plain of a great river, where it is certain to be periodically inundated.

Lately I read about the collapse of three giant cooling towers at a British power-station; they cost a million dollars each, but were not strong enough to withstand a good blow of wind.

I noted with interest that the indoor baseball stadium at Houston, Texas was found on completion to be peculiarly ill-suited to baseball: on bright days, fielders could not see fly balls against the glare of the skylights.

[9] The following excerpt is from *The Peter Principle* by Dr. Laurence J. Peter and Raymond Hull. Reprinted by permission of William Morrow and Company, Inc. Copyright © 1969 by William Morrow and Company, Inc.

incompetence, but this isn't really scientific.

I observe that appliance manufacturers, as regular policy, establish regional service depots in the expectation—justified by experience—that many of their machines will break down during the warranty period.

Having listened to umpteen motorists' complaints about faults in their new cars, I was not surprised to learn that roughly one-fifth of the automobiles produced by major manufacturers in recent years have been found to contain dangerous production defects. . . .

I have stopped being surprised when a moon rocket fails to get off the ground because something is forgotten, something breaks, something doesn't work, or something explodes prematurely.

I am no longer amazed to observe that a government-employed marriage counsellor is a homosexual. . . .

As I write this page, the woman in the next apartment is talking on the telephone. I can hear every word she says. It is 10 P.M. and the man in the apartment on the other side of me has gone to bed early with a cold. I hear his intermittent cough. When he turns on his bed I hear the springs squeak. I don't live in a cheap rooming house: this is an expensive, modern, concrete highrise apartment block. What's the matter with the people who designed and built it? . . .

Education, often touted as a cure for all ills, is apparently no cure, for incompetence runs riot in the halls of education. One high-school graduate in three cannot read at normal fifth-grade level. It is now commonplace for colleges to be giving reading lessons to freshmen. In some colleges, *twenty percent* of freshmen cannot read well enough to understand their textbooks!

Having established his case (once he gets going he causes the reader to supply another thousand of his own examples!), Mr. Hull goes on to describe his meeting with "Dr. Laurence J. Peter, a scientist who had devoted many years to the study of incompetence." Together they offer the reader a scientific analysis of incompetence and how it can ultimately be prevented.

The "Peter Principle" itself amounts to this: things go wrong because the whole American hierarchical system—business, education, the military, the government, and so on—is predicated on promoting competent people until each of them achieves *a level of incompetence:* that is, finally gets a job that he doesn't understand and can't do well. At this point he has reached what the authors call "final placement," and vegetates at his post. Since he can't function well anymore, he loses interest and enthusiasm and starts bungling things. In other words, promotion itself, based on the fundamental American desire to "get ahead," is at the root of all the evil. In a Utopia, so the authors imply, people would be allowed to function and be suitably rewarded in jobs they enjoy doing and can do creatively without being continually tempted by the thought of going higher and higher.

"Hierarchiology" in a very real sense does become at least a pseudo-science in this book. Despite the satiric attitude and underneath the ridicule the authors do make a strong point and keep increasing the degree of credibility by dissecting the subject thoroughly and carefully. Chapter after chapter piles up inventive terminology as this new science is systematized and made applicable to every aspect of American life. A concluding chapter is called "The Darwinian Extension" (to the whole development of humanity), wherein the authors note that mankind itself may have reached its "final placement," may be bungling itself out of existence by having reached a level of evolution at which it is hopelessly incompetent.

To prevent one's own promotion to oblivion, it is necessary, of course, for the reader to decide to resist final placement. He does this through "the power of negative thinking," whereby he avoids bucking for promotion by realizing in advance all of its disadvantages. The authors also suggest trying "creative" or "irrelevant incompetence," whereby one pretends to bungle his present job (but actually does it successfully) in order to discourage others from promoting him. If such subversion were widespread enough, then, the authors comment with pretended hopefulness (masking their actual cynicism).

> The net result? An enormous store of man-hours, of creativity, of enthusiasm, would be set free for constructive purposes.
> We might, for instance, develop safe, comfortable, efficient rapid-transit systems for our major cities. (They would cost less than moon-ships and serve more people.)
> We might tap power sources (e.g., generator plants powered by smokeless trash burners) which would not pollute the atmosphere. Thus we would contribute to the better health of our people, the beautification of our scenery and the better visibility of that more beautiful scenery.
> We might improve the quality and safety of our automobiles, landscape our freeways, highways and avenues, and so restore some measure of safety and pleasure to surface travel.
> We might learn to return to our farm lands organic products that would enrich, without poisoning, the soil.
> Much waste that is now dumped might be salvaged and converted into new products, using collection systems as complex as our present distribution systems.

Otherwise useless waste might be dumped to fill abandoned open-pit mines and reclaim the land for constructive purposes.[10]

Sobering? Indeed! The whole trick is the labeling and categorizing they do on almost every page. We are told, for example, of the "power of Push"—the thrust toward promotion; of "The Alger Complex," the rags-to-riches disease that nearly every American catches; of the Pseudo-Achievement Syndrome; the Final Placement Syndrome; even the Generalized Life-Incompetence Syndrome, which refers to "neuroses, anxiety, psychosomatic illness, amnesia, and psychosis" through which many people become triumphantly and brilliantly unable to function well in any capacity whatever!

The delicious "gimmick" (if that word is proper here) of *The Peter Principle* is being so straight-faced and statistical—having graphs and charts—about the subject of bungling. We cannot help being amused by the whole idea behind the book, but at the same time, we are transferring our amusement from the authors' style to their targets. That is, we find ourselves smiling at army generals, high-ranking politicians, business executives, and educational administrators. We suddenly see these people, whom we may once have admired for the very prestige that "promotion" normally connotes, as possibly having achieved their final placement and occupying a lofty level of incompetence. Through satire the authors have brought us face to face with a most serious possibility. By pretending to be scientific they have accomplished the same goal as a real scientific tract would have done: persuasion.

EXERCISES

1. Using the science of "Hierarchiology," as explained in this section, analyze any institution to which you are in any degree related. The purpose of your paper is to imitate the Peterian method of satire and to account for the reason things always go wrong in this institution in terms of the people who have been promoted to their level of incompetence.

    In order to prevent your paper from becoming a monotonous listing of occupations, give it variety and originality by trying to draw as amusing a portrait of each incompetent as you possibly can. Show him at his job and point out some of his most "endearing" characteristics. Does he sit, for example, at a desk that is

[10] From *The Peter Principle* by Dr. Laurence J. Peter and Raymond Hull. Reprinted by permission of William Morrow and Company, Inc. Copyright © 1969 by William Morrow and Company, Inc.

perfectly in order, containing no books or papers or any other visible signs of work? Does he keep filling his desk pen and straightening his clean blotter? What kind of evasions of work is he capable of?

Here's a suggested list of choice incompetents:

the ex-drill sergeant
the C.O.
the chairman of the ———— department
the high school principal
the coach of the ———— team
the foreman
the supervisor

2. Select one incompetent whose steady rise to the heights of incompetence you have observed. Do a character study of this person as an example of why this world is so fouled up.

3. Write a paper describing your own conflicts with the hierarchical system in America. Have you, for example:

   a) tried to get ahead in your place of employment but been held back by all the blockheads higher up?

   b) been forced to keep things going because of the incompetence of your superiors but, at the same time, been paid far less than they?

   c) been yourself the victim of the promotion system, whereby you were aware of having been elevated to a level of incompetence?

   d) attempted to resist the stagnation that comes from final placements?

   e) been, as a student, the victim of a teacher's having achieved his level of incompetence? (Give details. In your opinion should this teacher have remained a lab assistant? a paper grader for someone else? a student?)

   f) been the victim of unjust treatment at the hands of a department chairman, dean, or other administrator, who was stagnating in his final placement?

   g) been prevented from functioning as you might in your fraternity, sorority, or other campus club because of the incompetence of an officer in this society?

   h) become yourself an officer in a campus organization and discovered what it means to achieve a level of incompetence?

". . . getting into things that prove too vast and overwhelming to admit of even conceivable change."

9

GRIPES,
GROANS,
AND METHOD

Putting stylish touches and witticisms in your prose, adding humorous stories, or writing parodies and satires will not do on every occasion, as we both know. This book would hardly be complete without finally coming to terms with the "traditional stuff," the kind of writing that Miss Prendergast, everyone's high school English teacher, called expository prose. This is the prose in which you're supposed not only to have something to say but to have some method in your madness; in which enthusiasm, involvement, even style aren't quite enough; in which you're graded on that elusive thing Miss Prendergast called *form* or *structure*. Remember the old topic sentence? the outline *before* writing? Remember the torture and the torment?

The question before us now is whether Miss Prendergast was putting us on. Is it really necessary to do any pre-planning? Does outlining really work? Isn't it enough to get turned on by the subject itself? Doesn't thinking about writing beforehand diminish the spontaneity, dull the enthusiasm, and deaden the final product?

In all honesty, if I thought the best method for writing was to have no method at all, I'd come out and say it. Who is Miss Prendergast to me, or I to Miss Prendergast by now? We haven't spoken since the day she asked me in class to explain what Shakespeare was "trying to tell us" in *Julius Caesar* and I answered, "To do that I'd have to read the whole play out loud."

So it is not to preserve the Prendergast legend that I come out now in favor of method. I do so because I think method—the feeling you impart to the reader that you know exactly what you're doing—is what finally makes it for you on paper. Indeed, doesn't it stand to reason that this book, devoted as it has been to self-realization through prose, should be especially concerned at the very last with something that, in distinguishing your prose, will have a great effect on your search for identity?

There will always be a place for spontaneous enthusiasm in writing. There will always be a need for inspiration, and some of the best pieces ever penned have been done in a swirling fog, with the writer working on literary radar. But inspiration can't *always* be counted on. In these final two chapters we want to consider what you do when you calmly sit down to communicate to both yourself and others serious thoughts about your life, your time in history, and the one and only world you may ever have to live in.

How To Succeed Without Miss Prendergast

My Miss Prendergast was about as liberal and swinging as a drill sergeant. Her aim was to make of our class nothing less than a crack rifle team. We were to be better trained than Pavlov's dogs. She just had to say "theme" and any one of us would be able to salivate a topic sentence on the spot.

"Find your general area of interest first," was her advice. I always supposed she meant, "Say the first thing that pops into your head," as a psychiatrist does. One day, after she had given the usual command, I happened to turn my head and catch sight of a travel poster scotchtaped to the wall. (Our classroom doubled as a foreign language lab.) The poster advertised two glorious weeks in Hawaii, though I doubt that they taught Hawaiian in our high school. At any rate, I saw this hula-hula girl, and my mind started a fantasy at once. But Miss Prendergast, whose eagle eye never missed a thing, sensed I might be gone in two seconds, so she brought me back rudely by asking me to start theme drill for the day.

"Your general area of interest?" she asked with a smirk.

"Hawaii," I popped back.

"I see," she smiled, glancing over at the poster. Some of the finks in the class giggled. "A noble subject. Now give me a topic sentence."

Desperate, I started ransacking my brain, and lo and behold! something must have been knocked into place and started a chain reaction. All of a sudden the Prendergast mysteries were made clear to me. As in a trance, I became high priest of a beautiful cult. I spoke as an oracle of the goddess of Planned English Themes. Without going through the formal process of thinking, I said divinely, "Hawaii should not have been granted statehood."

As I look back on this incident, I suppose this inane notion came to me because my subconscious was secretly thinking that Miss Prendergast should not have been granted a teaching certificate. At any rate, I had committed myself to the foolishness, and there was no going back. I want you all to know what a magnificent exhibition of pre-planning I went on to give, proving once and for all that it is possible to write a Prendergast theme on any subject, no matter how idiotic it may be.

Testing my new-found mettle to its utmost, she sent me to the blackboard to write my outline, which I did without batting an eye:

First Para.:	Statement of purpose of paper—to show just cause why Hawaii should not have been granted statehood.
Second:	Hawaii inhabited by people with native customs and strange way of life.
Third:	Hawaiian natives out of touch with rest of country. (Give examples.)
Fourth:	Important for American citizens to know what is going on.
Conclusion:	Turn Hawaii into a reservation.

The class applauded, but Miss Prendergast pursed her lips, arched her nose, and folded her hands over what was presumably her bosom. She sensed that I was making fun of her and her methods. Honest, I wasn't! I had become a perfect little theme-producing machine.

As you can see, the fallacy of the Prendergast Method is that it is possible to achieve the illusion of meaningfulness if you become skillful enough in handling artificial structure. We grew to consider strained connections and illogical transitions the student's best friends. I remember a classmate once commenting, "you can get an A as long as it *looks* like it makes sense." I also remember being bothered by this. Why shouldn't I want to make sense for the sake of making sense? But it was so hard, so very hard, to locate myself anywhere in that raw skeleton of an outline. How did I go from Me to a writing method?

What Do We Communicate?

The answer to the problem may lie buried in the whole phenomenon of communication. Why do we write if not to communicate? And why do we communicate if we don't have to? There we have it: the big question. *Do we really have to? If so, why?*

Let's forget for the moment that we're talking about written communication. Let's consider the most common form our communications take: namely, oral. Here's a list that occurred to me of the reasons we generally bother to say something to somebody else:

1) to get some needed information ("Where's Gate 21?")

2) to give some requested information ("I don't know.")

3) to keep open the channels of communication even if you have nothing to say (When you pass a friend on the street, you're required to stop and pass trivial conversation, because if you don't, you won't have any friends at all in case you ever really need them!)

4) to use oral communication as a means of letting out your pent-up tensions (Notice how often people who live alone tend to call others up and chatter on for hours; if they didn't, they'd be climbing the walls.)

5) to exchange thoughts with people you respect and enjoy being with; to stimulate them and in turn be stimulated yourself

If you stop for a moment and contemplate this list of motives for communication, you'll probably agree that although #1 and #2 serve practical purposes, #3 and #4 constitute the usual reasons we talk to others. (Number 5 can be the most stimulating, but it isn't easy to get a good intellectual bull session going.) Most of the time we are jabbering away with our friends simply because they *are* friends and it's fun to be with them. Why do people enjoy going to parties? Is it not for what is generally called "idle" conversation on almost any subject, from Brahma bulls to the atmosphere of Venus? It has little purpose other than enjoyment and comradeship, and no direction whatsoever.

But what generally comes to the surface during this unstructured conversation? Isn't it one complaint after another: people sharing each other's aggravations and even trying to outdo each other? Even as I write this, I am conscious of chatter coming from the courtyard of the apartment house in which I live. I walk out into the living room and stand close enough to the window to eavesdrop without being observed.

MRS. X: Oh, my husband is even worse than that. When he comes home, he . . .

MRS. Y: Oh, don't they all, my dear? But the tuna casserole is the answer. Why in God's name should we spend all day cooking?
MRS. Z: Sure, and the prices they charge for meats! I swear I can't keep up with it.
MRS. X: What about rent? If I *told* you what he's charging for the top floor . . .
MRS. Y: And for what? So you can break your back walking up the stairs. As far as I can see, the elevator's always being repaired.
MRS. Z: Because it's made of junk. Junk. Like everything else nowadays.
MRS. X: Our car is falling apart, and it's only a year old.

This is no exaggeration. They kept on. I left. I'd learned what I came to find out. Most nonintellectual bull sessions are Gripe Fairs at which each participant displays his grievances and hawks his wares by trying to outscream everyone else.

In all probability the intellectual bull session amounts to the same thing, except that you'll hear complaints being registered on all sides about "the inflationary spiral" rather than the price of meat, and "United States urban policy" rather than how rotten it is to go downtown nowadays because it's so filthy and crowded.

Behind the bull session there is an atmosphere of tension and uneasiness. People seldom meet together to be perfectly tranquil and enjoy the *silent* pleasures of companionship. (Lovers do when they are very much in love, and when they meet, they usually have no need of spoken communication.) The longer the bull session lasts, the more the participants let off steam. The conversation becomes increasingly excited—and increasingly undirected and disorganized.

But we'd all perish without these Gripe Fairs. If anything is sure, it's that none of us can sail through life in absolute calm. Living means getting rubbed the wrong way by life's failure to meet our expectations. Living means getting let down by other people; finding out that you yourself are not what you thought; discovering hundreds of possibilities and never quite being sure you have chosen the right course. Small wonder that we're continually agitated and have steam to let off.

But it isn't always possible to get together with others for a Gripe Fair. It seems to me that prose offers the most immediate chance for flipping your lid. By writing them down, one can have the fun of getting rid of his gripes, as he does in a bull session; he can also reach a little better understanding of what they truly are, where they come from, and what can be done about them. In a bull session it is seldom possible to finish a sentence. It is almost never possible to really explore any subject fully and reach any conclusions about it. Here's where writing has the advantage. Miss Prendergast never told us the secret. Expository prose begins with the gripe, and the gripe gives you a structure.

The Single Cell Theme: Just Gripe

They say life began with the simplest possible organism: the single cell. It makes sense to approach writing methods in the same way. Begin with a basic gripe and just let it out. You will immediately experience the gratifying difference between prose and bull sessions. In the latter nobody gives you a chance to finish. You hang there with your unexpressed agitation. You're not even a whole cell.

The basic gripe essay gives you a natural form because your own emotions will tell you when you're finished. Since there's nobody there while you're writing to shout you down, you can go until your instincts feel satisfied. The cell is bound to complete itself.

Here's what one high school student wrote who was thoroughly disillusioned by the whole educational system in which he felt himself trapped. From the roughness of the style I'd say he wasn't exactly the apple of his Miss Prendergast's eye. She probably never found out how much he had to say.

> High school is really and truly a drag. Standing on line for a goddam hour to see some crotchety old man and you can't smoke a cigarette so you settle for picking your nose and when you finally get into his office you're so up-tight that you forgot what you came down for and you couldn't care less and it's only second period on the first day and you know you ain't gonna make it for a whole year. And you realize, now that you're a senior, that the only things you learned in the last three years were how to roll a joint and how to rap your way out of suspension. For that you spend 8 hours a day of completely insane torture. Now you're a senior and you know how to sit in your assigned seat and raise your hand when you have to go. So why don't you drop out? Well, there's that thing they call the Selective Service System. Right?
>
> Did you ever notice that it's only the kids who're hip to the whole thing that they send to shrinks? Blessed be the ignorant.[1]

The Cause-and-Effect Essay

It's hard to find too much fault with the above essay. As far as it goes, it gets the job done. It wants to vent its spleen against the sys-

[1] From *How Old Will You Be in 1984?* edited by Diane Divorky. Reprinted by permission of Avon Books. Copyright © 1969 by Avon Books.

tem. It's had it "up to here," and it wants us to know it. To criticize the paper, you need to criticize the gripe. You need to tell this student, "This is bad writing because you have a bad attitude." Who's going to do that? When the paper *is* the gripe and the gripe *is* the paper, you've got a perfect single cell. You've got one of the miracles of the universe. Life begins; only this time it's prose life.

If there are grounds for any reservations, however, one can say it's not enough to spend your life merely griping. Sooner or later someone is bound to ask, "Yes, but why do you think things are like this? What makes you feel as you do?" The high school author doesn't tell us too much, really, about the educational system he so despises. He tells us about its effects. It's a "drag." The only thing he learned, he says, is "how to roll a joint and how to rap your way out of suspension." But what are some of the reasons these conditions have come about? I'm not even asking the writer how fair he is being. I'm not wondering how many were similarly affected. Weren't there, for example, some seniors, who knew how to do something beside roll a joint? who didn't even smoke pot? I'm recognizing his inalienable right to gripe, but I'm curious about the system and want to know more. I want to know whether *he* knows more, or is he satisfied just to gripe?

The following paper comes from the editorial page of a community college newspaper. Prose for prose it is not necessarily "better" than the first paper. It is possibly less "enthusiastic" about its gripe. But it does represent a step up in complexity of purpose and method. It has more than a single cell because it offers both the gripe itself (the effect) and an inquiry into at least one of the causes.[2]

Perhaps the best way to understand our American educational system of past eras is to take the time and glance through some very early copies of magazines, such as *Vanity Fair, Time, Look* and *Life.* Particularly around the years before the Great Depression, beginning with 1925.

In these volumes lie the hidden seeds of hints and suggestions made by men to show our country what was happening to college education in a time of great prosperity.

For example, February, 1925, *Vanity Fair* contained an article

[2] Reprinted by permission of *Falcon Times*, weekly student newspaper of Miami-Dade Junior College, North (Miami, Florida), and the author, Larry Grosswald.

by Stephen Leacock entitled, *The Rush to the Colleges, Its "Why"—Which is of More Importance—Its "Whither."*

Leacock explains: "There is no doubt that a great many boys are lifted along through school and lifted clean into college because there is nothing else to do with them."

In 1925, when Leacock said this, he tried to show the importance of a college education. What was happening to it? You put the fees in a slot and you draw out a salary.

It is this fact, he says, "which is turning the college curriculum up-side-down."

What Leacock is presenting is the idea that college has turned into a place for what is called "practical" studies. The student doesn't want to know anything. He wants be taught to do something.

The student has more of a demand for "knowing how" instead of finding out the—Truth, which proves to be unfindable.

Is it not like this, today in our educational system? Futile studies, each in someway taught to show the importance it has upon making money, disillusioning the student from the true purpose of an education.

In another article appearing in January, 1925, *Vanity Fair* John Jay Chapman explains how higher education in America is today (1925) controlled by big business. His article is *"The American University" A Plea for the Emancipation of Our Culture from Well-Meaning Commercialism.*

We would have to agree with Mr. Chapman in many places, that business men have been substituted for scholars even in our own educational system today.

But what do we do now?

Where do we look for help?

Who will speak for higher education?

Our professors? They sit in silence on their points of view, every once in a while catching a wondering student to explain. Dare they try and tell the Administration?

As a college newspaper reporter, I am not surprised at all to hear an instructor agree with things said in disfavor towards the Administration. But at the end of each criticism I am not disturbed also to hear, "Please don't quote me as saying that."

As John Jay Chapman said back in 1925: "I do not laugh at this. Far from it. The realities of life and the ways of human nature loom so distinctly, and I say, What then? Where shall we look for help?"

LARRY GROSSWALD

You can tell this author thought about his gripe in advance. He wondered how he might put his finger on one of the reasons for his own discontent with the educational system. Then he traced the system's problems to an educational philosophy: forget learning for its own sake; concentrate on the practical. The author decided he'd look further into the matter and appears to have made a trip to the library to look into some of the causes of the philosophy itself. Or perhaps he ran across these books and found in them a key to his gripe. Either way, he committed himself to prose when he had both cause and effect—to his satisfaction at least—in his hand.

The writer of the editorial knew in advance what his purpose was. He also had a plan of attack, an approach, a *method*. He must link cause to effect. He must describe an educational philosophy that arose during the 1920s and then show the effects it is having half a century later. *Purpose determines structure.* The single celled paper doesn't need a plan of organization because it does only one thing. It doesn't move from one point to another. To grasp this principle is to begin to see that the reverse of the proposition may also be true; namely, that when a paper gets complicated and has many parts, the absence of any sort of structural principle may well signify the lack of clear purpose. And this is no laughing matter.

EXERCISES

1. Put into practice what you have learned about structure so far. Just so you won't have to spend all your time thinking of a subject, why not begin with the very same gripe that both of the student authors had? Surely there must be many things about the high school or college system that agitate you.

   Do the assignment in two parts. First, write a single-celled essay in which you gripe as fully as you want. Let your hair down, as it were. Don't worry too much about style. Let off steam. Let your prose take you where it will as long as you don't go beyond the boundaries of this one gripe. Don't, for example, jump from dissatisfaction with the educational system or some parts of it to your anger at the way the country is going, war, discrimination, and so forth. Learning to stay within the cell is the basic exercise in putting discipline into your writing.

   Second, take the same gripe and expand it into a cause-and-effect essay. Include more details or specific instances that illustrate some of the reasons for your gripe. If it is convenient, narrow the focus and use a particular class or teacher as typifying the system. Try to get at the sources of your discontent through an analysis of this person. Perhaps you had a Miss Prendergast of your own. What were some of her customary assignments? What reason, if any, did she give for them? Did she ever explain her grading system? Of what educational philosophy does she seem to have been the product?

Don't complicate your task any more than is necessary. If the gripe is about some aspect of the educational system, select the clearest possible causes, the ones that you can most easily and convincingly set down on paper. Don't get all tangled up in a profound analysis that will mystify the reader.

In doing the cause-and-effect essay, you don't always need to go back into the far past to find causes. For example, if Miss Prendergast's way of teaching turned you off, the cause can simply be Miss Prendergast's way of teaching. You're not duty bound to seek a super-cause, one that precedes Miss Prendergast, unless you feel compelled to do so.

Your teacher may read some of the cause and effect papers. As you listen to them, use these criteria to help you evaluate them. First, is the cause or are the causes clear enough? Do they seem convincing explanations of the effect(s)? Second, does the writer appear to have omitted some causes that could have been included? What makes you feel this way? Third, even if the cause explains the effect, does the writer seem to have reacted appropriately or to have overreacted? That is, does the cause seem strong enough for the gripe? Conversely, does the gripe seem adequate in view of the cause?

These are some realistic considerations to help you evaluate expository writing—at least when it is clearly based on a gripe. They should also help you to polish your own paper before you submit it.

2. If the Prendergast Method of subject-outline-conclusion sounds familiar to you, you can have a little fun right here by making a list of preposterous subjects—whatever comes to mind—and then doing an outline, as I did on the subject of Hawaii, before reaching my famous conclusion that Hawaii should be turned into a reservation.

On the other hand you can begin with a list of conclusions and then back one up with a parody of a logical outline. Some possible conclusions are:

a) Legalized gambling should be permitted in kindergarten.

b) Children under seven should not have immunity from the stop-and-frisk law.

c) Women should be drafted instead of men.

d) The voting age should be raised to fifty-three.

 The trick will be to see how logical and coherent you can make your paper. If you can persuade the reader that your conclusion is a sensible one, then you will have added further proof of the inadequacy of the Prendergast Method. If you can't, Prendergast will ride again, and we may never be able to control her!

3. Do a cause and effect essay on some institution other than the educational system: for example, the current federal administration, the state administration, the police, the Catholic Church, the Protestant sects, the various Hebraic sects, women's or men's fashions, our economic system, a middle-class morality, and so on. Indicate:

a) precisely how you feel

b) exactly why you feel that way

c) some specific examples of why this institution frustrates you so

Remember: the main requirement is that a cause-and-effect essay be clear and detailed. Try not to get so tangled up in your agitation that the reader is unable to understand the whole problem as you see it.

Agitation-Response

The single-celled and cause-and-effect gripe essays are fine for letting off steam and reaching some understanding of the main things that disturb your peace and equilibrium. But even when you undertake a careful analysis of causes, you still aren't dealing in solutions. A still more complex purpose, therefore, is to go beyond the agitation and express an appropriate response (or solution) to it. It need not be the only possible response, but it should be one the reader can understand; and if you go from one point to another with clarity of vision and purpose, you ought to be able to persuade the reader that your response is a logical one, perhaps even that it should be his.

 The agitation-response contains more cells, but, as long as you are master of the purpose, the structure should not pose an insurmountable problem. If the whole premise of this chapter is a sound one, structure should be inevitable, almost automatic, when you are acutely conscious of your intention. In this case it is to locate and express the gripe clearly and thoroughly and then indicate the solution you have either worked out and wish to suggest or prophesy as being inevitable even though you may not want it to happen.

The way to begin is to find the basic single cell, the gripe itself, and work up from there. Here's a random list of possible gripes:

the federal administration
the use of drugs by young schoolchildren
continuing racism
the weather

This time, however, you think of more than simply what's wrong in these areas. You think about what should happen, what could happen, or what probably will happen next.

Suppose you took the federal administration. As an illustration of what I mean by response, let's think of what could happen to improve matters up at the front office; what could happen to make you feel better about the government. You could:

vote it out in the next election
organize a national demonstration to protest a certain policy
write letters to Congressmen
write letters directly to the President

With such a large subject to work with, you'd end up with an extremely long list of possible responses. Then it becomes a question of deciding which ones are most appropriate, which ones seem to have priority. If the next election is three years off, organizing a demonstration may be more immediately profitable. Or writing a letter to the President. But any positive response is worth putting down on paper.

Even negative solutions can be valuable. Suppose you took the weather as your gripe. Or, better still, people who annoy you by constantly complaining about the weather when it seems perfectly obvious to you that nothing can be done about it. Can you do something about *them?*

Put them in an institution where they'll be locked up with hundreds of people who have also spent their lives griping about weather.
Install a weather-producing computer so that they'll experience nothing but extremes of cold and heat, blizzards, rain, and so on.
Allow them no reading matter: in fact, no form of diversion except complaining.

The negative response to an agitation is not as silly as it looks. First, it can offer you additional pleasure, if only to imagine such deeds.

Second, it can keep you from ever becoming like the people about whom you have this particular gripe. Third and probably most important—it can cause your reader to recognize the folly of behaving like these people.

After you've made your list of gripes, select the one toward which you have the strongest feeling of response. Analyze your thoughts completely so that you know exactly what the response is: whether it is positive or negative, whether you feel hopeful or pessimistic about improvements in this area. You now have an abundance of material for a rich and worthwhile piece of expository prose.

I asked a class of distinctly mixed writing backgrounds to do an agitation-response for me right there on the spot. The initial reaction was the usual panic. But I allowed the students to wander about the room or slump in their chairs or lie on the floor and just think about the assignment for about fifteen minutes. The only instructions given were to find an honest gripe and think of some way to take care of it. Here's what a black girl wrote. (Understand that no stylistic improvements were possible because of the time limitation. This paper represents a direct and sincere fulfillment of the assignment.) [3]

Understanding the Black Child

When a black child enters a classroom, he has a background of many other experiences than the white child. Many times the black child comes from a family where the father has left. And the mother is left with the task of supporting the family. Many black children suffer because of the lack of a father image. During the child's early years of imitation he doesn't have a suitable male figure to serve as a model for him to learn from. He doesn't have anyone to talk with about making important educational decisions. The family may not have neighbors, relatives, or friends in skilled occupations who might give the child the proper direction, encouragement, and information he needs to succeed.

In many black families the mother is the head of the household. The black mother is busy trying to earn a living. She doesn't have time to instill in the child the motivation of trying to do well in school. Black children see men working without an education earning money. This tends to make them think that education is unimportant.

[3] Printed by permission of the author, Arleyah Martin.

Many lower class homes are not verbally oriented. Parents are embarrassed by their own limitation and lack schooling. They do not encourage their children to ask questions.

The language and attitudes of the textbooks black children read may appear unreal, because the reader's ideas and way of life are drawn from middle class habits. The reader shows white children going on picnics, to zoos or on family vacations and other enjoyable adventures. The black children cannot identify themselves with these children. Many black children have never even been downtown shopping or eaten in a restaurant. These experiences are quite common to most white children.

A black child may express hostility to a white teacher. His attitude may have been transmitted from the home and parental experiences with white people. White store owners and employers may have treated the parent unfairly and the child may be conditioned to expect unfairness and raw deals from white people. Some teachers may openly make derogatory remarks within hearing of the black child. White teachers who teach in the black schools must realize life goes on after school. They must help train the child in some of the habits, manners, and customs the home did not accomplish. The teacher must have love and patience in order to help his students through many tasks. He must be kind and gentle in his work, but on occasion he must be firm and sharp. The teacher must take on many tasks and responsibilities in areas outside formal instruction. Many teachers may not like working in a black school, because the black school is not up to the standards of a white child. I do feel this is going to create many problems in the schools which are being integrated. A lot of work will have to be done.

ARLEYAH MARTIN

As a teacher, I can assure you I have read millions of gobbledegook words in educational journals dealing with the general subject of school integration and "teacher adjustments." I have seen words like "disadvantaged" and "deprived," but seldom is the impact as simple, direct, and eloquent as this sentence: "Many black children have never been downtown shopping or eaten in a restaurant." This student's gripe, I suddenly realized, was directed at precisely those educational journals with their fancy theories and remoteness from reality. As a result, I find I must carry her solutions very close to my conscience: "The teacher must have love and patience in order to help his students through many tasks. He must be kind and gentle in his work . . ."

Expository prose isn't something remote and formidable and dull. Structure isn't just something the rules of writing say we need to have; structure is beautiful because it takes us where it is distinctly *good* to go. Prose structure helps us to proceed from point to point in our thinking. And the agitation-response represents another step up because it stretches the structure to include the solution. I think what I'm trying to say is that we ought to be reaching out for more complex structures by way of strengthening our grip on things. I think the more *aware* one becomes, the greater the number of cells in his writing and the more solid the connection between them should be.

So many people gripe about so many things. But the accomplished writer is frequently the one who should be listened to. He goes further. Before the 1968 Presidential election comedian Dick Gregory decided to announce his own candidacy. He may not have seriously expected to win, but in imagining his own administration, he does offer solutions that strike at the conscience of the reader.[4]

PEACE AND FREEDOM

I offer myself as the independent candidate of all Americans who want to make their own declaration of independence this election year. I am issuing a call for a Write-In vote to all my fellow citizens who share my dream for America; whose concern for their country is greater than party loyalty; whose desire to solve the tremendous world and social problems confronting the soul of this nation supersedes an allegiance to a party platform.

To rid this nation of political decay we must create an independent army of determined voters who will march to the polls in November and emerge victorious. During America's World Wars, the designation "Democrat" or "Republican" had no meaning to the soldier on the front line of battle. Party labels are irrelevant to the defense of democracy. And the defense of democracy at home, in America's own political life, requires

[4] The following is from *Write Me In!* by Dick Gregory. Copyright © 1968 by Dick Gregory. By permission of Bantam Books, Inc. All rights reserved.

front-line soldiers who refuse to accept party labels or choices and who wage a just war according to their own strategies.

There are a variety of possible strategies. Each independent action should be designed to create a real alternative to the stale and decadent dominance of the two-party system. The use of pencil power and the creation of a personal, individual ballot of one's own choosing is one strategy. The current emergence of an active Peace and Freedom party in many states throughout the country is another. The creation of such a third party, a party based on the magnificent dream and the human aspiration of peace and freedom, exposes the shallow aspirations of the two-party system. Such a party offers a public forum for the expression of moral concern and provides a means of organizing those whose dream of democracy will not submit to or be stifled by current political realities. Any political strategy which makes possible the public exposure of the dreams of statesmen rather than the calculated partial commitments of politicians receives my wholehearted endorsement.

This is how I want to be President. I want to assume office in January of 1969 as the result of a political battle waged by an independent army of voters determined to save this great democracy and to save America from herself. Whatever the outcome of the vote in November, the waging of the battle is victory in itself. If I should happen to fail to receive the majority of that vote, I will still be the commander-in-chief of an independent voting army and will declare myself their President-in-Exile. That army will contiue to wage war for justice and dignity among men for years to come.

My Government-in-Exile would operate side-by-side with the other government in America. I will have my own Inaugural Ball on the evening of January 21st, though the music and food will probably differ from the other President's celebration. I will deliver my own State of the Union address on the same evening the other President delivers his message before a joint session of Congress. Whenever the occupant of the White House fails to respond to the just demands of human need, the independent army will bring their concerns to the Black House to their President-in-Exile. The new Government-in-Exile will offer political asylum to every man, woman and child in America who is devoted to freedom and true democracy. Ours will be an active exile, a functioning government and a marching army. For the first time since the Declaration of Independence, the voice of the democracy will be heard.

EXERCISES

1. Make a list of the major gripes that are currently disturbing you. Next to each one indicate a possible solution for it, whether it is a positive one (like the suggestions made for white teachers by Arleyah Martin or Dick Gregory's plan to become president) or an improbable one that is at least amusing to think about (like the idea of putting the weather-complainers all together in one place with a consistently bad climate). From your list select the gripe and solution you think will give you the most abundant and interesting material.

   A suggestion: try to find one that has a number of parts to it, for you may run out of gas somewhere in the middle of the paper unless your material is rich enough. Look for a gripe that has a considerable history. Here's a sample list of possible gripes that should provide rich material for writing (in addition to those already dealt with):

   a) the endless talk and lack of action in the matter of pollution

   b) the waning of quality in new cars and other appliances

   c) legislative control of morality (such as antiabortion and anti-homosexuality laws)

   d) the waning of religion among both older and younger people

   If you were to select one of these or one with a similar history, you would find that you've enough material for a paper that falls logically into three parts:

   a) an introductory section in which you offer a survey of the gripe's background: e.g., specific examples that you think demonstrate the decline in workmanship in cars and other things or a lack of a truly religious orientation in people close to you

   b) a middle section in which you offer specific instances of your own involvement with the institution or product or behavior causing your gripe

   c) a concluding section in which you offer the positive, or negative, solutions you have already thought about

   These suggestions are not intended to be hard-and-fast rules. It is obvious that, if you get inspired, you can do things instinctively and have them work. Arleyah Martin's written-in-class paper on integrated education was honest and moving without ever coming down from the level of generalities.

You will find, however, that the preliminary screening of your material will save you no end of trouble and generally produce a higher grade. The Institute for Intolerable Climate was introduced as a passing example. I doubt that it would make a good paper. The material is too thin to stretch far enough. Choose the subject that promises to have the most *details* for you.

2. This could be a classwide project. Have a family discussion in which the entire class as well as the teacher contributes some of its pet gripes. Eventually there will be a list on the board, no doubt including many of the ones prominently mentioned throughout this section.

Narrow down the choices until the class is satisfied these represent serious gripes as well as gripes for which a *positive* solution can be imagined. Thus:

a current war (if any)
apathy toward religion
resistance to integration of neighborhoods
governmental doubletalk
increase in drug use among the very young

By vote, one main gripe can be chosen: let's say it's the alarming statistics about the prevalent use of drugs among school-age children. The class then spends some time working on solutions, perhaps deciding on a communitywide campaign to make young people acutely aware of the dangerous consequences of drug use. The teacher can divide the class into smaller groups, or else each person can work individually. The idea is for the class *as a whole* to develop a response to the gripe. One group may come up with some posters (perhaps for actual distribution in the lower grades); another may work up a dramatization of the problem and get permission to perform it in some schools; still another may work up a pamphlet to be mimeographed and then distributed to school-children.

Incidentally, this assignment will focus the attention of the entire class on the apathetic members. It's always illuminating to find out who the people are that like to complain about everything but won't stir themselves into any action.

The Prophetic Response

Once you get too much scope to your gripes, however, you're getting into things too vast and overwhelming to admit of even conceivable change. "The spirit of the age," "the tempo of the times," "the way the world is going": we've all heard these phrases. We know they have meaning but are hard put to define them exactly. We live with a continual sense of *forces* working on us, a whole complex of influences that are steering the currents of history. Somehow we know history will go its own way no matter what we as individuals may do to improve the things that we can reach.

One way of responding to the BIG AGITATIONS is to project the present into the future; imagine what history will do to society in a generation or so. This may be the only possible means at your disposal to make your readers aware of some of the things that ought to be disturbing them *now*.

Here's an excerpt from Aldous Huxley's prophetic novel of 1932, *Brave New World*. The author had a frightening vision of a civilization entirely computerized, in which humanity had become so superfluous and bored that its only pleasure lay in taking week-end-long drug trips. All human emotions were discouraged, as was the sexual instinct, because perfect babies could be produced from test tubes. Without sex and without the intellectual stimulation derived from books, the population had "feelies" in addition to drugs. You can decide for yourself how close Huxley's vision has come to the present reality.

> The scent organ was playing a delightfully refreshing Herbal Capriccio—rippling arpeggios of thyme and lavender, of rosemary, basil, myrtle, tarragon; a series of daring modulations through the spice keys into ambergris; and a slow return through sandalwood, camphor, cedar and new-mown hay (with occasional subtle touches of discord—a whiff of kidney pudding, the faintest suspicion of pig's dung) back to the simple aromatics with which the piece began. The final blast of thyme died away; there was a round of applause; the lights went up. In the synthetic music machine the sound-track roll began to unwind. It was a trio for hyper-violin, super-cello and oboe-surrogate that now filled the air with its agreeable languor. Thirty or forty bars—and then, against this instrumental background, a much more than human voice began to warble; now throaty, now from the head, now hollow as a flute, now charged with yearning harmonics, it effortlessly passed from Gaspard Forster's low record on the very frontiers of musical tone to a trilled bat-note high above the highest C to which (in 1770, at the Ducal opera of Parma, and to the astonishment of Mozart) Lucrezia Ajugari, alone of all the singers in history, once piercingly gave utterance.
>
> Sunk in their pneumatic stalls, Lenina and the Savage sniffed and listened. It was now the turn also for eyes and skin.
>
> The house lights went down; fiery letters stood out solid and as though self-supported in the darkness. THREE WEEKS IN A HELICOPTER.

AN ALL-SUPER-SINGING, SYNTHETIC, TALKING, COLOURED, STEREOSCOPIC
FEELY. WITH SYNCHRONIZED SCENT-ORGAN ACCOMPANIMENT.

"Take hold of those metal knobs on the arms of your chair,"
whispered Lenina. "Otherwise you won't get any of the feely effects."

The Savage did as he was told.

Those fiery letters, meanwhile, had disappeared; there were ten
seconds of complete darkness; then suddenly, dazzling and incom-
parably more solid looking than they would have seemed in actual
flesh and blood, far more real than reality, there stood the stereoscopic images, locked in one another's arms, of a gigantic negro and
a golden-haired young brachycephalic Beta-Plus female.

The Savage started. That sensation on his lips! He lifted a hand
to his mouth; the titillation ceased; let his hand fall back on the metal
knob; it began again. The scent organ, meanwhile, breathed pure
musk. Expiringly, a soundtrack super-dove cooed "Oo-ooh"; and vibrating only thirty-two times a second, a deeper than African bass
made answer: "Aa-aah." "Ooh-ah! Ooh-ah!" the stereoscopic lips
came together again, and once more the facial erogenous zones of the
six thousand spectators in the Alhambra tingled with almost intolerable galvanic pleasure. "Ooh . . ."

The plot of the film was extremely simple. A few minutes after the
first Oohs and Aahs (a duet having been sung and a little love made
on that famous bearskin, every hair of which was separately and distinctly felt), the negro had a helicopter accident, fell on his head.
Thump! What a twinge through the forehead! A chorus of ow's and
aie's went up from the audience.

The concussion knocked all the negro's conditioning into a cocked
hat. He developed for the Beta blonde an exclusive and maniacal
passion. She protested. He persisted. There were struggles, pursuits,
an assault on a rival, finally a sensational kidnapping. The Beta
blonde was ravished away into the sky and kept there, hovering, for
three weeks in a wildly anti-social tête-à-tête with the black madman.
Finally, after a whole series of adventures and much aerial acro-
bacy three handsome young Alphas succeeded in rescuing her. The
negro was packed off to an Adult Re-conditioning Centre and the
film ended happily and decorously, with the Beta blonde becoming
the mistress of all her three rescuers. They interrupted themselves for
a moment to sing a synthetic quartet, with full super-orchestral accompaniment and gardenias on the scent organ. Then the bearskin
made a final appearance and, amid a blare of sexophones, the last
stereoscopic kiss faded into darkness, the last electric titillation died
on the lips like a dying moth that quivers, ever more feebly, ever
more faintly, and at last is quite, quite still.[5]

Not long ago I gave one of my writing classes an assignment
based on *Brave New World*. Each student was to offer a particularized
vision of an event or condition he saw as inevitable, however he

[5] From pp. 144–146, *Brave New World* by Aldous Huxley. Copyright, 1932, 1960
by Aldous Huxley. Reprinted by permission of Harper & Row, Publishers, Inc.

might hope to prevent its happening. The more details he could include, I indicated, the greater would be the likelihood of convincing his readers that he wasn't just being silly, that he really held a crystal ball in his hands. Here's what one student wrote: [6]

A LETTER TO THE FOLKS AT HOME

77 Utopia Street—Stall #4
Echo Valley, South Dakota
April 4, 1975

Dear Momma,

I know you have been waiting a long time to hear from me. I wanted to write earlier, but you know how it is. I had to find a place to live, a job and get myself situated. Everything was strange and wonderful and at first I had a bit of trouble getting settled, but now everything is just fine. After the city, it's wonderful to live in the country where the air is so clean and the streets are broad and new. Echo Valley is the prettiest of the new industrial-training towns.

You thought I would have difficulty finding a job, since I did not complete my training, but that is far from true. There are more jobs out here than there are people. There's so much space to stretch out in that industry is really growing in this part of the country. Right now I'm working in one of the new chemical plants. Mostly we manufacture fire control chemicals, but we do some work in gases and napalm, too. My salary is good, but I'm thinking of changing jobs. Just a few blocks from where I live a huge kennel is being started. You know how I always liked dogs. Of course, this kennel will specialize in Shepherds and Dobermans, but no matter. If I like it I can work my way up and become a trainer. Trainers of riot control dogs do very well salary wise. If I really do well in it, I may get a loan and start my own business. Of course I can never hope to do a large enough volume to supply the police or national guard, but I should be able to do quite nicely in distribution to private homes. I'm hoping that I can at least get started by my fourteenth birthday, so that next year when induction time comes, I can get a deferment because I am in defense work.

Tell Uncle Andrew that if he wants to come out here, I can

[6] Printed by permission of the author, Gloria Randolph.

find him a place in a bayonet grinder's shop. There are two or three right down the street from me.

Enough of work. I don't have much leisure but on the short three day weekend I do get a chance to see some things. Last week-end I went with some friends to the Modern Museum in the major sector. The actual trip was uneventful except that we were stopped by the usual police road blocks several times. At one place we were almost turned back because Red, one of the fellows in the crowd, didn't have his ID card. It was a little embarrassing because he has that curly hair and is very tan. We've told him to stay out of the sun.

The new exhibit at the Museum wasn't so exciting this time. Rufus Jackson's head and Sam Finklestein's hands were the only things of any interest. An attendant told us to come back in three weeks when the new exhibit arrives. The major sector was looking better this trip. All the police and guardsmen had new uniforms. Several of the public buildings that are not burned out were surrounded by barbed wire fences that are just covered with colorful spring flowers.

This week-end I think we'll go out to the training complex and watch the police and guardsmen at maneuvers. They have a new technique for bayonet practice. All the people on the streets after curfew time are taken to the camps for disposal.

Well, I had wanted to write more but it's nearly eight o'clock. They're very strict out here about the lights being out by eight and I do want to stay on the right side of the law.

Love and kisses to the girls. Answer my letter soon.

Your loving son,

George

P.S. I'll mail your food box as soon as my security clearance comes through.

GLORIA RANDOLPH

EXERCISE

1. Take a gripe you have whose source seems to you to be hopeless or at least far beyond any individual's or even administration's power to control. Of the ones mentioned prominently throughout this chapter of the book as a whole there are some that may be "more" hopeless than others.

Pollution?

The generation gap?

The draft system?

American involvement in foreign wars?

Inflation?

The waning of religion?

Tastelessness in the mass media of entertainment?

The computerization of the world?

The dehumanization of man?

The growth of the police state?

The drugging of the young into euphoria and apathy?

Campus disturbances?

The backlash of the educational establishment?

Racism?

White backlash?

Black militancy?

The reader may add dozens more of his own choosing. From the list, select the one that strikes you as having gone the furthest toward a point of no return.

Now project your imagination into the future and do an imaginative paper on what has happened as a result of this condition.

Do people wear gas masks to breathe?

Are people over thirty in concentration camps?

Are people under thirty in concentration camps?

Is there a great "military mind" as a result of so many decades of the draft?

Is America fighting twelve wars at once in places whose names no one can pronounce?

Are Americans bringing their salaries home in wheelbarrows?

Have all the churches been turned into discotheques?

These are random suggestions. You can no doubt think of much more powerful ideas. Your aim is to have impact on the reader and to use prophecy as the last desperate attempt to snap the reader into an acute awareness of a present state of affairs that has you frustrated.

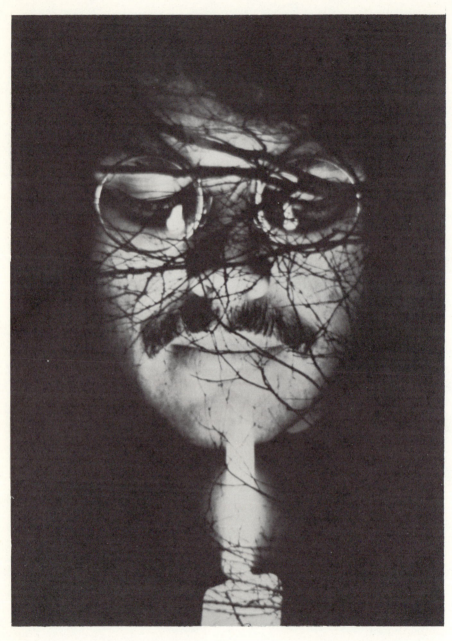

"Let's concentrate on some methods that have the feel of today about them."

10

PUTTING
THE **NOW**
IN THE PROSE

We began our prose adventure back in Chapter One with writing exercises that were strictly private. Remember "The deet fair indents while cobras wind big alsin grapples"? Nonsense language, secret countries buried deed in the unconscious, crazy mixed-up creatures from outer space, new animal species, and on and on into the innermost you. It didn't matter whether you had any readers or not.

Hopefully you've come a long way. Oh, you can still make occasional side trips to your secret land and play with the furry creatures of your imagination. But you should be able by now to put some strong stuff down on the page *with a reader* in mind and have some assurance you're going to communicate. Even if it's just a simple gripe, you've had practice in expressing yourself with some method or structure.

Method in writing bears a precise one-to-one relationship to method in living. When people are able to think of you in a clear and defined way, you have more than a *mere* identity: you have a pronounced identity. It's the difference between being someone who's "sort of fun to be with" or "a pretty nice person" and being "the man for the job" or "the girl with a future." The strong feelings about you and your accomplishments or potential that people have can only be supplied by you, and the strength, the mastery, the *cool* you display on paper will help give you that pronounced identity. *If you know what you're doing in prose you probably know what youre doing in general.*

So that's why we wind up this book with some really jazzy methods that you can use to attract readers. After all, just look at how much stuff is published. Look at all the magazines and paperbacks in the drug store, not to mention what's in the library. It stands to reason there's more to it than just griping. What we did in the preceding chapter constitutes the barest beginnings of experimenting with what can truly be called prose techniques. There's so much else, and now is not too soon to begin to get into some of them.

In fact, N * O * W should be our theme song. Let's put aside the million-odd techniques that Miss Prendergast learned, practiced and taught. Let's concentrate on some methods that have the feel of today about them. I propose in this final chapter that we should go from the "Now-Traditional" and work way further out to the "Supernow."

PERSUASION THROUGH PROSE

Persuasion is one of the enduring purposes of all writing. In one sense you're aiming at it whenever you commit yourself to paper with a reader in mind. Even if it's fiction or poetry, even if you are simply sharing feelings as one human being to another, you surely aren't hoping the reader will put you down. You'd prefer to have the reader agree with you.

But persuasion is also a specific use that can be made of expository prose. You have an idea that is so compelling that you aggressively *want* to influence the reader's thinking. Perhaps, as a member of the Now Generation, you want to convince a Yesterday person of the need to change his ways. In fact, if you're interested in changing society and the behavior of its members, persuasive writing is something you absolutely have to know how to handle.

Borrowing from Socrates

Socrates lived during most of the fifth century B.C. In 399 he was convicted of preaching atheism and other corrupting ideas to the young men of Athens. For this he was executed. But his martyrdom has remained a permanent symbol for each new generation of non-conformists who go out to do battle with the Establishment. In a very real sense, the youthful followers of Socrates, including Plato himself, were real Athenian swingers, and the master mind was the first of the great Now people. We can still learn a lot from him.

Despite the fact that he continually claimed to be ignorant, Socrates was just plain sharper than most of his contemporaries—and he knew it. His ignorance was of the ultimate mysteries of life, but, as he looked around him, he saw people frittering away their lives on trivialities like the pursuit of wealth. He made it his mission to persuade them of the beauty of thinking and of being with other people and of sharing ideas with them.

Persuasion came to be a great art with Socrates. It turned him on to challenge someone to an intellectual duel and then defeat him. He loved especially to play cat-and-mouse with people who pretended to wisdom; to trap his opponent into declaring himself on a certain issue and then to take his argument apart item by item until it could no longer be defended. This was his way of exposing the phonies, the people who pretended to have a lot of cool, but whose thinking couldn't stand up under the scorching heat of Socratic analysis.

As recorded in Plato's Dialogues, the Socratic method of persuasion usually comes down to these steps:

1. Socrates announces a subject without dropping even a hint of his own feelings about it, though he has secretly reached an unshakable position.

2. In a very friendly, disarming manner, Socrates invites someone else to present his view(s).

3. Socrates then asks some left-field questions that seem to have nothing to do with the issue. The other person answers them truthfully, not suspecting the trap.

4. Socrates then uses those very answers as the means of destroying the logic of the person's original position.

5. The opposition is brought to his knees by being forced to admit the faultiness of his thinking. Socrates therefore has won without having had to offer a total defense of his own position.

Here's an example of Socrates himself at work. Let me recreate in my own fashion part of the debate in Book I of Plato's *Republic* between Socrates and Thrasymachus the Sophist. A Sophist was a member of a fashionable clique who comprised the faculty of a kind of early law school where students were taught the arts of persuasion and skill in rhetoric. The Sophists were well known for their belief that no such thing as absolute truth existed, that the truth of any matter was whatever one could make people accept. But Socrates was personally convinced that this wasn't so. He believed absolutes did exist. They are here debating the question of whether there is absolute justice.

THRAS: No such thing as absolute justice exists. Justice is to be defined as that which is in the best interests of the ruling class, the people in power.

SOC: I see. That makes considerable sense. (Socrates is fond of putting his opposition at ease, then totally unhinging him because he isn't expecting it. See how he takes a very *indirect* approach here. He circles around his victim, never coming head on.)

THRAS: Well, I should hope to tell you. I mean, what else can justice mean but what somebody makes it mean? And that somebody has to be the one with the power to make it go.

SOC: You amaze me with your profundity.

THRAS: Think nothing of it.

SOC: Oh, by the way, Thrasymachus, just tell me one thing. Would you say that rulers are incapable of making mistakes?

THRAS: Of course they can make mistakes.

SOC: In other words, it is just possible that they could pass a law that wasn't in their best interests.

THRAS: Yes, I suppose so.

SOC: But wouldn't you say that the people have to obey the rulers?

THRAS: Of course they must.

SOC: Precisely. Otherwise the rulers wouldn't be rulers, and what are we talking about anyway?

THRAS: You'd better believe it.

SOC: Thus what you are saying is that it is possible for the ruled to have to obey a law that was *not* in the best interests of the rulers.

THRAS: Now just a minute. . . .

SOC: These are your own ideas, Thrasymachus. But now, if someone were brought to trial for disobeying such a law and he were convicted because he had indeed broken the law, would we not have to say that justice had been done in this case?

(For the moment at least Socrates has the upper hand, though it takes the entire *Republic* to develop the full theory of what justice is all about. He has forced the opposition into a corner. If Thrasymachus says it is unjust to prosecute someone for disobeying a bad law, then the whole distinction between ruler and ruled falls apart and so does his argument. If the ruled can be arbitrary in what they obey or do not obey, the power of the ruler is diminished. Don't forget: the entire premise of Thrasymachus has rested on the belief that might makes right. If might isn't preserved, his definition of justice doesn't hold. But if might is sometimes preserved by forcing people to obey laws that are mistakes and that *don't* truly benefit the ruling class, then, again, Thrasymachus' definition of justice is contradicted. Socrates has won this round by allowing the opposition no further response.)

Socratic persuasion can be imitated without a great deal of difficulty. It can even be used to make a ridiculous point, though Socrates would not approve of such sacrilege (except that he's not around to stop us!). To show how workable and really up-to-date the method is, I came up with the following dialogue between a teacher and a student. I deliberately set out to make the teacher the defeated opponent and the student the Socratic winner. It's fun to experiment with the technique in this way so that, when you have it down pat, you can use it to win people over to an idea you hold in deadly earnest.

STUDENT: Would you mind, sir, if I spoke to you on the subject of my grade?

TEACHER: Why not at all. Come in, come in. Sit down.

STUDENT: Thank you. Now, sir, may I ask what you require for an A in your course?

TEACHER: Indeed. For an A I expect a student to demonstrate originality, skill, and interest.

STUDENT: I see. And I suppose you have some definite ideas about those terms and what they stand for.

TEACHER: Naturally I do. "Originality" means "doing something in a manner that is a little different; putting that unexpected touch in it that separates the unique from the mediocre." As for "skill," this means to me "the ability to work on his own, without assistance." And "interest" means "sincere involvement in the class; the indication that a student is making the subject relevant to his life, not just putting me on in hopes of getting a high grade."

STUDENT: These definitions strike me as being very reasonable.

TEACHER: I'm glad to hear it.

STUDENT: Tell me, sir, is nothing a something, the absence of something, or the presence of a nothing?

TEACHER: I don't quite see. . . . Oh, you want to play games, eh? Well then, as soon as you say "Nothing is . . ." you've agreed that you're talking about something.

STUDENT: In other words, in the same way that zero is said to be a number?

TEACHER: That's the idea.

STUDENT: But if nothing is something (of a sort) is it ever involved in one of your classes?

TEACHER: (Laughing) I sure hope not.

STUDENT: (Laughing with him) You needn't worry, sir. But then wouldn't you say that nothing would be distinctly the opposite of what you try to accomplish in class?

TEACHER: (Laughing harder) I sure would.

STUDENT: But suppose I wanted help in achieving nothing. Could I find it in your class?

TEACHER: (Hysterical by now) I hope not.

STUDENT: Ah, that means I'd be on my own.

TEACHER: 'Fraid so.

STUDENT: Suppose I were working on nothing as a project and couldn't get any help from you, I guess I wouldn't need to bother you during your office hours, would I?

TEACHER: Guess not.

STUDENT: Tell me, sir, the students who seek, as we say, "Brownie points": do they hang around your office much?

TEACHER: Oh, my, yes. Can't get rid of them.

STUDENT: This annoys you, doesn't it?

TEACHER: Why, sure, because you can't trust 'em, know what I mean? You never know if they're really interested or they're just out for the grade.

STUDENT: I sympathize with your plight. Well now, sir, let me tell you I won't be one of those people.

TEACHER: Good, good.

STUDENT: I don't have to be. I intend to do nothing in your course, and, by your own standards, I deserve an A.

TEACHER: I beg your pardon?

STUDENT: By doing nothing, I shall certainly be doing the unexpected, that which is clearly different from what you require of the other students. Because you cannot give me any help on this project, I shall be working on my own, without assistance, thus satisfying the definition of "skill." And since I shall not be one of those who hang around the office in hopes of getting a high grade, I cannot be untrustworthy and qualify, at least more than *they* do, to be labeled "interested."

TEACHER: That's ridiculous. That logic just doesn't hold up.

STUDENT: And, sir, I suggest that your standards do not either. Good-day.

Socratic debate isn't the only kind of persuasive writing that works. But you don't find it in the writing books, which I think is a dirty shame, and that's why I've introduced it here. In one sense, any method that ends up by persuading the reader is a raving success. Socratic persuasion is just a little surer, that's all. You know why? Because it dramatizes the argument; it captures the reader's attention and holds it better than a long, complicated, abstract argument is likely to; it gives the reader (and you, the writer) something more tangible, more concrete, more visual even than traditional expository prose; and, especially, it gains power by appearing to demolish objections—a technique you should bear in mind no matter what other methods of persuasion you employ. Squelch the objection before the reader has a chance to think of it. Think of it *for* him by inventing the character of the opponent.

EXERCISES

1. Do a Socratic dialogue on some subject that is being hotly debated at the moment and about which you hold strong convictions.

Drugs? Military service? The role of parents in shaping the moral character of children? Sexual freedom regardless of marital status?

The Socratic figure will of course, be you, and he will eventually persuade the reader to the position that you hold. Make the opponent represent the view of which you most seriously disapprove and which you would most enjoy destroying. An effective way to work up the dialogue is to think first of the opposition. That is, make a list of attitudes you *don't* hold. Locate a basic fallacy behind each one as you see it. Use the fallacy or contradiction in thinking as the target toward which your whole dialogue should be heading. Once you know what the fallacy in the opponent's thinking will be, you can arrange the debate in such a way as to force him into it.

Here's an example of what I mean by a "basic fallacy." Suppose an opposition viewpoint is: *Marijuana should be legalized.* (That is, suppose you do *not* believe this.) Now, instead of trying to think of a whole bunch of reasons to back up *your* belief, concentrate on finding one very glaring logical error that *could* be made by someone holding a viewpoint contrary to your own. For example:

> Marijuana is not harmful; it is not habit-forming, which means that I can take it or leave it; why not legalize it, then, so that I can get as much of it as I want?

Understand: this isn't the *only* possible error in thought. Your aim is only to locate some fallacy that you can use as the means to demolish the opposition.

Once you have your target, create the characters. Using the two models included in the text, have the opposition begin by stating its position (not the fallacy, just the position). Then have the Socrates figure circle around by asking some questions whose answers will eventually cause the opposition to wind up squarely in the middle of the fallacy. Here's how a mini-debate on the subject of marijuana might go:

OP.: Marijuana should be legalized.
SOC.: Are you presently enslaved to marijuana?
OP.: Of course not. I argue merely out of principle.
SOC.: I see. Perhaps then you have never tried marijuana and have no real authority to voice an opinion one way or another.
OP.: I assure you this is not the case. I have tried marijuana.
SOC.: Yes, but surely not enough to make a difference.
OP.: A great many times, sir.
SOC.: Is a slave someone who may take his freedom or not?

OP.: No. He has no choice.

SOC.: Then you have a choice of smoking marijuana or not.

OP.: Indeed.

SOC.: Tell me, is a law based on any principle other than an evaluation? Is there a guiding factor beyond the principle of good or bad in the formulation of a law?

OP.: I don't see how there can be.

SOC.: I would agree with you. Even the income tax, a most unpopular law, can be seen upon reflection to have the economic good of the country as the motive behind it.

OP.: Right.

SOC.: And the money taken in by the income tax, is it used for purposes that advance the welfare of the nation in any way? For example, does it go into social programs, education, relief funds, and the like?

OP.: Well, some of it does.

SOC.: And can we take or leave the welfare of the country?

OP.: No.

SOC.: That is, we must take it? must have it?

OP.: Indeed yes.

SOC.: Should we have as much of it as is possible?

OP.: I guess so.

SOC.: Similarly, a law, such as that forbidding murder, is desirable because murder is an evil?

OP.: I guess so.

SOC.: Can we take murder or leave it?

OP.: No. We must leave it.

SOC.: Then aren't laws at their best when they relate to values that are either completely good or completely bad? Should not laws try to promote as much as possible of the good things and as few as possible of the bad things?

OP.: Sounds all right to me.

SOC.: Do we need to waste time on laws that govern things that are neither good nor bad? Things, that is, that can be taken or left?

OP.: I don't see why we do.

SOC.: But if you can take marijuana or leave it, as you say, are you not admitting it is neither wholly desirable nor wholly undesirable? Why then should there be a law to make it available when it is not, by your own definition, a good?

If you intend to take the argument apart, I think I'll leave by the back door. Socratic persuasion doesn't always stand up under analysis, but it is effective—especially when you are convinced of the rightness of your position. On these occasions you will be much cleverer in trapping, at least temporarily, your theoretical opponent.

2. An alternate or companion exercise is to try to locate the fallacies in the way the Socratic figure goes about doing his persuading. For example, I deliberately used a number of questionable transitions

in the above mini-debate. The biggest leap, of course, occurred when the Socratic figure summed up the case for the law by forcing the opponent to agree that laws were at their best "when they relate to values that are completely good or completely bad." Maybe many laws do this, but who says they're the best? Or that there aren't thousands of other approaches to the whole question of the law?

Suggest that the teacher read some of the more "now you see it, now you don't" debates. Listen to each very carefully and then write down the principal breaches of logic in the technique of the persuader.

3. See which member of the class can write the most persuasive dialogue on one of the following (or similar) viewpoints:

a) Tomorrow should be cancelled due to lack of interest.

b) People who do not support mental health should be killed.

c) Only a nudist movement will save the Establishment.

d) Strict censorship of the movies is necessary to save the young from moral damage.

e) There should be no minimum voting or drinking age.

f) The stop-and-frisk law is desirable.

g) The only way to save marriage is to go back to polygamy, or the practice of having several wives or husbands.

h) It is imperative to shower with a friend.

The Negative-Positive Effect

Let me reemphasize one of the major virtues of using Socratic persuasion in your writing: its lack of abstractness. The reader is more likely to get interested when there are two people talking and a conflict of interests is evident. Which one will win? He must find out.

I think we can also say that the degree of reader interest often has more to do with your method than with your idea. Learn this about readers: they're like children; they have high curiosity levels when they become intrigued but very low tolerance levels when they suspect they are being told something for their own good. "I have an important message for you" can be the kiss of death.

Most of us have had the experience of trying to win a child's approval. Most of us have made drastic mistakes too. Did you ever, for example, grab at some kid and rudely force him to occupy your lap while you bounced him up and down and sang some inane tune?

Chances are he struggled almost at once to wrench himself from your unwelcomed assaults on his time and fun. Adults, forgetting how enormous they seem to the very young, tower over, leer at, and generally turn kids off.

In this universal generation gap there is a lesson to be learned about persuasion in writing. Don't go after the reader. Let him come after you. Don't even suggest there's an attempt at persuasion on the way. Deceive him. Con him. The world moves so fast and so noisily that the screaming huckster stands very little chance of penetrating our awareness. You'll do better with young children by leaving them absolutely alone and never letting on you want to be their friend. Ignore them, and generally they'll come over to investigate. The Socratic method—because of its dramatic nature—is an indirect way of persuading. The Negative-Positive Effect is another such technique.

One of its most impressive uses has been by Deems Taylor in a verbal portrait of the composer Wagner: "The Monster." For three-fourths of the essay, Taylor bombards the reader with every unpleasant detail about Wagner's life and personality he can possibly think of. Example:

> He was equally unscrupulous in other ways. An endless procession of women marches through his life. His first wife spent twenty years enduring and forgiving his infidelities. His second wife had been the wife of his most devoted friend and admirer, from whom he stole her. And even while he was trying to persuade her to leave her first husband he was writing to a friend to inquire whether he could suggest some wealthy woman—*any* wealthy woman—whom he could marry for her money.

Wagner's colossal gall is particularized in the following paragraph.

> He had a genius for making enemies. He would insult a man who disagreed with him about the weather. He would pull endless wires in order to meet some man who admired his work, and was able and anxious to be of use to him—and would proceed to make a mortal enemy of him with some idiotic and wholly uncalled-for exhibition of arrogance and bad manners. A character in one of his operas was a caricature of one of the most powerful music critics of his day. Not content with burlesquing him, he invited the critic to his house and read him the libretto aloud in front of his friends.

But Taylor redeems Wagner in our eyes during the last quarter of the essay. The jist of his argument is that Wagner's outrageous conduct scarcely matters, for the world has so few geniuses it can afford to tolerate their "eccentricities." You may, of course, not agree with

Taylor's adulation of Wagner, but it's hard to deny the effectiveness of the emotional reverse.

> What if he was faithless to his friends and to his wives? He had one mistress to whom he was faithful to the day of his death: music. Not for a single moment did he ever compromise with what he believed, with what he dreamed. There is not a line of his music that could have been conceived by a little mind. Even when he is dull, or downright bad, he is dull in the grand manner. There is a greatness about his worst mistakes. Listening to his music, one does not forgive him for what he may or may not have been. It is not a matter of forgiveness. It is a matter of being dumb with wonder that his poor brain and body didn't burst under the torment of the demon of creative energy that lived inside him, struggling, clawing, scratching to be released; tearing, shrieking at him to write the music that was in him. The miracle is that what he did in the little space of seventy years could have been done at all, even by a great genius. Is it any wonder that he had no time to be a man? [1]

I'm not at all certain "The Monster" has quite the same punch now as it did when I first started teaching. Lately I've noticed an "Are you kidding?" undercurrent buzzing about the room whenever I take up the essay. Certainly the hero-worship is a bit old-fashioned. But no matter how you may personally feel about this fall-on-your-face-buddy-you're-in-the-presence-of-greatness stuff, you ought to be able to put the technique itself to good use. Disarm the reader. Lead him down one path. Then abruptly push him into another. Play games with him. He'll like it better, and, this way, if you've got something urgent to tell him, you've got his attention.

Novelist Sherwood Anderson, in a piece called "Discovery of a Father," begins by describing his father in a most unattractive light.

> He couldn't ride for shucks. He fell off the horse and everyone hooted with laughter, but he didn't care. He even seemed to like it. I remember once when he had done something ridiculous, and right out on Main Street, too. I was with some other boys and they were laughing and shouting at him and he was shouting back and having as good a time as they were. I ran down an alley back of some stores and there in the Presbyterian Church sheds I had a good long cry.
>
> Or I would be in bed at night and Father would come home a little lit up and bring some men with him. He was a man who was never alone. Before he went broke, running a harness shop, there were always a lot of men loafing in the shop. He went broke, of course, because he gave too much credit. He couldn't refuse it and I thought he was a fool. I had got to hating him.

It's hard not to get hooked when a writer comes on like this. He doesn't seem to be asking you for anything—only telling you how he feels. But such honest negation seems, at least for me, to beckon the reader further on. I want to know what happened finally. How was the hatred further intensified or else overcome? It isn't that I *care* whether anyone hates his father or not. It's that I can't help getting interested when the negative attitude comes first. (It's like ignoring the child, pretending he doesn't interest you or that maybe you don't even like him.)

Later on Anderson describes a night when his father came home and ordered him, mysteriously, to follow him somewhere. They arrive at the shore of a large pond, and there are claps of thunder and terrifying streaks of lightning.

> "Take off your clothes," he said. Still filled with wonder, I began to undress. There was a flash of lightning and I saw that he was already naked.
>
> Naked, we went into the pond. Taking my hand, he pulled me in. It may be that I was too frightened, too full of a feeling of strangeness, so to speak. Before that night my father had never seemed to pay any attention to me.
>
> "And what is he up to now?" I kept asking myself. I did not swim very well, but he put my hand on his shoulder and struck out into the darkness.
>
> He was a man with big shoulders, a powerful swimmer. In the darkness I could feel the movements of his muscles. We swam to the far edge of the pond and then back to where we had left our clothes. The rain continued and the wind blew. Sometimes my father swam on his back, and when he did he took my hand in his large powerful one and moved it over so that it rested always on his shoulder. Sometimes there would be a flash of lightning and I could see his face quite clearly.

Out of this incident there begins to emerge a most complex feeling about the father. Suddenly the boy sees the man in a totally different way, and I guarantee such emotional reverses almost never fail to move the reader deeply.

> It was as it was earlier, in the kitchen, a face filled with sadness. There would be the momentary glimpse of his face, and then again the darkness, the wind and the rain. In me there was a feeling I had never known before.
>
> It was a feeling of closeness. It was something strange. It was as though there were only we two in the world. It was as though I had been jerked suddenly out of myself, out of my world of the schoolboy, out of a world in which I was ashamed of my father.
>
> He had become blood of my blood; he was the strong swimmer

and I the boy clinging to him in the darkness. We swam in silence, and in silence we dressed in our wet clothes and went home.[2]

EXERCISES

1. Imitating Deems Taylor, select some famous historical personality about whom you have some knowledge. (Perhaps you did a research paper recently?) It could be someone who might be depended on to arouse negative feelings within the reader. (Examples: Benedict Arnold, or John Wilkes Booth. Are there extenuating circumstances? Are there things you've found out that you believe the average person doesn't know about these or similar "bad guys"?) Build up as negative an atmosphere as you can, and then pull the Taylor Switch: explain how the reader *ought* to feel, or, at least, show other responses to this person that can be made. You'll find it's much easier to persuade in this manner than by stating at the outset, "My purpose in this paper is to show how _____has been greatly misunderstood and deserves another chance."

   Or do with someone what Taylor did with Wagner: someone, that is, about whom the average reader probably has no reason to feel one way or the other. Tell all the dirt you know about him and cause the reader to believe you are describing the most miserable cur ever to exist. Then SWITCH. Make the reader see that this person had to be as he was (or is) in order to be great or to promote greatness in others.

   Possibilities:

   a) a famous football coach noted for his harsh discipline and winning teams

   b) a famous theater director, film director, ballet master who made everyone wretched but who produced great results

   c) a military leader whose strategy was, in your opinion, often misunderstood and derided but who, again in your opinion, was proved right by history

   d) a famous educator whose methods may not have been appreciated by those immediately involved with him but who, in your opinion, represents what education should be all about

2. There's always room for experiment and innovation. The world may now be ready for a Positive-Negative Effect. Why don't you be the first? Take one of America's "best-loved" personalities, some-

[2] The preceding three extracts are from Sherwood Anderson's *Memoirs*, edited by Ray Lewis White. Chapel Hill, N.C.: The University of North Carolina Press. Reprinted by permission.

one you think is probably as sacred as apple pie or motherhood. (I'd offer some examples, but I don't want to have this book banned.) Be sure you select somebody who you believe is overly popular with the masses of people, but who really rubs you the wrong way.

Build up a strongly positive atmosphere by describing all the reasons this person is "deservedly" popular with the general public. Then sock it to the reader with your own ideas about this person AND the general public!

3. Imitating Sherwood Anderson, select some figure from your own life, past or present, somebody toward whom your feelings have shifted from negative to positive. Perhaps you also had misgivings about your father. Or: mother; a high school teacher; an athletic coach; a minister, priest, or rabbi; a policeman; a staff sergeant; the C.O.; a doctor; a pot-smoking, nonconformist friend.

Narrate, as Anderson does, some specific incidents that bring out the worst side of this person and illustrate your earlier feelings. Then narrate an incident that caused these feelings to change. It is not necessary to spell out for the reader how you feel now. If you describe the incident sharply enough, the reader should share your feelings by the time he finishes the paper.

MAKE IT MOVE!

Both the Taylor and the Anderson pieces illustrate once again that the idea itself is sometimes less important than the way it is put across. Or, to put the matter differently, the reader's interest may be aroused more by the method than the purpose. Knowing that readers, like children, are curiosity seekers can help you to deliberately cultivate certain techniques, so that when you do have something of great moment to impart, you can see to it the reader doesn't get away from you.

Having a Plot

You turn on your television set. You hear, "The following program is brought to you in living color." Before your eyes is the familiar peacock with a color spectrum for a tail. But suppose, on one occasion, you see instead a tiny red dot at the extreme right of the screen. After a second or two it moves forward. Then it appears to be straining. Some force you can't see appears determined to push the dot back into the oblivion from which it came. But then a counter-force from inside the dot itself rises to the occasion and pushes ahead. For three or four minutes the struggle goes on: the dot tries to make it all the way across the screen; the unseen force tries to push it back. By the time the dot is *almost* to its destination the conflict intensifies. The dot becomes locked in a life-and-death struggle. Would you be able to turn the set off until the issue had been resolved? Could you go back to your homework, never knowing whether that poor red being had accomplished its mission or been defeated by the invisible, unnamed, horrible THING that despises red dots and seems bent on their destruction?

The dot's journey from one side of the screen to the other is a plot, or sequence. Your interest is aroused and sustained by the sequence and the way it is handled, *not* by your automatic concern for the cause of red dots. A red dot can be the world's most boring visual stimulus, but its agonizing journey across a blackened screen is made interesting because of the step-by-step movement *and* the promise that eventually there will be a resolution of the matter one way or another. The dot will triumph, or the dot will go down to defeat. The main thing is *you have to find out.*

Suppose the curtain rises on a play. You see a body lying on the stage. The police arrive and round up a room full of suspects. All of a sudden Uncle Ned cries: "All right. I did it!" Wouldn't you immediately expect to find out differently by the end of the play? Suppose you didn't? Suppose all that happened is the police found out it was all true? You'd demand your money back.

Which arouses a young man's concern more intensely? A note that says "Darling, drop by this evening to discuss the flowers for the wedding" or one that says "I must see you this evening on a most urgent matter"? Let us assume the intention is the same behind both messages. The second version is certainly more interesting. It creates a sense of anticipation. It makes the young man eager to get to the girl's house and discover what the "urgent matter" is. In writing, you can interest your reader by promising from the outset that he is going somewhere and making him awfully curious about what he will find when he gets there.

Of the following two beginnings, which could be the start of an interesting sequence? Which seems to require nothing beyond itself and therefore creates no suspense?

    A. Statistics show that incidents of lung disorder caused by smoking are alarmingly on the increase.
    B. How close are you to death at this very minute? This paper may provide the answer.

Beginning writers, unsure of themselves, tend to put down everything they have to say almost at once and then find themselves either hopelessly padding or handing in a mini-essay. When, however, you can set the reader up by creating the anticipation of a sequence and a conclusion that must be reached, you can take your time and enjoy writing the paper. The reader is virtually forced to stay with you until you get to the end.

Here's a very simple example of how you can get more mileage out of an idea by using a plot or sequence. Suppose the teacher assigns a paper to be written in class on the subject, "My family." One student plunges impulsively into the work, but without any apparent plan of attack:

> My family is just about the weirdest collection of characters you've ever met. My mother and father are both living, and I have two sisters and a brother. Everyone in my family is fiercely independent, and sometimes it's all we can do to come to a decision on where to go for a picnic.

I won't continue, because I haven't the faintest idea of how to do it. The next sentence would surely have to drop out of heaven. No structural principle is here to write it for me.

Now let's see how another student, this time with a plot, has an easier time of it:

> When you first enter the house I live in, you don't get the impression of its real size. My father had it built originally as a four-room love nest for him and my mother and an eventual bundle of joy. But since one nice bundle deserves another, the family found itself growing and so did the house. You come from the small front porch into a narrow hallway, which goes a long way back and then makes a left-hand turn. All you can see are doors, because each member of my family has a favorite room where he indulges in his favorite pasttime, and let me tell you, my family tops the list when it comes to weird hobbies.
> Let's peek into the first room off the hall—the living room, where we find my mother practicing her cello and watching her favorite soap opera at the same time without benefit of sound.

Perhaps you still couldn't care less about someone's family. But the second version of the assignment does use a structural device; it promises to put each member of the family in a different room. The reader expects to tour the house and meet the occupants and knows the paper isn't properly over until the tour is.

There's almost no end to the number and variety of plots that will work as ways of setting your paper up, but most of them have one thing in common. *They represent motion either in time or in space, or both.* Throw your window open and look at the world. Everything is moving from one point to another, from one moment to another. Our entire lives are geared to temporal and spatial sequences, and so it makes sense to reproduce these in writing. I can think of no surer way of capturing the reader's interest and creating suspense than to lead him through physical space or through a segment of time. I can think of no better way to make your writing less abstract than by putting time and space into it.

Time Makes it Tick

If a paper follows a clear time sequence, it is bound to move. Further, if it promises from the outset to cover a definite segment of time—say, the course of one entire twenty-four hour period—the reader will know that the paper is not meandering around aimlessly but is working toward its inevitable completion. He also expects something of importance to occur at the end of the time sequence, or else he expects the completed time segment to have given him greater knowledge of the subject.

One of the most famous plays of the contemporary American theater is Eugene O'Neill's *Long Day's Journey into Night,* in which an entire family is torn apart by the mother's addiction to drugs, an addiction that grows progressively worse during the course of a single day. By noting the title and by simply glancing at his program, the theatergoer is able to tell that the play will gather in force and tragic power as the day advances toward nightfall. He expects certain dramatic highpoints at various points of the day's passage and, by midnight, one final scene that should overwhelm him. Further, by removing the addicted mother for the first half of the long final act, O'Neill causes the viewer to sit there in mounting suspense, waiting for the woman's inevitable reappearance in what is sure to be a hopeless condition. O'Neill is a writer of surpassing power in any case, but the single-day structure of this drama makes it more effective than some of his other plays that lack its clear sense of direction.

One doesn't have to be an O'Neill, however, to use a time structure and to make something work because of it. I ran across the following paper in a collection of recent high school writing. Note how the author follows the routine of a single day at school and uses a period-by-period approach to make his comments about the educational system. Since the reader is generally familiar with the number of periods in a typical high school day, he has a definite sense that the paper is moving somewhere.

I am now in the 8th hour study hall recalling the importance of a student in this or any other school. Well, as you can guess,

I can't recall very much. No, it's not just this year. It's been like this every year I've been in school, and probably was the same when my parents went to school.

As the day starts off, I read another informative issue of our school newspaper. Wow! It's almost as good as the last one. The issue in which Dr. Brauer approves the plan for a new addition to the school. Now for the groovy articles in the new edition, they really turn me on. It has an All-Star cast of articles, such as "Student Council Lists Representatives," which was a very true article as told by the title.

The entire limit of power invested in the Council is having their names printed in the paper.

Get this! "Pupil Campaigns, Views America's Political System." As a start I'll quote a short paragraph to demonstrate the nonsense of this article and the paper in general.

"When asked what highlighted his trip to Chicago he decided that riding a fire truck with 'Humphrey for President' signs on it was a lot of fun."

Presenting such a whimsical view for such an historic and well remembered event gives true evidence of the contents of most of the articles.

What could I expect from a school paper is probably the question now in your mind. To start with the paper cannot be improved with the present hierarchy of our schools. As a result, this paper [*The Open Door*] has come into being. We have an entirely different paper filled with articles of interest, it is quite a difference from your gospel type school paper. So much for the paper.

I am now in English class and have just been informed that I am getting a zero for the day because I committed the number one sin, *wearing blue jeans*. I cannot imagine how wearing these infamous pants would have any effect on my work in school, the teachers, or anything else. I'm reaching a point of manic depression, everything that's happening seems unreal. Entering my third hour class I started to regain my senses. The hour goes well, and God sends the lunch bell.

After an hour of freedom the last place I wanted to go was back, but I have to graduate to get out. It's really sickening to think about how high a goal finishing school is, when people want to get out instead of getting a diploma.

It is now the fifth hour. I was only halfway into the room before the teacher kindly remarked, "Look, class, a real live farmer." Obviously referring to the hideous blue jeans I was wearing, of course. My tensions are rising to a mild state of hysteria. Sixth hour has now begun and I am glad to see we have a substitute teacher. After the first five minutes of class I've had my seat changed three times, my best and only guess for these changes is the fact that I asked the girl next to me for a pen. At this time I was getting disgusted and was about to tell the teacher what I thought of her methods. My better judgment decided against it since the least infraction of the rules would put me out of school as I am 18. The rest of the hour remained calm.

It is now time for seventh hour, a regularly uninteresting class. But today was different, the class starts out with a question on Vietnam. I quickly raise my hand to express my views, but I am not recognized since my views wouldn't agree with the teacher's and most of the class. I decide to stand firm and the teacher finally recognizes me. Could it be the pets of the class are afraid to stand up to their views? Well, it didn't last long anyway because the "Grand Duchess" has just decided that we'd had enough discussion for the time being.

As a conclusion to this article I offer the facts that: 1) not all teachers are bad, there are a few decent ones; 2) this is by no means representative of a majority of my days in school; 3) I'm sure everyone in school that doesn't shine the teachers' shoes has days like this. For my final statement I plead that there is no reason for these conditions and with support and petition they can be overcome.

P.S. I am not a degenerate, bum, or communist.[3]

Movement and direction in a paper aren't necessarily the same thing. Any ten minute segment of your life may get you nowhere. A paper is supposed to go *somewhere*. Here's a sample beginning that promises a time sequence but has no directional principle at all:

> I woke up at 8 A.M. and, after lying there for about ten minutes, I finally decided to get up and drag myself into the shower. The cold water refreshed me and so I managed to get myself dressed. By 8:30 I was ready for breakfast. It was then I remembered I had forgotten to do my math homework. I glanced at the clock and saw I'd have only ten minutes to accomplish an almost impossible task.

[3] "A Day in the Life," *How Old Will You Be in 1984*, ed. Diane Divorky. Reprinted by permission of Avon Books. Copyright © 1969 by Avon Books.

There may be a slim fluttering of suspense over the homework, but there's no hint of an overall direction for the paper.

In contrast, the student paper used to illustrate time-sequence writing starts off "I am now in 8th hour study hall recalling the importance of a student in this or any other school." As soon as he goes back to the first period, he has revealed his intention clearly: to take the reader period by period through a school day and to eventually reveal what the importance (or lack of it) of the student really is. Though the paper goes constantly out of focus and probably doesn't quite reach its avowed objective, it *does* have at least a rudimentary sense of direction.

Using almost any directional principle at all can rev up a paper practically at once. Let's rewrite the opening of the essay just above:

> I woke up at exactly 8 A.M. The school-day routine has trained me to do that. No matter how many times I've done this and gone through the routine, however, I'm always pretty hopeful at 8 A.M. I think to myself: "Maybe today will be different. Maybe things will change. Maybe . . ." Believe me, I try! So, without malice or forethought, let me take you to school with me on this particular day, a day I decide to be open to anything and to find all the good I can in the school, the faculty, and my fellow students.

I submit that this beginning is at least a shade more interesting than the first one. The narrator's hopefulness provides the sense of direction. The reader is now ready to go through the day with him and to discover how this hope will be crushed or perhaps how it will reach some insights into ways of improving the system.

The revelation of personality is another way to construct a piece of time-sequence writing. Do a portrait of Miss Prendergast, the high school English teacher. By day she's a prim and proper bastion of outmoded standards and techniques—conventional to the core. By night —wow! Promise this to a reader and you've got him hooked. The disclosure of character is, after all, one of time's main functions.

If you would know someone, study him in a given time segment; not too many minutes can go by without bringing to light some essential characteristics. If you tell me "My first love was the dearest, sweetest, most considerate . . ." I will answer "At ten o'clock or at eleven?" We generalize and categorize, we pigeonhole because we remember only scattered details about most people, not sustained chunks of time.

At the current moment one of the best-known painters of verbal portraits is Rex Reed, the controversial interviewer and advocate of tell-it-like-it-is journalism. A recent collection of interviews he calls

Do You Sleep in the Nude? contains an altogether delicious characterization of Barbra Streisand. Not only does it represent a total rejection of the old movie-magazine kind of star worship, but it utilizes the time-sequence method to bring the reader ever closer to understanding Reed's subject. Barbra Streisand is closely observed by her interviewer throughout the videotaping of a television spectacular: a time sequence of such mounting intensity that no aspect of the star's temperament and moods can escape attention. Whether the portrait seems fair you can of course decide for yourself.[4]

Word comes, from on high, that the superstar is ready for her audience. Three and a half hours late, she plods into the room, plotzes into a chair with her legs spread out, tears open a basket of fruit, bites into a green banana, and says, "Okay, ya got twenty minutes, whaddya wanna know?"

What's the new show like? "Like the old one. They're like book ends. The first one was great, ya know? So this one's gonna be as close as it can be. Whadda I know from TV? I hire the best people in the business, then I let them do everything for me. I don't take chances. I'm payin' the bill, it's my problem, right? I coulda got Frank Sinatra and Dean Martin to clown around just like everybody else does on their specials, but who needs it? I got complete creative control here, so I do it my way, right?"

How will the show differ from last year? "Instead of Bergdorf's, the first part's in a museum," she says, munching on a bunch of grapes. "I move around in front of the paintings and sometimes I turn into the paintings, get it? The costumes are mostly designed by me, borrowed, rented, or remade from my old hock-shop wardrobes. The second part's in a circus, and I sing to all the animals. The last part's the concert. Just like last year. Different songs, same feeling."

Eight people have moved into the room. All of them check their watches and make her very nervous. Some of them answer the questions for her. "Barbra does not like the image that comes with being a glamorous star," volunteers one. "She doesn't like parties; she's afraid people ask her because she's a celebrity, not because they like her."

"Yeah. Like whatchamacallit——"

---

[4] Reprinted by permission of the World Publishing Company from *Do You Sleep in the Nude?* by Rex Reed. An NAL book. Copyright © 1968 by Rex Reed.

"Joshua Logan."

"Yeah him. He threw this party for Princess Margaret, ya know? Elliott even wore a tuxedo. We were so miserable we cut out for a Ninth Avenue delicatessen, my favorite restaurant, where they still got great greasy french fries and the best rice puddin' in town. No raisins, ya know what I mean?

"Listen, all my life I wanted to be famous. I know from nothing about music. I never had a Victrola till I was eighteen. I used to buy clothes in thrift shops. Now I don't go there no more 'cause people bother me. Besides, they've gone up. I always dreamed of a penthouse, right? So now I'm a big star I got one and it's not much fun. I used to dream about terraces, now I gotta spend five hundred dollars just to convert mine from summer to winter. Let me tell you, it's just as dirty with soot up there on the twenty-second floor as it is down there on the bottom."

At 5 P.M. museum closes and the cameras are ready. An armada of armed guards line the doors with name tags for everyone official. Disgruntled reporters and unhappy photographers line up in a Renaissance hallway for clearance. "Barbra gets very upset if anyone who isn't official watches her," says a cameraman. Outside, the Philly branch of her fan club peers through the beaded glass windows carrying a sign that reads, "Welcome Barb." "Barbra has a fan club in prison," offers the pretty press agent.

At 7:30, Barbra emerges looking like a banana-split nightmare in a floor-length, op-art gown of hand-sewn sequins in twenty colors and six-inch triangle earrings with bolts of lightning through them like Superman emblems. Mondrian eyes sharpened with mascara and boyish hairdo slicked back behind her ears, she looks more like a male hairdresser than a girl, but she is ready for the first number. A twenty-five man production crew, a registered nurse, her personal staff, and a few favored members of the press watch as bongo drums blare from portable speakers and Barbra shimmies past walls filled with Cezanne watercolors and Matisse still-lifes shaking on their brackets. The number is repeated a dozen times before choreographer Joe Layton bounces through in white tennis shoes and white turtleneck sweater crying, "It's awful. It needs work."

Rest time. Barbra sits in a deck chair in front of the color receiver and eats salted nuts and Life Savers from a rumpled paper bag. There is no camaraderie, no teddy-bear playfulness with her crew, no exchanges of bon mots or even dirty jokes common to most sound stages. She speaks only when spoken to, trusts only those close to her, and ignores every one else. Mostly she just eats and stares at the gorillas peering out from a Rousseau jungle on the wall. When the nuts are gone, she brings out a half eaten bag of potato chips. A maid occasionally fortifies her with Kleenex to wipe her hands. A guard stops her from leaning against Renoir's "The Bather." "Cheez," she retorts, "just like New York. Pardon me for breathin'."

By 9:30 the test pattern is adjusted and the color cameras are ready for the fourth tape of the first song. A cameraman crushes out a forbidden cigarette on a valuable piece of a hundred-year-old Romanian oak while a guard isn't looking. "Let's go, Barb!" "I gotta get up?" cries the star. Hard looks from Joe Layton. Barbra gets up, pulling up her panties through her skirt.

"She's no dumb broad," says a CBS official. "She heads two corporations—one packages her specials, pays for everything, then the profit she makes is the difference between her expenses and what CBS pays her. This includes her salary. It's a one-woman show, so it would be very weird if she was not the boss."

By 1:15 she comes out in a floor-length black-satin maid's outfit with white over-apron, which she designed herself. Elliott Gould, her husband, arrives to hold her hand, wearing an official label so the guards will let him in. Barbra runs past twelve pillars and up thirty-five stone stairs singing "Yesterdays." Then she collapses in a corner eating hot pastrami, sour green tomatoes, kosher pickles, and stuffed derma from paper containers. "My gums hurt," she cries, sticking her fingers into her mouth. The crew throws color cables over the balcony of the museum's Great Hall, missing by inches a valuable Alexander Calder mobile and a priceless seventeenth-century Flemish tapestry. A museum official screams. Two guards rush forward. Barbra bites into a fish stick and adjusts her false eyelashes.

Barbra's manager, Marty Erlichman, comes over. Marty is a friendly, bearlike fellow who discovered her in the kitchen of the Bon Soir fresh out of Erasmus High School, a skinny, big-nosed girl with pimples who had a ninety-three average and a medal in Spanish. When he met Barbra he was a small-time talent agent working out of phone booths on Broadway. Now he heads his own company. "For nine months I tried to get her a job. Every record company in the business turned her down. 'Change the clothes, change the nose, stop singing the cockamamy songs.' Now it'll start all over when she hits Hollywood to make *Funny Girl*. They'll want to make her into Doris Day.

But she sells the public Barbra, nothing else. She's never been bastardized or exploited. The main thing she's gotta learn is not to trust too much. The public is very fickle. Ten million people love you when you're an underdog on the way up, but nine and a half million of them hate you when you hit the top."

At 2 A.M. a group of teenagers appeared at the museum with a kettle of hot chicken soup. "Just give it to her," they yell through locked doors. "Could she just wave?" Barbra is busily chewing sour green-apple gum (her current favorite) in a lavender-and-silver Marie Antoinette costume with lavender wig and purple ostrich plumes. "Get rid of the creeps. These jerks follow me everywhere. Sometimes they get my autograph three or four times in one night. Whatta ya think they do with all them autographs?"

The action continues through the next day, with no sleep. Barbra playing a guillotine scene in the French Revolution. Barbra doing "something based on Nefertiti" in the Egyptian Room. Electricians and reporters curl up on the table tops and behind potted palms, catnapping. "If the star gives up, everybody gives up, I gotta keep smilin'," says Barbra, swallowing an aspirin.

Back in New York, part two was achieved through sheer terror. Barbra danced out onto a pomegranate and pistachio-colored three-ring circus set. A baby elephant named Champagne roared so loud at the sight that a baby llama nearby did a somersault. Barbra sang "Funny Face" in an orange ringmaster's costume. The horse reared. The penguins got sick under the hot lights and had to be carted off to a refrigerated area behind the set. The leopard refused to pose. Barbra tripped and forgot her words. "Print it," yelled Joe Layton, "If nothing else we got the tiger's face in."

To make matters worse, the show was half live, half prerecorded. Barbra had to worry not only about being trampled to death, but when to come in on cue. Contempt hung in the air like moss. The show was behind schedule and the overtime was costing the star money. Four electricians chased a pig across the set and damaged part of the back-drop. The lion broke out of its cage and had to be replaced. As uncontrollable as their temperaments were the animals' nature habits, for which several takes were loused up by the broom-and-shovel detail. Barbra hated the animals and the animals were frightened to death of her. The only friendly moment came when she sang to an anteater named Izzy. "He must be Jewish," she said, as they touched noses.

More than thirty hours were spent on the circus segment, which runs only a few minutes on screen. Barbra's temper exploded. "Too many people not connected with the show. Too many people staring at me." The press was removed to the control room.

By week's end, there was nothing left but the concert. She came out in a pale creamy gown with pearl-drop earrings and pale-mauve lipstick, standing on a white spiral staircase under blue-turning-lavender lights, switching on the charm to the teased-hair girls, the screaming teenage fans—clowning, joking, kvetching with her little dog Sadie ("a hooked rug that barks"). For the first time in the week of temper tantrums, torment, uncertainty, and bleary-eyed exhaustion, she turned on her juices, and the talent showed. The Brooklyn accent was gone, the magic shone through. Barbra the terrible—rude, arrogant, anything but a lady—was Barbra the public figure—charming, almost appealing.

By midnight, 400 hours of hard work were over. The grips packed up, the set was struck. "Great show! She'll make millions on the reruns," said a control-room engineer. "Give me Julie Andrews anyday," said an electrician, wiping his forehead. In her dressing room the star of the show was told she could finally go home to bed and, for the first time that week, Barbra Streisand was on time.

EXERCISES

1. The student paper that retraced one entire day of attending classes in an outmoded educational system shouldn't be too difficult to imitate. If you have just recently come from a similar (or even worse) system, you may want to describe just such a typical day period by period. Perhaps you can add such things as physical education, sex education, or various efforts to bring the curriculum up to date with far-out techniques.

You may also take liberties with reality. You can put two classes back to back that really didn't come up that way, in order to make a stronger point. For example, if Classical Civilization bored you because it dealt with nothing but dead issues, you could pretend you went from that into a sex education class that proved just as inadequate, even though it presumably involved livelier issues.

Or you may want to make a dramatic contrast between a class that in your opinion was all right and one that was all wrong, or between an outmoded and a swinging teacher.

If your college experience is proving even less palatable, use the structure of a typical college day as the framework for your paper. Since college seldom involves going from one period to another for five or six hours, you may want to talk about inter-action with classmates, a visit to a dean, or a student demonstra-tion as part of the time sequence.

The biggest drawback to this particular kind of plot is its usual lack of mounting suspense, especially if your point is that one class hour is pretty much like another. If you know this in advance, however, you can make some adjustments, before you start writing, to insure at least a minimum of suspense. You could save your absolutely *worst* class until the last, pretending it came late in the day even if it didn't. Or reverse the process and find some way of letting the reader know that you are eventually coming to a class that represents your idea of what true education is all about.

2. Use the time-sequence method, but deal with some subjects other than education. Here are some suggestions:

a) a Presidential nominating caucus minute by minute—to show the wheeling and dealing that goes on behind the scenes

b) an imaginative treatment of the progressive pollution of an environment. Your paper can be the verbal equivalent of time-lapse photography (whereby you see flowers budding, bloom-ing, and then dying in a matter of seconds); start off with a new town and clean air and water and take it from there.

c) the development of a "high" from either drugs or alcohol—to demonstrate dramatically what happens to people under the influence

d) a day in the life of a typical middle-class American working man or woman, unified by the idea of the effects of machines and computers on the human personality

e) if you have been in the service, a day in boot camp or a day at the battlefront

f) a moment-by-moment account of a first date, designed to bring out the hangups—sexual and other—that complicate personal relationships

3. In addition to typifying a particular kind of structural principle, Rex Reed's interview with Barbra Streisand is good therapy, both

for author and reader. An essay like this allows one to let off steam about overly publicized, overly adored personalities. Do a paper on some famous person as if you had interviewed and observed him during a given segment of time. Be very specific about the time sequence: the shooting of a movie scene, going to address a graduation class, or even a typical day of various civic activities. Try to make the sequence progressively reveal the person's "true" nature, at least as you think it is.

Have fun! It doesn't matter how fair you are. Your subject will no doubt survive, even as Rex Reed's has. Find some gimmick to rev the paper up even more, like making the time sequence finally disclose a view of the personality that the public presumably never sees. Perhaps you will set up a contrast between this person in the early part of the day (kicking off a Girl Scout cookie campaign) and as revealed at midnight (performing some unfeeling action, like finding a box of cookies in the back of his car and laughingly hurling it from the window).

4. Not all time sequences must bring to light hideous realities and unpleasant truths about people. The method can work in reverse. That is, you can take a personality about whom you yourself have entertained adverse opinions or who you feel is misunderstood by many people—such as a black militant, a student protest leader, or even a college administrator—and have the reader accompany this person through a segment of time that gradually reveals a very different individual.

Taking a Trip

Like time sequences, motion in space offers a writer a ready-made structural principle, particularly if you find a clear unifying principle, such as a specific journey with a beginning and a destination. Using this relatively simple device, you can set the paper up by arousing the reader's curiosity about the outcome of the journey; you sustain his interest by promising him that both journey and paper will conclude with some important disclosure or recognition.

You don't, for example, begin like this: "The morning of our holiday finally dawned, and we just couldn't wait to begin our trip to the beach." True, a journey is promised, but there's no sense of direction to the paper—no principle, that is, of suspense. Instead, you begin like this:

> The morning of our holiday finally dawned. We hadn't visited our beach—a lonely and deserted stretch of shoreline we'd discovered

by accident years ago—for a very long time. We weren't even sure we could find it again because of the new roads and perhaps the new towns. In fact, we couldn't be sure of what our journey was going to be like and what we might find at the end of it.

Now you have the reader's curiosity aroused. He's determined to find out what lies at the end of your road.

Do you recall the example I used earlier in this section? about introducing one's family through the simple expedient of taking the reader on a tour of the house? Now that was a rudimentary kind of trip structure, more interesting than an undirected approach, but not truly suspenseful, because a house isn't built in a straight line. There isn't any climactic point in the house, but here's an example of how one could be created for the purpose of making the paper more interesting:

> When you first enter the house I live in, you don't get the impression of its real size. From the front it looks like a four-room cottage, and indeed that's what my father originally had built. But as the family grew in size, he kept adding on to the back of the house. There's a long hallway leading off from the kitchen and twisting and turning apparently without any end. There's a back room hidden away, a room that is always kept locked. I guess every family needs a place to store its skeletons.

Don't ask me what's in that room. I just made it up. But if you wanted to know, it means you got hooked on the promise that the paper (if there were any more to it) would eventually terminate in the locked room and in some significant disclosure.

But, you say, my house *isn't* built like that. I answer: how the devil does the reader know? We're not concerned with exact truth when we talk about time sequences or trips in space. We're talking about methods of structuring papers, of organizing thoughts, and of holding the reader's attention. The journey can be highly artificial. You can even start off with a totally abstract idea, do some random thinking about it, and then deliberately put together a journey out of the scattered memories of real trips you have taken. You can go from Los Angeles to San Francisco for the purpose of writing an effective paper even if you never made the trip in one straight line and all at once. As long as you can put it all together in your mind, you're in business. Let's see how it can be done by tracing the history of one paper from original idea to final product.

The assignment is, let us say, "The Inner City." Nothing else is given. We are at liberty to take any approach we want. Presumably the first thing we do is mull over our feelings about the inner city—the sprawling, often decaying downtown area from which few major American cities are free. Whenever a writing exercise revolves around an explosive or controversial topic, one's feelings about it almost inevitably amount to agitations and gripes, and I doubt that this subject would be an exception. For my own part I can think of some random gripes relative to the inner city:

1) I am appalled when I witness how some people are forced to live.
2) I am disturbed by the thought of how many Americans seem utterly indifferent to the continued existence of slums and will not lift a finger to help in abolishing them.
3) I am disgusted by the endless amount of talk and wasted energy that bog down every honest effort to improve conditions in the slums.

From these three gripes I make the final selection of a subject, using as my guide this simple question: which one seems to promise the most material?

But answering this question isn't necessarily simple. On the face of it there's little reason for choosing one of these agitations over the others. You'll admit, I'm sure, that all of them deserve a hearing; all are red-hot responses to red-hot issues. I hit a stone wall, therefore, unless I give my imagination a big lift at this point. If I let ideas just swirl around in my mind, I may very likely become more and more confused. I find it's easier to let my mind play around with real images.

I begin to see parts of a black ghetto. Slums. I see a shopping center whose parking lot ghetto children have to use as a playground and some of them are run over from time to time. I think back to hot summer nights when I've driven along the main drag of the black district, and I remember an old fat woman leaning up against a rickety porch post and trying her best to breathe; I remember how some black child must have pried the water loose from a hydrant and about twelve naked kids were dancing around the God-sent icy torrent laughing for joy as if this were the most fun they'd ever had and maybe it was; I remember. . . . It keeps coming, more and more of it, and suddenly I've found my structure. I'll take an auto tour of the ghetto on a particular night in summer.

All of the images that come to me aren't from the same time or even the same place. Some are impressions remembered from Harlem, some from Watts, others from Liberty City. Naturally, I never saw all of them on the same night. But in writing I can take such a liberty.

But what do I plan to say through this journey? Is it enough to let the glimpses of ghetto life speak for themselves? Yes, perhaps. But I think back to my gripes. All three of them relate meaningfully to my images of ghetto life, but does any of them fit into the idea of the journey through the ghetto? Can I use the journey, in other words, to express one of those gripes?

Gripe number one—"I am appalled when I witness how some people are forced to live"—doesn't seem to need a structure of any kind. It doesn't matter where you go in a ghetto, you can still have *that* gripe. But I'll also have a paper without a specific plan or direction, a paper that is a series of glimpses into ghetto life. This is fine, but, if I want to do a paper that has a structure, I need something else.

Gripes number two and three, dealing with the seeming indifference of many Americans to inner-city slums and the political double talk that stymies many efforts to bring about significant change, seem closely related and could benefit from the trip structure. That is, a journey from a white point of origin through the heart of the ghetto and back again to the white community could conceivably allow me to make a strong point about the continued existence of these two separated worlds. Even if I said nothing directly, would not the contrast itself say it for me?

Here, finally, is the paper I write:

It's hot in Florida in August. Maybe it doesn't get hotter than it is in June or July, but, by the time you've had three straight months of heat, you're sensitive to the merest whisper of a breeze. If you've got air conditioning—as you do if you're sensible or have enough money to afford it—you wall yourself up in your apartment, draw the drapes against the cruel persistence of the sun; you play your stereo, you read your magazines, you invite friends in for tall, cool drinks, and you get on tolerably well. If you must go out for supplies, you choose the sleek modern shops opening onto air-conditioned malls. Of course they're expensive, but it's so hot in Florida in August you don't really care.

The nights are the worst. Then whatever breeze there was dies down. Absolutely nothing can move in that thick heat. Even the scent from the night-blooming jasmine seems to hang in the dense air. It settles nowhere. You can't escape the aroma, and it comes to mean the summer and the heat to you. That's why you hardly ever go out at night if you can possibly help it.

One night in August I heard my air conditioner make a low whistling sound; I saw it vibrating as if struggling for its life; and then—silence. Inside of five minutes the appalling fact could not be denied. My air conditioner had given out, and I was marooned in all that terrible heat. I could go sit on the front steps and risk the mosquitoes and stifle from the cloying odor of the jasmine, or I could go for a ride and enjoy the artificial hot breeze that all Florida motorists know who buy the economy-model cars without "factory air."

I just drove, not knowing or caring where. Suddenly I began to notice a gradual deterioration of landscape. I had driven off the expressway as a one-man protest against the monotony of modern driving and found myself in one of the older neighborhoods of the city. Spanish-style homes mostly, and here and there a concrete block rectangle that called itself modern fifteen years ago and was now all cracked and faded and dirty, the kind of dwelling you see all over Miami. What struck me about this street was that nearly every house had a FOR SALE sign on the front lawn. Some of the signs looked old, as if the owners had been trying unsuccessfully to get out from under a bad deal. If too many houses are for sale, there won't be any takers.

Further on down the street I began to see black children riding bikes or just sitting on steps, and I knew that the FOR SALE signs meant white people were desperate to get out but the blacks couldn't meet their prices—or else were waiting to get the houses at whatever prices they wanted to pay. It was all starting again, the same old pattern.

I reach N.W. 62nd Street, which is the main drag of the ghetto they call Liberty City. I drive by a shack with a tin roof that looks like it's about to roll off. Part of it is hanging over the front steps, and I wonder how the inhabitants can get in or out. Next door there's another shack whose roof seems pretty solid, but the posts that hold up the porch aren't. There's an old fat black woman on the porch, and she's holding onto one of the rickety posts, trying her best to breathe.

Further along I come to a bright lime green apartment house that curves in a semicircle around a cement courtyard. A lot of kids are playing ball there, and a ball rolls out into the street. I slow down so a little kid can chase it and not get killed, at least by me. The speed limit says 30, but I notice people go a lot faster than that.

I pass a hydrant with water gushing out of it. Some black

child must have pried it loose, and there's about twelve naked kids dancing around in the God-sent icy torrent laughing for joy as if this were the most fun they're ever had and maybe it was.

I notice there aren't any playgrounds anywhere along this street, and there must not be any very close either because all the kids seem to be playing right on the sidewalks or in the gutters. Further up, at the corner of 27th Avenue, there's a shopping center, and it's filled with young blacks playing ball or just standing around. It's also full of broken glass and potholes, and I wonder whose responsibility it is to fix it up. I know I don't want to drive into that parking lot. I know I'd be afraid of flat tires, and the sight of so many young black people doesn't inspire too much confidence. I feel awfully damned white all of a sudden. I'm not exactly scared, but the heat is getting the best of me.

I'm not sorry when I turn up 27th Avenue, and people start looking white again. Soon I'm driving past the Northside Shopping Center with its smooth dark asphalt parking lot and its clean white parking spaces, and there's no broken glass or potholes or angry-looking young crowds just standing around. The windows of the air-conditioned shops are cheerful and have slim WASP mannequins modeling chic dresses. I could say: I'm home. But am I?

Why can't I forget the sight of that old woman gasping for breath? Or the children playing under the hydrant? Is it that I haven't the right to? What about all those community people with their graphs and statistics? Sure, they drive down 62nd Street all the time. They have seen what I saw. But when they reach 27th Avenue, do they relax and blend into the white world once again, their jobs done for the day?

EXERCISES

1. You will find it not hard at all to imitate the process by which I wrote the paper on the ghetto. First, make a list of gripes you have relative to a certain subject. (Perhaps your teacher will suggest the subject.) Second, let your mind wander around the general "area" of the subject until it hits upon some specific images. For example, if the subject is "Pollution," you could list such things as flying over an industrial metropolis and observing the smog; seeing dead fish washed up on a shore, apparent victims of pollution; tasting some water from a polluted well, and so on. Third, think of

some journey that you could take in the paper that would enable you to tie your images together and express one of your gripes. You might decide to go on an imaginary motorcycle trip through the United States, thus joining together your recollections of various places visited at different times. If one of your gripes were "pollution is killing off a beautiful earth," you could journey through smog-filled cities and along fish-strewn shorelines until you finally arrived at some remote spot, containing no population or industry, a spot that reminded you of how beautiful the world really can be. The contrast would express your gripe and give meaning to your paper. However you end your journey, make sure the reader expects it to go somewhere.

2. Another way to arrive at material for a paper is to take a mental journey *before* you have any particular ideas in your mind. At each place along the way try to make an idea-association. Suppose, for example, you chose or were assigned "A Trip around the Airport." You let your mind retrace a recent visit, jotting down certain spots that for one reason or another stay in your mind: a weighing-in counter, an arrival-departure board, a drug store, a duty-free shop, an escalator. Next to these and other specific places, you mention some thought that occurs to you. Thus:

> Weighing-in counter—how can they really check to see if anyone is carrying a bomb?
> Escalator—all these people, going up and going down, not looking at each other; so close, yet so remote.
> Arrival-departure board—all those people, staring up at it, so dependent on machines.

It doesn't matter how much sense the thought makes or how related or unrelated it is to the other thoughts. When you get through with your preliminary mental journey, you should have a couple of pages full of ideas.

Now try to put together those ideas that seem to have some relationship with each other. Of the three examples listed above, numbers two and three seem connected without my having planned it that way. I begin to see the possibility of doing a paper about people and machines. The airport starts looking more and more like an overwhelming collection of mechanical devices and a gathering ground for thousands of people who have forgotten they are human beings.

At this point in your prewriting deliberations you have a choice. You can simply tour the airport, as I toured the house in my first version of the "Weird Family" paper. You can make comments, either directly or by implication, at each point along the way. Or you can mentally turn the airport into a straight line, as I did with the house in the second version of the "Weird Family" paper. Select the place whose mechanical contraption strikes you as being *climactically horrible*—the place where you'll make the reader get the full impact of the dehumanization of people in a machine age. Perhaps the escalator will do the trick. Perhaps you need something more powerful: like standing on the observation deck and feeling the force of the jets taking off—monstrous tons of steel and roaring sound and turbulent air currents. Whatever you select, save this place for the last, and contrive the paper so that the reader knows from the beginning that he is going to arrive at some spot in the airport at which he will experience a pertinent realization. For example, you could drop a "hint sentence" in the first paragraph: "The sleek, modern cleanness, the shiny, scrubbed look of today's airport is pleasing to the eye when you first arrive, but this doesn't quite tell the full story: you have to walk around before you fully realize what an airport is all about."

Now: choose your own place. Take your trip. Arrange your images. Write your paper. Say something.

3. Forget ideas altogether. This time exercise the power of your imagination to concentrate on a journey itself. Imagine, for example, that you are in a space ship that has run into mechanical difficulties and must try to rush back to earth before oxygen runs out. The purpose of this paper is to practice building suspense in the reader, forcing him to stay with you until you reach the end. Whatever subject you choose, make certain you promise the reader an exciting finish, one he must reach, one it would frustrate him not to know.

TOWARD THE SUPER-NOW

Once you get into the prose swing of things, you'll find there are almost no limits to what you can do on paper not only to call attention to yourself but to call one hell of a lot of attention. Being witty, being funny, making your style crackle and snap, having structure and direction—even if you *could* excel in all these departments, you'd soon find you were getting restless. Move on! Conquer new worlds!

The really great thing about prose is there's almost nothing it can't do. What do people prefer nowadays to prose? Movies? Television? Sound? Psychedelic light shows? The new media are fine, but they're expensive; they often require technical knowledge that

". . . prose must continually explore new dimensions and experiment with new possibilities."

isn't come by all that quickly. A piece of paper, in contrast, is cheap and there are ways of putting sensible and important and exciting things down on it that aren't hopelessly beyond anybody's range.

In order to keep up with today's world and its new media of communication, however, prose must continually explore new dimensions and experiment with new possibilities. Its primary advantage is its solidity, its THERENESS. If you can't understand what you read, you can go back and read it over. You can't do that with a movie or a light show. Even stereophonic rock music often defies you to understand its words. You can play some records a thousand times and never quite catch all of the lyrics. Yet the solidity of prose in many quarters isn't enough. Prose needs to fly. This concluding section is dedicated to those who want to leave the ground, if only for a few minutes.

Camera Eye Technique

Since its advent on the scene three-quarters of a century ago, the medium of motion pictures has had a growing effect on prose style. Many writers have found that the camera can communicate with a directness, an immediacy, and a sensuous appeal that words can only approximate, and they have sought the means to make language function in an increasingly cinematic way. That cause today seems more urgent than ever. At a time when movies and television threaten to become *the* dominant media of world communication, when Johnny can't read and even those few remaining adults who can don't, the writer must make a critical decision. Should he bother at all? And if he does, must he not pay hard attention to what words on paper can be to make themselves as visual as the visual media themselves? Otherwise who will constitute his reading public?

Camera Eye Technique (CET) is the application to language of the objectivity the camera can give. It doesn't mean that what you say is any less your own property or that you can't express your subjective moods and fancies. It only means that you try to get your words down from the clouds, that you try to impart to the reader the visual images you see in your mind as you write. Camera Eye Technique discourages high abstractions. You don't talk, for example, about "liberty and justice for all." Rather, you describe as simply and visually as possible a scene from ghetto life. The reader sees what you see (though never as exactly, to be sure), and from the image he gets the idea. In short, Camera Eye Technique is a way of making words attempt to do whatever photography, either still or motion, can do. Many of the exercises that have already been included in this book have been pointing you toward using CET. The continual harping on specific details and actual incidents has been the effort to get you to start using your mind camera.

Camera Eye Technique is nothing new. All the great writers from Homer to John Steinbeck have labored to make the reader see what they see. Even the great philosophers have struggled against the deadly effect of the abstract in language and have usually been at their best and most communicative when they managed to find concrete and visual examples to illustrate their complex thoughts. Probably the best single example of CET in philosophy is Plato's Allegory of the Cave, in which he tells a highly visual story of prisoners in an underground cave in order to explain his theory of reality.

Is it Shakespeare? Are not some of his most memorable passages the most visual? Didn't Shakespeare have trouble with that barren little platform on which his plays were performed? No props, no scenery—only the visual stimulation his words could give to the listener's imagination. Through language Shakespeare creates the scenic and lighting effects we have in the theater today. Think of Juliet coming out onto her famous balcony. In a modern production there'd be a sudden burst of light to herald her entrance. Shakespeare has Romeo accomplish the same thing:

> But, soft! What light through yonder window breaks?
> It is the east, and Juliet is the sun.

Shakespeare knew, as did all the greats: *if you can't see it, you don't get it.*

The Camera Eye as Viewpoint

Today's writer has an advantage Shakespeare didn't possess, and that is a knowledge of movie technique. If you would sharpen your prose almost instantly, just relive in your mind the manner in which a movie you've seen recently makes a certain point, and then try to come as close to this as you can in words.

For example, the movies know exactly how to control the viewer's interest in the main character. Perhaps you see a woman's feet, and then the camera slowly travels upwards until it reaches her face. Just this simple visual trick is usually enough to attract the eye's attention, and the movies know that, when the eye is captured, the mind is too.

Here are the famous opening paragraphs of John Steinbeck's story "The Chrysanthemums." Note how the author's camera eye sweeps through a broad shot of the Salinas Valley in California and then gradually the focus gets narrower and narrower until we reach the woman who is to be central to the story. Once she is introduced in this cinematic manner, the reader is visually forced to think of her as important. The prose technique, imitating the camera, makes the woman appear to be central to nature as well.

> The high gray-flannel fog of winter closed the Salinas Valley from the sky and from all the rest of the world. On every side it sat like a lid on the mountains and made of the great valley a closed pot. On the broad, level land floor the gang plows bit deep and left the black earth shining like metal where the shares had cut. On the foothill ranches across the Salinas River the yellow stubble fields seemed to be bathed in pale cold sunshine; but there was no sunshine in the valley now in December. The thick willow scrub across the river flamed with sharp and positive yellow leaves.
>
> It was a time of quiet and of waiting. The air was cold and tender. A light wind blew up from the southwest so that the farmers were mildly hopeful of a good rain before long; but fog and rain do not go together.
>
> Across the river, on Henry Allen's foothill ranch there was little work to be done, for the hay was cut and stored and the orchards were plowed up to receive the rain deeply when it should come. The cattle on the higher slopes were becoming shaggy and rough-coated.
>
> Elisa Allen, working in her flower garden, looked down across the yard and saw Henry, her husband, talking to two men in business suits.[5]

This aspect of CET offers the same lesson as many other techniques we have been considering in these final two chapters: the method often outweighs the idea. Elisa Allen is to this story what the subject is to an expository essay. In both cases it's the way you seize the reader's attention and heighten his interest that does the job, that causes the communication to take place. Had Steinbeck opened his story with the sentence "Elisa Allen . . . looked down across the yard and saw Henry etc. etc." it would have been easier for a reader to comment "So what? Who's Elisa Allen anyway?"

After reading Steinbeck's cinematic opening to one of my classes, I gave an on-the-spot assignment, calling for each member to write an opening paragraph for a story in which a central character is introduced through the same or similar technique. One student used a closeup for a beginning and then little by little revealed a larger segment of reality. But it's still Camera Eye Technique.

[5] From *The Long Valley* by John Steinbeck. Copyright 1937, copyright © renewed 1965 by John Steinbeck. Reprinted by permission of The Viking Press, Inc.

She sat on the orange sofa with the composure of a familiar guest waiting for cocktails to be served. Beside her was a black plastic handbag almost of attaché-case size. She toyed with a pair of white gloves in her lap as she looked straight ahead, apparently oblivious to her surroundings. An occasional lurch scarcely jarred her awareness more than just enough to make her brace her feet and grasp the sofa arm with her right hand. At those times, her cheeks stained briefly with color under the dirty parchment skin, and the pucker-string of her mouth drew tighter. Not once did she glance behind or beside her, at the chairs, dresser, upended mattress and box springs, tables, and cartons roped securely to the sides of the moving van. There she sat, riding her sofa, traveling forward but looking backward.[6]

So beautiful is the control achieved by this student writer, as far as I'm concerned, this paragraph is a complete whole all by itself. Do we not feel sympathy for this woman? Can we not fill in many of the details about her life, her past and her future—details that CET has made unnecessary for the author to spend time giving us?

This control we can call *viewpoint*, and though it is a matter of life and death in fiction, it is something one should *always* be concerned with. No matter what you're writing, you are you, and the words on the page represent what you see and think. But the writers don't always make this clear (just as people when in real life forget they are communicating their own views rather than the way things necessarily are!).

You become more sharply conscious of viewpoint when you hold a camera in your hand. Whatever the lens is picking up is your vantage point. You can move forward or back. You can stand upside down. You and you alone can control the kind of imagery the camera is going to record. Similarly, you can practice viewpoint in writing by pretending, again, that your mind is a camera. Never lose consciousness of this. Whatever you describe is what your camera can record. If you concentrate on putting down your images exactly as they come to your mind's camera, you are thus controlling the reader's response—in a way that isn't possible if you just plunge into the act of writing.

EXERCISES

1. Take the reader on a camera tour of a specific place, one that you have visited so often you can close your eyes and see it sharply as if you were actually there. Pretend you *are* there, holding a

[6] Printed by permission of the author, Kathleen Merrill.

camera. Begin at one point and proceed with the tour. Write down everything you see exactly as your camera could pick it up.

Ask the teacher to read a number of papers. As you listen to each one, decide whether the writer is staying with the Camera Eye viewpoint throughout. You might even devise some method of interrupting the reading whenever you or anyone else thinks the viewpoint has been switched or gone out of focus, such as pounding sharply on the desk. Decide on the spot what the trouble is. It's a good way to improve your own handling of viewpoint.

In addition to worrying about the viewpoint, it is also necessary to make absolutely certain the language doesn't "cheat" and say things that aren't truly visual. For example, if your tour is of the zoo, you can't write, "The mother bear looked at me maternally." Or can you? It's fun to see whether everyone in the class will agree that a given word or phrase is visual or not. Perhaps the class could agree on another way of interrupting the reading whenever the language becomes "un-camera." A whistling noise? This assignment will teach you a great deal about how visually you can write. If your paper gets whistled at continually, you may begin to suspect you're not communicating very effectively.

2. Select any character you wish and contrive a way of introducing him to the reader by using CET. Imitate either John Steinbeck or Kathleen Merrill. One worked from the general to the particular, from the broad panorama to the specific character and thus made her assume an importance she might otherwise not have had. The other reversed the process in that she began with a closeup of the woman on the orange sofa and then moved back slowly to encompass a broad panorama. Both techniques worked perfectly for the purpose they served. Decide whether you want to zero in on somebody (and why you want to do it) or whether you want to withhold the full reality from the reader (again, why?).

There are other movie techniques for introducing characters. If one of them appears to serve your purpose better, by all means use it. Here are some possibilities:

a) *beginning with one part of the body*—say, hands or feet—and working up to the entire person. (But make the method seem relevant to the subject; perhaps the character is a ballet teacher and she is described, hands first, then neck, then shoulders and arms, then face, then graceful torso, and finally she is shown occupying a wheel chair.)

b) *beginning with an action and then showing the person.* (In a student paper I once received, various warlike activities were described—shooting, bayoneting, hurling a hand grenade—

and then the reader was shown that the "soldier" was a little
boy playing war games.)

c) *beginning with the effects of your character on other people.*
(Show their facial expressions—boredom, wonder, admiration,
anger, horror—and then finally reveal the person who is responsible for such effects; this can be very effective in grabbing the
reader's attention. Like a child, he will demand to know what
you're holding back from him.)

d) *beginning with a sound coming from the character.* (This is
especially effective if it's a weird sound, like a twanging
noise or a moan or a fiendish laugh. You can also record what
the person is saying—such as a lecture on sex education—and
withhold the sight of the actual speaker. Know what the sex
educator looks like? You're right!)

It's fun and informative to have the teacher read samples of
these exercises to the whole class. You can discuss which writers
seem to arouse the greatest degree of interest in their characters
and how they manage to do it. Also, which writers violate CET by
telling about their people ("The ballet teacher was sitting in a
wheel chair experiencing unbearable pain and envying the lithe,
free movements of the young dancers.") instead of *showing*
the people. ("She was sitting in a wheel chair, looking at the
young dancers.")

Outside In, Not Inside Out

When you begin to experiment with your visual abilities as if your
mind were an actual camera, you make an interesting discovery. You
realize that the camera is limited to images from visible, not invisible,
reality. (And I think this is a Super-now discovery to make. You
begin to wonder how many times in the past you have reported
things about what certain people were like inside without any first-
hand knowledge of the subject.)

Old-fashioned fiction and modern fiction that uses a nineteenth-
century model, tend to perpetuate the myth that it is really possible
to reproduce the inner life of a person in prose. Here's an example
of what I'm talking about, taken from a satire on ladies' magazine
fiction:

> Suddenly she felt his presence, and she turned quickly. He was
> standing there, grinning that crooked grin that always made her
> heart turn over. . . . He was at her side with one step, and then
> he was crushing her to him, and her little white face was pressed
> tight against the warm roughness of his tweed shoulder. He buried

his hands in the thick mass of her hair, and then he lifted her face up to kiss her. She's so little, he thought. He was always surprised at how little she was.

"Jim, darling," Carol said, "let me get my breath." (*He mustn't suspect, she thought. I'll tell him tomorrow.*) [7]

Now of course people *do* think, but nobody thinks like the people in this story do. Nobody goes around saying internally, "She's so little. I'm always surprised at how little she is." The more psychology, philosophy, and anthropology investigate the workings of the mind, the less we really know for certain about it and the more absurd it becomes to try to suggest in 1-2-3 language what goes on inside a mind.

Camera Eye Technique teaches us to back off and not even try. That is, it teaches us to describe the visible and then to *infer from that* the nature of the invisible. Let's look at a few examples of expressing similar ideas through old-fashioned or conventional prose and CET. You'll see at a glance how drastically different the result are.

The Law

CONV.: The defendant sat there, freely perspiring, nervously twisting and untwisting his hands as the massive weight of evidence against him began to take its toll.

CET.: The defendant sat perfectly still as the testimony of the witness was given. The only apparent sign of tension was the twisting and untwisting of his hands.

(The conventional version could have been written by a columnist bent on getting the defendant convicted. It strongly suggests guilt because it presumes to be an authority on the inner life of the accused. The CET version presumes no accurate knowledge of the inner life. The reader is free to interpret the external evidence as he wishes. The man may be expressing guilt or simply fear, and there is quite a difference!)

Education

CONV.: As I passed the note to the girl next to me, the teacher looked up sharply and then gave me a terrifying glance, the look of triumph that the powerful can give to the defenseless.

CET.: The teacher glanced up as I was passing the note. There were three flushed faces in the room, but he looked only at me.

(The first version sounds nice, but what does it really mean? The CET version, while not completely clear, at least spurs the interest and imagination of the reader. The

[7] Elinor Goulding Smith, "Story for the Slicks," New York: Pocket Books, Inc., 1946.

teacher's glance, by being left vague and indefinite, acquires heightened significance. The reader begins to speculate on what the teacher may be expressing. Of course, if such a sentence is to work, it requires a wider context.)

Religion

CONV.: The cock crew for the third time, and Jesus directed to Peter a look of unutterable sadness as he recognized that the demands of this world are sometimes too much for even the purest in heart and intention.

CET.: There was a distant sound. Jesus looked up, smiled slightly, and then turned toward Peter.
(The first version actually comes from an unpublished novel. The second is my invention, but it illustrates the manner in which a writer could handle such subject matter. If the story line makes it clear that the sound heard is that of the cock crowing, a full delineation of the moment and its significance becomes unnecessary. CET, in other words, substitutes simplicity for wordiness and can prove far more powerful than detailed description.)

As a writing technique, especially when it comes to characterization, CET can be very powerful indeed. Whether you're doing fiction or writing a narrative account of a past experience, don't tell the reader how people think and react. Show what happened, and the reader will infer from the external event what the internal feelings of the characters are. CET teaches us to treat words as enemies. Words obscure more often than they make clear. The less you can say, the better. "She looked at him" usually works better than "She shot him a withering glance, a long, lurid look of loathing hatred."

See how this student writer (an extremely gifted young lady) was able to make us feel a great deal of sympathy for both the characters in this story about a mother and her son. This was consciously written with CET. Note how nothing is told that could not be caught by a film camera following the action. Note that a minimum of details are given and that no effort is made to go into the feelings of either character. The action is allowed to speak for itself, but the author controls our understanding of it and reaction to it by keeping a tight hold on the camera: [8]

Sluggish grey clouds moved across a leaden sky. The streets glistened darkly after the cooling rain, and pigeons strutted about puffing out their feathers. The boy sat on the front stoop

[8] Printed by permission of the author, Ceil Katchen.

wearing a pair of oversized shorts and scuffed brown shoes. He held the broken wing of a toy airplane in gentle hands and spoke to it in an earnest voice. "She didn't have to break you," he said. "I worked hard to make you nice and paint you real good and Mama didn't have to get mad at me and break you all up like that." His skinny body made his shaggy head look too large. He sat perched on the damp step like a scrawny bird. His shoulder blades stuck out on his back like budding wings. "But I didn't cry," he said, "I didn't cry." His eyes were large and dark in the pinched face and his pink ears stuck out on either side of his head like sad flowers. He leaned over the stoop and dropped the smashed airplane wing into an open trash can.

Pushing open the heavy front door, he entered the dingy hallway and trudged up the stairs. The wooden steps creaked and echoed dismally under his feet. On the third floor, he reached into his pocket and removed the large safety pin that held his door key. Once inside the apartment he locked the door behind him and emptied his pockets on the table. He put the bottle cap, smooth stone and blue marble into the shoebox of valuables hidden under his bed. The dead fly, which he had saved for scientific purposes, was transferred to a small jar behind the radiator.

At the sound of a key in the lock, he went into the bathroom and began to wash his hands. The woman came in, sighed heavily and dropped her handbag on the chair. Dark lines were etched under her eyes and drops of perspiration trembled on her pallid face. "Wash up and set the table," she said.

"Okay, Ma," his small voice echoed in the bathroom.

He decided upon the tablecloth with the faded yellow flowers on it. Smoothing it carefully on the table, he set out the two chipped blue plates, centering them precisely.

"Ma?"

"What?"

"You think maybe we can go to the park on Saturday?"

"No," her weary voice came from the kitchen. "We have to visit your grandmother's grave on Saturday. I told you that yesterday."

"Maybe after, Ma? Maybe after we can go to the park?"

"Oh, for God's sakes!" she turned a strident voice on him. "Will you stop pestering me? I've been working like a dog all day and I'm dead tired. Besides its only Wednesday. Leave me alone, will you?"

She looked at his small face, closed and silent, and her voice softened. "I brought you something," she said. "It's over there in that little container. Mind you take care of it now." He walked slowly to the chair, and lifting the lid of the container, looked inside. He drew in his breath sharply.

The goldfish glowed orange-gold, and its fan-like tail swept back and forth in the clear water. The boy stared at its round blank eyes, at the gulping mouth and the rhythmic pumping gills. His eyes took in the paler orange of its round belly, the graceful sweep of the delicate fins.

With great care, he lifted the container and held it before him in both hands. He walked into the bathroom and tilted the contents of the container into the toilet. He stood and watched the goldfish flick its tail with excitement and swim quickly about examining its new surroundings. The boy pressed the tank handle. Water rushed into the bowl, caught the fish and whirled it around, around and down. He watched until the surging water carried the fish out of sight, watched until the water grew calm again.

Going into the kitchen, he reached into a drawer for the knives and forks and set them neatly out on the table.

CEIL KATCHEN

When one has recovered from this story, one notes the sparsity of adjectives and adverbs. Only those most necessary for identification of place or of objects. But the author makes no attempt to guide our response by putting a value label on things. The nineteenth century threw words around as if they were going out of style (and they just about have). "I am exhausted," she said wearily—lines like this abound in Victorian fiction. Or: "How her heart leaped for joy at the thought that she would soon be wrapped once more in the warm, comforting, safe, and strong arms of her beloved Roger." Adjectives and adverbs are like background music in movies: they're at their best when you don't notice them at all. "The freckled boy" is all right because it tells you who it is, but "the scheming brother-in-law" is bad because it tells you how you're supposed to feel about him. It's insulting to your intelligence.

EXERCISES

1. Let the class disperse, each member going for a walk in the immediate vicinity of the classroom, but absolutely alone. Let him

converse with no one. Let him pretend he is only a movie camera and not a person at all. Let him absorb with fierce intensity all the sensations he can. After fifteen minutes or so, the class reassembles, and, without saying a word, each one begins to write down exactly what he saw and heard as faithfully as possible.

This assignment is designed to force you to forget your own personality during the time you are absorbing from your surroundings so that you will be less likely to encumber your writing with evaluative terminology, less likely to keep interpreting the world for the reader and more likely to put things down accurately and simply.

Ask the teacher to read some of the papers out loud. Using the interruptive methods mentioned earlier—banging on the desk or whistling—or any other method you want, indicate when a writer violates CET and either becomes too abstract or too evaluative.

2. Try to describe a simple action, such as starting an automobile or the process of removing laundry from the washing machine and hanging it up to dry, without using a single adjective or adverb. It won't be easy, and you'll find it's well nigh impossible to write for very long without these aids. But do the best you can.

Do the same assignment a second time but allow yourself the delicious privilege of adding adjectives and adverbs that describe reality. Continue to keep your feelings out of it. It is to be hoped that the experience will make you acutely aware of the difference between reality words and evaluation words and greatly enhance your powers of translating visible reality into prose.

3. Instead of writing a complete paper, for this assignment make a list of famous but abstract statements from the Old Masters. (Perhaps the teacher and the class can work up a list together.) In order to practice the Show-Don't Tell aspect of CET, rewrite each statement, being as visual as you can. Your CET version need not communicate exactly the same thing as the original. It just has to be what a camera could show.

Examples:

Original	*CET*
To be or not to be: that is the question. (Shakespeare)	The man stood on the very brink of the shallow ledge and looked down at the crowd twenty stories below. He was completely motionless but poised and tense.

Original	CET
A little learning is a dangerous thing. (Pope)	The two powders I had mixed together in the testtube made the prettiest blue color, and I was fascinated by it as I held it over the knife-like flame of the Bunsen burner. Suddenly the girl next to me screamed and cried, "That's gunpowder you're cooking!"
All the world's a stage. (Shakespeare)	The green curtains that led to the mysterious rear quarters of an apartment were suddenly flung open, and she stood there holding tightly to them for a full minute. She waited until every last whisper of conversation had died away and every pair of eyes was focused directly at her before she honored us with her rich and vibrating "Hello."

4. From the "film library" of your memory draw forth some visual images of some person who meant a great deal to you, or one that still does. Write a characterization of this person without ever stating why you remember him or what he means to you. Simply give the reader a Camera Eye description; show the person in action. Let the pictures speak for themselves. Stay out of it altogether. Reread Ceil Katchen's story of the boy and the goldfish. Try to find a similar action involving your person—that is, one that conveys an instantaneous meaning without your having to make any comment at all.

Jazzed-Up CET

Using the Camera Eye as a means of controlling the way the reader sees what you're describing and using it to stimulate the reader's imagination about the invisible reality you don't describe are techniques that have been around for some time now. Ever since movies were invented, those two basic methods were available for prose imitation. But we're living in an era of fantastic visual effects on the screen. New technology, new processes can make the camera do things that its inventors may never have dreamed of. It's only natural that prose should want and need to keep up with the times.

One of the major influences on both the new prose and the audiovisual media of today has been Marshall McLuhan, an educator-philosopher who points out a striking difference between prose and other media. What he has to say may well bring about extraordinarily different uses for written language, and, though his total philosophy is exceedingly complex and hard to summarize, the gist of his thinking about prose is of interest to our study.

Man, says McLuhan, is an animal endowed by nature with five senses. His survival is supposed to depend on their proper functioning, and no one sense is intended to dominate others. But with Johann Gutenberg's invention of the printing press in the late fifteenth century, a sensory imbalance was created. In order to read print on a page, man must suffer a diminishing use of his other senses. That's not the whole tragedy either. In staring at the printed page, people aren't seeing the world of reality. They're not looking at what their eyes were meant to look at. Instead they're staring at a highly artificial medium that communicates meaning step by step, word by word. Such "linearity" gives people a distorted way of thinking about reality.

Take this sentence:

> Dave looked up and was aware that the front door had blown open from the wind, a stream of water was coming down from the leak in the ceiling, and the tree outside the window was banging so hard against the pane he was fearful the glass would soon shatter.

You've no doubt seen hundreds and thousands of sentences just like this on the pages of countless books. If you're any sort of habitual reader, you have probably never given a thought to the fact that neither Dave nor anyone else could experience these things the way the words describe the event. In reality, Dave would be aware of the parts of the total event with a simultaneity the written sentence cannot even approximate.

Obviously the camera can come closer to this simultaneity than prose can. The jazzed-up photography of today's movies and television can bombard the eye and the ear with sights and sounds that are dramatically different from what McLuhan sees as the increasingly outmoded linearity of prose. In many quarters, a total revolution against the written and printed page is going on. Some composition teachers are going so far as to abandon writing altogether in favor of still photography and filmmaking.

One advantage that I believe prose still has is the relative calm in which it can be read, reread, contemplated, and then absorbed. It isn't possible to do much thinking when your senses are being assaulted on all sides. When you see and hear a Cinerama spectacle with a hundred-foot screen and a sixteen-channel stereophonic sound track blaring at you it's hard to do much of anything but surrender to the "trip." Prose may be one of the tranquilizers we can't afford to give up.

Nonetheless prose *can* go further than it has in the past. If the visual impact of prose is an important part of writing today, there's no reason that prose can't use the *quick cut* (imitating the camera jumping from one scene to another so rapidly you don't catch the change) or even the *split* or *multiple screen* (imitating the use of simultaneous images as a way to speed up the communication.)

Here's a story written by a black student, deliberately making use of jazzed-up CET. Note how swiftly the action moves. Note how much is said on the theme of prejudice and discrimination by visual means, without the author having to comment at all. Note how the transitions are what the camera could catch, and the reader simply has to keep up with them. Pay particular attention to the way the author handles the checker game. Time passes very quickly; at the same time the visual immediacy is somehow not sacrificed.[9]

A Friendly Game of Checkers

The new pine counter of Zeke's Grocery and Market was conspicuous against the worn gray color of the shelves. The store was in a converted shotgun house. Store at the front and Zeke's bed, stove and other necessities in the back with a beaver board partition in between. On the wall behind the counter was a yellow and white kitchen clock with the greasy cord hanging down. The clock was attached to the wall with a bent nail on either side. The clock showed nineteen minutes after seven. Next to the clock, but slightly below and to one side of it, was a soiled calendar which was turned to August. Through the grimy glass window, weak rays of sun were shining on a few wilted vegetables in a bin. On the counter between the cookie jars and boxes of penny candy were several loaves of fresh bread. The steamy meat case contained several kinds of lunch meat, a pan of sausage, a pan of hamburger and several empty pans. Zeke, a tall black man, walked out from behind the meat case tying on a clean white store apron. He picked up the loaves of bread, carried them over to the bread rack and began arranging them.

The door opened and the ice man walked in. He wore well used work shoes, gray work pants and a faded blue shirt. He was young and his neck was sunburnt and very wrinkled. His smile revealed crooked slightly yellow teeth. He had scraggly blond eyebrows above pale gray eyes. Ambling over to the

[9] Printed by permission of the author, Gloria Randolph.

corner on the other side of the window he lifted down three heavy wooden empty milk crates from a stack. When he had arranged them in a row he reached behind the stack of crates, pulled out a dogeared rigid wooden checkerboard and placed it on the center crate. Seating himself on one of the crates, he pulled it up to the checkerboard and waited.

Zeke was through putting up the bread and was wiping off the sweating red cola machine. He wiped his hands on the rag, stuck it in his back pocket, walked over to the empty crate, threw one leg over it and eased down. The ice man reached under the bottom shelf and took out a cigar box. He opened it and poured onto the checkerboard twelve black checkers, eleven red checkers and a red soda bottle cap.

"Heads up for red," said the ice man.

"O.K."

Tossing the coin, he caught it and turned it over onto the checkerboard.

"Looks like you got black, ice man," said Zeke.

The ice man began to pick out the black checkers and arrange them on his side of the checkerboard. Zeke arranged his red ones.

The little girl with the tightly plaited stingy braids came into the store. Walking on bare feet with badly fallen arches she moved over to a little table in front of the meat case. She picked up a small brown bag tied with white cord, and walked behind the counter where she got a small can of tomato paste. She continued to the back of the meat case, slid open the glass door, picked up a long crooked link of sausage and closed the sliding door. Coming out from behind the counter, she got a bag and dropped all three items into it. Twisting her bag at the top, she hobbled over to Zeke and put a quarter in his hand. Skipping as best she could she hurried out of the screen door, slamming it.

The ice man pulled out some crumpled dollar bills from his pocket. Straightening each one precisely, he stacked twelve of them up. Neatly he twisted them into a half roll lengthwise and stuck them into the top of an empty milk bottle which he set on the floor.

The first game began. The ice man moved. Zeke moved. The ice man moved. Making a second move, Zeke said "O.K. Rack up!" The ice man took a dollar bill from the bottle, put it on Zeke's side of the checkerboard and reached for the red checkers and the red bottle cap. Zeke arranged the black checkers.

Smiling, the ice man moved first. Zeke moved. The ice man moved, this time cautiously. Zeke shoved his second black

checker. The door opened and a man came in. With a "Mornin',
Zeke," he got a loaf of bread, placed twelve cents on the counter
and left. The ice man studied the checkerboard, moved and
picked up two of Zeke's checkers. Smiling broadly, he settled
more comfortably on his seat. Zeke eased another checker
forward and took a red checker. The ice man jumped it and
claimed it. Zeke moved again. The ice man jumped three
checkers and made the king row. Zeke moved a checker at the
far side. The ice man jumped three checkers with his king,
moved the king into safe territory and picked up Zeke's three
checkers.

"Your game," said Zeke.

He handed back the dollar. Ice man took it. Zeke got up, cut
off the lights, put the twelve cents for the bread into his
pocket, came back, and sat down. Ice man had arranged the
checkers. Again he had the red checkers.

The game began. Three moves and Zeke said "Rack up!"
Ice man handed him a dollar. Another game. Ice man studied
the board and made his move. Moving quickly, Zeke said,
"Rack up!"

"Wait a minute," said the ice man, wiping his face with a
dirty handkerchief. He moved again. "Rack up!" The ice man
scrambled the checkers and handed Zeke another dollar.

The games continued. Zeke kept winning. Zeke had eleven
one dollar bills stacked on his side of the checkerboard.

"You got to gimme back my money, Zeke."

"I won it."

"You cheated."

"I didn't."

Kicking over the checkerboard, "You stinking black bastard!
You cheated me!"

Zeke got up. "Watch your mouth, white man."

Snatching up the money from the floor, the ice man crumpled
it and jammed it into his pocket. Zeke put out his hand and
took the ice man's wrist. Yanking it out of his pocket, he held
the ice man's wrist, squeezing until the fingers relaxed and the
bills floated down to the floor. Snatching away his hand, sweating and trembling, the ice man backed toward the door.

"I'll be back, Zeke. And I won't be by myself!" He left,
slamming the door.

From outside a woman's voice, "Hey Zeke. I got a gallon
of kerosene. Pay you tonight."

"O.K."

Zeke walked to the back room of the store, put the night latch on the back door, reached under his bed and pulled out a rifle. Picking up a chair, he carried both into the front of the store. Placing the chair squarely in front of the meat case and the rifle across his knees, Zeke sat down.

GLORIA RANDOLPH

Long before the new screen techniques came along, the Welsh poet and prose stylist Dylan Thomas was experimenting with rapid imagery and sound in language. The following passage from his "Child's Christmas in Wales" almost makes you forget you are looking at words on a page:

> One Christmas was so much like another, in those years around the sea-town corner now and out of all sound except the distant speaking of the voices I sometimes hear a moment before sleep, that I can never remember whether it snowed for six days and six nights when I was twelve or whether it snowed for twelve days and six nights when I was six. All the Christmases roll down toward the two-tongued sky that was our street; and they stop at the rim of the ice-edged, fish-freezing waves, and I plunge my hand in the snow and bring out whatever I can find. In goes my hand into that wool-white bell-tongued ball of holidays resting at the rim of the carol-singing sea, and out comes Mrs. Prothero and the firemen.

Thomas had a tremendous ear for sound and a great gift for making lifeless marks on a page turn into stereo speakers, as when, in the same piece, he talks about the firehouse gong "bombilating" through the snow. You can have some fun practicing the direct translation of sounds into prose.

Bells	Clang	(Better than "toll"?)
	Tintinabulate	
	Tinkle	
	Boom	
Guns	Crack	(Better than "sharp retort"?)
	Zing	
	Ahahahahahahah	
	Blam	
Automobile taking off	Errrrooooozzzzzzzzz	
Crashing	Eeeeeeeeeeessssssspllllllluuuuuush	

You can go further. You can alter the very appearance of the page, so as to get away from what McLuhan calls linearity. By startling the reader with an unusual format for setting language down on paper, you may seize his attention and stand a better chance of communicating with him.

In poetry the revolution against print has been going on for quite a while. In 1923 the poet E. E. Cummings was doing things like this:

O SWEET SPONTANEOUS EARTH

O sweet spontaneous
earth how often have
the
doting

     fingers of
prurient philosophers pinched
and
poked

thee
, has the naughty thumb
of science prodded
thy
     beauty   , how
often have religions taken
thee upon their scraggy knees
squeezing and

buffeting thee that thou mightest conceive
gods
     (but
true

to the incomparable
couch of death thy
rhythmic
lover

     thou answerest

them only with

     spring) [10]

Surely you can experiment with some far-out methods of putting sentences on paper, for no doubt your children will see

```
ma      U
  n    s
 y un  u              Y           i      P
        a          w;a  s of sE-Tt- n   U  Pr (in): T
      l (TO US)                    g
```

[10] Copyright, 1923, 1951 by E. E. Cummings. Reprinted from his volume, *Poems, 1923–1954* by permission of Harcourt Brace Jovanovich, Inc.

You can use a split-screen technique. Example:

The dean shook the president's hand; the president shook the hand of the chairman of the board of trustees; the chairman of the board shook the governor's hand; all smiled warmly and then sat around the huge oak table, each lighting up an enormous cigar.	There were only five of them standing down by the lake, but their bearded faces were grimly set, and they had determination in their eyes as they looked toward the white administration building standing high and solid on the other side.

The prose of the space-age future may well demand that you learn how to read two or more columns simultaneously. It may be the prose for the "sense-expanded" human being. In fact, the expository essay of the future may look like the following theme written by one of my students after the Liberty City (Miami) riots in 1968. Here is multiple-screen imagery jazzing up what could have been "straight" prose.———————————————————————————————————→

EXERCISES

1. Make a list of all the screen techniques of the moment that you can think of, such as the pan, the closeup, the quick cut, the fade-out, the fade-in, the split screen, and the multiple screen. Experiment by putting next to each one an example of its prose equivalent. Some examples:

   a) *Pan:* From Oakland to San Francisco the Golden Gate Bridge spanned the shimmering waters of the Bay.

   b) *Closeup:* His face was a twisted mass of wrinkles, perspiration, and grime. As he grinned, you could see his crooked, yellowed teeth.

   c) *Quick Cut:* "I'll never drink again, darling," he said as he left the house. The jukebox throbbed out a quiet rhythm as he spun the quarter around on the smooth, polished bar that reflected the pink lights.

   d) *Fade-Out and Fade-In:*

   He stood there on the porch watching the car drive off down the road and finally disappear into the distance. The leaves were blowing along the pathway, and the sky was a leaden gray.

   He hung the raincoat up carefully in the closet and brushed some lint from the shoulder.

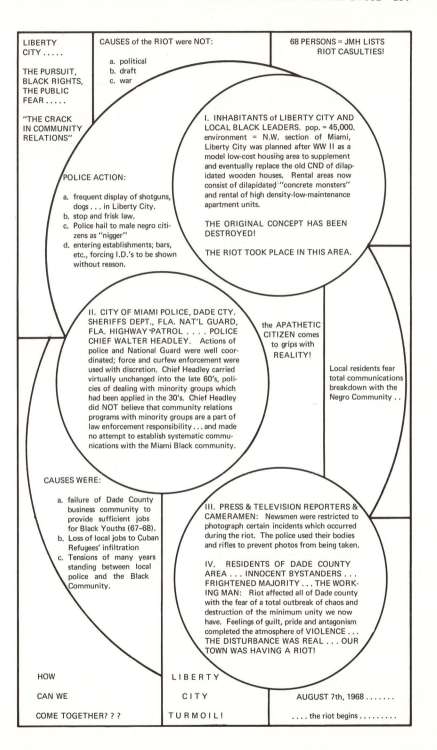

LIBERTY
CITY . . . . .

THE PURSUIT,
BLACK RIGHTS,
THE PUBLIC
FEAR . . . . .

"THE CRACK
IN COMMUNITY
RELATIONS"

CAUSES of the RIOT were NOT:

a. political
b. draft
c. war

68 PERSONS = JMH LISTS
RIOT CASULTIES!

POLICE ACTION:

a. frequent display of shotguns,
   dogs . . . in Liberty City.
b. stop and frisk law.
c. Police hail to male negro citizens as "nigger"
d. entering establishments; bars,
   etc., forcing I.D.'s to be shown
   without reason.

I. INHABITANTS of LIBERTY CITY AND
LOCAL BLACK LEADERS. pop. = 45,000.
environment = N.W. section of Miami,
Liberty City was planned after WW II as a
model low-cost housing area to supplement
and eventually replace the old CND of dilap-
idated wooden houses. Rental areas now
consist of dilapidated·"concrete monsters"
and rental of high density-low-maintenance
apartment units.

THE ORIGINAL CONCEPT HAS BEEN
DESTROYED!

THE RIOT TOOK PLACE IN THIS AREA.

II. CITY OF MIAMI POLICE, DADE CTY.
SHERIFFS DEPT., FLA. NAT'L GUARD,
FLA. HIGHWAY ᐧPATROL . . . . POLICE
CHIEF WALTER HEADLEY. Actions of
police and National Guard were well coordinated; force and curfew enforcement were
used with discretion. Chief Headley carried
virtually unchanged into the late 60's, policies of dealing with minority groups which
had been applied in the 30's. Chief Headley
did NOT believe that community relations
programs with minority groups are a part of
law enforcement responsibility . . . and made
no attempt to establish systematic communications with the Miami Black community.

the APATHETIC
CITIZEN comes
to grips with
REALITY!

Local residents fear
total communications
breakdown with the
Negro Community . .

CAUSES WERE:

a. failure of Dade County
   business community to
   provide sufficient jobs
   for Black Youths (67–68).
b. Loss of local jobs to Cuban
   Refugees' infiltration
c. Tensions of many years
   standing between local
   police and the Black
   Community.

III. PRESS & TELEVISION REPORTERS &
CAMERAMEN: Newsmen were restricted to
photograph certain incidents which occurred
during the riot. The police used their bodies
and rifles to prevent photos from being taken.

IV.   RESIDENTS OF DADE COUNTY
AREA . . . INNOCENT BYSTANDERS . . .
FRIGHTENED MAJORITY . . . THE WORK-
ING MAN: Riot affected all of Dade county
with the fear of a total outbreak of chaos and
destruction of the minimum unity we now
have. Feelings of guilt, pride and antagonism
completed the atmosphere of VIOLENCE . . .
THE DISTURBANCE WAS REAL . . . OUR
TOWN WAS HAVING A RIOT!

HOW

CAN WE

COME TOGETHER? ? ?

L I B E R T Y

C I T Y

T U R M O I L !

AUGUST 7th, 1968 . . . .

. . . . the riot begins . . . .

2. Try to tell a connected narrative by means of the various Camera Eye techniques you've experimented with in the previous exercise. Perhaps you can begin with a subject, such as prejudice, the generation gap, a moral conflict. Let your mind play around with it for a time. Try to concentrate on specific people and events. When you think you have an action to describe, one that embodies or illustrates how you feel about the subject, put it on paper, using the new techniques. Let your mind camera dictate what you write and how you do it. For example, don't waste time on statements like "After promising my parents to do my homework, I went up to my room and sat there for a full two hours, waiting for the inspiration to strike." In a flash you can go from downstairs to upstairs without bothering to fill the reader in. What if he *is* confused? It's good for him!

3. Experiment with new ways of putting words down on a page—to get away from "old-fashioned" linearity. Here are some suggestions:

   a) If you're writing on religion, put your prose in the shape of a cross.

   b) If you're writing a protest against war, use the peace symbol.

   c) If you want to illustrate the dangers of drug trips, make your words explode on the page in some kind of design.

   d) Try an "X" design, allowing the prose to roar down the page from the left and right corners, intersecting in the middle, so that the reader can read either column first—or both together.

   e) If the world confuses you, write in the shape of a question mark.

   Your departure from linearity doesn't, of course, have to *look* like something. You can paint a design with prose—just for the sake of the experiment. If it leaves the teacher or the class cold, shrug your shoulders and try again.

4. Experiment with multimedia techniques by combining prose with visual forms of expression. Do a series of slides on a given subject and write a prose narration to go with them.

   Give a presentation before the class that involves both a film, which you have made, and a talk, which you have written.

   Show slides rapidly moving. Cut to a short film you have made. All the while you can be playing a tape of something you wrote.

   If you don't know how to make a film, here's a word of advice which I asked two of my more visually oriented students to write for you.[11]

[11] Printed by permission of the authors, Gordon E. Price and Philip Obrecht.

If you have decided to make your first film there are several important factors which you should consider. You must decide on the type of equipment which you feel should be used to record the visual and/or audio components of your film. The higher the sophistication of your equipment, the fewer imposed limitations there will be on your product. However, the equipment which you may use ultimately depend on that which is available—through ownership, loan, or rental—and also upon your purposes and objectives for making the film. If available, 16mm film and equipment will allow you to benefit from extra laboratory services, though this will increase your production costs. Black and white film is available in all film formats and will enable you to film at reduced expense. Should you decide to add sound to your film you may choose either a synchronized tape-recorder, which you will play simultaneously as your film is being screened, or have a magnetic strip added to your film, in which case you will require a magnetic-sound recording projector.

The equipment which you will use for your first film may actually be secondary to the content (and intent) of the film. It is most important that you know in some detail what it is you wish to film and wish to show by your film. When you are aware of what it is you are attempting to capture on and in your film you will be better prepared for making judgments concerning the type of equipment which you should use. Deciding upon where—the location—you wish to shoot may likewise help you decide—sometimes by necessity—on the equipment which can or should be used.

It is advisable that you write a script for your film, the detail of which is dependent on the demands of your particular film. This script may be nothing more than a crude outline, but it will be invaluable for avoiding the exclusion of scenes or ideas during your shooting schedule. The asset which you as an independent filmmaker have is that you may improvise ideas on the spot; the script will provide you with the base outline on which you may make alterations, additions or deletions.

Should your film require the use of actors you should keep in mind that the camera has the tendency to magnify all actions and, unless your film expressly calls for it, overacting should be avoided; subtlety should be the rule.

Remember: acknowledge your capacities, remain within your capabilities, but do not shy from experimentation.

GORDON E. PRICE
PHILIP OBRECHT

A PARTING WORD

If you'll turn back to the very beginning of this book, you'll find a preliminary exercise, *Who Are You?*, that you were supposed to do without any guidelines to follow. It was tempting to end the book with the same exercise. But I decided against it. By now I doubt that you could handle that question in the space of one short paper. At least you shouldn't be able to.

I also hope your interest in prose as the key to identity has been quickened and intensified. If it hasn't, if your finger is absolutely itching to seize hold of that camera and you can't wait to be off, why then—GO.

But I'll be sorry. I really will. I still believe prose is the principal means we have of coming to know who and what we are. I still believe it's the anchor of human intelligence.

Experiment with the other media, yes. But don't forget it's prose that doesn't warp or tear or fade. It's prose that can't be folded, spindled, or mutilated by unsympathetic and inhuman machines.